Paul Georg Meyer

Descriptive English Linguistics

An Introduction

Fourth, completely revised, supplemented and updated edition

With contributions by Elma Kerz and Timo Lothmann

In collaboration with Judith Bündgens-Kosten, Andreas Frühwirth, Birgit Haupt, Andreas Kohn, Peter Marsden, Paula Niemietz and Tanja Oelkers

gnⱱ Gunter Narr Verlag Tübingen

Prof. Dr. Paul Georg Meyer ist Inhaber des Lehrstuhls für Anglistische Sprachwissenschaft an der RWTH Aachen.

Bibliografische Information der Deutschen Nationalbibliothek

Die Deutsche Nationalbibliothek verzeichnet diese Publikation in der Deutschen Nationalbibliografie; detaillierte bibliografische Daten sind im Internet über http://dnb.d-nb.de abrufbar.

4., vollständig neu bearbeitete Auflage 2008
3., überarbeitete Auflage 2005
2., unveränderte Auflage 2003
1. Auflage 2002

Die 1.–3. Auflage ist unter dem Titel „Synchronic English Linguistics" erschienen.

© 2008 · Narr Francke Attempto Verlag GmbH + Co. KG
Dischingerweg 5 · D-72070 Tübingen

Internet: http://www.narr-studienbuecher.de
E-Mail: info@narr.de

Druck: Gulde, Tübingen
Verarbeitung: Nädele, Nehren
Printed in Germany

ISSN 0941-8105
ISBN 978-3-8233-6400-9

Preface to the fourth edition

This fourth edition of our linguistics textbook from the English Department of RWTH Aachen University, hitherto entitled *Synchronic English Linguistics*, includes many major revisions and additions.

Many disturbing factual and typographical errors could be corrected and many improvements of formulations carried out. Special thanks in this connection are owed to Judith Bündgens-Kosten, who gave innumerable valuable hints for improvement from her hands-on teaching experience.

In accordance with its new title, the book now contains a fully-fledged historical component: Not only was the chapter on language change (Ch. 3) supplemented by new subchapters (for the most part written by Timo Lothmann) on the history of the English language and linguistic changes that are still relevant for understanding the present-day language or differences between English and German. Historical remarks and cross references were added throughout the book where this seemed elucidating. In the same way, the contrastive component of the book was strengthened.

Wherever this seemed helpful, comparisons with structures in German and other languages were drawn. We hope that this helps fulfil the need for a textbook in courses covering both synchronic and diachronic linguistics and serving both bachelor and teacher training programmes.

Due these substantial additions, and in the interest of price stability, it was necessary to dispense with the former chapter on psycho-, neuro and biolinguistics in the printed version. This chapter will remain available at www.narr-studienbuecher.de .

For the first time, this book will be accompanied by an on-line component: in addition to the chapter mentioned above, an electronic glossary will be available which explains all technical terms used in the book, along with German equivalents if available and provides a wealth of additional explanations and examples. If this catches on, futher components will be added.

The authorial team also wishes to thank the many users who contributed suggestions that led to improvements, and the publishing house that made this new edition possible.

Aachen, July 2008
On behalf of the authorial team
Paul Georg Meyer

0 Introduction

0.1 What is linguistics?

Linguistics (*Linguistik, Sprachwissenschaft*) can be very simply and broadly defined as the systematic study of language in all its properties and in all its inter-relations with other human phenomena. People who are engaged in this kind of study usually call themselves **linguists**.

> ☛ Note that the word *linguist* has a completely different meaning here from its most usual everyday meaning: Ordinary educated speakers of English, on hearing the word *linguist*, will expect such a person to be able to speak many different languages. A linguist in the technical, i.e. linguistic, sense of the word, however, does not necessarily need to speak many languages. Just as mathematicians do not necessarily have to be good at doing sums, linguists don't necessarily have to be good at languages, although in both cases, it must be said, the practical skill will be helpful.

The above 'definition' of linguistics is not shared by all linguists, maybe not even by most of them. Many linguists have very specific ideas of what linguistics is, what kind of study is a 'proper' occupation for a linguist, and what kind of study isn't. This introduction deliberately takes the broadest possible view, so as not to prejudice your decision about what you find interesting about language and worth studying, no matter whether some linguists call that kind of study 'linguistics' or not.

The first chapter will deal with the uncontroversial core area of linguistics, **grammar**. This area will be familiar to some of you from your language classes at school, but you will soon notice that the way linguists do grammar is somewhat different from the way it is done there. Emphasis is not so much on established knowledge and rules that can be learnt by heart, but on interesting generalisations and theoretical problems.

From grammar we proceed in chapter 2 to another core area of linguistics, the study of the sounds of language, **phonetics** and **phonology**.

Chapter 3 deals with the **history** of the English language and with different kinds of language **change**. We will primarily discuss changes that are observable in or relevant for present-day language.

Chapter 4 is concerned with the remaining core area of linguistics, the study of linguistic meaning, in particular, word meaning. This area, known as **semantics**, having been neglected by the most influential schools of linguistics during most of the 20th century, is now gaining more and more importance, although it is one of the most difficult subfields of linguistics.

Chapter 5 addresses an area which has been very much debated in linguistics, but not only in linguistics, during the last three decades or so. This is the study of language use in contexts, or: **pragmatics**. Some linguists, mainly interested in formal aspects of grammar, have regarded pragmatics as lying outside the domain of linguistics 'proper'. Other linguists, however, have declared pragmatics to be the very core area of linguistics, on which the study of all other subfields should be based. Between these two extremes, many interesting observations can be made and theories have been constructed concerning the relationship between the system of language as it is laid down, e.g., in a grammar, and the use of language, as it is observed in real-life situations.

The next chapter, 6, is also concerned with language use, but concentrates on the fact that language is mainly used in texts and conversations. For the study of texts, a separate branch of linguistics has been establishing itself over the last three to four decades, **textlinguistics**, while the **analysis of conversation** has also attracted the attention of many linguists.

The last two chapters examine further aspects of language, which can only be studied on an interdisciplinary basis. Chapter 7 discusses certain phenomena and questions arising from the interaction of language and society, a branch of linguistics usually called **sociolinguistics**.

Chapter 8 is not a proper chapter in the sense that it deals comprehensively with one branch of linguistics. As it concludes the book, we call it an epilogue, and it raises the fundamental question of the species-specificity of human language.

In the appendix, you will find exercises (chapter 9), an extensive bibliography (chapter 10) and a subject and name index (chapter 11) which will help you find individual topics and technical terms.

0.2   Useful hints for the user

This textbook is intended to introduce you to English linguistics. For an introductory textbook, it contains an unusual amount of material, and we hope that doesn't deter you. The book may thus well accompany you throughout your studies in linguistics. Our objective is to help you get growing into true professionals of the English language and linguistics who enjoy doing linguistics and reflecting about language. This involves, i.a., the use of a professional language, that is linguistic terminology, and development of a professional attitude towards language and communication. This, above all, is what will distinguish you in your later professional life. Therefore, we place great emphasis on explaining the difficult and sometimes confusing terminology of linguistics, to eventually enable you to read technical linguistic literature (which is indispensable in studying linguistics), and we argue vehemently against unprofessional views and attitudes towards linguistic problems.

We think that a fruitful occupation with linguistics cannot be restricted to learning definitions (only half understood and quickly forgotten in the worst case). We want you to understand the concepts explained in this textbook, i.e., develop concepts of your own of linguistic phenomena, and see their usefulness and necessity for handling language professionally. For this purpose, it is important for you to develop a network interconnecting your knowledge in different branches of linguistics and integrating it with the rest of your knowledge. That's why, i.a., we frequently refer to languages other than English, primarily German, drawing on your native language competence. That is also why this book contains a huge amount of cross references between its different sections to help you find your own way in the maze of language and linguistics. Some important concepts are taken up in several places in the book, to show that they figure in various branches of linguistics, and to have you construct your own concept.

We also use a number of logos and other graphic devices which help you decide what is important for you at the moment and know what kind of information you are dealing with. These logos are explained in the following box, beginning with typographical conventions.

✎ All important technical terms which are explained in the text are printed in **bold** face, when they appear for the first time (with alternative terms for the same phenomenon and German equivalents following in brackets), and when they are used again, to mark a new topic or to add further explanations.

Bold italics are used in examples to draw attention to the phenomena under discussion.

Italics are used for sentences and individual words given or mentioned as examples. German equivalents for English terminology, wherever they exist and have a spelling that is different from the English term are also printed in italics. They are also used to mark other non-English expressions that are used as normal words in the text.

'Single quotation marks' mark explanations of meanings, but are also used for other purposes, say, to mark expressions that we think are not quite appropriate, but that we use because we don't know a better expression or because we think that this expression is better known and more comprehensible than the 'correct' expression ('scare quotes').

"Double quotes" are used to really quote, either from other authors, or from examples given in the text. Longer quotes from other authors are not put in "quotes", however, but presented in a separate indented paragraph in smaller print.

Underlined words are meant to be read with emphasis. Underlining is occasionally used for other purposes, too.

SMALL CAPITALS mark names of linguists mentioned in the text. These are also used *ad hoc* in some cases for other purposes.

The use of **abbreviations** is kept to a minimum. Basically, we only use abbreviations that are in general use in English, e.g. *e.g.* Abbreviations used in formal linguistic descriptions are explained *ad hoc*. The more important ones are listed in the index (→ 11).

* We mostly use the asterisk as is customary in <u>synchronic</u> linguistics, i.e. to mark sound sequences, expressions or sentences that are not well-formed according to the rules of the language in question. The asterisk is also occasionally used for explanatory footnotes in tables. Note that in the literature on <u>historical</u> linguistics, the asterisk usually marks reconstructed, non-attested sounds, forms or words from extinct languages. We will also occasionally make use of this convention in this book, not without drawing attention to this fact.

? is occasionally used to indicate marginal acceptability of an expression.

Orientation aids:

Highlighted numbered boxed passages explain general theoretical concepts of linguistics whose scope goes beyond the questions discussed at the point where they are found.

→ We generally use this arrow to refer the reader to other sections of this introduction. References are to section numbers or to figure or box numbers only, not to page numbers. To find the page, please use the table of contents (p. X), the list of boxes (p. X), or the list of tables and figures (p. XVII).

☞ marks unnumbered boxes which are used to clarify points of terminology.

✍ boxes explain notations.

☀ is used to warn you against extra stupid frequently-made mistakes (FMM), folk linguistic superstitions, linguistic false friends and badly confused terminology.

📖 boxes contain suggestions for learning and practising activities you can engage in on the basis of what you've just read, on your own or in a tutorial.

➢ marks boxes and paragraphs that give historical linguistic background, with frequent cross references to Chapter 3.

◉ boxes contain additional information concerning a comparison with German or other languages.

△ marks boxes which deal with true or apparent exceptions to a regularity just mentioned.

⊟ marks passages containing elucidating extended examples, elaborate argumentations meant to serve as didactic examples of linguistic argumentation, or little case studies.

We use the signs •, –, and - in lists to indicate different degrees of importance.

• Important terminological dichotomies and categorial distinctions are indicated by this dot.

– The long hyphen is used for lists of important theses or observations.

- The short hyphen is used for lists of examples, steps in an argumentation, and similar items.

Further notational conventions are explained in highlighted boxes marked by ✍ wherever they are used.

Table of contents

0   Introduction VI
    0.1 What is linguistics? VI
    0.2 Useful hints for the user VII
1   The core area of linguistics: grammar 1
    1.1 Grammar in general 1
        1.1.1 What kind of thing is grammar? 1
            1.1.1.1 Grammar as knowledge 1
            1.1.1.2 Grammar as a societal phenomenon 3
            1.1.1.3 Discourse as a window to grammar 3
            1.1.1.4 Written grammars 6
            1.1.1.5 Summary 9
        1.1.2 Subdivisions of grammar and the notion of *word* 11
        1.1.3 General concepts of grammar 15
            1.1.3.1 Word classes 15
            1.1.3.2 Grammatical categories of the noun 18
                1.1.3.2.1 Number 18
                1.1.3.2.2 Gender 19
                1.1.3.2.3 Case 21
            1.1.3.3 Comparison of adjectives 22
            1.1.3.4 Verbal categories 23
                1.1.3.4.1 Tense 23
                1.1.3.4.2 Aspect 24
                1.1.3.4.3 Orientation 26
                1.1.3.4.4 Person and number 28
                1.1.3.4.5 Voice 29
                1.1.3.4.6 Mood and modality 30
                1.1.3.4.7 Finiteness 32
    1.2 Syntax 33
        1.2.1 Traditional structural categories in the sentence 33
            1.2.1.1 The notion of valency 33
            1.2.1.2 Syntactic functions: subject and object, adverbial and complement 35
                1.2.1.2.1 Subject 35
                1.2.1.2.2 Predicate 37
                1.2.1.2.3 Object 38
                1.2.1.2.4 Subject predicative and object predicative 38
                1.2.1.2.5 Adverbials and the complement – adjunct distinction 39
            1.2.1.3 Compound and complex sentences 42
        1.2.2 Generative Grammar: the description of constituent structure 45
            1.2.2.1 Requirements on a syntactic description 45
            1.2.2.2 The major constituents of an English sentence. Heuristic tests 48
            1.2.2.3 Types of phrases in the English sentence 52
            1.2.2.4 Structure within constituents: Head and modifier 55
            1.2.2.5 Resolving syntactic ambiguity 56
            1.2.2.6 Thematic roles 57
            1.2.2.7 Formal vs. functional approaches in syntax 59
        1.2.3 Construction Grammar 60
            1.2.3.1 The development of Construction Grammar. Different approaches 60

	1.2.3.2	The notion of construction	62
	1.2.3.3	Examples of constructions	66
	1.2.3.4	The figure / ground alignment	70
	1.2.3.5	Further properties of constructions	70
	1.2.3.6	Generative vs. Construction Grammar	72
1.3	Morphology		73
	1.3.1	Why morphology?	73
	1.3.2	Morphemes	74
	1.3.3	Allomorphs and morphological processes	77
	1.3.4	Inflection vs. derivation	80
	1.3.5	Further strategies of word-formation	82
	1.3.5.1	Conversion	82
	1.3.5.2	Compounding	83
	1.3.5.3	Blending, secretion and neoclassical compounding	86
	1.3.5.4	Reduplication	89
	1.3.5.5	Abbreviations	90
	1.3.6	Productivity in morphology	91
	1.3.7	Summary	93
1.4	Language typology and linguistic universals		94
	1.4.1	Parameters of typological comparison	95
	1.4.2	Traditional morphological language typology	96
2	**Phonetics and Phonology**		99
2.0	A brief note on phonetic transcription		99
2.1	Phonetics		99
	2.1.1	Articulatory phonetics	100
	2.1.1.1	Vowels	101
	2.1.1.1.1	Parameters of vowel description. Kinds of vowels	101
	2.1.1.1.2	The vowels of English	103
	2.1.1.1.3	Contrastive observations on the monophthongs	105
	2.1.1.1.4	Observations on the English diphthongs	108
	2.1.1.1.5	Observations on the English vowel system	109
	2.1.1.2	Consonants	110
	2.1.1.3	Approximants / Glides / Semi-vowels. The sonority continuum	115
	2.1.2	Acoustic phonetics	116
	2.1.3	Auditory phonetics	119
2.2	Segmental phonology		120
	2.2.1	Phonetics vs. phonology. The phoneme	120
	2.2.2	Phonemic and phonetic transcription	122
	2.2.3	Phoneme vs. allophone	124
	2.2.4	Neutralisation	132
	2.2.5	Morphophonology	133
2.3	Suprasegmental phonology		135
	2.3.1	Phonotactics	135
	2.3.2	Syllables	136
	2.3.3	Word stress	138
	2.3.4	Intonation	140
	2.3.4.1	Theoretical preliminaries: What is special about intonation?	140
	2.3.4.2	The function of intonation in language systems	145
2.4	The phonetics and phonology of connected speech		148
	2.4.1	Weak forms	148
	2.4.2	Assimilation	151

2.4.3   Linking /r/ and intrusive /r/ 152
2.5   Writing 153
2.5.1   Graphemics and spelling 153
2.5.2   English spelling 155
2.5.3   Non-alphabetic writing systems 157

3   The history of English 158
3.1   External history 158
3.1.1   The onset: the formation of Old English 159
3.1.2   The transformation: Middle English 161
3.1.3   The eve of modernity: Early Modern English 162
3.1.4   Becoming global: Late Modern English 163
3.1.5   New communicative modes: Present-Day English 164
3.2   Internal history and types of language change 165
3.2.1   Sound change 166
3.2.1.0   Comparative reconstruction. The Indo-European language family 166
3.2.1.1   What Grimm's Laws tell us 167
3.2.1.2   Internal reconstruction of a phoneme split 170
3.2.1.3   Umlaut 171
3.2.1.4   Ablaut 172
3.2.1.5   The Great Vowel Shift 174
3.2.1.6   Phoneme merger 175
3.2.1.7   Phoneme loss 176
3.2.1.8   Phonetic attrition 177
3.2.2   Morphological change 178
3.2.2.0   Mechanisms of morphological change 178
3.2.2.1   Declension of nouns 179
3.2.2.2   Declension of adjectives 180
3.2.2.3   The pronoun system 180
3.2.2.4   Verb inflection 182
3.2.2.5   Changes in word formation 183
3.2.3   Syntactic change 185
3.2.3.1   Word order changes 185
3.2.3.2   Developments in the verbal syntagm 185
3.2.3.3   Grammaticalisation 189
3.2.4   Semantic change 194
3.2.5   Lexical change 197
3.2.5.1   Borrowing 198
3.2.5.2   Neologisms 203
3.2.5.3   Lexicalisation 204
3.2.5.4   Other lexical changes 205
3.3   Why do languages change? 206

4   Semantics 209
4.0   What is semantics? 209
4.1   General key concepts of semantics 210
4.1.1   Reference vs. sense and related dichotomies 210
4.1.2   Ambiguity, homonymy and polysemy;
         metonymy and metaphor; vagueness 212
4.1.2.1   Two kinds of ambiguity: homonymy and polysemy 212
4.1.2.2   Metonymy and metaphor 215
4.1.2.3   Vagueness 216

4.2   Structural semantics: semantic fields, sense relations and
      componential analysis 216
      4.2.1   Semantic fields 217
      4.2.2   Sense relations 220
      4.2.2.1   Synonymy 220
      4.2.2.2   Hyponymy 221
      4.2.2.3   Partitive relations 222
      4.2.2.4   Antonymy 222
      4.2.3   Componential analysis: the semantic feature approach 224
4.3   Cognitive semantics 225
      4.3.1   Central tenets of cognitive semantics 225
      4.3.2   Prototypes. Metaphors 228
      4.3.3   Frames 230
4.4   Formal semantics 233
      4.4.1   Truth values and truth conditions 233
      4.4.2   Logical connectives 234
      4.4.3   Logical relations between propositions 237
      4.4.3.1   Entailment 237
      4.4.3.2   Paraphrase 238
      4.4.3.3   Presupposition 238
      4.4.4   Logical properties of propositions 241
      4.4.4.1   Contradiction 241
      4.4.4.2   Tautology 241
      4.4.4.3   Anomaly 241
      4.4.5   Predicate logic 242
      4.4.5.1   Simple statements 242
      4.4.5.2   Quantification 243

5   Pragmatics: the context of language use 245
5.0   What is pragmatics? 245
5.1   Illocution 247
5.2   Conversational maxims 251
      5.2.1   Speakers' maxims: GRICE 251
      5.2.2   Hearers' heuristics: LEVINSON 253
5.3   Relevance theory 255
5.4   Pragmatic inferencing and language change 256
5.5   The notion of context 258

6   Textlinguistics. Conversation analysis. Discourse analysis 261
6.1   Textlinguistic approaches to text analysis 261
      6.1.1   Grammar beyond the sentence: cohesion phenomena 262
      6.1.2   Cohesion as text constitution 264
      6.1.3   Thematic progression 266
      6.1.4   Coherence relations 269
6.2   The analysis of conversation 272
6.3   Discourse in the technical age 273
      6.3.1   The oral – written dichotomy 273
      6.3.2   Media discourse 278

7   Sociolinguistics 280
7.0   The realm of sociolinguistics 280
7.1   Dialect, sociolect, and the standard 281
      7.1.1   Dialect vs. language vs. accent 281
      7.1.2   Sociolect 288

7.1.3 The standard 291
7.2 Languages in contact.. 294
7.2.1 Minority vs. majority.. 294
7.2.2 Bi- and multilingualism 295
7.2.3 Language policy 298
7.3 English as a world language... 300
7.4 Pidgins and creoles 305
7.4.1 Pidgins 305
7.4.2 Creoles 307
7.5 Language and gender 309
7.6 On variation and conditioning factors of its use 313

8 Epilogue: Specific characteristics of human languages
vs. animal communication 317
8.1 Arbitrariness.. 317
8.2 Duality / double articulation 318
8.3 Displacement.. 319
8.4 Creativity / productivity and recursiveness...................................... 319
8.5 Can animals learn human language?... 320

9 Exercises.. 322
9.1 Exercises relating to chapter 1 322
9.1.1 Grammar in general... 322
9.1.2 Syntax 322
9.1.3 Morphology 323
9.2 Exercises relating to chapter 2 324
9.3 Exercises relating to chapter 3 325
9.4 Exercises relating to chapter 4 326
9.5 Exercises relating to chapter 5 327
9.6 Exercises relating to chapter 6 328
9.7 Exercises relating to chapter 7 330
9.8 Exercises relating to chapter 8 331

10 Bibliographical section... 332
10.1 Some useful links for linguists... 332
10.1.1 General sources 332
10.1.2 Grammar 332
10.1.3 Phonetics and phonology.. 333
10.1.4 Lexicology and semantics 333
10.1.5 Sociolinguistics... 333
10.1.6 Psycholinguistics 333
10.1.7 Corpus linguistics 333
10.2 Important basic literature 333
10.2.0 General literature 333
10.2.0.1 Bibliographies.. 333
10.2.0.2 General readers 333
10.2.0.3 Reference works 334
10.2.0.4 Basic theoretical literature / Classics of linguistics.................... 335
10.2.0.5 General introductions.. 335
10.2.0.6 Schools of linguistics 336
10.2.0.7 Exercises 337
10.2.1 Grammar 337
10.2.1.1 Grammars of Modern English.. 337
10.2.1.2 Syntax 337

 10.2.1.3 Morphology 338
  10.2.1.3.1 Theory. General 338
  10.2.1.3.2 Word-formation 339
 10.2.1.4 Typology and universals 339
 10.2.2 Phonetics and phonology. Graphemics.................................. 339
 10.2.3 The history of English 340
 10.2.3.0 Introductions to historical linguistics............................ 340
 10.2.3.1 History of the English language.................................... 341
  10.2.3.1.0 Language histories. Historical grammars.
             Historical and etymological dictionaries 341
  10.2.3.1.1 Old English 341
  10.2.3.1.2 Middle English 342
  10.2.3.1.3 Early and Late Modern English 342
 10.2.3.2 Language change 342
  10.2.3.2.1 General 342
  10.2.3.2.2 Grammaticalisation 343
 10.2.4 Lexicology and semantics 343
 10.2.4.0 Dictionaries. Lexicography... 343
 10.2.4.1 Introductions to semantics 343
 10.2.4.2 Structural semantics... 344
 10.2.4.3 Cognitive semantics.. 344
 10.2.4.4 Formal semantics 345
 10.2.5 Pragmatics 345
 10.2.5.0 Theory / Introductions 345
 10.2.5.1 Speech act theory 345
 10.2.5.2 Conversational maxims.. 346
 10.2.5.3 Relevance theory 346
 10.2.6 Textlinguistics. Conversation analysis. Discourse analysis........... 346
  10.2.6.1 Textlinguistics... 346
  10.2.6.2 Analysis of conversation:... 347
  10.2.6.3 Discourse in the technical age.................................... 347
   10.2.6.3.1 Orality / literacy 347
   10.2.6.3.2 Media language 348
 10.2.7 Sociolinguistics and dialectology 348
  10.2.7.0 General 348
  10.2.7.1 Dialects, accents and the standard 349
  10.2.7.2 Bilingualism.. 349
  10.2.7.3 Varieties around the world.. 349
  10.2.7.4 Pidgins and creoles 350
  10.2.7.5 Language and gender 350
 10.2.8 Psycholinguistics. Neurolinguistics. Biolinguistics.................. 351
  10.2.8.1 Psycholinguistics 351
  10.2.8.2 Neurolinguistics 352
  10.2.8.3 Biolinguistics 352
 10.3 Literature mentioned in the text 352

11 Index.. 361

List of boxes

Box 1:   Mentalism vs. empiricism in linguistics   2
Box 2:   Object language vs. metalanguage   4
Box 3:   Corpus linguistics   5
Box 4:   Competence vs. performance. *Langue* vs. *parole*   6
Box 5:   Scope   8
Box 6:   Core vs. periphery in language   11
Box 7:   Agreement   19
Box 8:   Natural and grammatical gender   19
Box 9:   Perfective vs. imperfective   24
Box 10:   Markedness   28
Box 11:   Adjunct vs. complement   40
Box 12:   Sentence vs. clause   42
Box 13:   Descriptive vs. prescriptive   46
Box 14:   Transformations in transformational grammar   47
Box 15:   Recursiveness   55
Box 16:   Compositionality   60
Box 17:   Cognitive Linguistics   61
Box 18:   Fuzziness   62
Box 19:   Arbitrariness and PEIRCE's concept of 'symbol'   63
Box 20:   Lexicalist vs. derivationalist   74
Box 21:   Compound or noun phrase?   85
Box 22:   Comparative vs. contrastive linguistics   94
Box 23:   The notion of 'opposition' or 'contrast' in modern linguistics   121
Box 24:   Content vs. expression, form vs. substance   130
Box 25:   Discreteness   141
Box 26:   Iconicity   142
Box 27:   Indexicality   144
Box 28:   Tone languages   146
Box 29:   Diachrony vs. synchrony. Historical linguistics   158
Box 30:   Etymology   167
Box 31:   Areal typology: Sprachbünde   172
Box 32:   Analogy   178
Box 33:   Free variation   186
Box 34:   Metaphor   196
Box 35:   Etymological doublets   200
Box 36:   Structuralism in 20th century linguistics   216
Box 37:   Trajector vs. landmark   226
Box 38:   Pragmatics vs. semantics, competence vs. performance, *langue* vs.
          parole   246
Box 39:   Theme vs. rheme / topic vs. comment   267
Box 40:   Modality, medium, channel   274

List of tables and figures

Fig. 1:	Different aspects of grammar	10
Fig. 2:	Differences between morphology and syntax	15
Fig. 3:	Minor word classes in English	17
Fig. 4:	An example of different word classes in a complex English sentence	18
Fig. 5:	Natural and grammatical gender in German	20
Fig. 6:	Gender and number agreement in English pronouns	21
Fig. 7:	The two aspects of English	25
Fig. 8:	English tense and aspect combined	25
Fig. 9:	Examples of complex verbal syntagms in English	27
Fig. 10:	Personal pronouns of Present-Day English, subject case	28
Fig. 11:	Objects, complements, adjuncts: diverging terminologies	41
Fig. 12:	Tree diagram: *She served them there*	51
Fig. 13:	Tree diagram: *The distressed waitress solemnly ...*	54
Fig. 14:	Tree diagram: *He saw the boy with the telescope*, first reading: 'He used the telescope to see the boy.'	56
Fig. 15:	Tree diagram: *He saw the boy with the telescope*, second reading: 'He saw the boy who had a telescope.'	57
Fig. 16:	The symbolic nature of a construction	65
Fig. 17:	Examples of constructions	67
Fig. 18	An example of a hierarchical network of constructions	71
Fig. 19:	Lexical vs. grammatical morphemes	75
Fig. 20:	Tree diagram *Second language acquisition conference*, reading I	85
Fig. 21:	Tree diagram *Second language acquisition conference*, reading II	86
Fig. 22:	Kinds of morphemes	94
Fig. 23:	Anatomy of the vocal tract	100
Fig. 24:	Short (lax) vowels of English (phonetic descriptions)	103
Fig. 25:	Long (tense) vowels of British English (Received Pronunciation) (phonetic description)	104
Fig. 26:	Vowels of English (Received Pronunciation)	104
Fig. 27:	Vowels of English (General American)	105
Fig. 28:	Transcription of sounds by place and manner of articulation in IPA	111
Fig. 29:	Examples for English obstruent consonants	112
Fig. 30:	Examples for English sonorants	112
Fig. 31:	Examples for the use of some variants	112
Fig. 32:	Examples of consonants not used in English	113
Fig. 33:	Terminology for places of articulation	115
Fig. 34:	Spectrogram I	117
Fig. 35:	Spectrogram II	118
Fig. 36:	Spectrogram III	118
Fig. 37:	The major allophones of English /k/ and their complementary distribution	126
Fig. 38:	Content / expression vs. form / substance (table)	131
Fig. 39:	Content / expression vs. form / substance (graph)	131
Fig. 40:	Allomorphs of plural -s in English	134
Fig. 41:	Examples of morphophonological alternations in English*	134
Fig. 42:	Syllable structure	137
Fig. 43:	Words with several syllables	137

XVIII

Fig. 44:	Examples of stress patterns	139
Fig. 45:	Weak forms (clitics) in British English	149
Fig. 46:	Examples of linking /r/ and 'intrusive' /r/	152
Fig. 47:	'Silent letters' in English	156
Fig. 48:	Dialects of Old English	160
Fig. 49:	The family tree of English	167
Fig. 50:	Cognates in Old English and Old High German	168
Fig. 51:	Some fricative phonemes and their allophones in Old English	170
Fig. 52	The Old English umlaut pattern	171
Fig. 53:	Old English ablauting verbs	173
Fig. 54:	The Great Vowel Shift	175
Fig. 55:	The Great Vowel Shift ff.: examples	175
Fig. 56:	Old English noun declension: examples	179
Fig. 57:	Old English personal pronouns (nominative forms)	181
Fig. 58:	The fate of English verbal inflection, present tense	182
Fig. 59:	Examples of broadening and narrowing	195
Fig. 60:	Meaning development of verbs of perception	197
Fig. 61:	Celtic and early Latin loans in English	200
Fig. 62:	Norman French loans	201
Fig. 63:	Loans from all over the world	203
Fig. 64:	Examples of homonymy	213
Fig. 65:	Example of homophony	213
Fig. 66:	Example of homography	213
Fig. 67:	English and Welsh colour adjectives	218
Fig. 68:	'cousin' in English and German	218
Fig. 69:	*neck* in English and *Hals* in German	219
Fig. 70:	English loans in German and their synonyms	221
Fig. 71:	Hyponymy / hyperonymy	221
Fig. 72:	Meronymy	222
Fig. 73:	Contradictory contrast	223
Fig. 74:	Polarity	223
Fig. 75:	Converses	223
Fig. 76:	Semantic feature analysis	224
Fig. 77:	The extension of English *boy* as intersection of three sets	225
Fig. 78:	Image schema for *through*	226
Fig. 79:	The commercial transaction frame with its lexical realisations	231
Fig. 80:	Logical connectives and their names	234
Fig. 81:	Truth table for '&'	235
Fig. 82:	Examples of presuppositions	239
Fig. 83:	Examples of selection restrictions in English	242
Fig. 84:	The domains of semantics and pragmatics: some antitheses	246
Fig. 85:	Illocutions	247
Fig. 86:	Performative utterances and their illocutionary force	250
Fig. 87:	Conversational maxims	251
Fig. 88:	The three spheres of the context of an utterance	259
Fig. 89:	Situation elements, speech events and text types	277
Fig. 90	BIBER's factor one: interactive vs. edited	278
Fig. 91:	Approaches to language and society	280
Fig. 92:	Lexical differences between English dialects	283
Fig. 93:	Grammatical differences between English dialects	283
Fig. 94:	Traditional vs. modern dialects	285
Fig. 95:	Pronunciation differences between English dialects	288

Fig. 96:   Grammatical differences between American and British English   292
Fig. 97:   Different degrees of formality   293
Fig. 98:   The spread of English   301
Fig. 99:   English as a world language   304
Fig. 100: An example from Tok Pisin   306
Fig. 101: An example from Hawaiian Pidgin   308
Fig. 102: Prominent conditioning factors of language use   314

1 The core area of linguistics: grammar

1.1 Grammar in general

1.1.1 What kind of thing is grammar?

We will start out by explaining what we mean by the word *grammar*. For most of you, this word will probably refer to a kind of book, which you used when you learnt English at school, and which you will (hopefully) have on your bookshelves at home. Now you will have noticed that there are many such books, small ones, for use at schools, and large ones, for use at universities, and many different sizes in between. So it seems there is no <u>one</u> such thing as 'grammar'. Instead, we find many kinds of grammar<u>s</u>. It seems that 'grammar' in the singular is something beyond the different books that you may have on your shelves. It is something that the different books try to describe.

So we must say that the word *grammar* has at least two different meanings: In the sense you are most acquainted with, it means a kind of book which describes 'rules of grammar'. In the second sense, in which linguists usually use the word *grammar*, it means just these 'rules'. In this second sense, a **grammar** (*Grammatik*) is not something that you can touch or look at, but an abstract system that can be viewed from different angles: It can, among other things, be viewed as a psychological phenomenon: It can be said that a grammar is something that people have in their heads.

1.1.1.1 Grammar as knowledge

People <u>know</u> their grammar, even if they've never gone to school. The vast majority of the roughly 6,000 languages that are spoken in the world have never been written, and the vast majority of unwritten languages have never been described in a grammar book. Nevertheless all speakers of each of these languages have <u>a</u> grammar of that language in their heads. They simply know how to use their language. They automatically use the right word order, use the correct forms of words. Even if they make mistakes, they will know they've made a mistake when it is pointed out to them. And the grammar rules which they follow may be much more complicated than any rules of a language that any of us may know. So the first important thing we have to learn about 'grammar' is: A grammar of a language exists independently of its description in a grammar book.

It exists, first of all, in people's heads as a kind of **knowledge** as to <u>how to</u> use their own language. This is a very special kind of knowledge: a kind of knowledge which is usually not learnt at school, but in life. It is knowing how to do things. Just as you know how to walk, how to swim, how to drive, how to open a milk bottle (this may turn out to be the most difficult of all these), you also know how to speak, how to use your own language. So all this is knowing <u>how to</u>, not knowing <u>that</u>. Knowing <u>that</u> something is the case is typical of the kind of knowledge that you learn at school or from books. You learn and then know that Goethe died in 1832 (or was it 1838?). You know that the present Queen of England is named Elizabeth and that Paris is the capital of France.

> 📖 Find other examples of things that you know-how-to and that you know-that!

In this sense of 'knowing that', you may also know a lot of things about English grammar: You may know, e.g., that subject, verb, object (SVO) is the normal word order in an English sentence. This means, in very simple terms, in a normal English sentence like:

The linguist shot the albatross

the doer of an action, normally expressed by the subject of a sentence (*"the linguist"*), is mentioned before the action, normally expressed by the verb (*"shot"*), followed by the undergoer of an action, normally expressed by the object of a sentence (*"the albatross"*). (More on the notions of subject and object will be said in section → 1.2.1.2.) And yet, though you may have known this for a long time, you may have made mistakes, because of course you know that English word order is SVO, but sometimes forget how to implement this knowledge.

Linguists are primarily interested in people's knowing how to, not in people's knowing that. Grammar is knowledge of language in the sense of knowing how to use a language.

There is an important school of linguistics that particularly emphasises this basic idea that the object of linguistics is grammar in this sense, as knowledge in the sense of knowing how, as knowledge of native speakers of their language. This theory was first formulated by the famous linguist Noam CHOMSKY (1957) and has become known under the name **Generative Grammar** (*Generative Grammatik*). CHOMSKY says that it is the task of a grammatical description to describe "what the speaker of a language knows implicitly" (1972, 9) (→ Box 4; 1.2.2). Grammar as knowledge, however, is also invoked by **Construction Grammar**, a major alternative approach to Generative Grammar, that will also be presented in this introduction (→ 1.2.3).

Box 1: Mentalism vs. empiricism in linguistics

Approaches which concentrate on structures in the human mind as the primary object of linguistics are often called **mentalistic** approaches. Opposed to this would be an **empiricist** view which maintains that empirically gained linguistic data should be the object of linguistics. This view, e.g., is subscribed by many sociolinguists (→ chapter 7) and also by most corpus linguists (→ Box 3).

1.1.1.2 Grammar as a societal phenomenon

But grammar is not just individual knowledge. Grammars are also a societal phenomenon. Grammars can define **speech communities** (*Sprachgemeinschaften*).

> ☞ A speech community is a group of people sharing a certain amount of linguistic norms, such as in grammar, phonology, lexicon, etc., no matter whether they are laid down anywhere in writing or not, and using them in regular mutual interactions.

If language was just an individual phenomenon, it would be possible for individuals to have a private language not shared by anybody else. But what use could such a private language have? Everybody could use it to write their own private diaries, or to indulge in soliloquy. But language could not fulfil one of its most important functions, that is, communication. To fulfil this function, languages have to have grammars and vocabularies that are more than individual. Individual grammars in a speech community must be similar enough to make individual languages a tool for communication with others in that speech community. We shall return to speech communities and the social relevance of language in section → 7.1.1.

1.1.1.3 Discourse as a window to grammar

There is yet a third angle from which you can look at grammar in the linguistic sense. Discourse is the process in which language is used. We will come back to this in Chapter → 6. Grammar may be seen as an abstraction from people's linguistic behaviour in **discourse**. This is an important aspect of grammar that is often overlooked. The problem with grammar as a psychological phenomenon and grammar as a societal phenomenon is that it is not directly accessible. For all the progress made in psychological and neurological research in recent years, it is still very difficult to look into people's heads. You may ask people questions about what they think the rules of their language are, but the answers you get will often be very unsatisfactory. People's intuitions, people's true knowledge of language is not directly accessible to introspection and questioning. In the same way, grammar rules as a societal phenomenon are difficult to assess in their own right. Again, inculcated norms and attitudes may weigh more heavily than people's intuitions if you ask them what the rules of grammar in a certain community are. To put it briefly: People are not very reliable when asked to make **metalinguistic** statements and assessments, that is, statements about their language. The best you can get from ordinary native speakers of a language is statements or other language behaviour in their language. This is difficult enough to accomplish.

4

Box 2: Object language vs. metalanguage

Linguists are bound to make metalinguistic statements all the time and are thus careful to distinguish between **metalanguage** and **object language** (*Metasprache, Objektsprache*). Metalanguage is the kind of language they use when they speak about language in contrast to the object language we all use when we speak about other things in the world. In principle, all expressions in a language can be used metalinguistically, i.e., when we speak about the linguistic expression, and not the thing it refers to. In this book, we use *italics* to indicate that an expression is used metalinguistically.

Thus, if we write "Butter melts in the sun", this is a true statement about real butter, if, however, we chose to write "*Butter* melts in the sun", this would be plain nonsense because the word *butter* does not melt in the sun (unless, perhaps, it is written in something that happens to melt in the sun). On the other hand, a statement such as "Butter has six letters" is plain nonsense because butter cannot have letters, whereas the sentence "*Butter* has six letters" is fine.

It can also be said that in the sentences without italics, we **use** the word *butter* to make an ordinary statement about butter, whereas in the other two cases, where *butter* is written in italics, we just **mention** the word *butter* to make a statement about that word. This is a distinction that is not always maintained in everyday discourse, but that is crucial when doing linguistics. Failure to maintain the use – mention distinction has often led to severe misunderstandings, as the distinction does not only apply to individual words, but also to sentences. Incidentally, it is, among other things, crucial for an understanding of irony and related phenomena (SPERBER / WILSON 1981).

With respect to empirical studies, the **observer's paradox** (*Beobachterparadoxon*) is an inherent problem when collecting linguistic data, e.g. the recording of samples of spoken language. It is the recording situation itself which is paradoxical: the observer wants to observe people as to how they behave normally, i.e. when they are unobserved. A result of this is that the recorded data is not as 'natural' as it could have been without somebody observing. For example, a person asked to tell a certain story will do so very differently, i.e. possibly more carefully when being confronted with a microphone or camera. The problem is not solved by hiding e.g. a tape recorder somewhere in a room where it is not detected by the prospective informants so that the observer can be physically absent. On the one hand, it might be difficult to obtain precisely the kind of data the observer is interested in – what if the structures I am studying simply do not occur in the material? Thus, the body of data collected in the observer's absence may lack representativeness and focus. On the other hand, even if the observer is present during surreptitious recording (which might ensure the right kind of output), his or her mere presence renders the communicative situation artificial and will most probably bias the output of the informant(s). What is more, there is always the possibility that the informants might – for various reasons – never have agreed to their utterances being recorded and analysed. This raises serious ethical problems which cannot be ignored. Thus, minimising the effects of this dilemma should be a major aim of the observer who wants to collect reliable data.

Still, linguists have learnt to overcome these difficulties by employing methods of empirical research developed in the social sciences, so meanwhile we have a fair and ever-increasing amount of authentic language data available, samples of language behaviour, both spoken and written, much of it collected in huge computer-readable corpora.

Box 3: Corpus linguistics

The term *corpus* is now almost exclusively used to refer to a large and structured collection of authentic written texts or transcribed speech provided in a machine-readable form and representative of the language or language variety in question. More generally, a corpus is any large collection of texts in whatever form.

Corpus linguistics (*Korpuslinguistik*) has become an expanding and extremely fruitful field of linguistic studies. It is certainly now the dominant paradigm for empirically oriented linguists. It can be said that the use of computer corpora has largely replaced more traditional ways of data-gathering. Corpus linguistics is not to be understood as a specific linguistic theory; but certain theories have more uses for corpus linguistics than others.

Corpus studies are used as an empirical basis for a wide range of topics within linguistics, including lexicography (→ 4.0), all sorts of grammatical questions, language variation (→ 7.6), historical linguistics (→ Chapter 3), contrastive linguistics (→ 1.4), translation theory, natural language processing, etc.

There are different types of corpora, varying in size, and composition and serving different purposes, e.g. the **British National Corpus** (BNC) (a contemporary British English 100-million-word corpus), the **American National Corpus** (ANC), and the **Helsinki Corpus** (a historical corpus). Although the bulk of available corpus data is still from written sources, corpora of oral language are increasingly being built.

One of the major objectives of corpus-based studies is to reveal typical patterns of use, replacing the traditional eliciting of judgements of grammaticality from native speakers. With the help of corpora we can examine the frequency distribution of syntactic patterns, lexical association patterns, the use and function of morphological characteristics, etc.

The most commonly used tool in corpus linguistics are **concordances** (*Konkordanzen*): A software program displays all occurrences of a selected word together with their immediate contextual environment. Concordances also facilitate the study of **collocations** (*Kollokationen*) (→ 4.1.1).

But there is a problem with authentic language data. Look at the following example of a transcript of a real-life conversation (braces { } indicate breaks in the flow of speech):

6

The one {} one of the things I {} I'm told, {} I gather from Alec, {.} this morning, {u:m} that {uh} Oscar feels very sore about, {.} is, that he sees this {uh} as a breaking of the consortium...

When we speak and don't finish a sentence before we start a new one, as in the above example, we cannot say that this is what is stored in our heads, that is, it is not a rule of our grammar to speak with a lot of '*uhs*' and '*ums*' and other hesitation phenomena, or to keep leaving sentences unfinished. And it is not something that defines our speech community, either.

Box 4: Competence vs. performance. *Langue* vs. *parole*

> The difference between edited and authentic language, or between what is accepted as flawless speech in a speech community and what is actually spoken is the difference that CHOMSKY (1972, 9) had in mind when he distinguished between
> - **competence** (*Kompetenz*), that is the know-how of the speakers of a language, and
> - **performance** (*Performanz*), that is the actual use of language.
>
> This distinction is a late 20th century reformulation of a distinction made in the early 20th century by the Swiss linguist Ferdinand de SAUSSURE ([1]1916] 1965, 112), between
> - *langue* and
> - *parole*.
>
> These are two terms taken over from French into international linguistic terminology which could be reformulated in English and German as the
> - **system of language** (*Sprachsystem*) and the
> - **use of language** (*Sprachgebrauch*).

Grammar, of course, cannot be directly read off the authentic data. But these data are our most reliable source of the grammar that people have in their heads and that is accepted in their speech communities. If we want to study grammar we want to look at competence, not performance. But performance, or discourse, is a <u>window</u> to competence. And discourse, as we shall see in section → 3.2, is also the most usual place where language change originates.

1.1.1.4 Written grammars

Grammars as they are written down in books may be of several kinds. Traditionally grammars were written in order to prescribe and teach the 'proper' use of a language to native and non-native speakers. Such grammars are therefore called prescriptive or pedagogical grammars. Linguists' grammars are different. Linguists are more interested in the way language is actually used and less in the way some people <u>think</u> they or other people should use language. Incidentally, such beliefs about language norms, often advocated by self-appointed experts with great conviction, are often not in accordance with the same people's actual language usage (see below for examples).

Thus, while **prescriptive** grammars (*präskriptive Grammatiken*), and also **pedagogical** grammars (*Schulgrammatiken*) to a certain extent, lay down rules of correctness as to how language should be used, **descriptive** linguists' grammars (*deskriptive Grammatiken*) try to describe the facts of linguistic usage as they are. To give a few more concrete examples:

A prescriptive grammar might tell its users that

> *The man whom I saw*

is correct English, while

> *The man who I saw*

is incorrect, contrary to actual contemporary usage by the vast majority of English speakers and writers in the vast majority of cases. It is just because prescriptive grammarians of English happen to have noticed that English grammar has been changing in this point, and happen to have decided to stop this change. Descriptive grammars, on the other hand, might note that *whom* can be used in the sentence in question in formal written style, whereas informal speech prefers *who*, keeping the form *whom* only after prepositions, such as in

> *The man to whom I spoke,*

where, however, in many cases informal speech prefers

> *The man I spoke to.*

The latter example also raises another issue, one that prescriptive grammarians have fought a heroic battle about for centuries: so-called stranded prepositions, that is prepositions that are 'stranded' at the end of sentences or clauses, like the preposition *to* in the above example. (For more on the notion of preposition → 1.1.3.1). In this hopeless battle, prescriptive grammarians were probably influenced by the etymology (→ Box 30) of the word *preposition*: According to its Latin origin, a preposition is something that is <u>pre</u>-posed, that is, put before something else; so it seemed logically impossible to have a preposition alone at the end of a sentence. Descriptive linguists will only note that stranded prepositions are a very normal phenomenon not only in English, but also in other languages, including some varieties of German:

> *Nachgestellte Präpositionen im Deutschen? Da will ich nichts **von** hören!*

They will then proceed to explain this phenomenon in their respective grammatical framework. In fact, stranded prepositions are so normal in English that even people fighting against them cannot help using them occasionally. It's like in the old schoolboys' joke about a teacher who used to say

> *"A preposition is not a proper word to end a sentence with".*

Another pet issue of prescriptive grammarians is the so-called "split infinitive" (on infinitive clauses, → 1.1.3.4.7), as in the following example:

*She decided **to gradually get** rid of the teddy-bears*
(TRASK 1999, 246).

What is meant by *split infinitive* is the insertion of an adverb between *to* and the infinitival verb form. Now for various reasons, this insertion is very much within the logic of English grammar. If it wasn't, the construction would have been unlikely to arise at all. (On the notion of 'construction', see → 1.2.3.2). In the above example, there is actually no choice if you want to avoid misunderstandings:

*She decided **gradually to get** rid of the teddy-bears*

has a different meaning because the **scope** of *gradually* is different, and in

*She decided to get rid of the teddy-bears **gradually**,*

the scope of *decided* changes (see Box 5). For some inexplicable reason, prescriptivists have objected to constructions of this kind for centuries.

What is interesting to note about prescriptivism is that it seems to concentrate on banning certain ways of using language rather than actually giving advice to language users on how to use language. So, instead of being concerned with pre-scription, they indulge in proscription.

But to end this section on a conciliatory note: Writing prescriptive grammars can be a very useful occupation, and maybe linguists should pay more attention to the practice of writing prescriptive grammars for insecure language users and learners. But prescription should be based on description, and on a sound knowledge of grammatical facts and principles.

Box 5: Scope

Scope is an important and widely-used technical term in linguistics which is easy to comprehend but difficult to explain. Every language presumably has expressions that have, or as is often said, **take scope** (*Skopus, Reichweite*) over other expressions. Let us call such expressions **operators**. Taking scope means that other expressions, usually in the same sentence, are affected by the operation referred to by the operator. Usually the scope of an operator is the whole sentence, or what follows the operator in the sentence, or the sub-clause of which the operator is part (on *sentence* and *clause*, see Box 12).

In the above example, the critical operators are *decided* and *gradually*. The questions are: What exactly is the scope of the decision? How far does the scope of *gradually* extend? That means: What in the sentence is it that is decided, and what exactly is gradual?

In the formulation *"... to gradually get rid of ..."*, *gradually* is inside the *to*-clause and can thus only take scope over this clause. So the "split" infinitive yields the intended meaning that not the decision is gradual, but the getting rid of the teddy bears. The scope of the decision is the whole *to*-clause.

If you put *gradually* outside the *to*-clause, as some prescriptivists would have it, *gradually* takes scope over the whole sentence, and so it would be the decision that is gradual. This, however, is obviously not the intended meaning.

If you put *gradually* at the end, as in the last example, which would also be acceptable to prescriptivists, it receives more weight because this is an unusual position for a small adverb. In consequence, the scope of *decided* is now the adverb *gradually* alone, which means that the decision to get rid of the teddy-bears must have been taken earlier, and that now the decision was taken to achieve this gradually. Again, this is not the intended meaning in the 'split infinitive' sentence.

Scope is most often discussed in connection with negation (asking: What actually is negated in the sentence?). It also plays an important role in formal logic (→ 4.4).

☛ *scope* is also often used quite untechnically in this textbook.

1.1.1.5 Summary

We can thus see that *grammar* has a variety of different senses. As an abstract system it can refer to a psychological and societal phenomenon determining the use of language in discourse. As a book, it can refer to a prescriptive (normative), pedagogical, or descriptive account of the grammar of a language.

Having thus clarified from four different angles what kinds of things grammar can be, we present a very brief summary of all this in a diagram (Fig. 1) showing the interrelatedness of these different aspects of grammar. It shows how different approaches to linguistics have different concepts, or concentrate on different aspects, of grammar, and it shows how these different aspects are interrelated.

Individual competence, grammatical norms of a speech community and discourse all shape and influence each other. By using language in discourse, individuals show their individual competence. This competence, of course, cannot remain uninfluenced by the social norms that the speaker accepts as a member of a speech community: If a speaker keeps violating the linguistic norms, this will lead to communication difficulties to the point of miscomprehension or incomprehension. The norms of the speech community are largely shaped and maintained through discourse: By using norm-conforming language, speakers rehearse their knowledge of these norms; the correction of eventual errors, of course, also takes place through discourse. To reverse the circle, discourse not only maintains the norms, but is clearly also shaped by them. The grammatical norms, in turn, are nothing but the sum of individual competences, and they cannot persist if too many or too influential individuals no longer conform to them. Individual competence, in turn, is of course influenced by the use of language in discourse: by the feedback that people get in discourse to their use of language and by how people hear other members of the speech community use language. Discourse is the basis of all empirical study in linguistics; corpus linguistics (→ Box 3) is the best example of this.

Fig. 1: Different aspects of grammar

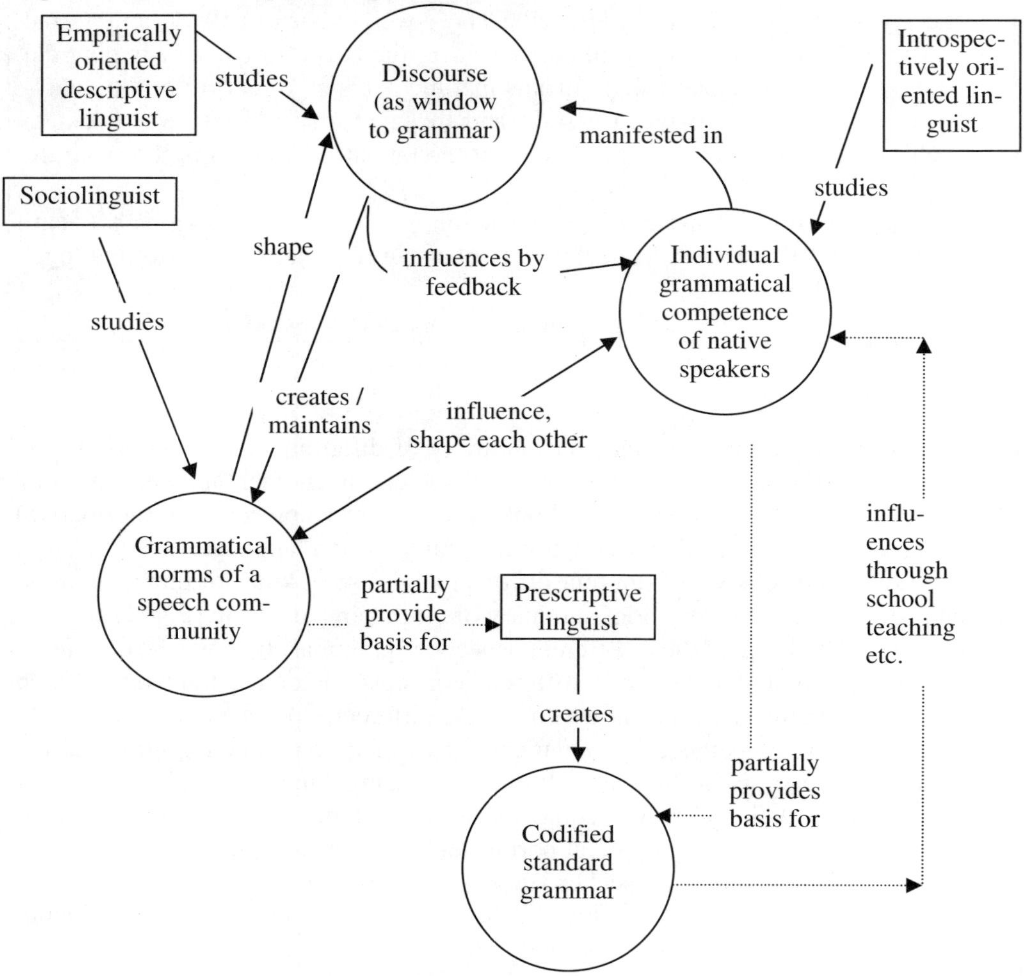

Empirically oriented descriptive linguist — studies → Discourse (as window to grammar)

Introspectively oriented linguist — studies → Individual grammatical competence of native speakers

Discourse (as window to grammar) — manifested in ← Individual grammatical competence of native speakers

Sociolinguist — studies →

shape

influences by feedback

creates / maintains

influence, shape each other

Grammatical norms of a speech community — partially provide basis for — Prescriptive linguist

Prescriptive linguist — creates → Codified standard grammar

influences through school teaching etc.

partially provides basis for

Linguists who believe that individual competence should be the sole object of study in linguistics are, as we saw above, said to take a mentalistic view of language and their method is often **introspective**, that is, they more or less study their own grammatical competence and that of a few friends and colleagues. The norms of speech communities belong to the realm of sociolinguistics (➔ Chapter 7), whose method is largely empirical. Prescriptive linguists are of course also concerned with norms, but their method is seldom empirical, but introspective. They usually take what they take to be the linguistic norms of their own, usually a rather narrowly defined speech community (usually so-called 'educated' speakers of a certain socially defined standard language variety, ➔ 7.1.3) as the basis for their prescriptions (➔ 1.1.1.4).

1.1.2 Subdivisions of grammar and the notion of *word*

The study of **grammar** (*Grammatik*) as seen by linguists is usually divided into two parts: morphology and syntax. **Morphology** (*Morphologie*, *Formenlehre*) deals with the inner structure of words; **syntax** investigates how words can be combined to form sentences.

Although this sounds easy enough, the distinction is difficult to explain in strict theoretical terms. Obviously, the distinction hinges on the notion of *word*, and linguists have sometimes found it extremely difficult to define what a word is, although naïve speakers of most languages have some kind of notion that corresponds to what English speakers usually call a word.

The problem is that these intuitive notions are sometimes contradictory (just think of the permanent controversies about '*Getrennt- und Zusammenschreibung*' in German orthography!), and they usually only work for a core set of unproblematic cases.

To come back to the notion of *word:* Speakers who have learnt to write in a traditional spelling system may be influenced in their judgements by spelling, so that in many European countries, people have a notion of *word* that is influenced by the spelling system, rather than a spelling system determined by people's notion of *word*.

Box 6:   Core vs. periphery in language

This phenomenon, namely that rules and generalisations do not always work without exception, is not restricted to laypeople's linguistic notions, however. While this is still a major problem for some traditional approaches to linguistics, many linguists nowadays have come to accept that in dealing with language, we often have to distinguish between a

- **core** (*Zentrum*) set of well-behaved phenomena, for which all theoretical generalisations hold, and a
- **periphery** (*Peripherie*), where we find surprises, exceptions, irregularities and other kinds of linguistic misdemeanour.

This statement is more or less true of all subfields of linguistics.

Thus, on the level of sounds, languages such as English and German have peripheral sounds, such as the sound of disapproval usually transcribed *tut-tut* in English, *dz-dz* in German. This sound is phonetically exceptional in both English and German, and it would never form part of a word in these languages; but it may be central in other languages, as it is indeed in Zulu, spoken in South Africa, where it is combined with other sounds to form words.

Looking at the level of words, there are thousands of everyday words in English forming the core of its vocabulary, but many more peripheral words known only to special groups such as hunters, computer specialists, or drug dealers, respectively.

In all these cases it is useful to distinguish a core from a periphery. The phonetic characterisation of English would become very awkward if sounds such as *tut-tut* had to be included in it. And many generalisations about English words could not be made if they had to be made to include all slang words, special vocabulary, etc.

During the twentieth century, many linguists came to the conclusion that *word* should not be a technical linguistic term at all, because it was impossible to define rigorously. The same linguists often tended to neglect the morphology – syntax distinction.

On the other hand, the usefulness of the division between morphology and syntax has become increasingly apparent, and linguists have now come up with a set of criteria that can be used both to define what a word is, and to draw a boundary between syntax and morphology.

Such definitions usually distinguish several different kinds of notions. The first question that must be asked is whether we are talking about the word as a unit of the *langue* or as a unit of the *parole* (➔ Box 4). Defining the word as a unit of the *langue* means asking how many words there are in the lexicon of a language or whether two different word forms belong to the same word or not. This question will be taken up in section ➔ 4.0. Defining the word as a unit of the *parole* amounts to the question whether a given string of sounds is one word, several words following each other, a part of a word or even parts of different words. This is the question we are asking in this section.

Two notions which must clearly be distinguished here, and which are usually mentioned in the literature, are the

- **phonological** word and the
- **morphosyntactic** word.

The two are not necessarily identical, and it is precisely this occasional discrepancy which has led to the confusion mentioned above.

The phonological word is recognisable by phonological criteria, which may be highly language-specific. Thus, in some languages, words may have a clearly defined phonological structure, e.g. in terms of number of syllables (➔ 2.3.2), stress patterns (➔ 2.3.3) etc. In English, phonological criteria are only applicable indirectly, but they often play a decisive role.

The morphosyntactic criteria have to do with the morphological structure of words and the role words play in syntax.

In this introduction, we would like to approach the problem practically-minded, and suggest a number of criteria which can be applied to decide whether a given string is a word or not.

We can thus now say that a **word** (*Wort*) is a linguistic unit that

- can be moved around relatively freely in a clause (whereas units smaller than a word cannot),
- can be stressed (➔ 2.3.3), and
- can be pronounced naturally on its own.

As you will notice, the first criterion is syntactic, the last two are phonological. To these may be added a fourth, syntactic criterion that may be applied when the first three don't provide a conclusive result:

– a word can usually be inserted between two other words, but not in the middle of a word.

Taking the two German clauses

Ich werde heute Abend Essen kochen
Ich werde heute Abendessen kochen

which differ only in the number of words (it's not easy to find examples like this in English), some of these properties of the word can be demonstrated. If *Abend Essen* are two words, they can be moved around separately in the clause:

Heute Abend werde ich Essen kochen
Essen werde ich heute Abend kochen.

Abendessen as one word, however, can only be moved as a whole:

Abendessen werde ich heute kochen.

The same applies to the criterion of stress. *Abend* and *Essen* as separate words can be stressed separately. (Stress is indicated by capitals here).

Ich werde heute Abend ESSEN kochen
Ich werde heute ABEND Essen kochen.

Abendessen as a single word can only be stressed in one place:

Ich werde heute ABENDessen kochen
*Ich werde heute AbendESSEN kochen.

✍ Remember: We use the asterisk (*) in synchronic linguistics to mark expressions or sentences that are not well-formed according to the rules of the language in question.

Criterion 3 (pronounceability) cannot be applied to the above example because *Abend* and *essen* could always be words on their own and could thus be pronounced on their own. But there are many linguistic units in both German and English that are smaller than a word and that can never be a word on their own.

Let us take the complex English word *theatricality* or the complex German word *einheitlich*. They can be divided into smaller units which will be discussed in more detail in section → 1.3.2.

Let us say, for example, that *theatricality* consists of the word *theatre* with several 'endings' attached to it which are familiar to anybody learning English: *-ic*, *-al*, and *-ity*. It is clear that, of these parts, only *theatre* has a natural pronunciation when used on its own. *-ic, -al* and *-ity* never occur on their own in natural English speech. They only occur in linguistic description, and they don't really have a natural pronunciation of their own (just try to pronounce them if you are not sure what we mean). And it is also obvious that *-ic, -al,* and *-ity* cannot be moved around as freely as an English word can. They have to find their specific place in an English word, and they cannot be permuted nor can they 'float' around in a word as words sometimes do in a sentence: There is no *ity-theatr-al-ic*, and there aren't too many words in English which are able to host the suffixes -ic, -al, or -ity. Words usually can be combined much more freely. A similar argument could be built for the complex German word *ein-heit-lich*.

The fourth criterion (insertability of a word between words) can be applied to all our examples. Thus, if *Abend* and *Essen* are two words, another word can be inserted between them:

> *Ich werde heute Abend schnell Essen kochen.*

This is not possible if *Abendessen* is one word. *Abendschnellessen* is, to say the least, unusual. In the case of *theatricality* and *einheitlich*, it is not even conceivable what word could be inserted in the middle of these words, so that it is abundantly obvious that they are words and not groups of words.

The fourth criterion, that of insertability, is also the criterion that tells us that articles in English (*the, a(n)*), prepositions, auxiliaries and other **function words** (→ 1.1.3.1, ☞ box) are actually words. With these, the other criteria are not applicable or give the 'wrong' results. Articles and some of the other function words cannot be moved around freely, but are fixed to certain positions in the clause. If they are stressed, their pronunciation often changes, so that it may be doubted whether the stressed versions of *the, a,* or *can, has* etc. are actually the same words as their unstressed counterparts. The only criterion that 'saves' these units from losing their word status is the criterion of insertability:

Given the clause

> *The linguist shot the albatross*

we may insert words between *the,* and *linguist* and *albatross*, respectively:

> *The stupid linguist shot the protected albatross.*

Otherwise, *thelinguist* and *thealbatross* would have to be regarded as single words. The same can be argued for *can* and *has*:

> *John can (certainly) do the washing-up*
> *Mary has (repeatedly) offended Jane.*

The insertability of *certainly* or *repeatedly* is evidence that *cando* and *hasoffended* are two words rather than one.

📖 Find examples which argue for the word status of prepositions like *in* or *with*.

We thus get the following characteristic differences between morphology and syntax:

Fig. 2: Differences between morphology and syntax

	Syntax	Morphology
Domain	Above word boundary (*Theatricality*) (*may* (*frighten* (*the boy*)))	Below word boundary (((*theatr*)-*ic*-*al*)-*ity*)
Mobility of smallest units	Relatively free mobility *May theatricality frighten the boy?*	Relatively rigid combination **ic-theatr-ity-al*
Integration of smallest units	Units may be pronounced separately. *Theatricality ... may ... frighten ... the ... boy*	Units cannot be pronounced separately **theatr ... ic ... al ... ity*
Largest unit to be formed	Sentence *Theatricality may frighten the boy*	Word *Theatricality*

1.1.3 General concepts of grammar

There are numerous concepts in the grammar of English and other languages which affect syntax as well as morphology. This is why we should concern ourselves with them first. It should, however, be noted that it is not the aim of this introduction to replace a reference grammar. It is, on the contrary, presupposed that students are acquainted to a certain degree with the grammatical phenomena of English and are able to use a reference grammar (we recommend QUIRK et al. [12]1994 and BIBER et al. 1999). This introduction emphasises theoretical aspects of these phenomena and discusses detail only in order to illustrate certain points. Occasionally, we will give bibliographic hints as to where the facts can be ascertained.

1.1.3.1 Word classes

The four most important word classes (parts of speech; *Wortklassen*) of most languages are:
* **noun** (*Substantiv, Nomen, Hauptwort*),
* **adjective** (*Adjektiv, Eigenschaftswort*),
* **verb** (*Verb, Tätigkeitswort*).

  * Within the verbs, we have to distinguish a special subclass, the **auxiliaries** (*Hilfsverben*), which in turn have to be divided in several subclasses with specific characteristics. What all auxiliaries have in common, however, is their obligatoriness in negation and questions:

  *The linguist **didn't** shoot the albatross.*
  *The linguist **won't** shoot the albatross.*

*The linguist **hasn't** shot the albatross.*
*The linguist not shot the albatross.
***Did** the linguist shoot the albatross?*
***Will** the linguist shoot the albatross?*
***Has** the linguist shot the albatross?*
*Shot the linguist the albatross?

The fourth 'major' word class of English are
- **prepositions** (*Präpositionen*).

The word classes will be characterised in more detail in → 1.2.2.3. At the moment it may suffice to illustrate them by way of an example. Thus, in the following sentence

The waitress served a gigantic portion of muffins to Aunt Martha

- *waitress*, *portion* and *muffins* are nouns,
- *gigantic* is an adjective,
- *served* a verb and
- *of* and *to* are prepositions.

It is very difficult and perhaps even impossible to provide universal definitions of the different word classes, i.e., definitions which account for all languages. There are some universal tendencies only. On the other hand, if individual languages are considered, it is not too difficult to define their major word classes. We distinguish several ways of defining word classes:

- The traditional view: semantic criteria
  Traditionally, word classes were distinguished by their meaning. It was said that nouns designate things, verbs actions, processes and events, and adjectives properties and states. But what kind of 'thing' is, say, an exam, what kind of 'event' is looming, and what kind of 'property' is being busy? Isn't it more appropriate to say an exam is an event, looming a property, and being busy an activity? Despite these difficulties, the traditional semantic definitions of word classes have their heuristic value, and recent theories of cognitive grammar have taken them up in a more sophisticated form (LANGACKER 1988, → 1.2.3).

- Syntactic criteria
  In English, word classes are primarily determined according to syntactic criteria: They fit into particular slots in a sentence, i.e., words of different classes follow each other in sentences according to certain recognisable patterns so they rather describe syntactic functional classes than qualities of words (for more on this question, see → 1.2.2.3).

- Morphological criteria
  In most languages, nouns and verbs in English can also be recognised by the different morphological forms they may assume (→ 1.3.4). Thus,

  - words taking an -s in the plural (→ 1.1.3.2.1) (*boy, boys*) are certainly nouns whereas

- words that may be substituted by forms ending in -*ed* or irregular forms such as *sang* (from *sing*), thus showing that they have a past tense (→1.1.3.4) can safely be regarded as verbs in English.

There are a number of other, minor word classes in English. The following tables give an overview of the most important types and subtypes and some of their characteristics (Fig. 3 below) and a sentence which contains most of the word classes mentioned (Fig. 4 below). For explanation of some of the syntactic terminology used, see → 1.2.1.3; 1.2.2.3; 1.2.2.4.

Fig. 3: Minor word classes in English

Word class	Subtypes and examples	Characteristics
conjunctions (*Konjunktionen*)	**coordinating** (*koordinierend*): *and or but*	Connect clauses or phrases of the same type with each other
	subordinating (*subordinierend*): *while although if because*	Connect subordinate to superordinate clauses.
adverbs (*Adverbien*)	**temporal** (*Zeitadverb*): *yesterday, then* **local** (*Ortsadverb*): *abroad, here* **manner** (*Adverb der Art und Weise*): *quickly, badly, hard*	Modify verbs or adjectives
articles (*Artikel*)	**definite** (*bestimmter*): *the* **indefinite** (*unbestimmter*): *a(n)*	Introduce noun phrases
pronouns (*Pronomina, Fürwörter*)	**personal** (*Personalpronomen*): *I me you he him she her it we us they them*	Replace whole noun phrases
	demonstrative (*Demonstrativpronomen*): *this that*	Replace whole noun phrases or articles
	possessive (better: **possessive determiner**) (*Possessivpronomen*): *my your his her its our their*	Replace articles
particles (*Partikeln*)	*only even just*	See * in box below

> ***Particles** form a residual category with sometimes unusual syntactic properties which is difficult to characterise, there are probably several subcategories.
> ☞ Articles, and possessive and demonstrative pronouns which can replace them, are often grouped together in a superordinate word class **determiner**. This is particularly relevant in syntactic description (→ 1.2.2.3).

Auxiliary verbs, prepositions, conjunctions, determiners, pronouns and particles are often called **function words** (*Funktionswörter*) because they fulfil grammatical functions. All the others are **content words** (*Inhaltswörter*) because they are believed to provide the 'content proper' of each sentence.

Fig. 4: An example of different word classes in a complex English sentence

When	subordinating conjunction	*she*	personal pronoun
the	definite article	*didn't*	auxiliary verb
poor	adjective	*even*	particle
waitress	noun	*dream*	verb
came	verb	*of*	preposition
into	preposition	*serving*	gerund (noun <u>and</u> verb)
the	definite article	*her*	personal pronoun
room	noun	*the*	definite article
and	coordinating conjunction	*incredibly*	manner adverb
only	particle	*dry*	adjective
saw	verb	*muffins*	noun
Aunt	noun (as part of name)	*on*	preposition
Martha	proper noun (proper name)	*an*	indefinite article
sitting	participle (adjective <u>and</u> verb)	*exquisite*	adjective
there	local adverb <u>and</u> demonstrative pronoun	*silver*	adjective
unashamedly	manner adverb	*dish*	noun

The major word classes – except prepositions – have abstract so-called **grammatical categories** (*grammatische Kategorien*) associated with them in many languages. These categories give the speaker different choices for modifying the meaning or grammatical function of the respective noun, adjective or verb. These different choices we will call the **values** of the respective grammatical category. The most frequent categories in European languages are:

- with nouns: number (→1.1.3.2.1), gender (→ 1.1.3.2.2), case (→ 1.1.3.2.3);
- with adjectives, in addition to the preceding: comparison (→1.1.3.3);
- with verbs: tense (→1.1.3.4.1), aspect (→ 1.1.3.4.2), person/number (→ 1.1.3.4.4), voice (→ 1.1.3.4.5), mood, modality (→ 1.1.3.4.6).

All these categories will be discussed in the above-mentioned sections in turn.

1.1.3.2 Grammatical categories of the noun

1.1.3.2.1 Number

Number (*Numerus*) provides information on the number of things to be described by a noun. There are two such numbers in German and English: singular and plural.

> ➤ Old English still had some relics of a third number (**dual** for the number two).

In English, number is marked on the noun (and the verb, → 1.1.3.4.4), but not on the adjective or determiner:

some-ø good-ø book-s.

> ✍ In morphology, the ø sign is sometimes used to indicate that a certain category is not signalled although one might expect this. It is used in a somewhat loose manner here to simply draw attention to the fact that determiner and adjective, in contrast to the noun, are not marked for number.
> ⭕ In other languages, the 'ending' of adjectives depends on the associated noun as well. In German, this concerns so-called **attributive adjectives** (*attributive Adjektive*) (→ 1.2.2.4) only, as in *gut-e Büch-er*, but in Latin, **predicative adjectives** (*prädikative Adjektive*) are affected as well, cf. *Die Bücher sind gut-ø. Libr-i bon-i sunt.*

Box 7: Agreement

> ☞ In linguistic terminology, this kind of correspondence between words belonging together in terms of grammatical categories is called **agreement** or **concord** (*Kongruenz*). Agreement means that the value of some grammatical category on a certain word (in the above examples, the value 'plural' of the category 'number' of the word *Bücher*) must be repeated on some other word in the same sentence (in this case, the adjective form *gute*) according to certain rules.
> The only kinds of agreement found in Standard Present-Day English are the number agreement between subject and verb (→ 1.2.1.2) and perhaps a kind of gender agreement as described in section → 1.1.3.2.2. Substandard varieties of English frequently show so-called **negative concord** (aka "double negation"), → 3.2.3.2.
> ⭕ In a number of other languages, including Old English, German, and Latin, agreement plays a much more important role. Look out for remarks in the following sections.

1.1.3.2.2 Gender

Gender (*Genus*) designates the more or less arbitrary division of all nouns of a given language into classes, which behave differently in terms of agreement and related phenomena.

Box 8: Natural and grammatical gender

> In order to discuss gender in linguistics, it is necessary to distinguish
> • **natural gender** (*natürliches Geschlecht*), for which the terms *female* and *male* are used in Fig. 5 below, from

- **grammatical gender** (*grammatisches Geschlecht*), which is traditionally subcategorised into **masculine**, **feminine**, and as **neuter** (*Maskulinum, Femininum, Neutrum*).

O As far as persons and higher animals are concerned, the division into genders is generally though not always motivated by the natural gender in most European languages. This makes linguistic gender a delicate problem for gender studies and feminist linguistics (→ 7.5).

German, like many other Indo-European languages (Latin, Greek, Russian etc.) has a rather antiquated system of grammatical gender inherited from Proto-Indo-European (→ 3.2.1.0) which presents one of the major obstacles to its non-native learners.

It distinguishes three different genders in a somewhat arbitrary manner. Gender is not only marked by the article, but also on attributive adjectives (→ 1.2.2.4). This means that agreement between noun and attributive adjective considers gender as well: *saur-er Wein, lausig-e Bedienung, alt-es Brot*. Gender sometimes also determines the way nouns are inflected.

The Romance languages have reduced this system to two genders, masculine and feminine.

The relation between grammatical and natural gender in German is somewhat complicated as the following data (in Fig. 5) show.

Fig. 5: Natural and grammatical gender in German

Form	Natural gender	Grammatical gender
die Frau	female	feminine
der Ochse	male	masculine
das Mädchen	female	neuter
der Fahrgast	female or male	masculine
die Person	female or male	feminine
das Kind	female or male	neuter

➤ The old, rather arbitrary Indo-European gender system that is still found in German was abandoned in English during the Middle English period due to the loss of practically all gender-determined inflection of nouns or adjectives (→1.3.4; 3.2.2).

Present-Day English now makes use of two different, rather inconspicuous systems of gender instead, only discernible through agreement (→ Box 7) and reference patterns:

–   The first system is concerned with the personal and possessive pronouns *he / him / his, she / her, it*, the use of which is almost exclusively motivated by the semantic parameters 'human' and 'natural gender' (if we disregard the use of *she / her* for ships and other vehicles). We could thus say that personal pronouns in

English agree with their antecedent noun in a specific kind of gender (and also in number if we regard the use of *they / them / their*):

> The linguist <female> *shot the albatross. Later,* **she** *regretted it.*
> The linguist <male> *shot the albatross. Environmentalists criticised* **him.**
> *The albatross was shot by the linguist.* **It** *was later recovered by the sailors.*
> *The linguist shot the albatrosses. Later, he regretted shooting* **them.**
> *The linguists shot the albatross. For this,* **they** *were criticised by environmentalists.*

– The other system of gender determines the use of the relative pronouns *who* (for persons) and *which* (for things), which agree with their antecedent according to this two-way distinction.

The system of gender / number agreement in English relative and personal pronouns can thus be summarised as follows:

Fig. 6: Gender and number agreement in English pronouns

	Personal and possessive pronouns		Relative pronouns
	Singular	Plural	
Male persons	*he him his*	*they them their*	*who whom whose*
Female persons	*she her*		
Ships, vehicles etc.	*she her*		*which*
Other things	*it*		

1.1.3.2.3 Case

Case (*Kasus*) is a grammatical category typical of Indo-European. It has to do with particular grammatical functions such as subject, object and the like (→ 1.2.1.2) which a noun assumes in a clause. In many Indo-European languages, such syntactic functions are marked by noun inflection (→ 1.3.4).

> ➤ Old English had a rich system of case marking like all older Indo-European languages which will be dealt with in section → 3.2.2.1.

Unlike in Old English and also German, the category of case is negligible as an inflectional category in Modern English. There are still a few formal differences based on case with some personal pronouns:

> *I – me, we – us etc.*

With nouns, case is expressed by the position of the noun in a given clause:

> *The boy saw the girl.*   vs   *The girl saw the boy.*
> *They joined Nancy.*   vs.   *Nancy joined them.*
> *The girl lent the boy a bicycle.*   vs.   *The boy lent the girl a bicycle.*

Besides, English uses prepositions to express what has to be expressed by case in other languages:

> *The girl lent a bicycle* **to** *the boy.*
> *The boy lent a bicycle* **to** *the girl.*

○ In a German clause, we do not need to maintain a particular sequence of elements in order to express case:

*Der Junge sah **das** Mädchen.*
*Den Junge-n sah **das** Mädchen.*
*Das Mädchen lieh **dem** Junge-n **ein** Fahrrad.*
*Dem Mädchen lieh **der** Junge **ein** Fahrrad.*
*Ein Fahrrad lieh **der** Junge **dem** Mädchen*
*Ein Fahrrad lieh **dem** Junge-n **das** Mädchen*

Due to German case-marking, the above sentence pairs are different in meaning despite the same sequence of elements and they can be interpreted, although some of them may sound somewhat stilted.

But note that the most important distinctions are only available in the singular of the masculine gender:

der Junge – *den Jungen*
das Mädchen – *das Mädchen.*
die Frau – *die Frau*
die Kinder – *die Kinder*

💣 It is thus not quite correct to say that "German can afford a free word order because it has case-marking." Case-marking does not carry very far in German and a preferred sequence can certainly be observed in German, too.

Agreement between an adjective and its corresponding noun considers case as well:

*ein gut-**es** Buch – mit ein-**em** gut-**en** Buch;*

in fact, the adjective is the element which often bears the load of case-marking alone:

*kalt-**e** Platten – kalt-**er** Platten – kalt-**en** Platten*
*gut-**er** Käse – gut-**em** Käse – gut-**en** Käse.*

1.1.3.3 Comparison of adjectives

In English, adjectives have a standard form which is unmarked (e.g., *loud, interesting*) as well as two marked forms: the **comparative** (*Komparativ*), marked by *-er* or *more* (*louder, more interesting*), and the **superlative** (*Superlativ*), marked by *-est* or *most* (*loudest, most interesting*). **Comparison** (*Steigerung der Adjektive*) is the only grammatical category that is relevant for the adjective.

○ In other languages, such as German or the Romance languages, adjectives also show gender, number and (in German) case (→1.1.3.2.3).
➢ This also used to be the situation in Old English, whose system was almost as complicated as the German one (→ 3.2.2.2).

1.1.3.4 Verbal categories

We shall describe the following verbal categories: tense, orientation, aspect, person, number, voice, mood and modality. The section will conclude with some remarks on finiteness, which is not on a par with the others, but constitutes a special phenomenon.

> ♦ The linguistic terminology in the field of verbal categories is rather inconsistent. Sometimes additional or different terms than the above-mentioned are employed, or different phenomena are included under the same heading, or the same phenomena are included under different headings. We will point this out wherever we are aware of such problems.

1.1.3.4.1 Tense

Tense (*Tempus*) is the grammatical expression of the temporal relation between the moment of speaking and the time of the event or situation talked about. In principle, speakers may talk about events or situations in the past, the present, or the future. But tense is language-specific, and different languages may make different distinctions of tense. A frequent source of misunderstanding is the confusion of formal grammatical distinctions of tense with meaning distinctions of time (*Zeit*), thus, e.g., present tense does not necessarily refer to present time.

> 📖 Find examples in English and German where present tense does not refer to present time, past tense does not refer to the past, und future 'tense' does not refer to the future. Hint: They can be found both in fictional literature and in everyday discourse.

In English, like in other Germanic languages, there are basically two tenses (*Tempora*) more or less universally agreed on by linguists: **present tense** (*Präsens, Gegenwartsform*) and **past tense** (preterite; *Präteritum, Vergangenheitsform*). Except for the 3rd person singular (see → 1.1.3.4.4) the present tense form is not marked.

- Past tense is usually marked by the ending *-ed*: *want-ed* (➤ presumably created in a very old grammaticalisation process from Proto-Germanic past tense forms of the equivalent of *do*, → 3.2.2.4; 3.2.3.3),
- sometimes by a so-called stem vowel alternation: *sing – sang* (➤ historically explainable by ablaut, → 3.2.1.4),
- and sometimes by a combination of both: *keep – kept* (➤ vowel alternation historically created by the Great Vowel Shift, → 3.2.1.5).

Many linguists recognise the **future** (*Futur*) as a third tense in English, but this categorisation has its problems. Formally, the *will/shall*-future is not a tense in English, but rather like a modality. It will therefore be treated under that heading below.

☞ There is also some disagreement about which category the **perfect** 'tenses' (present perfect (*I have gone*), past perfect (*I had gone*) and future perfect (*I will have gone*)) should be assigned to.

Some linguists regard the perfect as a tense, making a distinction between past and non-past tenses (rather than past vs. present), and thus integrating the different perfect tenses there (see next 💣 box and → 1.1.3.4.3 for further discussion of the perfect).

1.1.3.4.2 Aspect

The grammatical category of **Aspect** (*Aspekt*) is considered fairly widespread among the languages of the world and has attracted the attention of a large number of scholars. It is, however, far from easy to explain in a lucid way what aspect really is, let alone define *aspect* unmistakably. The category was introduced because it had been observed that many languages make additional distinctions in their 'tense' system that are somehow related to tense distinctions but do not really refer to a different time. Aspect concerns the way the speaker perceives a certain situation, be it past, present or future. This is what the original meaning of the term *aspect* implies.

Box 9: Perfective vs. imperfective

◗ In most languages that have an aspect system, aspect distinguishes between what is usually called **imperfective** (*imperfektiv*) and **perfective** (*perfektiv*) aspect. See Fig. 7 below for some semantic descriptions and examples from English. Russian and Greek (both Ancient and Modern) boast a highly sophisticated aspect system along these lines. The Romance languages make aspectual distinctions of a similar sort, but only in the past tense (French *imparfait* vs. *passé simple* or *passé composé*). Some of them are about to develop, in addition, a progressive comparable to the English progressive (Spanish *estoy cantando* 'I'm singing').

In English we distinguish the **progressive** aspect (*Verlaufsform*), formed by *be* + present participle (→ 1.1.3.4.7) (*I'm smoking*), from the **simple** aspect, expressed by unmarked forms (*I smoke*). Progressive and simple aspect in English may be said to correspond very roughly, but not quite, to imperfective and perfective aspect in other languages.

◗ Standard German lacks aspectual distinctions in its verbal system, which makes aspect difficult to understand for many German learners; but in West and South German colloquial language a kind of progressive is very common and in some varieties obligatory even with transitive (→ 1.2.1.1) verbs: *Ich bin am Überlegen* is fairly widespread; *Isch bin de Zeitung am Lesen* is typical of Rhenish Colloquial German.

Since aspect is a highly complex phenomenon that not infrequently seems to defy generalisable description, terminology that tries to capture its characteristics varies. Another corollary of this complexity is that we cannot give a full account of aspect in English here and have to refer the reader to the reference grammars (QUIRK et al. [12]1991, 197-213; BIBER et al. 1999, 162-166). Some of the most common descriptions are listed in the following table and applied to English examples (Fig. 7).

Fig. 7: The two aspects of English

Progressive ('imperfective') aspect	Simple ('perfective') aspect
Inner perspective: *John is smoking* means we are actually taking part in the situation.	Outer perspective: *John smokes* does not describe an actual situation at all, but rather a habit of John's.
Beginning and end of situation unknown (non-completion of situation) or irrelevant, but end of situation implied: *When we entered the room, John was smoking.* (He had not finished.)	Beginning and end of situation known (completion of situation) and relevant: *John smoked a cigarette, then left the room.*
Ongoing and temporary situation (limited duration of situation): *I'm smoking Cadets presently.*	Non-temporary situation: *God exists. He smokes Pall Mall.*

The progressive form in English, unlike aspectual categories in the Romance languages, can be combined with both present and past tense:

Fig. 8: English tense and aspect combined

I work	outer perspective: generalised; no specific process in the present
I worked	outer perspective: process completed in the past
I am working	inner perspective: ongoing process in the present
I was working	inner perspective: 'skips' into a past situation and from this perspective describes it as being an ongoing process or temporary situation

The use of one aspect form or the other also seems to be highly dependent on the semantics of the verb used and partly also on convention. Recently, the progressive is showing tendencies of expansion into new functional domains (cf. the fashionable "*I'm loving it*").

> ✒ There is a tendency to assign the **perfect** forms (*Perfekt*) to the category of 'aspect' as well, such as found in QUIRK et al. [12]1994 [[9]1991] ([1]1985), 188 ff., who mix up *perfect* and *perfective aspect*, which is all the more confusing as it is in flat contradiction to established terminology: If anything is 'perfective' in English, it is the simple past and not the perfect; see above.

The arguments for this categorisation are not very convincing, unless the notion of aspect is watered down in such a way that it is no longer of analytic value.

The new Longman grammar (BIBER et al. 1999, 451-475) is an improvement in that at least terminological confusion around 'perfective' and 'perfect' is avoided. The perfect, however, is also counted as an "aspect" here.

1.1.3.4.3 Orientation

Orientation (*Orientierung*) is a term introduced as a response to the difficulties in categorising the perfect (KORTMANN 1991). Though not generally accepted in linguistics, it is quite a helpful term. It denotes those grammatical categories that are used to look at the relevance of an event at a certain point of reference (*Referenzpunkt*).

This is, e.g., a central characteristic of the **perfect** in English and as you will notice, has nothing to do with aspectual distinctions, as it has nothing to do with inner or outer perspective or any of the other conceptions normally used to describe aspect. The point of reference is fixed by the speaker and can be located in present, past and future time.

The English perfect is formed by a form of the auxiliary (➔ 1.1.3.1) *have* plus the so-called past participle (➔ below on finiteness). Perfect forms denote that an event took place <u>before</u> the point of reference (**anteriority**; *Vorzeitigkeit*).

O The perfect can thus easily be mixed up with a past tense, and indeed, in many languages, perfect forms have historically developed into 'normal' past tenses such as in

- Latin, where the "perfect tense" is the normal perfective past tense, so that a new perfect using the auxiliary *habere* was 'invented' in the Late Latin period; then again in

- French, which had taken over the Late Latin *habere* perfect, which has, however, developed into the normal perfective past tense in modern colloquial French.

Something very analogous happened in Dutch, Yiddish and in major parts of the German-speaking area, but not in English! (DAHL 1985; 1994).

There have also been suggestions to explain syntagms with ***going to*** followed by the infinitive (also see ➔ 3.2.3.3) in terms of orientation. These forms denote that the event expressed by the infinitive will take place after the point of reference (**posteriority**; *Nachzeitigkeit*). It is thus interpreted as a kind of future tense.

O Future tenses on the basis of an auxiliary meaning 'go' are also commonplace across the languages of the world; cf. also the French *Je vais travailler aujourd'hui.*

Anteriority and posteriority can also be combined with each other and with all combinations of tense and aspect. Such combinations of auxiliaries with certain verb forms are often called **verbal syntagms** (*verbale Syntagmen*).

Fig. 9: Examples of complex verbal syntagms in English

Form	Meaning
I have written	Point of reference in the present; process in the past; relevance for the present
I have been writing	Point of reference in the present; process in the past seen from an inner perspective, as an ongoing process, with relevance for the present
I had written	Point of reference in the past; process before this point of reference
I had been writing	Point of reference in the past; process before this point of reference seen from an inner perspective, as an ongoing process
I'm going to write	Point of reference in the present; process in the future with relevance for the present (intention).
I'm going to be writing	Point of reference in the present; process in the future with relevance for the present seen from an inner perspective
I was going to write	Point of reference in the past; (intended) process after this point of reference
I have been going to write	1st point of reference in the present, 2nd point of reference in the past, process in the future (seen from the 2nd point of reference)

I was going to be writing, I have been going to be writing, I had been going to write and *I had been going to be writing* are theoretically possible combinations, but very unlikely in practice.

> ➤   This high complexity of the verbal syntagm in English is the result of a series of historical changes which enriched the expressive potential of English grammar (→ 3.2.3).

1.1.3.4.4 Person and number

Person and **number** (*Numerus*) are categories that are usually expressed together on the verb. In Present-Day English this is most commonly done by using personal pronouns (Fig. 10 below). The verb itself is only marked for person and number in the third person singular present tense:

> *I come – she comes.*

△ The fact that in English the 3rd person singular present of the verb is marked (*she get-s*), while all other person-number combinations are unmarked (*you get* etc.), is very unusual (→ Box 10) and calls for some explanation.

Fig. 10: Personal pronouns of Present-Day English, subject case

	1st person	2nd person	3rd person
Singular	*I*	*you*	*he she it*
Plural	*we*	*you*	*they*

⦿ German, in contrast, has a full-scale paradigm of personal 'endings':
   komm-e, komm-st, komm-t, komm-en
➢ The same can be said of Old English (→ 3.2.2.4).

Box 10: Markedness

We have now repeatedly been using the term **markedness** (*Markiertheit*). It plays a significant role in linguistic theory, but is sometimes used in a slightly confusing way. Applied to grammatical categories of a particular language, it first of all means that this category finds expression in that language.

But in many cases the use of this term means something beyond that: It is usually said that

* **unmarked** (*unmarkiert*) categories are more 'normal', frequent, simpler, easier to grasp, and more likely to be used in everyday speech than the
* **marked** (*markiert*) ones.

In consequence, the terms *marked* and *unmarked* are also used to refer to properties of a grammatical category irrespective of whether that category is actually expressed in a certain case or not. The term *marked* in some linguistic approaches is thus often used in the sense 'unusual, rare'. It might therefore be useful to distinguish between

* formal markedness and
* notional markedness.

Thus, the plural is usually the marked category in a number system in both senses: The singular is more frequent with most nouns, and indeed, in many languages the plural is marked by a special form (like the plural -*s* in English) whereas the singular is not marked. Moreover, as a result of this, the plural form is usually longer than the singular form.

> **○** Number systems in which the singular is expressed by a special form whereas the plural is not marked at all, or in which the singular form is longer than the plural form, are very rare. (Luxembourgish (→ 7.1.1), by the way, is such an 'exotic' language, but only in some of its nouns: E.g., *hon* is the plural of *hond* 'dog'.)
>
> In the same way, in most languages of the world, the 3rd person, the singular, and the present tense in verbs, if they exist, are less likely to be marked than the other categories they contrast with (→ Box 23), that is, the 1st and 2nd persons, the plural, and the past tense respectively.

1.1.3.4.5 Voice

Voice (*Diathese*; *genus verbi*) is a grammatical category that makes it possible to redistribute grammatical roles in a clause. In English there are two voices: **active** voice (*Aktiv*) and **passive** voice (*Passiv*). We will learn more about the passive in later sections, in particular see → 1.2.3.2.

Passive voice is formed by a form of the auxiliary (→ 1.1.3.1) *be* and the 'past participle' (→ 1.1.3.4.7) and can be combined with all other verbal categories.

> *The wall is painted every year.*
> *The wall is being painted today.*
> *The wall was painted last year.*
> *The wall was being painted yesterday.*
> *The wall was going to be painted when it started raining.*
> *The wall has been painted every year since it was built.*
> *The wall has been being painted for three weeks now.*
> *The wall had just been painted when John leant against it.*

More complex combinations of auxiliaries are in principle possible in English, but rather rare. However, in a computer-aided search of a huge corpus of newspaper texts from the nineteen-nineties (150 million running words long), Volker NOVAK (unpublished manuscript) found the following four examples of combinations of four or three auxiliaries:

> *He might have been being captured by the Iraqis but he wasn't*
> (Times 5.4.1991)
> *... the ... rules have always been being broken somewhere* (Times 2.8.1991)
> *... it has been being mended ever since* (Times, 6.12.1993)
> *... he had been being sent to his death* (Times, 13.11.1994).

> ➢ The combination of progressive with passive turns up rather late in the history of English. It did not become usual before the 19th century (→ 3.2.3).

The passive voice in English turns the object of an active clause, e.g. in

> *They paint **the wall** every year.*

into the subject (for the terms *subject* , *object*, etc., → 1.2.1.2):

> ***The wall** is painted every year.*

This also applies to indirect objects (in contrast to German):

*They awarded **the girl** a prize. =*
***The girl** was awarded a prize.*

*Here they will help **you**. =*
*Here **you** will be helped.*

* Das Mädchen wurde ein(en) Preis verliehen.
* Hier werden Sie geholfen.

⊙ In some varieties of colloquial German, however, there is a special form, known as the recipient passive (*Rezipientenpassiv*) to express this:
Das Mädchen erhielt (or *bekam* or better: *kriegte*) *einen Preis verliehen.*
Hier kriegen Sie geholfen. (→ 3.2.3)

In English the subject of the active clause can be added to the passive clause with the help of the preposition *by* (German: *von*):

This wall was painted by Michelangelo.
The girl was given the prize by the headmaster.

Under certain conditions, English (in contrast to German) may even form a passive from a so-called prepositional object such as in

This case has been provided for.
*Dieser Fall ist Vorsorge für getroffen worden.
but: *Für diesen Fall ist Vorsorge getroffen worden.*

This bed has been slept in.
*Dieses Bett ist drin geschlafen worden.
but: *In diesem Bett ist geschlafen worden.*

⊙ As can be seen above, German (in contrast to English) may use an **impersonal** (i.e., subjectless) passive (*unpersönliches Passiv*) in such cases.

1.1.3.4.6 Mood and modality

Mood (*Modus*) and **modality** (*Modalität*) are two categories which are difficult to distinguish. Both, roughly speaking, indicate the degree of probability of a state of affairs. A semantic distinction between the two categories that would apply to all languages is impossible to formulate.

✎ To make things worse, *modality* is used in a completely different sense in other branches of communication studies to refer to different ways of communication, e.g. in discussing the oral – written distinction (→ Box 40) or sign language, the language of the deaf community.

Regarding European languages *mood* usually denotes the categories that are marked by inflection (→ 1.3.4), i.e. in the verb form itself. *Modality*, in contrast, denotes those that are formed with the help of auxiliaries (→ 1.1.3.1). A corollary of this is that mood shows more symptoms of grammaticalisation than modality. This admittedly rather cryptic remark will be explained in section → 3.2.3.3.

- **Mood** in this sense is of little importance in Present-Day English (≻ on the situation in Old English → 3.2.2.4). Three different moods could still be distinguished in Present-Day English, though:
  - **indicative** (*Indikativ*),
  - **subjunctive** (*Konjunktiv*) and
  - **imperative** (*Imperativ*).

By far the most frequent mood is the **indicative**. The **subjunctive** is only distinguishable from the indicative

- in the 3rd person singular present tense (expressed by the omission of the *-s*)
- in negation (expressed through the missing auxiliary *do*) and
- in the form *be*.

The use of subjunctive forms, though, is very limited today and most likely to be found in (very formal) American English (see section → 3.2.3.3 for examples) and in fixed expressions (→ 1.2.3.1), such as *so be it*, *God **bless** the Queen*, etc.

The only difference between the **imperative** and the indicative is the missing subject (→ 1.2.1.2) pronoun (*you*) for the imperative. There is only a 2nd person imperative form in English. It is identical for singular and plural: *Come here! Take this!* Forms like *Let's go* are considered by some people to be a 1st person imperative form. In Ancient Greek, there is also a 3rd person imperative form that is used for orders to be passed on, the formulation of dogmas, etc. There is also a larger number of moods.

- **Modality**, though, is of much greater importance in Present-Day English. There is a comparatively closed paradigm of **modal verbs** (modals; *Modalverben*), which are a special kind of auxiliaries (→ 1.1.3.1), to express modality:

will	*shall*	*can*	*may*	*must*
would	*should*	*could*	*might*	etc.

These verbs share some specific grammatical characteristics and are used to express different degrees of possibility, desirability and probability.

Of these, *will* and *shall* have almost completely lost their modal meaning ('wollen', 'sollen') and as a complementary pair now constitute one of several (→ above section on orientation) possibilities to express **future** tense (*Futur*). In colloquial English, they are almost invariably reduced to the weak form *'ll*, as in

I'll be back soon.
He'll come later.

Thus some people regard them as tense markers rather than as modals. They still behave exactly like modal verbs and not like the tenses, though, and are thus mentioned here.

> ◉ The affinity of future tense to modality and mood respectively is no spe-
> cific feature of English. Future tense forms have often developed from modal
> expressions (in Latin and French, e.g.). This is evidence of a special semantic
> status of the future tense among the other tenses.

1.1.3.4.7 Finiteness

Finiteness (*Finitheit*) is a verbal category which is often described morphologically, but failing a decent verbal morphology in Modern English, syntactic categories must also be resorted to. Grammatical descriptions of many languages
make a distinction between finite and non-finite verbs (*finite / nicht-finite Ver-*
ben). Finite verbs are verbs that have a specific person, number and tense, no
matter whether these categories are marked on the verb form or not. In English,
as in most other European languages, finite verbs **agree** in person and number
(➔ Box 7) with the subject. (More on subject – verb agreement will be said in ➔
1.2.1.2.1.) In the following examples all finite verbs are shown in **bold print**,
non-finite ones in SMALL CAPITALS:

> *The linguist **shot** the albatross.*
> *The albatross **was** SHOT by the linguist.*
> *The linguist **has** SHOT the albatross.*
> *The linguists **want** to SHOOT the albatross.*
> *The linguist **is** SHOOTING albatrosses.*
> *The linguist **would** HAVE LOVED to SHOOT the albatross.*
> ***Doesn't** a linguist LIKE SHOOTING albatrosses?*
> ***Can** the linguist SHOOT the albatross?*

What is striking, not only about the above examples, is how often finiteness is
reserved for auxiliary verbs. Indeed, there is a growing tendency in English to do
exactly this. If this development continues, auxiliaries might some day become
obligatory for expressing finiteness. It is also important to note that in a simple
clause, only one finite verb is allowed at a time.

English main verbs (and also most auxiliaries) have three different non-finite
forms:
- The **infinitive** (*Infinitiv*) draws its name from being the most common non-
finite form. It is morphologically marked by zero in English, i.e., it displays the
'naked' verb stem: *shoot*. The infinitive is the form in which the verb is traditionally cited in most languages that have one, in English often accompanied, though,
by *to* to distinguish it from a possible noun of the same form (*to shoot*), and because indeed, in many constructions in English, the infinitive is preceded by *to*.
Only the verb *to be* has a special form for the infinitive, *be*, which is, however,
also used for other purposes (subjunctive ➔ 1.1.3.4.6). The infinitive is used in
many different constructions in English, some with, some without *to* (➔ 1.2.1.3).
- The **present participle** (*Partizip Präsens*) is the most regular of the English
verb forms. It is always formed by adding the 'ending' -*ing*: *shooting*. As we saw

above (→ 1.1.3.4.2), the present participle is used to form the progressive aspect in English. The so-called **gerund** (*Gerundium*) is identical in form to the present participle and is not distinguished from it in some recent grammatical descriptions (e.g., QUIRK et al. [12]1994, 1063); BIBER et al. 1999, 199; 739ff.). Traditionally, a gerund is a verbal noun, whereas a participle is a verbal adjective; but in many English constructions, the difference seems irrelevant. The form, whatever it is called, is used in a number of different constructions (→ 1.2.1.3).

  📖   Try to analyse the following examples of -*ing*-forms in terms of gerund (verbal noun) vs. participle (verbal adjective)! What criteria can be used? In which examples is a decision impossible?

> *She talked him into buying an engagement ring.*
> *A moped hit a pedestrian crossing the street.*
> *Looking back, this seems odd.*
> *She was looking for a temporary job before going back to school.*
> *Dog bark wakes baby falling asleep while eating.*
> *How to lose weight after having a baby.*

- The **'past' participle** (*Partizip Perfekt*) is regularly formed by adding the ending -*ed*: *loved*. The past participle is used to form both the passive voice and the perfect, and also occurs in further constructions (→1.2.1.3).

  ➤ Many English verbs form an irregular past participle: e.g. *shot*, *eaten*. These are relics of old **ablaut** (→ 3.2.1.4) patterns.

1.2 Syntax

1.2.1 Traditional structural categories in the sentence

We will begin this subchapter with the description of some traditional syntactic concepts some of which are actually very old, dating back to antiquity. In any case, they are part and parcel of every traditional syntactic description and theory, and they are also used, though often redefined, in more recent approaches to syntax. It should again be noted that the aim is not to describe English syntax, but to elucidate some theoretical notions.

1.2.1.1 The notion of valency

The meaning of a verb determines how many elements are necessary to form a complete sentence with that verb. It is said that the verb, often also called the **predicate** (*Prädikat*), takes a certain number of **arguments** (*Argumente*).

  ✒ The terms *predicate* and *argument* are used here in a sense adopted from predicate logic (→ 4.4.5.1). The term *predicate* has a slightly different use in traditional syntax (→ 1.2.1.2).

> Note that the use of the term *argument* in predicate logic has absolutely nothing to do with the colloquial sense of that word, in which we have also used it repeatedly in this book. Neither is it related to the notions of *argument* and *argumentation* as they are used in textlinguistics (→ 6.1.4).

This phenomenon is called **valency** (*Valenz*) and has a syntactic and a semantic side which do not always agree completely. Sometimes an argument may be regarded as obligatory from a semantic viewpoint but may nevertheless be left out in certain conditions:

> *John was eating (an apple).*

Of course, one always eats <u>something</u>, but this 'something' need not always be made explicit.

Taking the verb *sleep*, only one 'argument' is necessary, referring to the person who sleeps, to make a complete sentence:

> *John was sleeping.*

Linguists say that verbs like *sleep* take only one 'argument'. Such verbs are also called **intransitive verbs** (*intransitives Verb*) in English grammar. (In Latin and German grammar, there are further categories of intransitive verbs). The one 'argument' of an intransitive verb is the **subject** (→ 1.2.1.2) in English. In classical German, the only 'argument' of a verb need not be a subject: *Mich dürstet.*

Other verbs, invariably so-called **transitive verbs**, e.g. *take, join, shoot*, etc., obligatorily take two 'arguments' spelled out in noun phrases:

> *He saw the boy*
> 1   2
>
> *She took the bottle.*
> 1   2
>
> *They joined Nancy.*
> 1   2
>
> *The linguist shot the albatross.*
>   1   2

These two arguments are called the
- **subject** and
- **object**, respectively (→ 1.2.1.2).

There are even verbs that take three arguments in order to make a complete sentence, typically verbs of giving, selling and lending:

> *Mary gave John a book.*
> 1   2   3

In sentences such as this,
- the argument following the verb ("*John*" in the above example) is called the **indirect object** (*indirektes Objekt*),

- the following argument ("*a book*") then is the **direct object** (*direktes Objekt*) (→ 1.2.1.2).

It is important to note that arguments of a verb may also be spelled out in prepositional phrases in English, phrases introduced by a preposition (→ 1.2.2.3), such as in:

*Mary gave a book **to John**.*
1   3   2

*Mary was looking **at John**.*
1   2

1.2.1.2 Syntactic functions: subject and object, adverbial and complement

This section deals with the most important traditional **syntactic functions** (*Syntaktische Funktionen*).

1.2.1.2.1 Subject

The function of **subject** is so important and pervasive in syntax that we have mentioned it several times before, hoping you had a rough notion of the meaning of this term. This is where we explain in somewhat more detail what a subject is.

> ◉ Many languages have a grammatical category of subject, and English grammatical subjects have a number of properties found in similar categories in many languages all over the world.

The major clue to finding the subject of a sentence in English is **word order**:

In ordinary clauses, the subject is almost always found before the verb:

***John** smokes.*

– In yes-no and most other questions, it is found after the auxiliary:

*Does **John** smoke?*

> ☞ The phenomenon that a verb (contrary to normal word order) is put before the subject is usually called **inversion.** The verb is then said to be **inverted**. In questions, it must always be an auxiliary (→ 1.1.3.1 on auxiliary verbs) that is inverted.

Another criterion for subjecthood in English (as in many other languages) is **agreement**: (→ Box 7). The grammatical subject in English determines the number form of the verb (singular or plural):

He smoke-s.
They smoke-ø.

– The third criterion is found in **conjunction** (→ 1.2.1.3). If two sentences are conjoined by *and*, *or* or similar conjunctions, it is the subject that need not be repeated in the second conjunct:

The linguist shot the albatross and fell into the sea.
(=> 'The linguist fell into the sea.')

The albatross was shot by the linguist and fell into the sea.
(=>'The albatross fell into the sea.')

– The fourth criterion is applied in a **question test**: The subject of an English sentence always answers a question that has two characteristics:
– It is introduced by *who* (for persons) or *what* (for things).
– Contrary to usual questions, it does not show inversion of the verb, nor does it need an auxiliary because its subject is an interrogative pronoun which must always be the first word in the sentence.

Thus, in the first of the above examples, *"the linguist"* answers the question

Who *shot the albatross and fell into the sea?*,

and in the second, "the albatross" answers the question

What *was shot by the linguist and fell into the sea?*

As you will note, neither of these questions contains an inverted verb. **Questions** are a very common test method in syntax which will be discussed more extensively below (→ 1.2.2.2).

> **◉** In some languages other than English, the subject is marked by a special case, the so-called **nominative** (*Nominativ*) (→ 1.1.3.2.3). This was and is the case in Old English (→ 3.2.2), German, Latin, Greek, and all Slavonic languages.

The subject is an obligatory overt constituent (→ 1.2.2.2) of all finite clauses in Present-Day English. That means each clause with a finite verb (→ 1.1.3.4.7) in English must contain a subject.

> △ Exceptions to this can be found in **telegraphic style** (*Telegrammstil*)
>
> *Want some coffee?*
> (meaning 'Do you want some coffee?')
>
> *Sorry, didn't realise it was so late.*
> (meaning: 'I didn't realise it was so late.')
>
> or occasionally in advertisements:
>
> *Puts the T in BriTain.*
> (meaning: 'the advertised product puts the T in BriTain.')
>
> *Refreshes the parts other beers can't reach.*
> (You guess what it means.)
>
> ➤ In Old English, the subject was not obligatory: Personal pronouns in the nominative case could often be left out. The inflectional form of the verb (→ 1.3.4) already indicated the subject unambiguously (see also → 3.2.3.1).

○ According to the theory of Generative Grammar (→ 1.2.2), omissibility of the subject pronoun constitutes a major typological (→ 1.4.1) difference (the so-called "PRO-drop parameter"), which is denied by most other typologists (COMRIE 2001, 28f.). The same phenomenon can be found in most Romance languages, though not in French. Although the subject pronoun may not be left out in Present-Day German, except in telegraphic style like in English:

> *Bin an der Uni,*
> (in a note left on a kitchen table),

German does know subjectless finite clauses, the so-called **impersonal passive** construction such as in

> *Jetzt wird gefeiert.*

📖 How can you prove that *jetzt* is not the subject of the above sentence?

1.2.1.2.2 Predicate

Some linguists use the term **predicate** (*Prädikat*) to cover everything besides the subject in a clause. Thus, according to QUIRK et al. ([12]1994 [[9]1991] ([1]1985), 726ff.) all further elements of the clause are within the predicate.

> ♦ Note that the term *predicate* is used in a somewhat different sense in valency theory (→ 1.2.1.1) and predicate logic (→ 4.4.5).

A few examples may suffice to illustrate the major clause constituents (→ 1.2.2.2) before we explain them more closely in turn.:
S = **Subject**, V = **Verb**, O = **Object**, A = **Adverbial**, C = **Complement**

> ✍ The abbreviations are taken over from QUIRK et al. 1985, that's why we use C for 'complement', meaning 'predicative'. (See below, in particular → Box 11.)
> ♦ Don't mix up *predicate* and *predicative*! A predicative is only part of the predicate as defined here.

Words forming a constituent are all included in brackets ( ), respectively. The constituents forming the **predicate** are included in further brackets.

> *(Jane)   ((solemnly) (served) (the beer)   (on a tray)).*
> S   (A   V   O   A)
>
> *(She)   ((gave) (Aunt Martha)   (a fresh glass)).*
> S   (V   O   O)
>
> *(Aunt Martha) ((grew) (angrier) (from minute) (to minute)).*
> S   (V   C   A   A)
>
> *((Yesterday)) (they)((had elected)   (her) (fusspot of the year)).*
>   (A)   S   (V   O   C)

(Note that in the last example the predicate is discontinuous!)

1.2.1.2.3 Object

Objects can also mainly be recognised by word order in English: With very few exceptions, the object in Present-Day English always immediately follows the verb, and is never preceded by a preposition. It is thus clear that *"the beer"* and *"her"* in the above examples are objects, as indicated. They follow the verb and are not preceded by a preposition. Constituents such as *"on a tray"* or *"from minute"* cannot be objects because they do not follow the verb immediately and are introduced by a preposition. The question test can also be applied again: Objects in English always answer questions beginning with *who* or *whom* (for persons) or *what* (for things) and showing inversion with auxiliary:

> **What did** Jane solemnly serve on a tray? – The beer.
> **Who(m) did** she give a fresh glass? – Aunt Martha.
> **Who(m) had** they elected fusspot of the year? – Aunt Martha.

Some sentences in English, like the second example above, have two objects.
- The first object then usually denotes a person who benefits from the action described by the verb (*"Aunt Martha"*) and is called the **indirect object** (*indirektes Objekt*).
- The second object is more like a normal object and is called the **direct object** (*direktes Objekt*).

Languages exhibiting case (such as those mentioned above) usually have a special case for objects, the **accusative** (*Akkusativ*) and another one for indirect objects, usually called the **dative** (*Dativ*) (→ 1.1.3.2.3). Present-Day English has got special object forms in the personal pronoun, used for both direct and indirect objects and after prepositions, and the form *whom*, used mainly after prepositions (→ 1.1.3.1).

> ➢ Old English, like Classical German, distinguished three kinds of object by different cases (→ 3.2.2.1). In addition to accusative and dative, a **genitive** object was also possible, as is still the case in (somewhat old-fashioned) German: *Wir gedenken **der** Toten.*

1.2.1.2.4 Subject predicative and object predicative

Predicatives (**complements** in the terminology of QUIRK et al. [12]1994 ([1]1985), 728f.), *Prädikatsnomina, Prädikativa* in German, see → Box 11) are elements of the clause that designate properties or functions rather than entities and only occur with certain verbs such as *be, become, grow, remain*, or *elect, nominate, make*, etc. Predicatives are usually strongly associated with the subject or the object of the clause, in that the property mentioned is ascribed to either of these.
- Thus *"angrier"* in the above example is a property of *"Aunt Martha"*, mentioned in the subject of the clause, and is thus called a **subject predicative** or **subject complement** (*Subjektsprädikativum*),

- whereas *"fusspot of the year"*, again mentioning a property of *"Aunt Martha"*, who is this time mentioned in the object of the clause, is an **object predicative** or **object complement** (*Objektsprädikativum*).

> **O** In case-marking languages, subject and object predicative **agree** (→ Box 7) in **case** with the subject and object, respectively:
> *Der Mörder ist immer **der** Gärtner.*
> *Der Kommissar sah **den** Gärtner als **den** Mörder.*

One important syntactic property that distinguishes predicatives from **objects** is that predicatives cannot be made the subject of a passive clause, even if they are noun phrases. Thus, in the above example

> *Yesterday, they had elected her fusspot of the year.*

only the object (*"her"*) may be turned into the subject of a corresponding passive clause:

> *Yesterday she had been elected fusspot of the year,*

but not the predicative:

> **Yesterday fusspot of the year had been elected her.*

1.2.1.2.5 Adverbials and the complement – adjunct distinction

Objects and adverbials can be **obligatory** (*obligatorisch*) or **optional** (*fakultativ*). In the clause

> *Jane heard the explosion.*

the object (*"explosion"*) is obligatory, whereas in

> *Jane was painting (a picture of Aunt Martha),*

the object is optional, i.e., it can be left out without harm to the syntactic integrity of the clause.

- **Predicatives** are always obligatory:

  > *Aunt Martha is an obnoxious fusspot.*
  > **Aunt Martha is.*

- **Adverbials** may be optional,

  > *Jane was painting (**in the drawing room**).*

but may also be **obligatory** quite frequently:

> *John put the tray **on the table**.*
> **John put the tray.*

Adverbials typically answer questions like *Where?*, *When?* or *How?*

Note that in a few cases, (optional) adverbials, in particular adverbials of time, do not need a preposition:

> *Jane was painting all day.*

Box 11: Adjunct vs. complement

✱ All obligatory constituents, even obligatory *that*-clauses, are called complements, e.g., in much of the literature on syntax nowadays, especially that committed to the framework of generative grammar (→ 1.2.2.2) such as HAEGEMAN / GUÉRON 1999, CARNIE 2002, or in BURTON-ROBERTS 1997, a commonly used textbook for syntax. In such approaches a general distinction is usually made between

- **adjuncts** (*Adjunkte*) (≈ optional adverbials, within the predicate typically those of time and place), which are not part of the valency (→ 1.2.1.1) of the verb and
- **complements** (*Komplemente*) (≈ obligatory adverbials) which are determined by the valency of the verb.

As this distinction is very common in the literature, we will also adopt it despite the danger of confusion with the still widespread terminology used in QUIRK et al. 1985, where **predicatives** are called "complements". It is simply the reality of the linguistic literature that terminology is not always used considerately and consistently.

The terms *adjunct* and *complement* are not restricted to major clause constituents. A complement is any constituent within a clause that is obligatory, i.e., demanded by the valency of the verb, and an adjunct is not obligatory.

Objects, in this approach, are only special kinds of complements because they, too, are determined by the valency of verbs. More on different kinds of adjuncts and complements can be found in section → 1.2.2.4.

As already mentioned, in those approaches in which the term *complement* is used for all obligatory constituents, complements in QUIRKs specific sense are called

- **predicatives**, and an analogous distinction is made between
  - **subject predicatives** and
  - **object predicatives**.

Furthermore, some of these approaches (BURTON-ROBERTS 1997, 85ff.) take it for granted that *"on the table"* in

   The tray is on the table

is a subject predicative. This terminology is also adopted by BIBER et al. 1999, 466. And in

   John put the tray on the table

it would be an object predicative (BURTON-ROBERTS 1997, 88ff.). This classification makes sense since, in both cases, the tray <u>is</u> on the table. This object predicative, however, would be called an obligatory adverbial in QUIRK et al. [[1]1985] [12]1994, 466 and, inconsistently, in BIBER et al. 1999, 151.

BIBER et al., on the other hand, use the term *prepositional object* for complements of verbs which are very closely associated with a specific preposition, such as *look at*, *insist on* etc.

QUIRK et al. ([¹1985] 1994, 508f.) suggest two alternative analyses for these. On the one hand, in the example *John looked at Mary*, "*at Mary*" could be seen as an obligatory adjunct. The alternative would be to regard *look at* as a transitive verb with an object. BIBER et al. (1999, 129) call these objects *prepositional objects*, BURTON-ROBERTS (1997, 90f.) speaks of *prepositional complements*.

In this textbook, we are going to use the adjunct – complement distinction, which seems to be most widespread, as consistently as possible and apart from that try to avoid misleading terminology. In particular, we will use the term *complement* to refer to all kinds of complements, including complement clauses and complements of prepositions.

Fig. 11 summarises the terminological chaos in a simplified, idealised form. 'Mixed' systems are also in use in the literature.

Fig. 11:   Objects, complements, adjuncts: diverging terminologies

	Examples (relevant constituent in **bold** print)	QUIRK et al. 1985ff.	BIBER et al. 1999	BURTON-ROBERTS 1997
I	*John saw **Mary**.*	object	object	object
II	*John is **a teacher**.*	subject complement	subject predicative	subject predicative
III	*John called Mary **a friend***	object complement	object predicative	object predicative
IV	*John met Mary **in the park**.*	optional adverbial adjunct	adjunct	adjunct adverbial
V	*John is **in the park**.*	obligatory adverbial adjunct	obligatory adverbial	subject predicative
VI	*John is **in good spirits***	subject complement	subject predicative	subject predicative
VII	*John sent Mary **into the park**.*	obligatory adverbial adjunct	object predicative	object predicative
VIII	*John looked **at Mary**.*	obligatory adverbial adjunct*	prepositional object	prepositional complement

*   As mentioned above, QUIRK et al. also suggest an alternative analysis for this example.

Note: Everything that is not called an "adjunct" is regarded as some kind of complement in BIBER et al. and BURTON-ROBERTS. Even QUIRK et al. speak of "complementation" in connection with objects.

>   📖   Why do you think some approaches distinguish between type V and VI in Fig. 11? Could it have to do with the question test (→ 1.2.1.2.1; 1.2.2.2)?

1.2.1.3 Compound and complex sentences

The preceding sections explain the basic concepts used by linguists to describe so-called simple (main) clauses in English (and in some other languages). This section is now concerned with more complex structures, consisting of several clauses.

Box 12: Sentence vs. clause

> ☞ English, it must be noted, has two words, *sentence* and *clause*, where German has to make do with one, *Satz*.
> - A **sentence** is the largest unit that can be analysed in syntax, that is, a syntactic unit that is not contained in any larger syntactic unit. A sentence may contain several clauses, but need not.
> - A **clause** (*Teilsatz*) is a linguistic unit consisting of one and only one verb along with its subject, object(s), and maybe adverbial(s) etc. It may not contain another clause, though other clauses may have a function in it (see below). A clause may be smaller than a sentence, but need not be.

A sentence consisting of more than one clause may be a
- **compound sentence** (*Satzreihe*) or a
- **complex sentence** (*Satzgefüge*).

A compound sentence consists of two or more main clauses which are connected in some way, e.g. by coordinating **conjunctions**, such as *and, or, but* etc. Such conjunctions, by the way, may connect any two syntactic units of the same type, including whole clauses (last example below):

> *The linguist shot an albatross but fell into the sea.*
> *The linguist shot an albatross today or last week.*
> *The linguist shot an albatross and the sailors got mad at him.*

Complex sentences contain **embedded** or **subordinated clauses** (*Nebensätze*).

> ⊙ In German, subordinate clauses can be more easily distinguished from main clauses than in English because they have a special word order: The finite verb always comes second in main clauses, and at the end in subordinate clauses:
>
> > *Gestern **war** er gekommen.*
> > *… weil er gestern gekommen **war**.*

Complex sentences will not be dealt with in much detail here, but it can be said that in principle the same categories of analysis as in the sections above apply:
- Compound sentences are syntactically no different from sequences of simple sentences.
- Finite (→ 1.1.3.4.7) subordinate clauses in English are structurally no different from main clauses internally, and

– externally they can be seen as constituents within the next superordinate clause, that is, they have a function in that clause (see below). Subordinate clauses are thus another example of the principle of recursiveness (→ Box 15). According to the function they have in their superordinate clause, we distinguish different types of subordinate clauses:

- Subordinate clauses introduced by **subordinating conjunctions** such as *if*, *because*, *while*, *although*, function as adverbials (→ 1.2.1.2) in their superordinate clause, and accordingly are called **adverbial clauses** (*Adverbialsätze*):

  If Mary visited her parents yesterday, she should know about their problems.
  We had an accident because there was oil on the road.
  I learnt all about flowers while we lived in the country.
  His English accent is perfect although he has never been to the United Kingdom.
  (KORTMANN 1997, 84ff.)

- **Relative clauses** (*Relativsätze*) are in most cases part of a noun phrase, and are accordingly used as **attributes** (→ 1.2.2.4), which can be seen from the following set of examples:

  Good suggestions
  Suggestions capable of quick realisation
  Suggestions which are capable of quick realisation

  - In the first example, the simple adjective "*good*" is used as an attributive adjective to the noun "*suggestions*".
  - In the second example, the attribute is more complex and is therefore put after the noun.
  - In the third example, the attribute is a full relative clause introduced by the **relative pronoun** (*Relativpronomen*) *which*. Relative pronouns always have a double function in Present-Day English: In addition to establishing the relation to the noun phrase they belong to, they also have a syntactic function within the relative clause (in the latter example, *which* is the subject). Other relative pronouns in Present-Day English are *who*, *whom*, and *that*.

- Not all clauses introduced by *that* are relative clauses, however. Subordinate clauses introduced by *that* within which *that* doesn't have a syntactic function are called **that-clauses**. The *that* in this case is not a relative pronoun, but a subordinating conjunction (also called **complementiser**). Such clauses as a whole always have a syntactic function in the main clause. They may occur in the function of

  - **subject clause:**

    That he had shot two hundred albatrosses was astonishing to the linguist (answering the question: *What was astonishing to the linguist?*)

- **object clause**:

*The linguist regretted **that he'd shot two hundred albatrosses**.*
(answering the question: ***What** did the linguist regret?*),

- or something confusingly called **noun attribute** (→ 1.2.2.4), or **noun complement** (slightly better, → Box 11):

*The fact **that he'd shot two hundred albatrosses** didn't make him exactly popular.*
(answering the question: ***What fact** didn't make him exactly popular?*).

The latter type of *that*-clause may be difficult to distinguish from a relative clause at first sight as it also modifies a noun phrase (in the above case, *the fact*). But the *that* in the above example does not have a function within the subordinate clause; it only connects it to the main clause. This is what distinguishes it from the relative pronoun *that*.

All subordinate clauses described so far are **finite clauses** (*finite Sätze*), i.e., they contain a finite verb (→ 1.1.3.4).

- In addition to these, English has several kinds of subordinate **non-finite clauses** (*Nicht-finite Sätze*) centred around an infinitive, a participle or a gerund (the latter two are not always distinguished in the literature). They may have different functions in their superordinate clause:

- **subject clause:**

***To shoot albatrosses** is ecologically incorrect.* (infinitive)
***Shooting albatrosses** is every linguist's favourite hobby.* (gerund)

- **object clause:**

*He likes **to shoot albatrosses** early in the morning.* (infinitive)
*He likes **shooting albatrosses**.* (gerund)

> ☞ The latter type of clause is often grouped together with finite *that*-clauses of the same function in a category called **complement clause** (*Komplementsatz*) (→ Box 11). These clauses are often discussed jointly under the heading of "(verb) **complementation**", as the question which of these clauses should be used is often an issue for learners.

- **adverbial clause:**

*The linguist went to the Pacific **(in order) to shoot albatrosses**.*
(infinitive of purpose, optionally introduced by *in order*)

***(When) shooting albatrosses**, linguists tend to get nervous.*
(participle expressing a temporal relation with ot without conjunction)

***Being a linguist**, he shoots albatrosses every weekend.*
(participle expressing a causal relation without conjunction)

- **relative clause:**

  *The first linguist **to shoot an albatross** was Chomsky.* (infinitive)
  *The linguist **shooting the albatrosses** is Chomsky.* (participle)

Non-finite clauses usually don't have a subject of their own, but 'borrow' it from surrounding clauses.

There are, however, special constructions in which non-finite clauses do have a subject:

- *for ... to* **infinitive clauses** (a construction which has only been recognised as such recently and has considerably been increasing in frequency, especially in American English):

  ***For Obama to win** was very important to African Americans in the USA.*

- **absolute constructions** (*Absolute Konstruktionen*) (rare), consisting of a subject and a predicate in participle form:

  ***The weather being fine**, they went for a walk.*

A lot more could and would need to be said on complex sentences in general and non-finite clauses in English in particular. But we have to refer the student to the large reference grammars which are able to give a more complete picture (QUIRK et al. ^{12}1994, 915-1234; BIBER et al. 1999, 192-201; 608-750; 818-852).

1.2.2 Generative Grammar: the description of constituent structure

1.2.2.1 Requirements on a syntactic description

It is agreed in all linguistic approaches that syntax is based on the fact that sentences are neither inextricable jumbles, nor simple chains of words, but complex, hierarchically structured and ordered sequences of constituents put together according to certain language-specific rules. As we said, syntax is concerned with the structure of clauses and sentences in a language, in particular the constituents of clauses and the function of words and word classes in them.

A school of linguistics which has contributed much to our understanding of constituent structure is **Generative Grammar** (CHOMSKY 1957; 1965; 1995; HAEGEMAN 1997; RADFORD 2004; see especially HAEGEMAN / GUÉRON 1999 for the most advanced and detailed application to the description of English grammar).

Most linguists within this framework agree that a syntactic description of a language must meet certain requirements in order to be considered adequate.

– First of all, a syntactic description must make a distinction between 'grammatical' (i.e., grammatically correct) and 'ungrammatical' (i.e., grammatically incorrect) sentences.

Box 13: Descriptive vs. prescriptive

In the light of section → 1.1.1.4. you may well ask: What's the difference, then, between a linguist's **descriptive** grammar and a **prescriptive** grammar? After all, both allow certain constructions and prohibit others.

The difference is that a descriptive grammar allows everything that competent native speakers will accept in their own vernacular speech (→ 7.1.3, ☞ box), whereas prescriptive grammars usually disallow a number of constructions that competent native speakers will use every day.

The relation between prescriptive and descriptive grammar is actually more complicated in highly literate languages such as English, German, Arabic, Greek, or French because many speakers are influenced by norms that are laid down in prescriptive and pedagogical grammars and propagated through school teaching, self-appointed language experts and even language columns in newspapers. Certain social groups in many countries are preoccupied with some hazy notion of 'correct' English, German, French, Greek, or Arabic, and may even tend to regard their own use of language as incorrect and deficient (→ 7.1.3).

Linguists pay attention to norms because they influence people's language behaviour. But they also believe that all native speakers of a language have their own grammar in their heads, which is, of course, constantly being checked against other people's language.

It is this internalised system of rules, as accepted in a speech community, regardless of whether it is influenced by exposure to normative grammars, that linguists try to describe, and it is in this sense, based on the intuition of native speakers as it is manifested in their own usage and judgement, that linguists speak of 'grammatical' or 'well-formed' sentences.

— A further requirement for an adequate syntactic description is that it should take account of certain regular formal relationships between certain constructions, such as the relations between the following sentences:

The linguist shot the albatross.
The albatross was shot by the linguist.
Who was the albatross shot by?
Which albatross did the linguist say he shot?

I had ransacked my mother's kitchen for a sharp-pointed knife.
It was a sharp-pointed knife that I had ransacked my mother's kitchen for.

Box 14: Transformations in transformational grammar

In Generative Grammar such relationships used to be described in terms of **transformations** (*Transformationen*) transforming one sentence into another by certain formal operations, such as changing the order of words, inserting function words ($\rightarrow$ 1.1.3.1, ☞ box), etc.

That's why this approach has often been called **Transformational Grammar** (*Transformationsgrammatik*).

The use of transformations to explain syntactic phenomena has been drastically reduced in recent treatments of Generative Grammar, now allowing only one kind of transformation, the **movement**, that is, a change in word order. Thus, the sentence

Yesterday, the linguist shot an albatross

would be derived from the more 'normal'

The linguist shot an albatross yesterday

by a movement rule of fronting or extraction.

Movement rules are widely used in Generative Grammar to explain all kinds of complex syntactic phenomena, not only the just mentioned fronting, but also things like questions, relative clauses, and even passive constructions ($\rightarrow$ 1.2.3.2).

A deeper understanding of movement rules requires a rather sophisticated knowledge both of syntactic structure and of abstract questions and principles of generative syntactic theory, which would be beyond the scope of this introduction.

– The third requirement on a syntactic description that is usually mentioned is that it must be able to explain what are called **syntactic ambiguities** (*syntaktische Ambiguitäten*), that is, ambiguities of sentences which are not due to the presence of ambiguous words but which must be sought in the syntactic structures of the sentence, such as in

He saw the boy with the telescope.
(old linguistic folklore)

One witness reported sex between two parked cars in the street.
(inspired by PINKER 1995, 109)

The above sentences do not contain any ambiguous words. Their ambiguity can be explained by assigning to them several syntactic structures. In the first sentence, the telescope can be the instrument by means of which the boy is seen, or it can be an accompanying object of the boy.

The second sentence is not really ambiguous, but the fact that it may give rise to an interpretation where two cars are 'having sex together' leads to some hesitation in its processing, followed by hilarity as this possible meaning 'dawns' on the reader / hearer.

> 📕 Try to explain the last ambiguity using the notions of 'complement' and 'adjunct' (or 'obligatory' and 'optional' adverbial) (→ Box 11).

In the next section we will consider how these different syntactic structures may be described.

1.2.2.2 The major constituents of an English sentence. Heuristic tests

There are many different models and theories of syntax, making divergent assumptions about the scope and principles of syntax, its place in a linguistic description, and even about syntactic facts and their analysis. But there are some questions that most linguists agree upon. One of these is that sentences have a **constituent structure** (*Konstituentenstruktur*), which is revealed by the analysis of sentences into different parts, each having a specific function, internal structure, and designation. Let us take the following example:

> *The distressed waitress solemnly served the incredibly dry muffins in the weedy garden.*

If we want to analyse this sentence, we can apply several heuristic tests that are commonly used in linguistics. They are usually called **constituency tests**.

• We might, e.g., ask which of the elements in the sentence are perhaps redundant and which are indispensable to provide the general meaning (**deletion test**; *Weglassprobe*). Deleting all the elements that seem dispensable at first sight, we arrive at something like the following:

> *The waitress served the muffins in the garden.*

This sentence still carries the general meaning of the original sentence: It still describes the same kind of event, leaving out 'unnecessary' (though possibly interesting) detail. This reduced sentence gives us a clearer idea of the general structure of the original sentence, making it easier to handle. How do we set about analysing its structure?

Here we can use two further, closely related methods that are often used in linguistics:

• The **question test** (*Fragetest*) is based on the fact that all the major constituents of a sentence can be used as answers to questions concerning this sentence.

Suppose you have just heard a sentence spoken, but there is some part of this sentence that you could not hear properly, let's say, due to some noise. You may then ask a question to get the speaker to repeat the part that you did not hear properly. Since you have already gained a certain idea as to the structure of the sentence you will use specific question words to ask for specific constituents of the sentence, so that the other speaker does not have to repeat the whole sentence.

Thus, depending on what it is you haven't heard properly, you may ask, concerning the above example:

Who served the muffins in the garden?
What did the waitress serve in the garden?
Where did the waitress serve the muffins?

A well-formed answer to each of the above questions will be precisely one major constituent of the sentence concerned: *the waitress*, *the muffins*, or *in the garden*. By means of such questions, we can thus not only find out the major constituent structure of a sentence, but also what their syntactic function (in terms of subject, object etc.) is (→ 1.2.1.2).

– Asking for the subject of a clause, you use the interrogative pronouns *who* or *what*, and since your question does not have a further subject, you do not need an auxiliary that is to be put before the subject.

– Asking for the object, we use *who* (*whom* in old fashioned grammar) or, as in this case, *what*, but this time your question has a subject so that you need an auxiliary that you can put before it.

– Asking for an adverbial, we may use a number of different question words, depending on what kind of adverbial we think it was we are asking for. In this case, we use *where* because we have already understood that it was an adverbial of place. Other interrogative pronouns asking for adverbials are *when*, *why*, and *how*. You may also use any combination of a preposition with *whom* or *what* if you think you have heard that preposition (*with whom*, *concerning what*, etc.).

– Asking for the verb in a clause is slightly more complicated. The question usually concerns the whole predicate (→ 1.2.1.2), i.e., the verb together with object and adverbial, always uses some finite form (→ 1.1.3.4), which contains some additional information concerning tense, aspect, modality (→ 1.1.3.4) and the like that you may presume to be included in the sentence. The answer to such a question is, then, the 'naked' predicate, that is, it only contains the main verb in a non-finite form:

What did the waitress do? – Serve the muffins in the garden.

From this, linguists have drawn further conclusions concerning the structure of a predicate in English (cf., e.g. HAEGEMAN / GUÉRON 1999, 97ff.) which also have a bearing on the other test, discussed below.

• The other method, closely related to the question test, is the **substitution test** (*Ersetzungsprobe*): In this case, we try to replace all parts of the sentence, except the verb, with pronouns (usually abbreviated Pro in generative grammar). There is usually only one way of doing this. Applying this test to the above sentence, we obtain:

She   served **them**   **there**.
(The waitress   served *the muffins in the garden.)*

To prove that there is no other way of reducing the above sentence to pronouns, we could try to find other chunks of the sentence that are replaceable by pronouns. It becomes immediately obvious that there is no pronoun to replace, e.g., the strings *"waitress served"* or *"served the"* or *"muffins in"*. In this way we obtain a fairly clear picture of the overall constituent structure of the above sentence.

Putting the omitted detail back in, we obtain:

(The distressed waitress)   (served)
She   served

(the incredibly dry muffins)   (in the weedy garden).
them   there.

Under this analysis, our sentence would consist of four parts. These are, indeed, the most common major sentence constituents usually recognised by traditional grammar (→ 1.2.1.2), that is, in the case of our sentence, **subject**, **verb**, **object**, and **adverbial**.

Modern linguists, however, are not content with this analysis. And indeed, we may ask whether further analysis is possible. Applying further deletion, question and substitution tests, we are able to show that our sentence has a slightly more complex structure. We could argue, e.g., that *She served them (the muffins)* could under certain conditions be replaced by *She worked*, still covering roughly the same meaning. We thus obtain:

She worked (= served the muffins) there (=in the garden).

Note that while *there* is this substitution for *served them*, there is no substitution possible for *them there* or *she served*. And you may also formulate a question to which *"serve the muffins"* is the answer:

What did she do in the garden?

But there is no conceivable question to which *them there* or *she served* would be the answer.

• A different way of showing that *served the muffins* forms a constituent of its own is another useful substitution test, the so-called **do-so test**. Those constituents that are most closely associated with the verb (such as the object(s)) are usually and obligatorily covered by a *do so* substitution, whereas other constituents (such as adverbials), less closely linked to the verb, are not covered by such a paraphrase:

Jane served the muffins in the garden, and Mary did so on the verandah.
(= 'Mary served the muffins on the verandah.')

*Jane served the muffins in the garden, and Mary did so.
(*do so* does not cover the adverbial, so this sentence is incomplete.)

*Jane served the muffins in the garden, and Mary did so the cookies.
(*do so* obligatorily includes the object, so it cannot be combined with a new object.)

• On the other hand, applying the <u>inverted</u> substitution **so do** (instead of *do so*), which includes verb, object and adverbial in the scope of its paraphrase, shows that these three constituents together form one larger constituent which is called the **verb phrase** (*Verbgruppe*) (corresponding to the **predicate** in traditional terminology):

> *Jane served the muffins in the garden, and so did Mary.*
> (= 'Both Jane and Mary served the muffins in the garden.')

> *?Jane served the muffins in the garden, and so did Mary on the verandah.*
> (Inverted substitution includes adverbial, so it cannot take a new adverbial.)

> **Jane served the muffins in the garden, and so did Mary the cookies.*
> (*so do*, not even allowing a new adverbial, does not allow a new object.)

Also applying the deletion test once more, we may see that *there* is not indispensable in our sentence, so that ultimately its minimal structure could be represented by something like:

> *She (= the waitress) worked (= served the muffins in the garden).*

It can thus be seen that the minimum of constituents in an English clause is two (in traditional terminology: subject and predicate).

> ➢ This was not always the case in the history of English. As in Old English a subject pronoun could be left out, person and number being expressed by the form of the verb, the minimal Old English clause thus consisted of just one verb form (→ 1.2.1.2, 3.2.3).

The above tests also show that the four major constituents (subject, verb, object, and adverbial) of our sentence are not on one level, but are arranged in what is called a **hierarchy** (*Hierarchie*) in linguistics. Some groups of constituents form larger constituents, which in turn are grouped together to form even larger constituents, and so on, until the level of the complete sentence is reached, the sentence being the largest unit that can be analysed in syntax.

The hierarchical structure of a sentence is often represented by **tree diagrams** (*Baumdiagramme*), as they are called. We might thus represent the overall constituent structure of our sentence in the following way:

Fig. 12: Tree diagram: *She served them there*

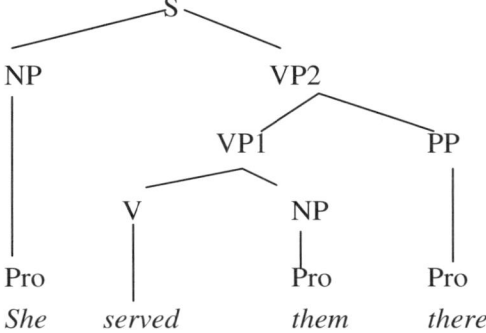

Generative Grammar in particular has become notorious for its elaborate tree diagrams. (The abbreviations for constituents used in this diagram will be explained presently.)

> ✍ In this introduction we are using tree diagrams in a somewhat simplified manner, approximately as they are used by generative grammarians, especially in HAEGEMAN 1997, RADFORD 2004, and HAEGEMAN / GUÉRON 1999, without following all their theoretical implications, nor imitating generative analyses in every detail.

In the version of Generative Grammar underlying the above diagram, a subject can thus be defined through the tree structure as that **NP** (**noun phrase**, *Substantivgruppe*) directly dependent on the **S** (**sentence,** *Satz*) node. And an object is an NP directly dependent on an VP node. Preceding sections, however, have shown that there is much more to be said about subjects and objects than that (→.1.2.1.2).

To fully understand the above tree diagram, we must discuss some further basic assumptions of Generative Grammar (RADFORD 1981; 1988; 2004; HAEGEMAN ^{2}1994; 1997) in the next section.

1.2.2.3 Types of phrases in the English sentence

In the syntactic analyses provided here, we assume that every English sentence consists of a Noun Phrase (NP) and a Verb Phrase (VP), as is shown in the above diagram. These are two major types of constituents found in sentences of languages all over the world.

The NP preceding the VP in an English sentence is what is traditionally called the **subject** (*Subjekt*).

In our above example, the first NP of the sentence is only represented by the pronoun (Pro) *she*. Pronouns such as *he*, *she*, or *it*, i.e., personal pronouns (→ 1.1.3.1) always stand for a full NP in English. Full noun phrases are centred around a noun (N) and may have additional constituents, which we will look at below.

The VP (VP2 in the above diagram) ("*served them there*") is centred around a verb (V) and may contain further constituents. The first is in our case another NP. This VP corresponds to what is traditionally called the **predicate** (*Prädikat*). The NP contained in the VP is traditionally called the **object** (*Objekt*) (→ 1.2.1.2). The object in the above example is only represented by the pronoun *them*, but of course objects may be full noun phrases, just like subjects.

> ☝ Beware of the discrepancy in the use of the term *predicate* between traditional grammar on the one hand and valency theory (→ 1.2.1.1) and formal logic (→ 4.4.5) on the other!

The verb ("*served*") and its object ("*them*") are once again grouped together under the label VP (in this case: VP1) in the tree diagram to show that these two constituents already form a legitimate full VP. *She served them* would be a complete English sentence, fully satisfying the valency of its verb (→ 1.2.1.1), and are in closer association with each other than with the other constituents within the larger VP.

✍ Notations such as V', N' (spoken "V-bar", "N-bar") and even N" ("N-double-bar"), V" etc. are widely used in publications on Generative Grammar for such smaller constituents within constituents of the same type to show the internal hierarchy within phrases. We are abandoning this notation here because it has led to more confusion than clarification in earlier editions of this introduction and has really been made redundant by recent developments of the theory (cf. HAEGEMAN / GUÉRON 1999, 80f.). Note, however, that our notation is not the same as is normally found in the generative literature.

Adverbials (*Adverbiale*) often give additional information on **place** and **time**, on **manner** or other **circumstances** of the event. In our example, the adverbial is labelled PP, which means 'Prepositional Phrase', although it is only represented by the pronominal adverb *there* (labelled Pro). But this adverb actually stands for a full prepositional phrase, that is a phrase introduced by a preposition (→ 1.2.2.3), such as *in the garden*, just like some pronouns can stand for whole NPs as we saw above.

Having thus clarified the overall structure of our simplified sentence, let us now look at the internal structure of constituents in more detail. Each constituent is centred around a word of a specific word class (→ 1.1.3.1) and named after that word class.

To achieve this, we put the omitted detail back in, representing the sentence structure in a complex tree diagram shown in Fig. 13 on the following page (some words are abbreviated). From this diagram we can, among other things, learn more about the internal structure of NPs, VPs, and PPs in English. We can see that the first NP ("*the distressed waitress*") has an article (labelled D for 'Determiner' in the diagram), and an adjective (A), "*distressed*".

In the second noun phrase ("*the incredibly dry muffins*") we can see that adjectives in turn may form a phrase of their own (AP) because they may be modified by an adverb (Adv).

Prepositional phrases (PP) usually consist of a preposition (P) and an NP, but may in some cases contain additional elements as well. In our case, the preposition "*in*" is followed by the NP "*the weedy garden*".

54

Fig. 13: Tree diagram: *The distressed waitress solemnly ...*

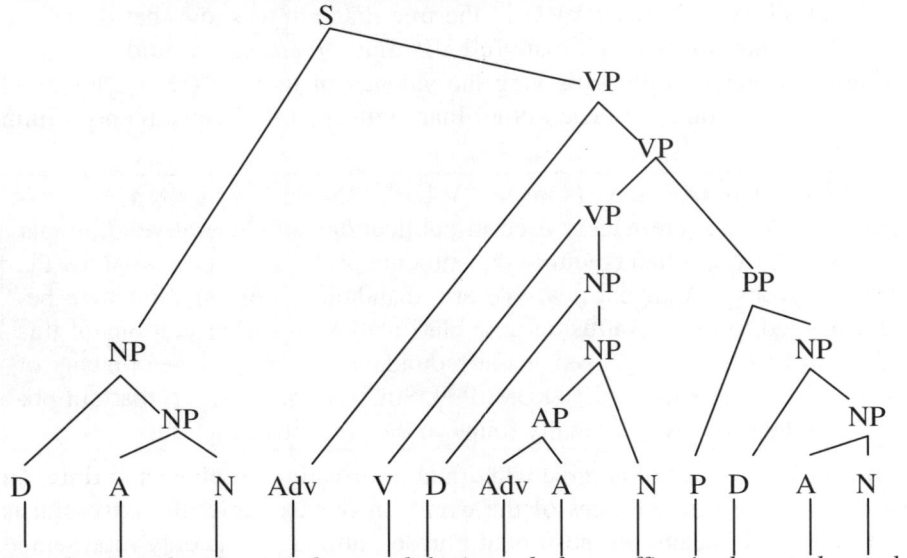

The distressed waitress sol. served the incred. dry muffins in the weedy garden

The possible **phrase structures** (*Phrasenstrukturen*) of a language may be described by **phrase structure rules** in Generative Grammar.

The relevant phrase structure rules (plus a few other important ones) for our sample sentence are the following:

S	→	NP VP
NP	→	(D) NP
	→	(AP) NP
	→	N (PP)
	→	Pro
AP	→	(Adv) A
VP	→	VP (PP)
	→	(Adv) VP
	→	V (NP)
PP	→	P NP
	→	Pro

✎ Constituents in brackets may be omitted according to the rules of English grammar.

These rules are said to **generate** (*erzeugen*) the structure of the above sentence. This is why we speak of a **Generative Grammar**. The above rules, in fact, are capable of generating most English simple sentence structures. Note that the rules generate sentence <u>structures</u>, not individual sentences. If you insert appropriate words in the above structure, you may obtain an entirely different sentence, though with the same syntactic structure. One such sentence would be

> *The stupid linguist deliberately shot the strictly protected albatross in a stormy night.*

Box 15: Recursiveness

A further important fact about the grammar of human languages can be seen from the above phrase structure rules. You will notice that some of the symbols (such as NP, PP) occur both on the left and on the right-hand side of the arrow. This means that constituents such as NP or PP may be embedded in other constituents, and that the rules describing their internal structure may be applied several times in the generation of a sentence structure.

Thus, the rule generating NP structures is applied three times in the generation of the above sentence to generate the NPs, *"the distressed waitress"*, *"the incredibly dry muffins"*, and *"the weedy garden"*. This explains how an infinite multitude of sentence structures may be generated by the application of a finite, even small, set of rules.

Rules that allow this, due to a multiple application of the same rules, are called **recursive rules** (*rekursive Regeln*). The principle of recursive rules was formulated by Noam CHOMSKY (1957; 1965) and in his theory serves as an explanation for the mystery of **linguistic creativity** (*sprachliche Kreativität*): how speakers manage to "make infinite use of finite means" (→ 8.4)

1.2.2.4 Structure within constituents: Head and modifier

All sentence constituents consisting of more than one element have an asymmetrical internal structure, in that one of its elements is the **head**, and the others are **modifiers**. The head determines the type of constituent, and is named in the label of the constituent. Thus, the head of a noun phrase is the noun, the head of a verb phrase the verb, etc.

Modifiers may be divided into **adjuncts** and **complements** (→ Box 11). Complements are obligatory, that is, they cannot be left out without destroying the structure of the phrase or changing its meaning drastically. Adjuncts are not obligatory, i.e. optional.

The modifier in a noun phrase is usually called **attribute** (*Attribut*), unless it is a determiner (→ 1.1.3.1, ☞ box). Thus in the NP *good books*, *"good"* is the attribute, *"books"* the head of the phrase. We also say, as already mentioned, that *"good"* is an **attributive adjective** here. In the NP *the books on the table*, *"on the table"* is also called an attribute.

Attributes may be very complex themselves (For further examples see → 1.2.1.3). Since attributes are usually not obligatory, i.e., **adjuncts** (→ Box 11), most attributes may also be called *noun adjuncts*. Some nouns, however, may also have **complements** (→ Box 11): The phrase

books on American history

may be a case in point, because the noun *book* may be said to have a kind of valency (→ 1.2.1.1) which, at least implicitly, demands information on the content of a book, but not on the place where a book happens to be located. But noun complements are sometimes difficult to distinguish from adjuncts. (For another type of noun complement, viz. *that*-clauses, see → 1.2.1.3.)

Modifiers in the verb phrase are the **object** and the **adverbial**. Objects are practically always obligatory, i.e., they are complements. Adverbials, as we have seen (→ 1.2.1.2), may be optional (adjuncts) or obligatory (complements).

Even prepositions have modifiers. The preposition is the head of the prepositional phrase, and the noun phrase following it is its modifier, in most cases obligatory. We thus say that a preposition usually takes a noun phrase as its **complement** (→ Box 11).

1.2.2.5 Resolving syntactic ambiguity

Phrase structure rules can also be used to explain syntactic ambiguity, thereby fulfilling one of the most important requirement for a syntactic theory according to → 1.2.2.1: Syntactically ambiguous sentences have several descriptions in terms of phrase structure (→ 1.2.2.2), one for each syntactically possible reading. To return to our above example

He saw the boy with the telescope,

the two possible readings can be represented in the following tree diagrams:

Fig. 14: Tree diagram: *He saw the boy with the telescope,* **first reading: 'He used the telescope to see the boy.'**

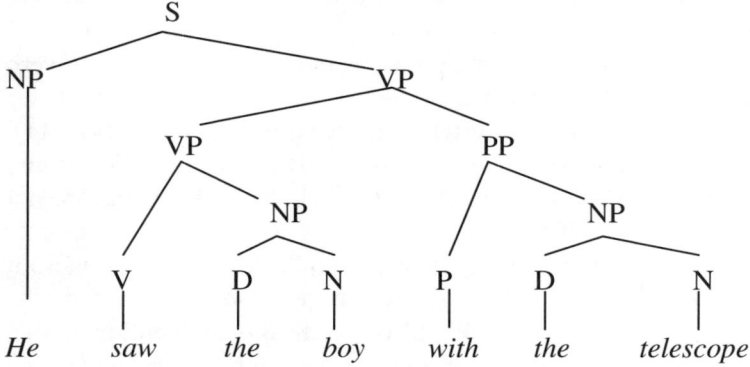

Fig. 15: Tree diagram: *He saw the boy with the telescope*, **second reading:**
'He saw the boy who had a telescope.'

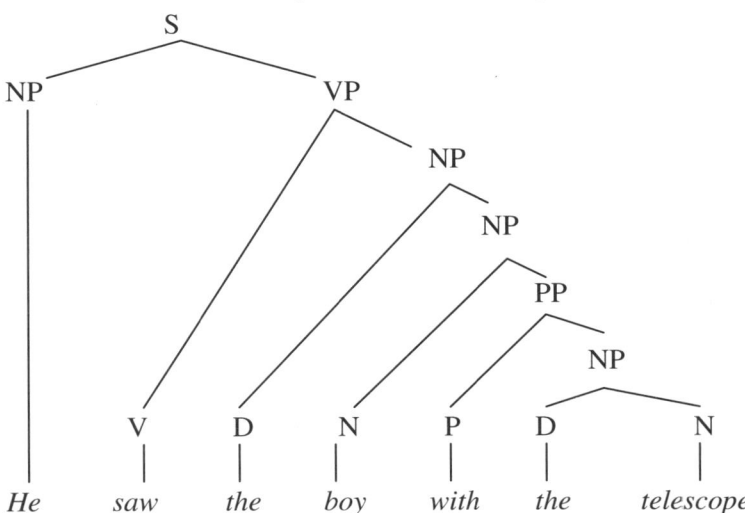

Technically speaking, in the first reading, the PP "*with the telescope*" is an adverbial in the verb phrase, in the second reading the PP "*with the telescope*" is part of a NP, modifying "*the boy*".

1.2.2.6 Thematic roles

Knowing the different constituents of a sentence and learning about how they are put together hierarchically does not tell us much about the function, or the role, of these constituents in a sentence.

To characterise more precisely the semantic role of the NPs and PPs in a sentence vis-à-vis the verb, many linguists use a small set of roles originally called **case roles** (*Kasusrollen*) (FILLMORE 1968). The so-called case grammar FILLMORE had developed became an important precursor of functional (→ 1.2.2.7) and cognitive (→ 1.2.3.6) approaches to syntax.

   Case roles were also adopted by mainstream generative grammarians under the name of **thematic roles** or θ-roles (pronounced 'theta-roles') (GRUBER 1976).

☞ The term *thematic role* is a 'good' example of unnecessarily infelicitous terminology in linguistics. The term was chosen because one of the most common roles of this kind is (equally infelicitously) called the *theme* (see below). This term, however had long been used in European linguistics for something that is completely different (→ 6.1.3) which can, however, easily be mixed up with the theme in the sense of thematic roles, since both terms usually refer to noun phrases as parts of clauses.

> Due to the prestige of generative approaches within linguistics, the term is now almost universally used by linguists of different schools. As practically no other term is available for this thematic role, we adopt it as well.

The following roles are most commonly distinguished nowadays (HAEGEMAN [2]1994, 49f) (further roles have been discussed in the literature):

"AGENT/ACTOR: the one who intentionally initiates the action expressed by the predicate.

PATIENT: the person or thing undergoing the action expressed by the predicate.

THEME: the person or thing moved by the action expressed by the predicate.

EXPERIENCER: the entity that experiences some (psychological) state expressed by the predicate.

BENEFACTIVE/BENEFICIARY: the entity that benefits from the action expressed by the predicate.

GOAL: the entity towards which the activity expressed by the predicate is directed.

SOURCE: the entity from which something is moved as a result of the activity expressed by the predicate.

LOCATION: the place in which the action or state expressed by the predicate is situated."

> ✒ HAEGEMAN uses the term *predicate* in a sense here which is somewhat ambiguous: It could mean the predicate of traditional syntax (→ 1.2.1.2) as well as the sense in which it is used in predicate logic (→ 4.4.5). The difference is not important here.

HAEGEMAN ([2]1994, 50) gives the following examples for these roles:

Galahad   gave   the detective story   to Jane.
AGENT   THEME   BENEFACTIVE/GOAL

Constance rolled the ball towards Poirot.
AGENT   THEME   GOAL

The ball rolled towards a pigsty.
THEME   GOAL

Madame Maigret had been cold all day.
EXPERIENCER

Maigret likes   love stories.
EXPERIENCER THEME

Love stories please Maigret.
THEME   EXPERIENCER

Poirot bought the book from Maigret.
AGENT   THEME   SOURCE

Maigret is in London.
THEME   LOCATION

Thelma abandoned the project. (from HAEGEMAN / GUÉRON 1999, 26)
AGENT   PATIENT.

The roles THEME and PATIENT are sometimes conflated as they are not easily distinguished. The relationship between thematic roles and syntactic roles such as subject and object is not arbitrary, but on the other hand somewhat complicated. It depends on the verb, but also on other factors, such as the voice of the verb, which argument (→ 1.2.1.1) is selected for which syntactic position.

In English, there is a certain preference for **agent** (*Agens*) and **experiencer** (*Experiens, Erfahrender*) NPs to appear in subject position, a tendency which is even stronger in German, and for patient and theme NPs to surface as syntactic objects. But as we said before, this is only a tendency, not a strict rule.

In summary, it must be said that the theory of thematic roles is very much in need of elaboration and clarification. It is a promising approach to establish a connection between the structure of a sentence and its meaning, and is also important common ground between Generative Grammar and other approaches to syntax (→ 1.2.3.6). The difference between Generative Grammar and functional and cognitive approaches lies, among other things, in the importance they assign to the thematic roles: In Generative Grammar thematic roles are a *post hoc* interpretation of the formal structure of a sentence, whereas functional and cognitive approaches take the thematic roles as primary determinants of sentence structure.

1.2.2.7 Formal vs. functional approaches in syntax

Generative Grammar is now the most influential and widespread approach to syntactic description (CHOMSKY 1981; 1995; HAEGEMAN [2]1994; 1997; HAEGEMAN / GUÉRON 1999; RADFORD 2004). The theory is developing very rapidly so it is difficult to keep pace with it. It tries to formulate generalisations on syntactic structure that are based on purely formal criteria. This has led to analyses of sentence structure becoming more and more abstract and more and more removed from 'common sense' categories. This very fact, however, is embraced by adherents of this theory as welcome progress towards a truly scientific study of language. Categories of modern physics or computer science, it is said, are not 'common sense' either. Thus, arguing about and with Generative Grammar amounts to arguing about the epistemological status of linguistics as such: Is linguistics a science just like chemistry, biology, or physics, or is it still part of the humanities?

Generative Grammar has been severely criticised from within linguistics for various reasons. We would like to point out just one line of argument that is relevant for the analysis of sentence structure. The theory has greatly improved our understanding of constituent structure in a sentence. It has little to say, however, on the function of constituents in a sentence. Categories such as *subject*, *object*, or *adverbial* do not exist independently in Generative Trasformational Grammar; they are defined by their place in the tree structure alone. Moreover, this theory starts from the formal structure of a sentence and then assigns a semantic interpretation to this structure, which is dependent on the meaning of the verb. **Functional approaches** to syntax (HALLIDAY 1985; WIERZBICKA 1988, GIVÓN 1984;

function

1990, FOLEY / VAN VALIN 1984), by contrast, maintain that it is the meaning of a sentence that determines its form. TG could thus be accused of putting grammar upside-down. In the following section (→ 1.2.3), we will get to know a version of Construction Grammar as an advanced functionally oriented approach to the description of syntax.

1.2.3 Construction Grammar

1.2.3.1 The development of Construction Grammar. Different approaches

Construction Grammar is an alternative approach to the analysis of syntactic structures, alongside the mainstream generative grammar. It originally emerged from the necessity to explain **idioms** contradicting **FREGE's compositionality principle** (→ Box 16), such as

> *to come out of the closet on sth.* 'sich zu etw. bekennen' or
> *to riot away one's days* 'sich ausleben'.

Box 16: Compositionality

Compositionality of the meaning of complex patterns counts as a clear indication of a linguistic structure. The compositionality principle says that the meaning of most complex words, phrases, or sentences may be said to be **composed** of the meaning of its parts according to certain rules to be formulated in linguistic descriptions. Such linguistic expressions are called **compositional**. This principle (also called **FREGE's principle** (*FREGE-Prinzip*) to honour the German philosopher Gottlob FREGE, who first formulated it) is an important, but unresolved issue in many branches of linguistics (→ 1.2.3.2; 1.3.4; 1.3.5; 2.3.4.1; 3.2.3.3; 3.2.5.3; 4.4).

Idioms as in the above examples are often adduced as counterexamples to the principle as their meaning is wholly unpredictable on the basis of the meanings of their parts. From within Cognitive Linguistics (→ Box 17) both the compositionality principle as a general rule and the assumption that idioms are totally opaque have been questioned. Even the most 'transparent' construction is non-compositional to some degree. And even idioms like the above retain some conceptual structures that hint at their total meaning. In any case, the term *idiom* is often used for fixed expressions that seem perfectly compositional (such as *God save the Queen!*). Compositionality thus turns out to be a key issue in Construction Grammar. All this will become clearer, we hope, while you read this section.

The analysis of idioms led to the rethinking of the syntactic representation laid down in the generative framework, since the semantic and syntactic unpredictability of idiomatic constructions represents a problem for the generative theoretical framework. Idiomatic expressions cannot be generated by the rules of the componential generative model (→ 1.2.2.2), and are conventional, thus must be stored and processed in the speaker's mind as a whole. The meaning of the construction does not correspond to the sum of meanings of lexical items occurring in this construction and thus contradicts **FREGE's compositionality principle** (→ Box 16). This need to represent linguistic knowledge in terms of constructions led to the development of a cognitive grammatical framework, known as Construction Grammar, whose major assumptions and guiding principles will be outlined in the following section.

The term *Construction Grammar* is used to refer to a family of cognitive approaches to grammar which share certain guiding principles.

Box 17: Cognitive Linguistics

> Construction Grammar can broadly be assigned to the framework of **Cognitive Linguistics** (*Kognitive Linguistik*), which is now the major alternative paradigm to Chomsky's generative grammar in linguistics. One of its most typical characteristics is that no clear boundary can be drawn between syntax and semantics. This and other basic tenets of this approach will become evident in the following discussion. Since the organisation of this introduction presupposes such a boundary we try to raise relevant issues of cognitive linguistics separately in the chapters on syntax and on semantics. (→ 1.2.3, 4.3)

There are four variants of Construction Grammar within the cognitive paradigm, i.e.

- **Construction Grammar** (KAY / FILLMORE 1999),
- **Cognitive Grammar** (LANGACKER 1987, 1991),
- **Radical Construction Grammar** (CROFT 2001),
- the **Construction Grammar** of LAKOFF (1987) and GOLDBERG (1995; 2003; 2006).

Due to lack of space, it was not possible to provide a detailed account of all those variants here. Instead, we will introduce some basic concepts which reflect more or less common tenets of these constructionist approaches.

Most current approaches follow a so-called **usage-based model** (LANGACKER 1987; 2000; TOMASELLO 2003; GOLDBERG 2006). This means that they regard **discourse**, or language use as the window to linguistic competence and to language structure (→ 1.1.1.3). The model furthermore assumes that the statistical properties of the input shape the language user's repertoire of linguistic configurations. A usage-based type of modeling a language thus requires statistical, as opposed to categorical observations. In fact human cognition in general is considered to be **probabilistic** (→ Box 18 below). This means that all generalisations and inferences can only be made with a certain probability. As far as linguistic method is concerned, commitment to the usage-based approach of course means a strong commitment to methods of corpus linguistics (→ Box 3).

Box 18: Fuzziness

This is in line with one of the basic tenets of Cognitive Linguistics maintaining that natural language categories are **fuzzy** (*unscharf*) and probabilistic. MAN-NING and SCHÜTZE (1999, 15) argue that "the argument for a probabilistic approach to cognition is that we live in a world filled with uncertainty and incomplete information."

Hence a felicitous interaction with the world requires our capability to deal with this type of information.

The notion of fuzziness is used in many linguistic argumentations, not only about natural language categories, but also about analytic categories of linguistics themselves. Many traditional distinctions of linguistic theory have meanwhile been argued to be fuzzy, i.e., to represent a continuum (*Kontinuum*) of phenomena rather than clear-cut separate categories. We will repeatedly return to this issue (see index s.v. 'continuum' and 'fuzziness').

1.2.3.2 The notion of construction

☞ The term **construction** *(Konstruktion)* as used in Construction Grammar constitutes a broadening of the traditional notion. In traditional grammar, the term is used in a somewhat loose manner and usually refers to a rather abstract, recurrent configuration of morphosyntactic categories which is typically smaller than a sentence and larger than a word, such as the infinitive construction, the participle construction etc. A construction in this sense seldom contains specific lexical material, and if so, only so-called function words (→ 1.1.3.1, ☞ box). As will be seen below, the notion of construction in Construction Grammar differs from this. A construction – and this is true of Construction Grammar constructions as well as of constructions in the traditional sense – may, but need not be coextensive with a constituent in the sense of Generative Grammar.

Constructions in Construction Grammar are linguistic units of varying complexity and abstractness which map items of **form** (phonological, morphological and syntactic structures) with items of meaning (any conceptual **content**).

◖ The term *form* is also used in variable meanings in linguistics. Note that *form* in Construction Grammar terms does not correspond to HJELMSLEV's notion of *form*, but is more analogous to his notion of *expression* (→ 2.2.3, Fig. 38 and Fig. 39).

Since these mappings, as we saw, are not always predictable, linguists say that they are, at least to a certain extent, **arbitrary** (→ Box 19 below).

Box 19: Arbitrariness and PEIRCE's concept of 'symbol'

The notion of **arbitrariness** (*Willkürlichkeit, Arbitrarität*) may be explained with reference to PEIRCE's ([1931-1958] 1998, 2.247-2.249) basic classification of signs into **symbols**, **icons** (→ Box 26) and **indices** (Box 27). (See also section → 8.1; cf. LYONS 1977, 100ff.).

PEIRCE did not develop a theory of language, but a general theory of signs, called **semiotics** (*Semiotik, Allgemeine Zeichenlehre*), of which linguistics was conceived to be a part. PEIRCE's concept of **symbol** rests on SAUSSURE's ([¹1916] 1965, 100) thesis of the **arbitrariness** of the linguistic sign, i.e. the **conventionality** of the relationship between an **expression** and a **content** (→ Fig. 38; Fig. 39). A symbol stands in a signifying relationship with its object only because there exists a convention that it will be interpreted in that particular way. That's why they are often also called **conventional signs**. It is also often said that symbols, in this sense, are not **motivated**, except by convention, whereas icons and indices are motivated by other factors.

It must be noted here that the principle of arbitrariness is originally only meant to be valid for simple linguistic signs (consisting of only one morpheme, → 1.3.2), but not necessarily for complex signs, which are relatively motivated by their components. Thus *Handschuh* can be said to be more motivated than *glove*. Although a *Handschuh* is not a shoe, it is to the hand what a shoe is to the foot; thus the designation is motivated by an **analogy** (→ Box 32). It certainly makes more sense to call a glove *Handschuh* than to call it *Apfelkuchen*. *glove*, on the other hand (if the pun is allowed), is completely arbitrary as a designation. Any word pronounceable in English could be used instead.

Arbitrariness does not necessarily hold for complex constructions either, which may be iconic to a some degree (→ Box 26).

☞ Note that in literary studies, and also in everyday usage, the term *symbol* is used to refer to something rather different. "Symbols" as defined in literary studies are also signs in SAUSSURE's and PEIRCE's sense, but they are typically non-arbitrary (CUDDON 1992, 939-942). If Brandenburg Gate in Berlin is called a "symbol of German unity", then this is not just an arbitrary convention, but is historically motivated. From now on, we will use the term *symbol* exclusively for arbitrary signs in this linguistics textbook.

➤ This terminological choice (or should we say chaos?) may be infelicitous, but Saussure could base his usage on a tradition in French-language mathematics and sciences to use the term "*symboles*" for conventional signs used in their technical language Thus, in French chemical texts, *O* is called a "*symbole*" for 'oxygen'. A similar usage exists in English. Thus SAUSSURE's term was adopted into PEIRCE's English without much ado.

It should also be pointed out that actually SAUSSURE's and PEIRCE's definition is closer to the original concept of 'symbol' in Ancient Greek: *sýmbolon* originally denotes a very special kind of sign whose meaning is established by explicit convention.

The explicitness of the convention, of course, does not hold for all symbols in PEIRCE 's sense.

For example, a flag at the beach may signify that swimming is safe; but there is neither any resemblance between the flag and the state of the tide, nor any direct natural causation from the tide to the flag. The only thing that qualifies the flag for signifying that swimming is safe is the general conventional practice of using flags in this way. This practice presumably rests on some explicit convention laid down in some regulations.

Language usually shows a different kind of conventionality. In English there is a word *tree*, in German there is a word *Baum*, and in French there is a word *arbre*. Each of these expressions has very much the same meaning and may be used to refer to the same class of objects, although they are quite different in form. No one of them is more naturally appropriate to signify trees than the other two. Neither *tree*, nor *Baum*, nor *arbre* can be said to be in any way naturally or functionally representative of trees or of their distinctive properties. It just happens to be the case that these words are used to denote such things. It can be said that it is a convention that underlies this usage, but this convention is only in rare cases a convention agreed upon by language users explicitly. Such a rare case are terminological and notational conventions in the sciences, e.g. In vernacular language (→ 7.1.3, ☞ box), 'conventions' are handed down from generation to generation, but are also subject to often unnoticed changes under certain conditions (→ 3.3). These changes, however, are not likely to make the convention less arbitrary (→ 8.1).

Symbols in language are thus arbitrary correlations between **expression** (= **form** in cognitive linguistic terms) and **content** (= **meaning** in cognitive linguistic terms) (see also → Box 24).

Note: To characterise this dichotomy, the terms *form* and *function* are also widely used. (cf. → Fig. 38, Fig. 39).

As already mentioned, non-arbitrary signs can be **icons** (→ Box 26) or **indices** (→ Box 27).

Far from denying that grammar may have non-arbitrary traits, cognitive linguists do emphasise the arbitrary nature of both lexical units and grammatical constructions. They say a grammatical construction is a **symbolic form-meaning pairing** (see → Fig. 16 below).

Fig. 16: The symbolic nature of a construction
(adapted from CROFT / CRUSE 2004, 258)

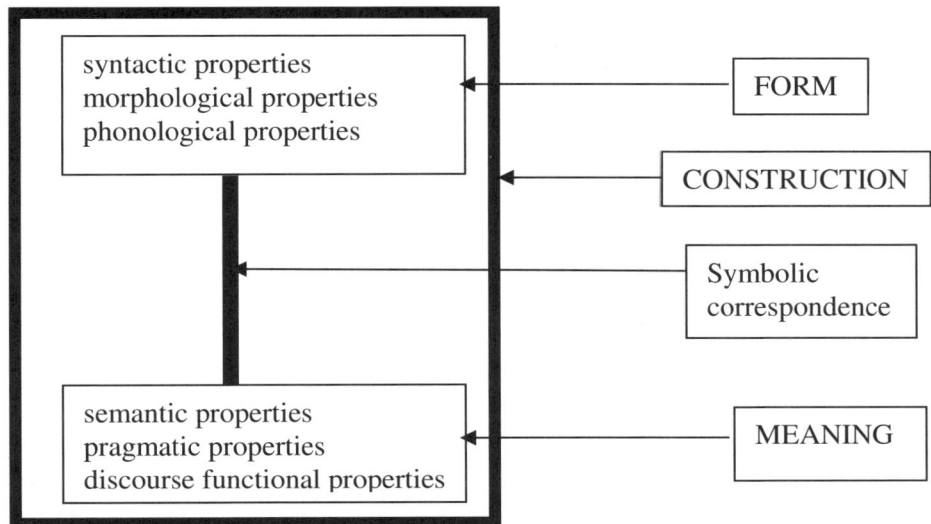

☞ The credit for this conceptual gestalt goes to SAUSSURE, of course ([1916] 1965, 97-100; 1966, 65-67). His concept of the linguistic sign, as we can see above, has become seminal for reasoning about sign theories and signs all through the 20ᵗʰ century right into the present. SAUSSURE called the two sides of 'his' sign that are mysteriously and inseparably linked in language users' minds *signifiant* ('signifier') and *signifié* ('signified'). SAUSSURE's model is often presented to explain the nature of word meaning (→ 4.1). In cognitive linguistics, it is extended to all constructions, words being regarded as a kind of construction, too. SAUSSURE's model of the linguistic sign also underlies HJELMSLEVs statements about **expression** and **content** (→ Box 24).

A construction in Construction Grammar is considered to be a basic unit of **linguistic knowledge** (In Generative Grammar, generative rules are these basic units). Constructions vary considerably
–   in size: ranging from
    –   morphemes via
    –   words and
    –   phrases to
    –   whole sentence patterns.
–   They also vary in abstractness: from
    –   substantive (i.e. fully lexically filled) idioms via
    –   partially lexically filled to
    –   fully schematic (abstract) linguistic patterns.
Thus, linguistic knowledge at all levels can be characterised as constructions, i.e. form-meaning pairings.

1.2.3.3 Examples of constructions

To illustrate the notion of construction, the table below (Fig. 17) contains a few examples of constructions, varying in size, abstractness and complexity.

✍ Before giving examples, a few remarks on the notation may be in order:
Notation for the representation of constructions in the different versions of Construction Grammar varies considerably and is often used in a somewhat unreflected way. The categories used come from
- traditional grammar (subject, object etc.) (→ 1.2.1.2) as well as
- generative grammar (NP, VP, etc.) (→ 1.2.2.3) and
- case grammar (agent, theme etc.) (→ 1.2.2.6), but also
- from the cognitive framework itself.
Among the latter are, e.g.
- **actor**, an agent- or experiencer-like case role, likely to turn up as subject
- **undergoer**, a patient- or theme-like case role, likely to turn up as object
In this introduction, we use an *ad hoc* though, we hope, consistent notation following CROFT / CRUSE 2004 and GOLDBERG 1995 as much as consistency allows,
- trying to capture the schematic, i.e. more abstract categories involved at that level of schematicity (abstractness) that appears to be the most sensible for the construction in question while at the same time
- trying to specify more substantive (i.e. lexically filled) slots as precisely as possible.
Accordingly, in the following, we use the following conventions and abbreviations:
- Constructions, and also relevant constructions within constructions, are included in square brackets [ ], assuming that confusion with a phonetic notation is unlikely.
- Optional elements are put in parentheses ( ).
- Substantive, i.e., lexically specified elements are given in ordinary spelling in *italics*, names of schematic (abstract) elements are abbreviated and shown in CAPITALS (with a few self-explanatory exceptions; see below).

Syntactic roles:		Constituents:		Word classes:		Case roles:	
SBJ	Subject	S	Sentence / Clause	D	Determiner	AG	Agent
V	Verb			N	Noun	EXP	Exper.
OBJ	Object	NP	Noun phrase	Aux	Auxiliary	PAT	Patient
ADV	Adverbial	VP	Verb phrase	V	Verb	THE	Theme
SP	Subject predicative	PP	Prepositional phrase	P	Preposition	BEN	Benef.
OP	Object predicative	AP	Adjective phrase	A	Adjective	LOC	Location
				Adv	Adverb	GOA	Goal
						INS	Instrument
						Act	Actor
						Und	Undergoer

- **Subcategories** may be indicated by lower-case subscripts:

V_{trans}	transitive verb
V_{intr}	intransitive verb
V_{caten}	catenative verb (see QUIRK et al. [12]1994, 146f.)
V_{papa}	verb in the 'past participle' form ($\rightarrow$ 1.1.3.4.7)
N_{count}	countable noun
ADV_{time}	adverbial of time

- Information from different levels may also be combined by subscripting:

LOC_{PP}	A location given as a prepositional phrase
PP_{LOC}	A prepositional phrase which gives location information

(These two notations are of course equivalent; their choice depends on what information is most relevant).

ADV_{PP}	An adverbial in form of a prepositional phrase
ADV_{Adv}	An adverbial in form of an adverb.

Fig. 17: Examples of constructions
(adapted from GOLDBERG 2003, 220, with some additions)

Construction type	Form / Example	Meaning / Function
Morpheme	e.g. [*un-*], [*bio-*], [*-aholic*], [*-ness*], [*-ing*]	To be described individually in lexicon or in morphology
Word	e.g. [*sheep*], [*advice*], [*and*]	To be described individually in lexicon
Complex word	e.g. [*dare-devil*], [*shoo-in*], [*talk show*]	Mostly to be accounted for by word formation rules
Idiom (filled)	e.g. [[*spill*]$_V$ [[*the*]$_D$ [*beans*]$_N$]$_{NP}$]$_{VP}$	To be described in lexicon and in grammar
Idiom (partially filled)	e.g. [[*under*]$_P$ [[[*the*]$_D$ [*auspices*]$_N$ [[*of*]$_P$ NP]$_{PP}$	To be described in lexicon and in grammar
Catenative verb construction	[SBJ [V$_{caten}$ *to* VP]$_{VP}$]$_S$ (e.g. *Sam came to realise the problem*)	Finer distinctions of aspect and modality
Ditransitive (double-object) construction	[SBJ [V$_{trans}$ OBJ1$_{BEN}$ OBJ2$_{THE}$]$_{VP}$]$_S$ (e.g. *She gave him a Coke; He baked her a muffin*)	Transfer of possession

As can be seen from the above table, a **grammatical construction** is a unit of syntactic representation which in many cases may also involve one or more specific lexical or grammatical (**substantive**) items. This is a major innovation on generative grammar.

What is also important to note is that the conceptual content of a construction need not be wholly predictable from the meaning of its individual parts. The construction itself contributes content that is not necessarily contained in the meaning of its individual elements. Why should a sequence of two noun phrases A and B like in the ditransitive construction signify transfer of B to A? It does this only by virtue of the <u>construction</u> in which the two noun phrases are involved. To show the significance of this, we give a few more examples of partially lexically filled constructions:

– *let alone* **construction**: [A *let alone* B], where A and B are constituents of the same type (cf. FILLMORE et al. 1988), as in

*It takes science to come along and tell us that what is going on under these circumstances is a BRAIN process, **let alone** to tell us WHICH brain process it is. BNC: A0T 172*
*We hadn't SEEN a fish, **let alone** HOOKED one. AS7 1089*

Both A and B must contain some negative element. Thus, other sources of knowledge cannot tell us what science can. And A and B must be in a certain semantic relation in that B is in some way stronger than A on a certain scale: Hooking a fish is more difficult than seeing one. The *let alone* construction is used in a very specific speech situation in which the speaker imputes a certain misconception to the hearer and tries to correct it.

– *have a* $[V]_N$ **construction** ($[V]_N$ stands for a noun converted ($\rightarrow$ 1.3.5) from a verb): as in

have a drink,
have a nap.

WIERZBICKA (1988, 293-357) has shown that the *have a* V_N construction can only be used under fairly restricted semantic conditions and systematically changes the meaning of the verb. Thus, she tries to explain why it is possible to have a drink, but not to *have an eat.

> 📖 Find examples of the *have a* V_N construction and try to describe their conceptual content.

– V_{intr} *away* **construction**, where V_{intr} stands for an intransitive verb ($\rightarrow$ 1.2.1.1) as in:

*I munched **away***
'Ich mampfte drauf los'.

Again, the meaning of the construction is not identical with the sum of the meanings of its parts. The meaning of *away* is quite different from the usual meaning of this adverb.

On the other hand, there are many constructions which are purely formal (**schematic**) and do not involve any specific lexical material, as with the

- **resultative construction**, which occurs in several variants, e.g.,

[SBJ	V_{trans}	OBJ	OP]
You	*killed*	*it*	*stone-dead.* (S. Maugham, *Altogether*)
I	*had brushed*	*my hair*	*very smooth* (Ch. Brontë, *Jane Eyre*)
She	*sneezed*	*the napkin*	*off the table*

  (Cognitive linguists' folklore)

that is, in the traditional sense, a kind of object predicative construction (→1.2.1.2.4), or in:

[SBJ	V_{intr}	SC],
The river	*froze*	*solid.*
The vase	*went*	*to pieces*

  (cf. GOLDBERG 1995, 180f.)

a subject predicative construction.

In particular, the napkin-sneezing example is elucidating: It will be noted that *sneeze* is not really a transitive verb. But its use in the resultative construction gives it a new meaning and we understand that the sentence describes a result of an act of sneezing, however bizarre the circumstances may be.

Another very common and much discussed construction that is almost purely schematic and uses only little lexical material is the

- **passive construction**, which also occurs in several variants, e.g.
  - **"direct passive"**

[NP$_{Und}$	[*be* (Adv)	V_{papa}	(*by* NP$_{Act}$)]$_{VP}$]
The armadillo	*was (fatally)*	*hit*	(*by a car*).

  - **"indirect passive"**

[NP$_{Und/BEN}$	[*be* V$_{papa}$	NP$_{THE}$	(*by* NP$_{Act}$)]$_{VP}$]
The poor thing	*was given*	*an injection*	(*by the highway vet*).

  - **"prepositional passive"**

[NP$_1$	[*be*	V$_{papa}$	P$_1$	(*by* NP$_{Act}$)]$_{VP}$]
This service was		*paid*	*for*	(*by the car driver*).

    (☞ The subscript "1" in the last example indicates that the NP and the P belong together; the precise thematic role of the NP depends on the meaning of the preposition.)

The passive construction in particular has been subject to many debates and theoretical considerations in Generative Grammar, which cannot be repeated here (→ Box 14, cf. HAEGEMAN 1991, 180-187; 295f.). It is granted that Generative Grammar provides a more 'elegant', i.e., parsimonious analysis of the passive construction than CxG because it does not need three different descriptions to cover all the variants. The question remains which analysis is 'psychologically real', i.e., best reflects the grammatical knowledge of the naïve native speaker.

This knowledge may well be redundantly organised and not 'elegant' and parsimonious at all.

1.2.3.4 The figure / ground alignment

However elegant purely formal analyses may be, generative linguists overlook one important aspect of the passive construction which is certainly part of the native speaker's linguistic knowledge: This construction codes a different conceptualisation of the same scene coded by the corresponding active construction. The major discourse-functional property of the passive construction is that of making the object more prominent (or, in Cognitive Linguistics terms, making it the **figure**), and thus backgrounding the agent (i.e., turning it into the **ground**) or leaving it out altogether.

The **figure / ground** alignment is a central concept in Cognitive Linguistics which is not only relevant in passive constructions and not only in syntax. According to LANGACKER,

> "The figure within a scene is a substructure perceived as "standing out" from the remainder (the ground) and accorded special prominence as the pivotal entity around which is the scene is organized and for which it provides a setting" (LANGACKER 1987, 120).

This can be additionally illustrated by the following example:

> *The train station is next to McDonald's.*
> *McDonald's is next to the train station.*

The difference between these two sentences is described in cognitive linguistics in terms of a figure / ground alignment. In the first example, the train station is conceptualised as the figure (hence corresponds to a grammatical subject) and MacDonald's as the ground, whereas in the second we have the reversal of the figure / ground roles. In other words, we would select the first sentence if the train station is in the focus of our attention. E.g., if we are looking for the train station, the first sentence would be the appropriate answer to a pertinent question. The reverse is true for the second sentence. What this last example also shows is that the passive is only one of several possible instantiations of a more general principle, i.e. figure / ground alignment.

> ☛ The figure-ground alignment is sometimes erroneously equated with the **theme – rheme** distinction in functional syntax and textlinguistics. On the difference, see → 6.1.3, in particular Box 39.

1.2.3.5 Further properties of constructions

This means that Cognitive Linguistics and Construction Grammar also make use of generalisations, but in contrast to the generalisations of generative theory, which are purely based on formal properties of syntactic rules (→ 1.2.2.7), thereby hoping to isolate a linguistic module in our brain that is independent of our general cognitive abilities, cognitive approaches are based on people's general cognitive abilities, in this case the ability to conceptualise or construe the same scene in multiple ways (→ 4.3.1), and the ability to conceptualise analogous scenes in analogous ways.

As we saw above, within a construction certain elements are lexically open (**schematic**) and others are lexically fixed (**substantive**); there is a continuum (→ Box 18) from schematic to substantive (the **syntax-lexicon continuum**). According to this approach, words, e.g., are grammatical units, and word classes are schematisations of these grammatical units.

– A construction has its own conceptual content and sometimes its own pragmatic meaning (on pragmatics, → Chapter 5); thus a construction is an amalgamation of phonological, syntactic, semantic, and pragmatic information. This can be seen in the examples given above: Each of these constructions has not only got a (morpho)syntactic structure, but also a specifiable conceptual content and a pragmatic function.

– Constructions are viewed as units learnable on the basis of the input and general cognitive mechanisms and are expected to vary cross-linguistically (GOLDBERG 2003, 219).

In Construction Grammar, grammar is seen as a structured inventory of constructions. This inventory can be represented as a network. Within this network we encounter, as we saw above, different levels of schematicity (abstractness). Several levels of schematicity, e.g., can be identified between the idiomatic phrase *kick the bucket*, which is a substantive construction and which is an instance of the more schematic construction 'verb phrase'.

Fig. 18 An example of a hierarchical network of constructions
(adapted from CROFT / CRUSE 2004, 264)

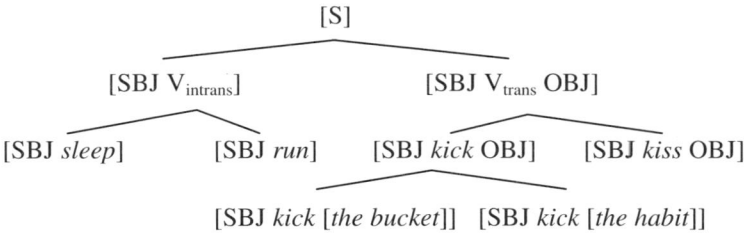

> ♠ The above tree diagram looks deceptively similar to a tree diagram in Generative Grammar (→ 1.2.2.2 ff.), but shows something completely different: Although both diagrams have the symbol S, meaning 'sentence', at their top, a tree diagram in Generative Grammar shows the constituents, i.e. <u>parts</u> of a sentence, whereas the above diagram shows <u>kinds</u> of sentences, i.e. different construction <u>types</u>. In semantic terms, it could be said the relations in the above tree are hyponymic (kind-of) relations (→ 4.2.2.2), whereas a tree in Generative Grammar always shows meronymic (part-of) relations (→ 4.2.2.3).

Note that the fact that Generative Grammar mainly uses meronymic tree diagrams in syntax, whereas the above tree diagrams are used to show hyponymic relations, is entirely coincidental and does not describe an essential difference between the two grammatical approaches.

1.2.3.6 Generative vs. Construction Grammar

In contrast to Chomskyan Generative Grammar, **Construction Grammar** rejects the autonomous, modular status of syntax, i.e. the assumption that syntax is a module that is completely independent of other levels of linguistic description and other cognitive abilities. According to Construction Grammar, syntactic phenomena can never be described adequately without reference to semantics and pragmatics. An insightful analysis into syntactic patterns cannot be provided in terms of abstract syntactic principles alone but only in terms of the language user's intended meaning in a particular context. The process of joining words into larger patterns is

> "handled, not by a special syntactic component of the grammar, but in terms of constructions" (TAYLOR 2002, 561),

which as we said above, are pairings of a certain form with an array of functions. Construction Grammar assumes that it is not possible to draw a clear borderline between facts pertaining to the lexicon and facts pertaining to syntax. An adequate analysis of grammatical phenomena has to take the meaning of items into account.

The main underlying assumption of Construction Grammar is that a language is a symbolic system (→ Box 19), devised to code meanings generated by the cognitive processes of language users, with their experiences of the world figuring in these processes. Sentences will be perceived as maximally natural ('normal') if the meanings they code coincide with natural ways of conceptualising the relevant situation (LEE 2001, 17). Judgements about the grammaticality of sentences in question are based on our everyday experience of the relevant situation rather than on some formal abstract set of rules. In other words:

– The generative framework assumes that the structure of the language system can best be described in terms of rigid, formal syntactic rules independently of their semantic functions.

– Construction Grammar abandons the idea that language users generate sentences via rules specifying which grammatical categories are combinable to form phrases and sentences. Grammatical properties are not decisive for the constructional process but it is meaning that is the principal determining factor for the combinability of linguistic units.

– As already mentioned, constructionist approaches to grammar consider constructions as an amalgamation of multiple levels of linguistic structures: phonological, syntactic, semantic and pragmatic. Consequently, Construction Grammar assumes a syntax-lexicon continuum (a continuum from substantive, i.e. fully or partially lexically filled patterns of different size to schematic, i.e. fully abstract phrasal patterns). This contrasts strongly with the generative modular view, which assumes that various levels of linguistic knowledge, in particular grammar and lexicon are strictly separated and separately stored and processed.

1.3 Morphology

1.3.1 Why morphology?

Morphology (*Morphologie*, *Formenlehre*), as we said earlier, is the study of the internal structure of words. We will now have to clarify what this means. Let us look at the following more or less well-known words:

talk talks talking talked (verb)	*talk-back*
talkable, talkability	*talking-to*
talkative, talkativeness	*talk-master*
talker	*talk show*
talkie	*talkfest*
talky	*talkathon*
talk talks (noun)	*talkee-talkee*

They're all English words, although you may not know all of them. It seems obvious that they are all somehow related. This is also suggested by their meanings. (If you don't know the meanings, look them up in a good dictionary, → 10.2.4.0). It is obviously no coincidence that the words in the above list are related both in expression and in content (meaning) (→ Box 24).

It is this non-coincidence that morphology is concerned with. Every language has large numbers of such groups of words that are related in expression and in meaning. This amounts to saying that every language has morphology, i.e. that every language has at least some words that are morphologically complex, that have a **morphological structure** (*morphologische Struktur*).

Linguists would not be content with a description that listed all the above words and described their meaning separately. Not even dictionaries, which are basically nothing but lists of words, do this.

If you look up *talk* in a dictionary, you will find that at least the first four words are treated specially. Sometimes the words *talks*, *talking*, and *talked* are not even listed, but given in an abbreviated form together with *talk* (*talk, -s, -ing, -ed*). This is because many people feel that these 'words' are not really words on their own, but just 'forms' of the word *talk*. Linguists say they are **inflectional forms** (*Flexionsformen*) of *talk* (→ 1.3.4).

Indeed, it is almost impossible to describe the 'meaning' of a word form like *talked* without resorting to the meaning of *talk*. In any case, the easiest way to describe the word form *talked* is to say that it is the past tense and the past participle of *talk*.

But then we see that there are many word forms ending in *-ed*, having quite an analogous (→ Box 32) meaning: *walked* may be described as the past tense of *walk*, *pillaged* as the past tense of *pillage*, and *measured* as the past tense of *measure*, and so on for thousands of English verbs. If we were content with listing all these verb forms and describing their meaning in one way or another, we would thus be missing an important fact about the English language: the fact that the past tense in English is regularly formed by adding *-ed* (in writing) to the present tense form. Stating this fact is a much more elegant way of describing the thousands of regular past tense forms of English than listing them, and it is also much easier for learners to learn the rule of forming the past tense and to memorise only the exceptions. And exceptions there are, of course, as you will know. We come to those later (→ 1.3.4).

Box 20: Lexicalist vs. derivationalist

☞ The argument we have been developing here is an argument that is quite typical of linguistic reasoning. It concerns a question that may be asked about many linguistic phenomena: Should the phenomenon be listed in the dictionary or should it be described by a grammatical rule? This question (also known as the **lexicalist** vs. **derivationalist** controversy) is not always as easy to answer as in the case of the regular English past tense (and not even on that do all linguists agree). It was one of the most frequently debated questions in linguistics in the second half of the 20th century and keeps coming back in different guises (see also → 1.3.4, 1.3.6).

1.3.2 Morphemes

So far we have only discussed the word forms *talk*, *talks*, *talking* and *talked*. We saw that they are best described by formulating a **morphological rule** (*morphologische Regel*). How should such a rule be formulated? Most approaches to morphology assume that the relation between the form *talk* and its inflectional forms *talks*, *talking*, and *talked* should be described by analysing the inflectional forms into smaller units, in the following way: *talk-s*, *talk-ing*, *talk-ed*. These smaller units are called morphemes. **Morphemes** (*Morpheme*) are the smallest meaning-bearing units of a language.

Those linguists who use the term morpheme, and most of them do, can also define morphology as the study of how morphemes combine into words, or to put it in a more general way, the study of the **morphological structure** (*morphologische Struktur*) of words.

ANDERSON (1992, 71 f.) says that there are

"...two basic intuitions underlying the morphemic account of word structure:
(...)   a. Words that are related in meaning are (often) related in form as well. This is captured by saying that they contain the same morpheme(s).

   b. The constituents of a word's form can be organised into a hierarchical structure which also represents the internal organisation of its meaning and relation to other words."

Applying the notion of 'morpheme' to our above data, we thus find four different morphemes in the above examples: *talk*, *-s*, *-ing*, and *-ed*.

• For most linguistic models, a distinction between **lexical** and **grammatical morphemes** (*lexikalische* vs. *grammatische Morpheme*) is essential. It is, however, far from easy to draw. As we saw in section → 1.2.3.2, the assumption of a grammar-lexicon continuum is very plausible. It thus seems to make more sense to speak of 'more or less grammatical' and 'more or less lexical morphemes'. Criteria to assess the degree of grammaticalness or lexicalness of an item come from both content and expression (→ Box 24). Often, they are themselves fuzzy and vague. Fig. 19 tries to give some preliminary rules of thumb:

Fig. 19: Lexical vs. grammatical morphemes

Lexical morphemes	Grammatical morphemes
Lexical items tend to have a clear conceptual meaning that is rather specific: *dog, freedom, paraphernalia, easy, big, find, consider, …*	Grammatical items tend to have rather general, vague, or abstract meanings, such as 'past', 'dative', 'necessity', 'plural', 'passive', '2nd person', …
Lexical meanings are constrained as to their combinability in complex expressions: *the idea slept; *colourful idea; *sleep furiously*	Grammatical morphemes have a wide application across the lexicon: Tense combines with all verbs, number with most nouns etc.
Lexical morphemes form an **open class** (*offene Klasse*), that is, new lexical morphemes can be added without much difficulty, usually by borrowing (→ 3.2.5.1).	Grammatical morphemes form a **closed class** (*geschlossene Klasse*); that means that languages do not easily acquire new grammatical morphemes. (That does not mean that they never do, → 3.2.3.3; 3.2.5.1). Open vs. closed class is one of the most often-quoted criteria distinguishing lexical and grammatical morphemes.
Most lexical morphemes in English are **free** (*freie Morpheme*), that is, they can occur as words on their own. Some lexical morphemes, however, are **bound** (*gebundene Morpheme*); in particular, these are the combining forms (→ 1.3.5.3) and the unique morphemes (→ 1.3.6).	Grammatical morphemes are typically **bound,** as we see in the above examples. But English has also got a large number of **free** grammatical morphemes, the so-called **function words** (*Funktionswörter*), in particular determiners, prepositions, auxiliary verbs and the like (→ 1.1.3.1, ☞ box).

• Morphemes such as *talk*, which have a clear conceptual meaning and which form the basis of the inflectional forms, are clearly **lexical morphemes** (*lexikalische Morpheme*) by the above criteria.

- *-s*, *-ing*, and *-ed*, but also *-able*, *-ity*, *-(t)ive*; *-ness*, *-er*, *-ie*, and *-y* from the above list are **grammatical morphemes** (*grammatische Morpheme*), whereof
  - *-s*, *-ing*, and *-ed*, to be more specific, are **inflectional morphemes** (*Flexionsmorpheme*),
  - the others are **derivational morphemes** (*Derivationsmorpheme*, *Ableitungsmorpheme*) (For more detail on this distinction → 1.3.4).
- Bound grammatical morphemes are called **affixes** (*Affixe*).

> ➤ What is striking about Modern English derivational morphology is the unusually large number of derivational affixes that were borrowed from French or Latin, such as *pre-*, *sub-*, *super-*, *-able*, *-tive*, *-ation*, *-ify* etc. (→ 1.3.4; 3.2.2.5; 3.2.5.1).

- What is left over if you take away the inflectional affixes in a word is called the **stem** (*Stamm*).
- When discussing a particular derivation, such as the derivation of *consideration* from *consider*, then the stem to which the derivational morpheme is attached is called the **base** of the derivation. In *consideration*, we say *consider* is the base of the derivation *consideration*. A base is thus always the base of something specific, viz., of a specific derivation, whereas a stem can be discussed in isolation. We can thus say: "*consider* is an English verb stem", but not *"*consider* is an English base". However, we might say: "*consider* is the base of several derivations in English, such as *consideration*, *considerate*, *considering*, *considerable*".
- Affixes which are always attached at the end of a stem are called **suffixes** (*Suffixe*). A morphological rule generating the above word forms (*talks*, *talking*, ...) would then be formulated by saying that certain inflectional suffixes are added to the verb stem. This does not mean that all suffixes are inflectional, though (→ 1.3.4).
- Morphemes that are attached to the front of a stem are called **prefixes** (*Präfixe*). English does not use prefixes in inflection any more, but in other areas of morphology (→ 1.3.4).

> ◉ German uses the prefix *ge-*, together with a suffix *-t* in the regular verbs, to form the past participle: *ge-koch-t*.

Suffixes and prefixes never occur alone (except in linguistic descriptions). They are always attached to a stem. They are the two main kinds of bound morphemes.
- Stems which cannot be analysed further into morphemes are also called **roots** (*Wurzeln*). Most stems occurring in the everyday language of English are in this sense roots. Stems may, however contain derivational morphemes, roots not. In this sense, *talkative*, *talkability*, etc. in the above list are stems (consisting of a root, *talk*, plus one or more derivational affixes), but for this very reason they are not roots.
- Roots and stems in English are usually **free**.

> ○ Roots in Latin and Greek, and to a certain extent also in German, usually do not occur alone, but are connected with suffixes to form a stem or a word:
> Latin: *Naut-a vin-um am-at*
> German: *D-er Knab-e komm-t ge-lauf-en*
> That the root is actually *Knab-* and not *Knabe* can be seen from the word *Knäb-lein* which shows the root in an umlauted (→ 3.2.1.3) form.

• However, **bound** roots or stems of Latin and, more often, Greek origin (known as **combining forms**) (*audio-, bio-, ethno-, phono-, -logy, -graphy, -cracy, -philia* etc.) are generously combined with each other and with native words in English to form so-called **neoclassical compounds** (→ 1.3.5).

The distinction between **free** and **bound** morphemes is not always easy to draw, providing another example of the fuzzy character of many linguistic categories. In fact, to escape the dilemma of having to decide between only two categories, 'bound' and 'free', linguists have introduced a third category in between: **clitics**. Clitics may be said to behave like bound morphemes on the level of pronunciation, but are equivalent to free morphemes on the level of syntax.

In English, most clitics appear as the **weak form** (*Schwachtonform*) of a stronger form which is a full-fledged word phonologically. A typical example of a clitic in English is the auxiliary verb form *'s* (weak form for *is* or *has*) which in pronunciation is always attached very closely to whatever word it happens to follow, but which in syntax stands for a word of its own, equivalent to the strong form, receiving its own node in a syntactic tree diagram (→ 1.2.2.2). As this is mainly a question of pronunciation, we will come back to these forms in section → 2.4.1.

1.3.3   Allomorphs and morphological processes

Morphemes often occur in different variants, called **allomorphs** (*Allomorphe*).

Thus, the German root *Knab-* 'boy' can be said to have an additional umlauted allomorph *Knäb-* used in the diminutive *Knäblein*. The German verb root *seh-* 'see' has an additional allomorph *sieh-* that is used in the 2nd and 3rd person singular: *du sieh-st, er sieh-t*. These allomorphs of German morphemes are **morphologically conditioned** because the form of the morpheme varies depending on other morphemes that it is combined with. The allomorph *Knab-* is determined by the suffixes *-e* and *-en* that it occurs with (*Knab-e, Knab-en*). The allomorph *Knäb-* is determined by the diminutive suffix *-lein* which regularly brings about umlaut in the stem it is attached to. In the same way the allomorph *seh-* and *sieh-* are conditioned by the various suffixes that follow them.

Note that it is the morphological status of the suffix and not its phonological shape that determines the stem allomorph here: A suffix *-t* is used for the 3rd person singular and the 2nd person plural, but it is only the 3rd person singular suffix that occasionally creates stem allomorphy: *er sieh-t, ihr seh-t*. We have thus got the curious situation that the difference between two inflectional forms is in the stem <u>allomorphs</u>, whereas the suffixes are alike.

Morphologically conditioned allomorphs exist in English, too, but as there are phonological questions involved as well, they will be discussed in section → 2.2.5 below.

There are other types of allomorphs. In English the prefix *in-* (used to form the opposite of certain adjectives of Latin or French origin) has several allomorphs in writing (some of which also differ in pronunciation), as can be seen from the following words:

in-efficient, im-possible, il-literate, ir-regular.

This allomorphy, though observed in writing, is clearly **phonologically conditioned**, and can thus only be exhaustively explained after we have done phonology (→ 2.2.5).

Yet another type of allomorphy is found in the irregular English noun plurals. Most nouns in English take a suffix *-s* or *-es* (in writing) to form the plural. The *-s* suffixes form a group of phonologically conditioned allomorphs that we will come back to later (→ 2.2.5). There is, however, a small number of nouns in English which do not take *-s* in the plural, but which instead take another suffix or no suffix at all.

> ➤ Historically speaking, they are relics of an earlier stage of English in which (like in German until today) several other strategies of plural formation were in use (→ 3.2.2.1), i.a.:
> - the ending *-en* like in *oxen* (cf. German *Ochsen*);
> - umlaut (→ 3.2.1.3) like in *feet* (cf. German *Füße*);
> - 'zero' plural like in *sheep* (This form obviously results from the loss of a final *-e*, commonplace in the history of English, → 3.2.1.8. It is preserved in German *Schaf-e*).

From the viewpoint of the present-day language, one must say that *-en*, e.g., is a **lexically conditioned** allomorph of the plural morpheme in English, because it occurs only with certain words. But now look at the following examples:

man – men; woman – women; foot – feet; goose – geese; mouse – mice.

The above are forms which correspond historically to German umlaut plurals. One could say that the plural here is formed by changing the stem vowel (**vowel alternation**).

Generations of linguists have tried to come to grips with such examples, trying to analyse them in terms of morphemes. What is the 'allomorph' of the plural morpheme here? Several solutions have been proposed within a framework that uses the notion of 'morpheme', none of which is fully satisfactory and adequate.

○ Some might be tempted to say that these are only a few exceptions that we shouldn't bother too much about. But what is an exception in English, is the rule in other languages. Arabic, like all Semitic languages, makes ample use of vowel alternations in its morphology, as can even be seen in the two Arabic loanwords *Muslim* and *Islam*, which are formed from the same Arabic root, *s...l...m*, a root which only consists of consonants, by prefixation and vowel insertion.

We need not even go as far as Arabic to find examples of this kind; just look at the following German words, which are all undoubtedly morphologically related:

brechen bricht brach bräche gebrochen Bruch Brüche.

Here, *ö* is the only vowel letter that does not occur within the *br...ch* root. Historically, these vowel alternations are caused by ablaut (→ 3.2.1.4) and umlaut (→ 3.2.1.3).

The best solution is to admit that the notions of *morpheme* and *allomorph* have their limitations, and only work for a certain number of cases. One needn't go as far as abolishing the concept of 'morpheme' altogether (as done by ANDERSON 1992). But it might be a good idea to use the notion of **morphological processes** (*morphologische Prozesse*) in addition to it. It could then be said that English uses several kinds of morphological processes:

– adding morphemes such as suffixes and prefixes to a stem:

   talk-ed, talk-ative, im-possible, sub-conscious,

– vowel alternation:

   sing – sang, foot – feet,

– consonant alternation:

   advice – advise, half – halve, extent – extend, house (noun) – house (verb)
   (Yes, there is a consonant alternation here, because the s in house is pronounced differently in the verb: It is voiced, → 2.1.1.2).

– stress shift:

   im'port – 'import
   im'port is a verb, *'import* a noun, and the two are derived from each other by a morphological process which would be very awkward to describe in terms of morphemes.

The notion of 'morphological process' may also be useful to describe certain types of allomorphy more elegantly than just by listing allomorphs. In section → 2.2.5 we will briefly come back to this.

An embarrassment for an analysis in terms of morphemes and morphological processes alike is the 'occurrence', in some cases, of so-called **zero morphemes** or **zero allomorphs** (*Nullmorphem, Nullallomorph*). Thus, in English (and in

German, too), some nouns have a plural form that does not differ from the singular in any way:

> *one sheep – two sheepø*
> *one fish – a dozen fishø*
> *ein Lehrer – hundert Lehrerø.*

A descriptive linguist will not be content with the historical explanation given above that these forms arise from the loss of an ending. A **synchronic** description (➔ Box 29) is wanted. In these cases it is usually said by morpheme-and-allomorph addicts that the plural is formed by a zero allomorph. This does not seem to make much sense, but a 'zero process', it must be admitted, does not make much more sense either. Nevertheless, such phenomena exist, and must be handled in morphological theory and description.

It may be a viable compromise to admit zero <u>allomorphs</u> where other allomorphs of the same morpheme are actually visible or audible, as in the case of the English plural. Great caution, however is indicated when postulating zero <u>morphemes</u>, that is morphemes that are never realised on the surface.

1.3.4   Inflection vs. derivation

As we have already seen, there is another basic distinction that is usually made in morphology, that between
* **inflection** (*Flexion*) and
* **derivation** (*Derivation*, *Ableitung*).

It applies to morphemes and morphological processes alike.

* We had already said that *talks*, *talking* and *talked* are inflectional forms, so the morphological rule forming them is an inflectional rule. **Inflection** is one important part of morphology.

> ❂ In Present-Day English, inflection plays only a minor role. (➔ 3.2.2). Other Indo-European languages have much more inflection than Present-Day English. The few forms listed above are the only inflectional forms of the verb *talk*. A verb in Ancient Greek may have more than 300 different finite inflectional forms, a verb in Latin 86, in Present-Day French 44, and in Old English 26. These would be impossible to learn if all these forms had to be listed in the lexicon and learnt individually by the learner. This is where morphological rules are really useful.

> ☞ Traditional grammar makes a terminological distinction between the inflection of verbs and auxiliaries on the one hand, and nouns, pronouns and adjectives on the other. The inflection of verbs including auxiliaries is called **conjugation** (*Konjugation*), the inflection of nouns, pronouns and adjectives **declension** (*Deklination*).

• The other important part of morphology is **derivation**. The difference between inflection and derivation has been the subject of heated debates among
linguists. There is a certain amount of evidence that the boundary cannot be
drawn clearly. But for the present purposes the criterion already hinted at above
will do: Inflection creates different forms of the same word, derivation creates
new words. This criterion, it must be admitted, is largely intuitive in its application and more rigid criteria are actually necessary (SCALISE 1988; PLANK 1981).
Most of the examples in our above list are examples of derivation.
We will first deal with the following:

> *talkable, talkability*
> *talkative, talkativeness*
> *talker, talkie, talky*

All the above words are formed by adding a suffix to a stem.

> ➢ What is remarkable historically is that although *talk* is of Germanic origin,
> three of the seven suffixes used in the above examples (*-able*, *-ity*, and *-tive*)
> come from Latin or French.

> ❍ Such 'mixtures' of morphemes of heterogeneous origin are called **hybrid
> formations** *(Hybridbildungen)*. These are very characteristic of English (➔
> 1.3.2; 3.2.2.5; 3.2.5.1) and not nearly as usual in German, where, after all, both
> Germanic and Latin-French suffixes are used, but only in combination with
> Germanic and Latin-French stems, respectively: cf. *kind-isch*, but *infant-il*.
> △There are very few exceptions to this (*bursch-ikos, Liefer-ant*).

There are a few more things we can learn about derivation from these examples:
– Derivational suffixes may be added one to another, but only in a strict order
to be described in rules. This order often reflects historical chronologies of derivation. Thus, it is possible
- to add *-ity* to the suffix *-able* to yield *-ability*, or
- *-ness* to *-(t)ive* to yield *-(t)ive-ness*,
but not vice versa: There is no *talkityable*, or *talknessive*.

> ❍ This, by the way, is also true for inflectional suffixes, if not in Present-Day
> English, then certainly in Old English and German: *du wart-et-est* contains a
> sequence of two inflectional suffixes: one for the past tense and one for the 2nd
> person singular. Again, this sequence is irreversible.

– Derived forms may themselves be inflected if they belong to an appropriate
word class. Thus, you may form
- a plural *talker-s* from the noun *talker*, or
- *talkie-s* from the noun *talkie*.

Note that inflectional suffixes always come after all derivational suffixes;
talk-s-er or *talk-s-ie* are not possible words in English.

It is an almost universal principle across all languages in the world that inflectional morphemes are put outside derivational morphemes (seen from the stem), another possible criterion distinguishing between derivation and inflection in certain cases.

△ One possible, but doubtful exception to this is German ?*Kind-er-chen*, where the inflectional plural morpheme is inside the derivational diminutive suffix.

– Derivational suffixes are invariably used to form new words from old ones. Very often, but by no means in all cases, they change the word class. Thus, the examples above are all derived from the verb *talk*, but none of them is a verb itself. Inflectional suffixes, by contrast, never change word class.

– The meaning of the derived words is certainly related to the meaning of the stem, but it is not always wholly predictable.

- *talker* and *talky* may be the easiest to guess, but
- *talkable* and *talkative* might make you wonder and want to look the words up, although the meaning of the suffix -*able* seems clear enough.
- The meaning of *talkie* is completely unpredictable. It is formed on the model of *movie* and was used as long as movies with talking in them were something unusual. It is now only used historically, that is, when talking about the first 'talkies' that eventually replaced the silent movies.

☞ Whenever the meaning of a derived word is not fully predictable from the meaning of its components (→ Box 16), linguists assume that a process of **lexicalisation** (*Lexikalisierung*) has taken place. Lexicalisation is an extremely powerful mechanism of language change, but also well observable in present-day language. It will be taken up in section → 3.2.5.3.

❧ The term *lexicalisation* is used in a completely different sense in lexicology and semantics (→ 4.2.3).

Apart from suffixes, English has also got a large number of derivational **prefixes**:

- *pre-* as in *pre-war*,
- *in-* as in *indistinguishable*,
- *mis-* as in *miscalculation*, etc.

Prefixes in English usually do not change the word class (note, however, that *pre-* in *pre-war* does!) and modify the meaning of the word in different ways than suffixes. (On the history of English prefixes, see → 3.2.2.5.)

1.3.5 Further strategies of word-formation

1.3.5.1 Conversion

Our original list of examples from the *talk*-family is not exhausted yet. There are still some examples left. Let us start with the first item:

talk, talks (noun)

The noun *talk* provides an example of a very special and 'very English' type of word-formation: **conversion** (*Konversion*). Conversion is the use of a stem belonging to one word class in another word class, without any recognisable morphological processes. Thus, in our case, the verb stem *talk* is simply used as a noun as well. The only way in which this noun differs from the verb it has been derived from is that it takes noun inflection instead of verb inflection: The form *talks*, when it is a nominal form, is the plural of *talk*, and not the 3rd person singular of the verb *talk*. There has been considerable controversy among linguists about the exact nature of this phenomenon. It is very typical of English, made possible by the loss of much of the inflection from Old to Modern English (→ 3.2.2), so that most forms of nouns and verbs are without suffixes anyway; these uninflected stems can thus easily be used in different word classes.

- Some linguists have claimed the presence of a zero-morpheme in the converted form: A noun *talk-ø* would then be derived from the verb *talk* by a 'zero suffix'. As we said already above, postulating zero morphemes is rather problematic.
- Other linguists would claim that no morphological process at all is involved in the switch from the verb to the noun; *talk* is simply a syntactically multifunctional stem.

☞ Again we have a **lexicalist-derivationalist** controversy (→ Box 20). The term *conversion* may be seen as a compromise between the two positions: It allows us to describe the process as derivational without having to postulate problematic zero entities.

One problem, however, remains for all the derivational treatments of the conversion problem in morphology: There is no clear indication as to which of the forms is derived and which is basic. Above we have assumed that the noun *talk* is derived from the verb *talk*. How do we know it isn't the other way round?

A decision is sometimes difficult to make; but in many cases, the meaning of the morpheme may be of help. Talking is an activity, and thus it seems more natural to assume that the verb is basic. Besides, it is easier in this case to define the meaning of the noun on the basis of the meaning of the verb than vice versa. This is confirmed by the treatment of *talk* in the Oxford English Dictionary (OED), where the meaning of the noun is simply described as

"<t>he action or practice of talking",

whereas the verb is given elaborate paraphrases such as

"<t>o convey or exchange ideas, thoughts, information, etc. by means of speech, ... ".

1.3.5.2 Compounding

Let us now turn to some of the remaining examples:

talk-back, talking-to, talk-master, talk show

These exemplify further types of word-formation.

- *Talk-back* and *talking-to* are **compounds** (*Komposita, Zusammensetzungen*), though less typical ones which will not be dealt with here.

- *Talk-master* is a more typical English compound. Compounds are new words formed by joining two existing words. That is, each part of a compound must be able to occur on its own as a word. The final part of a typical compound is the **head** of the construction, determining its word class and much of its semantic properties, and is preceded by the **modifier**. Further typical examples of English compounds are

  houseboat, room-mate, seasick, skinhead, sitting-room, flycatcher

Note how the head determines the semantic properties of the whole construction to a large extent: A houseboat is a boat and not a house, a room-mate a mate and not a room, etc.

△ This does not work with all compounds, however. A jelly fish is not a fish, a skinhead is not a head, and a walkman is not a man.

📖 Can you find other examples of either kind?

➤ Compounding is a very old, typically Germanic word-formation strategy which already existed in Old English (→ 3.2.2.5). The form it mostly takes in English, i.e., just placing two complete words next to each other, with the modifier preceding the head, is sometimes called **juxtaposition**. As the older forms of French and Latin are not very compound-friendly languages, few compounds were borrowed from them; the English strategy of juxtaposition can, however, be freely applied to words of any origin:

The recent language acquisition conference was characterised by a curious kindergarten weltanschauung.

language acquisition conference is a compound of three words of French origin which could never be formed in French. *Kindergartenweltanschauung*, incidentally, could also be a German word because German word formation strategies are similar to the ones in English (though not precisely the same → 1.3.5.3).

On so-called neo-classical compounds and compounding in other languages see → 1.3.5.3.

The spelling of English compounds is somewhat inconsistent, variants with or without hyphen or in two words are common. It is also a controversial question whether two-word combinations spelled in two words can be called compounds (*talk show* in contrast to *talk-master*, e.g.). Quite a few of them are listed in dictionaries, and *talk show* is certainly lexicalised (→ 1.3.4, 3.2.5), because the meaning of that word combination cannot be predicted.

Box 21: Compound or noun phrase?

There is some insecurity in English language description as to how far the notion of *compound* extends, or whether some combinations of nouns should be regarded as syntactic constructions (noun phrases) rather than as compound words.

Words such as *silver* in *silver tray* are regarded as attributive adjectives (→ 1.2.2.4) rather than as compounded nouns, but the criteria for this are somewhat unreliable and sometimes difficult to apply. It is usually said that compounds are stressed (→ 2.3.3) on their first element, whereas noun phrases are stressed on the head noun. To quote the most famous example:

BLACKboard is a compound noun, whereas
black BOARD is a noun phrase.

In longer compounds or noun phrases, however, the position of stress (→ 2.3.3) becomes less clear. Premodifying elements in noun phrases may be very complex themselves, consider the following example:

United Nations Conference on Afghanistan Media Center
(text of a banner seen on a boat on the Rhine during the conference)

In this noun phrase, *media center* is a compound, forming the head of the phrase. *United Nations Conference on Afghanistan* pre-modifies it. That is, a whole complex NP may be used as a premodifier within another NP. In German, such structures count as compounds:

Gutenachtgeschichte.

In English, many such structures are much more complex, like the above example, and to regard them as a compound would be very awkward. It is clear that such examples are better handled in syntax.

To quote another authentic example, analysed by means of tree diagrams:

Second Language Acquisition Conference

Fig. 20: Tree diagram *Second language acquisition conference*, **reading I**

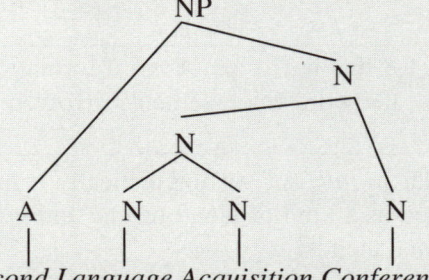

Second Language Acquisition Conference
'conference on language acquisition that took place the second time'

Fig. 21: Tree diagram *Second language acquisition conference,* **reading II**

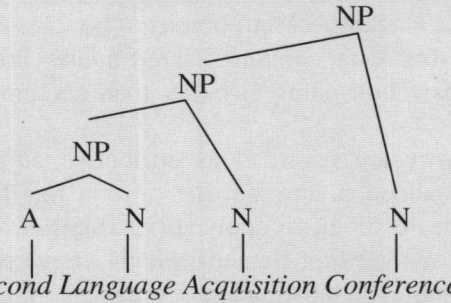

Second Language Acquisition Conference
'conference on second-language acquisition'

The tree diagrams show that this expression shows syntactic ambiguity, depending on whether *"second"* modifies a complex expression *"Language Acquisition Conference"* (first tree diagram below) or only *"Language"* (second reading).

In the second case, the German translation would be *Zweitspracherwerbskonferenz,* a typical German *Bandwurmkompositum* suggesting that the English equivalent might be a compound as well. This is probably not the case, but neither pronunciation (in particular, stress) nor spelling give us a clear indication. On the other hand, is the difference between *language acquisition* and *second-language acquisition* really so momentous as to warrant a completely different analysis, one belonging to syntax, one to morphology? There is no foolproof way of telling us where to draw the boundary between compound words and noun phrases. It may thus be said that compounding in English grammar closely borders on syntax.

1.3.5.3 Blending, secretion and neoclassical compounding

talkfest constitutes another very interesting type of word-formation. *-fest* does not occur on its own in English, but was borrowed as a kind of suffix from German words such as *Oktoberfest.* Its meaning is, however, too 'lexical' to make it a grammatical morpheme, a true suffix.

☞ There is no established term yet for this new type of word-formation. For want of a better solution, we will call the word-final elements involved **quasi-suffixes**.

Talkathon is superficially quite similar to *talkfest,* yet linguistically it may be a different category. It could be regarded as a kind of blend of *talk* and *marathon,* but it differs from the more conventional blends.

- A typical **blend** (*lexikalische Kontamination*) is usually a combination of two words, none of which is recoverable any more. Thus, *smog* arose as a blend of *smoke* and *fog,* but both these words enter into the blend in a mutilated form, none of them is actually recognisable. Some people nowadays, fifty years after the blend was blended, don't know that it is a blend.

- *Talkathon* is different in this respect. One element, *talk*, is still fully recognisable in the 'blend'. *Talkathon* could, therefore, also be regarded as a combination of *talk* and a quasi-suffix *-athon*. This 'suffix' was gained by taking the Greek word *marathon* apart, which is really only one morpheme, and treating its final element as a suffix. This strategy, which is known as **secretion**, has become increasingly productive recently. Another famous example of it is the new quasi-suffix *-(a)holic*: Gained from the word *alcoholic* in its meaning 'person addicted to alcohol' (the change in spelling remains mysterious), it has created a whole series of new (mostly humorous) words for all kinds of addictions:

> *workaholic, sugarholic, golfaholic, footballaholic, computerholic, news-aholic, spendaholic, bookaholic*

This strategy of taking all sorts of words apart (*Oktoberfest, alcoholic, marathon*) and using the parts to form new words is a typically English innovation in word-formation. It is much less common in German.

☞ Note that *blend* and *secretion*, as well as the following term *neoclassical compound*, characterise the <u>origin</u> of words, the way they were coined. That is, these terms belong to historical or diachronic linguistics They needn't all have the same structure when seen in a synchronic perspective (→ Box 29).

- Both blending and secretion in English may have been encouraged by the existence of so-called **neoclassical compounds**. These are words of mostly Greek, but also Latin and maybe other origin that are or could have been compounds in these languages, such as

> *geography, automobile, biology, holocaust*

and many others. So many of them have been borrowed into English over the last centuries that English readers and speakers became quite acquainted with the building-blocks of these words and began to form new words out of them. These building-blocks are usually called **combining forms**.

⊙ Note that neoclassical compounds are not really compounds in English (→ 1.3.5.2). Their parts often do not occur as independent words in English. And they are not formed by the English strategy of juxtaposition, but by a compounding strategy characteristic of Greek and also of German: The first part of the compound is not an independent word, but a special form of the stem.
- In Greek, this is usually the bare stem (but not the root!) of the first component, with the second component carrying the usual inflections. As Greek stems often end in *-o*, it had become the rule already in Ancient Greek that the first combining form ends in *-o*. In consequence, many Greek and also neoclassical compounds contain a linking *-o-* in the middle.

- In German, many compounds can be seen as originating from genitive constructions (*Amtsgebäude = des Amts Gebäude*), and thus many German compounds contain a linking *-s-* in the middle, even in cases in which the real genitive doesn't have an *-s* at all (*Hoffnungsträger*). In any case, it is often neither the citation form of the word nor the genitive that is used in German compounding. (Does *Schweinebraten* mean that it is made from several pigs? Karl Valentin's *Semmelnknödeln* come to mind.)
- Latin, as mentioned above, does not use compounding so often. A typical characteristic of a Latin compound is often the linking *-i-* in the middle (*patrilinear*, *multilingual*, etc.)
- French has followed its ancestor language in this respect for many centuries. Not many new compounds were formed; there were really only very few strategies available. One new common Romance word formation strategy, however, became rather productive: compounds directly formed from a verb phrase. The *portemonnaie* is the thing that carries (*porte*) money (*monnaie*). A *lave-vaisselle* is the gadget that washes (*lave*) dishes (*vaisselle*). This word formation strategy is only scarcely represented in Germanic languages, German *Taugenichts* or English *spoilsport* or the nickname *dolittle* being among the few examples.

Present-Day French is developing a new juxtaposition strategy, however, to form compounds, resulting from an omission of prepositions in lexicalising noun phrases. The resulting order of elements is a mirror reversal of the English and German order. The head comes first, followed by the modifier, as in most French noun phrases. Thus, *village de vacances de familles* becomes *village$_1$ vacances$_2$ familles$_3$*, as opposed to German *Familien$_3$ferien$_2$dorf$_1$*.

➢ Many of the people who coined neoclassical compounds from combining forms in the European languages also actually knew Ancient Greek and Latin, so that they had a lot more combining forms at their disposal than ordinary speakers of their respective language.

English educated writers apparently were especially keen on inventing new neoclassical componds. In this way a huge stock of words was created by English language users, usually made up of Greek (and some Latin) lexical stems or roots, e.g.

philo-dendr-ist   'lover of trees'
poly-morph   'of many forms'
caco-phon-ous   'ill-sounding'
auto-mobile   'capable of moving by itself'.

Most neoclassical compounds formed in this way did not exist in Latin or Ancient Greek and were formed by non-native speakers with sometimes imperfect knowledge of the source languages. The last example above is neoclassical in the full sense because it could never have been formed in antiquity, not because of its meaning but because it is a hybrid formation from a Greek (*auto-*) and a Latin stem (*-mobile*).

> ♦ It is therefore misleading to say that these words "come from Latin and Greek". They have been formed from combining forms that in most cases had already become part of the stock of lexical morphemes of English, according to rules which have long ago become rules of English and which are not identical to the Latin or Ancient Greek rules.
>
> ➢ Starting as early as the 18th century, English elements were increasingly put together with Greek ones, to quote just one surprisingly old example:
>
> *mob-ocracy* (attested in 1754),
>
> and a few more recent ones:
>
> *kisso-gram* (1982),
> *micro-wave* (1974 in the present everyday meaning).

Nowadays, not many neoclassical compounds are formed or find their way into everyday language. It seems, though, that women's and gay liberation have been most productive here recently:

> *hetero-sex-ism,*
> *phallo-crat,*
> *primo-genitur-ist,*

but also the media:

> *tele-matics,*
> *video-phile.*

It seems that neoclassical compounding as a standard strategy for gaining new words for relatively complex lexical meanings is being gradually replaced by blending and secretion which are probably not felt to be much different from neoclassical compounding by naïve speakers. As knowledge of the classical languages is generally declining, this tendency will certainly increase. It will no doubt lead to the creation of many new quasi-suffixes by secretion along the lines of *-athon* and *-aholic*.

1.3.5.4 Reduplication

We are left with the curious *talkee-talkee* to discuss. The word-formation pattern this is formed by is actually quite exotic in Europe nowadays: **reduplication** (*Reduplikation*). It consists in the repetition of a word, morpheme, or part of a morpheme, sometimes with vowel alternation, to form a new word or word form. In Modern English, reduplication plays a marginal role and is only found in a few words such as *sing-song, chiff-chaff* (with vowel alternation) and, maybe, *helter-skelter* and a few others.

> ❍ From German, we may add *wischi-waschi, Singsang, Holterdipolter, Tingeltangel, Krimskrams, Bimbam*, and *Hoppelpoppel*.

90

> ➤ It is interesting to note that reduplication in English and German often uses ablaut patterns like the 'strong' verbs (➔ 3.2.1.4). And indeed, reduplication is an ancient Indo-European morphological strategy and can be found

- in Ancient Greek verbal inflection, both in the present and the perfect:

  é-do-men   'we gave';
  dô-men   'let's give'
  dí-do-men   'we give';
  dé-do-men   'we have given'

  óp-s-omai 'I will see';
  óp-ōp-a 'I have seen'

- in Latin verbal inflection:

  pendet 'he hangs'*;*
  pe-pendit 'he hung'.

Proto-Germanic also had reduplication in its inflection, the only relic of this in Modern English being the irregular past tense *di-d* (see also ➔ 3.2.2.4, ➤ box).

◉ Some contemporary non-Indo-European languages outside Europe use reduplication regularly. Indeed, *talkee-talkee* originally comes from a variety of English in the West Indies that has obviously been in contact with such languages.

1.3.5.5 Abbreviations

Finally, a group of strategies of word-formation should be mentioned that is actually quite old, but has only recently become productive:

• Ever since the invention of alphabetic writing, people seem to have used **abbreviations** (*Abkürzungen*). An early well-known example is Latin *SPQR* for *Senatus PopulusQue Romanus*. But it is only recently that abbreviations were turned into spoken words and have actually formed the basis of further derivations and compoundings. Recent examples are:

  PC (which is actually used in at least two different meanings):
  'personal computer' and 'political correctness' or 'politically correct';
or:

  DAT 'digital audio type'.

Taking the first letters of each word or of some words of a longer expression is the most common strategy for abbreviations. There are two ways of pronouncing these abbreviations.

• In the case of *PC*, there is no real choice: You just pronounce the names of the letters: /piːsiː/. This type of abbreviation we call **initialism** (*Buchstabenwort*) because it consists of the initials of words pronounced separately. But in the case of *DAT*, another strategy is also possible: You pronounce the letters as if they formed a word: /dæt/.

- This possibility has turned out to be very productive in that it inspired people to actively look for or create abbreviations that could be pronounced as a word. These are called **acronyms** (*Akronyme*).

NATO and *Radar* are some older examples; a more recent, very productive one is *yuppie*. It is peculiar because its 'root', *yup*, does not exist in this meaning. The 'root' *yup* is meant as an acronym for 'young urban professional', but this root is never heard without the suffix *-ie*. This word, in turn, has become productive in a number of new coinings:

 yuppiedom, yuppieism, yuppieness, yuppyish, yuppify, yuppification.

We have just seen that some strategies of word-formation are very popular. In particular, some suffixes can be very productive. You may assume that all the suffixes in the *yuppie* examples are productive in English.

- Talking of abbreviations, one more strategy, typical of and originating in spoken language, should be mentioned: **clipping**. Over the last decades, it has repeatedly occurred that a certain new word became very frequent all of a sudden (because the thing it referred to became very frequent). It also often happened that the new word was much too long and difficult to pronounce. This is the typical situation in which **ZIPF's Law** (→ 3.3) applies and clippings are invented:

 professor becomes *prof*
 perambulator → *pram*
 bicycle → *bike*
 zoological garden → *zoo*
 nuclear (bomb, power station) → *nuke, etc.*

1.3.6 Productivity in morphology

A problem for morphological theory arises from suffixes which are constrained in their **productivity** (*Produktivität*) or which are no longer productive, but still transparent.

An example of the former case is the suffix *-ity,* which can be used to form nouns from adjectives, but only from certain adjectives. There is no **cleanity, *biggity,* or **blackity.* But even where it may be used, *-ity* competes with *-ness.* So why do we find *talkativeness* but not **talkativity,* whereas *productivity* is preferred to *productiveness*? Part of the answer seems to lie in the fact that *-ness* is more productive than *-ity.*

An example of the latter case, a suffix that is no longer productive, is provided by the suffix *-th* in

 strength, length, width etc.

The suffix is now only used with a small number of adjectives (most of them denoting size, interestingly) to form an abstract noun. The relation between the adjective and the noun is fairly regular semantically, but rather irregular phonologically. There is some 'funny' stem allomorphy involved:

long ~ leng-,
wide ~ wid-.

> ➤ An additional complication is raised by the fact that there are further words in English that end in *-th* and are historically derived from adjectives:
>
> *youth* (from *young*),
> *sloth* (from *slow*),
> *filth* (from *foul*).
>
> The problem is that they are lexicalised (➔ 3.2.5) to varying degrees, both in terms of their meaning and of their pronunciation. *youth* is certainly related to *young*, but not really in the same and regular way that *length* is related to *long*. In the case of *filth* the relationship could never be recovered unless we had the relevant historical knowledge (which ordinary speakers don't have).
>
> So the question arises which of these cases are really examples of the suffix *-th*. Lexicalisation (➔ 3.2.5.3) is a gradual historical process, and it never seems to affect members of a certain group of words to the same degree. But of course it is unsatisfactory to split up *-th* words into two or even more groups, and linguists may come to quite different solutions.

They provide examples for the **lexicalist-derivationalist controversy** mentioned above (➔ Box 20).

- Radical lexicalists will tend to say that all nouns ending in *-th* are so lexicalised that a "nominalising suffix *-th*" should not be mentioned at all in the grammar of Present-Day English.

- Derivationalists would argue that with such a description we miss an interesting generalisation, namely that some adjectives in English, most of them closely related in meaning (*long*, *wide*, *broad* etc.), form an abstract noun ending in *-th* and displaying some kind of irregular vowel alternation (*long – length*, *broad – breadth* etc.).

Questions of this kind are a big issue in morphology, and a challenge to any morphological theory (PLANK 1981). The answers given to them affects the whole architecture of linguistic theory as they concern the division between lexicon and grammar, the two most important parts of linguistic description.

A further productivity problem is presented by so-called **unique morphemes** *(unikale Morpheme)*. Such morphemes occur in combinations of which one part is frequent and productive, but the other part occurs only in that particular combination.

⚬ A famous example is *cran-berry*. We all know what a berry is, but what is a '*cran'?

> ➢ Historically, *cranberry* is an 18th century American borrowing (→ 3.2.5.1) from Low German *Kranbeere*; the berry originally wasn't found in England. The word *Beere* was apparently identified as *berry* by the borrowers, but *Kran* didn't seem to make sense. Actually, the word refers to the crane, a large, fairly common bird with a long neck, but it wasn't clear what the berry could have to do with a bird. The spelling *craneberry*, which seems slightly more motivated, also occurs in the 18th century, but was obviously abandoned.

Thus the status of the whole combination is somewhat dubious, since we had said that a compound should consist of parts that can occur on their own as words. But *cran-* wouldn't make a good prefix either. Its meaning is clearly lexical, quite unlike that of other prefixes. And what kind of prefix is used in only one combination?

By the way, the case of *strawberry* is not really very different except that we still think we recognise the word *straw* in it. *strawberry* existed in Old English already (in a different spelling, of course), when only wild strawberries were known. But what could strawberries have to do with straw? In fact, strawberry growers put straw into strawberry beds to protect the berries from snails and mildew, but none of the etymological dictionaries (dictionaries trying to elucidate and trace the origin of words and the development of their form and meaning) mentions this. In any case, there was no strawberry cultivation in Old English times. The only logical conclusion is that *straw-* in *strawberry* no longer means, or perhaps never meant, 'straw', but is actually a unique morpheme like *cran-*. Nevertheless, it is well conceivable that speakers of English with a knowledge of strawberry cultivation drew or draw the connection explained above, and for them, *strawberry* would be a motivated compound.

This, by way would then be a case of **folk etymology** (*Volksetymologie*) (→ Box 30). Furthermore, the case of *strawberry* would constitute an interesting case of interaction between linguistic knowledge and **encyclopaedic knowledge** (→ 4.3.1).

1.3.7 Summary

The following table summarises the different kinds of morphemes we have discussed and gives some additional examples:

Fig. 22: Kinds of morphemes

	Free	Bound
Lexical (open classes)	**Content words:**	**Unique morphemes:**
	albatross	*cran-* in *cranberry*
	cabalassou	*-ric* in *bishopric*
	go	**Quasi-suffixes:**
	contain	*-athon* in *talkathon*
	anger	*-aholic* in *workaholic*
	modest	*-fest* in *talkfest*
	free	**Combining forms:**
	black, etc.	*bio-* in *biology, biography* etc.
		-(o)logy in *biology, philology* etc.
Grammatical (closed classes)	**Function words:**	**Contracted ('weak') forms (Clitics):**
	and, the, in, that,	*'ll* for *will, shall; 'd* for *would, had*
	more, etc.	**Affixes:**
		Prefixes:
		post- in *post-war*
		un- in *unfair*
		Suffixes:
		-ed in *walked* (inflectional),
		-ise in *computerise* (derivational)

1.4 Language typology and linguistic universals

Language typology (*Sprachtypologie*) arises from the comparative (or contrastive) analysis of languages.

Box 22: Comparative vs. contrastive linguistics

In German-speaking linguistics, a distinction is usually made between **comparative linguistics** (*komparative Sprachwissenschaft, historisch-vergleichende Sprachwissenschaft*) and **contrastive linguistics** (*kontrastive Linguistik, konfrontative Sprachwissenschaft*).

In this sense, **comparative** linguistics is the historically orientated comparison between genetically related languages such as Latin and Greek, Latin and the Romance languages, or German and English. The emphasis is on tracing sound changes and establishing connections between words in the different languages by historical reconstruction (→ 3.2.1.0). Historical-comparative linguistics is dealt with in detail, i.a., in MOESSNER 2003.

Contrastive linguistics, on the other hand, is concerned with the comparison of (mostly living) languages regardless of their genetic relationship. The emphasis is on grammatical characteristics of the languages involved.

In the anglophone literature, the above distinction is not always maintained. Since we are exclusively dealing with grammatical typology in this introduction, this section is part of the grammar chapter.

1.4.1 Parameters of typological comparison

Two questions have been in the foreground of recent contrastive typology :
– In what respects can languages differ from each other? The answers to this question lead us to so-called **parameters of variation**.

❧ Note that the term *variation* is used here for the variation of certain linguistic phenomena <u>across</u> languages, whereas in sociolinguistics (→ 7.6) it refers to variation <u>within</u> a certain language. The terms *variant* and *variable* have a related technical sense in sociolinguistics (→ 7.1.2). As an adjective, *variant* is also (somewhat confusingly) used to characterise a language type (see below) and in this sense refers to language-<u>internal</u> variability.

Furthermore, the terms *variation*, *variant*, and *variable* are also widely used in a very untechnical, colloquial sense by linguists and also in this book. The term *variant*, in particular, is often used as an informal synonym for terms such as *allomorph* (→ 1.3.3), *allophone* (→ 2.2.3), etc.

HERMAN®

"We get a lot of foreign visitors."

If linguists ask, for example, how languages differ with respect to word order, they say they are studying the **parameter of word order**, which (for some cartoonists at least) seems to be a very salient parameter of variation between languages. (Cartoon taken from FROMKIN / RODMAN [5]1993, 72, Harcourt Brace College Publishers)

– The second question, which usually arises from trying to answer the first, is: In what respects can languages <u>not</u> differ from each other? The answers to this second question lead us to the so-called **linguistic universals** (*sprachliche Universalien*). Suppose that linguists found that in no language studied does the object regularly come before the subject. Then this could be formulated as a word-order universal.

In this way language typology and the study of linguistic universals are fruitfully intertwined with each other. Suppose that linguists studying universals found that there are a few languages, after all, in which the object is regularly placed before the subject. Then this would be an interesting result for typology, since 'OSV' languages would constitute an interesting, unusual language type. On the other hand, typological research supplies categories and parameters for universals research: Whatever is useful as a parameter in typological research, is also a possible universal. The parameters studied most commonly by linguistic typologists over the last few decades have been:

- word order
- morphology, i.e. in particular, the morphological structure of word forms (→ 1.4.2).
- the relation between thematic roles (agent, theme, etc. → 1.2.2.6) and syntactic categories such as subject and object (→ 1.2.1.2) or morphological cases (→ 1.1.3.2.3), an area where differences between English and German are striking.
- passive constructions (→1.1.3.4.5; 1.1.3.4.7; Box 14; 1.2.3.2), an area where vast differences are found across the languages in the world.

1.4.2 Traditional morphological language typology

The earliest typologies in the history of linguistics were made along morphological parameters: the way lexical and grammatical information is coded in a word or a clause, and how this affects the morphological structure of words.

The traditional typology, going back as far as, among others, Wilhelm von HUMBOLDT ([1825; 1836] 1963), which distinguishes between **inflecting**, **agglutinating**, and **isolating** languages (*flektierende, agglutinierende, isolierende Sprachen*) is still very much in use, although it has been scathingly criticised by modern linguists.

☞ Others use the rather infelicitous terms **analytic** (*analytisch*) for isolating languages and **synthetic** (*synthetisch*) for all the others, which also go back to the earliest typologists (e.g., August Wilhelm SCHLEGEL).

As a compromise between modern and traditional views, it has been suggested by COMRIE (1981; 2001), drawing on SAPIR (1921), that such global characterisations of languages should be replaced by a network of intersecting parameters, in which the traditional language types find their place. These parameters are called:

- degree of **synthesis** (or **fusion**),
- **analysability**, and
- **variance**.

Some examples are given below.

✍ The abbreviations for grammatical categories found in the **morpheme-by-morpheme translations** below are widely used in the typological literature. We use the following here:

1	1ˢᵗ person
3	3ʳᵈ person
AOR	Aorist, the Greek perfective aspect
IND	Indicative mood
MASC	Masculine gender
PASS	Passive voice
PAST	Past tense
PL	Plural
POSS	Possessor
PACO	Passé composé, the Colloquial French perfective aspect in the past tense
SG	Singular

Grammatical categories that are jointly expressed by one morpheme are linked by _ in the translation. Such morphemes are most typical of inflecting languages.

- The more **synthetic** (*synthetisch*) a language is, the more morphological information is usually packed in one word, just compare

> Turkish *ev   -ler   -im   -iz   -in*
> morpheme-by-morpheme translation:
> 'house -PL   -1_POSS   -PL_POSS -of',
> (one word, five morphemes)

with the English equivalent

> *of our house-s*
> (three words, four morphemes).

Turkish is thus more synthetic than English.

- The more **analysable** a language is, the more separable the different elements are from each other as morphemes. Look at the following example:

> French *il   a   ét-é   jet-é*
> word-by-word translation:
> 'he/it   has been   thrown'
> morpheme-by-morpheme translation:
> *il*   = '3MASC_SG'
> *a*   = 'PACO_3SG'
> *ét-* = 'PASS'
> *-é*   = 'PACO_MASC'
> *jet-* = 'throw'
> *-é*   = 'PASS_MASC'

Compare this with Ancient Greek

e	-bál	-ē	-ø

(of roughly the same meaning)

'PAST throw_AOR AOR_PASS 3SG_IND_PAST'

The suffix *-ē* expresses two grammatical categories jointly, aorist and passive, and is followed by a zero allomorph (ø) of a morpheme expressing three categories, 3rd person, singular and past. It could also be said that the overt suffix, consisting of one letter only, alone signals five different morphological categories. The category 'past' is also (redundantly) signalled by the prefix *e-*. The stem allomorph *bal-* also signals the aorist aspect, the perfective aspect of Greek.

French is thus more analysable than Ancient Greek. But note that also in French, just like in the equivalent English and Greek forms, the same information is sometimes encoded in several morphemes redundantly, and the suffix *-é* signals perfective past, passive, and masculine though not on its own.

• The more **variant** (see ❧ box on '*varia-*' terminology above) a language is morphologically, the more allomorphs (variants!) there are for a given morphological meaning. Thus, the Ancient Greek forms

báll-ei   'he/she/it throws',
é-bal-e   'he/she/it hit',
báll-e-tai   'it is thrown', and the above-mentioned
e-bál-ē 'it was thrown / he/she was hit'

display four different endings which all (among other things) signal '3rd person singular', and this list is not even complete! French has only got two morphemes to signal 3rd person singular, the personal pronouns *il* 'he' and *elle* 'she', and practically no suffixes on the verb for this meaning. Ancient Greek is thus more variant than French.

In this system of parameters, it can be said that

–   highly **inflecting** languages (*flektierende Sprachen*), such as Ancient (and Modern) Greek, Latin, Russian, and to a certain extent German, are all highly synthetic, tend to be rather variant, and are thus not very well analysable.

–   **Agglutinating** languages such as Turkish (the above example is typical), or Swahili are also fairly synthetic, but almost perfectly analysable and invariant.

–   Finally, **isolating** languages such as Vietnamese, Chinese and also English to a certain extent, are highly analytic, and, in consequence, highly analysable and invariant as well.

As a last caveat on traditional typology it should be pointed out that all these parameters and categories are a question of more-or-less rather than yes-or-no. Most languages represent mixed types, such as the Romance languages (*Romanische Sprachen*), which are highly inflectional with a low degree of analysability and a high degree of variance in the verbal system, but fairly isolating, that is analytic, in the nominal system. In sum, it could be said that every language is, in a way, a type of its own, representing a unique mixture of certain typological parameters and comprising a little bit of every type.

2   Phonetics and Phonology

Phonetics and **phonology** (*Phonetik und Phonologie*) are concerned with the sounds of language. We shall first explain what phonetics is (➔ 2.1) before we turn to phonology and explain how it differs from phonetics (➔ 2.2).

2.0   A brief note on phonetic transcription

Since most orthographic systems are more or less unreliable in reflecting the sound system of a language (➔ 2.5.1; 2.5.2), phoneticians have created so-called phonetic alphabets, enabling us to represent the exact value of each sound of any language.

This precise way of representing the pronunciation of a language is called (phonetic) transcription (*phonetische Transkription / Umschrift*). In order to distinguish a phonetic transcription from normal spelling, the signs are put in square brackets. [bɪt], e.g., would be the phonetic transcription of the English word *bit* (which in this case happens to be very similar its orthographic spelling), [wʊstə] would be the transcription of the English place name *Worcester*.

The most widespread phonetic alphabet is that of the **International Phonetic Association (IPA)** (*Weltlautschriftverein*; in French *Association Phonétique Internationale* (API)) and is known as the **International Phonetic Alphabet** (same abbreviation). The phonetic symbols used for English and German (and partly a few other languages) will be presented and explained below.

2.1   Phonetics

Phonetics is, very loosely speaking, concerned with the scientific study of the sounds of language. It is probably the most scientific branch of linguistics as it exclusively uses scientific concepts and methods. It describes

- how the individual sounds are formed: **articulatory** phonetics (*artikulatorische Phonetik*) using anatomical concepts (➔ 2.1.1);
- what acoustic properties they have: **acoustic** phonetics (*akustische Phonetik*) using methods of physics (➔2.1.2); and
- how they are perceived by the listener: **auditory** phonetics (*auditive Phonetik*) using methods of experimental psychology (➔ 2.1.3).

2.1.1   Articulatory phonetics

Articulatory phonetics is concerned with the way the different sounds of speech
are produced. As this is the aspect of pronunciation that is best accessible to 'introspection' (with some training, everybody can observe their own articulatory
movements while speaking), it is still the most relevant branch of phonetics for
practical purposes. To discuss articulatory phonetics we need a basic knowledge
of the anatomy of the human speech organs. Fig. 23 outlines the distinctions
made by articulatory phoneticians in describing the articulatory organs and articulatory movements.

Articulatory phonetics divides the sounds of a language up according to the
way and the place where they are produced in the **vocal tract** (*Vokaltrakt*). The
vocal tract comprises all the space leading from the larynx up to the lips and nos-
trils and may be thought of as a bent pipe.

Fig. 23: Anatomy of the vocal tract
        (MALMKJÆR 1995 [1991], 23, Routledge)

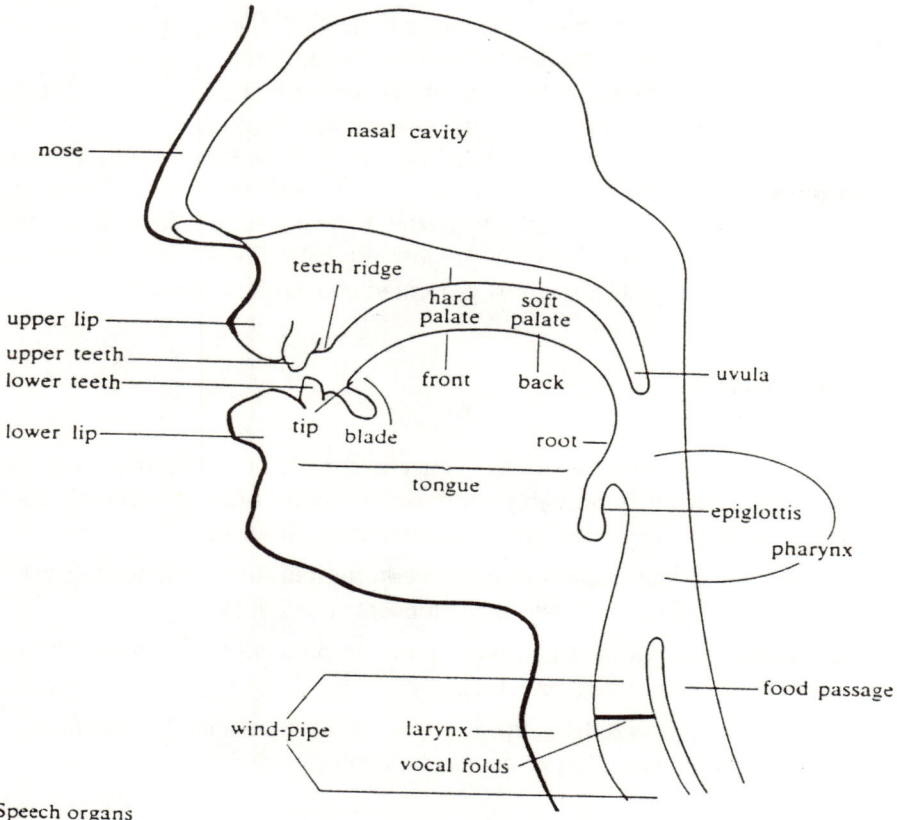

Speech organs

Furthermore, it should be noted that the description of articulation in terms of
'sounds' is really an idealisation. When we speak, we do not produce individual

sounds one after the other, but we perform smooth articulatory movements from which a phonetic description singles out individual positions of the articulatory organs as **segments** (*Segmente*). Individual positions or movements of the articulatory organs which can be isolated from the stream of speech in description, are sometimes called **articulatory gestures**.

In reality, however, speech production is a continuous articulatory process rather than a strictly segmental matter, i.e., sounds are not in fact discrete units in performance (see also → Fig. 36 below).

All actually produced speech sounds are therefore subject to considerable variation, which is dependent on their particular environment. When we abstract from this variation for the purpose of systematic investigation in phonology (→ 2.2), we cut the speech continuum up into individual segments (which we are used to calling 'sounds'), a segment being no more than a bundle of salient features of articulation in the flow of speech, realised at roughly the same time.

The most basic, universal (→ 1.4.1) distinction between sounds is that between **vowels** (*Vokale*) and **consonants** (*Konsonanten*). In the following, we describe the vowels, consonants and other sounds of English phonetically and also try to give a few hints for learners. This is meant to convince you of the usefulness of phonetic description because it is only in a precise phonetic description that we can communicate sensibly about sounds of a language.

2.1.1.1 Vowels

2.1.1.1.1 Parameters of vowel description. Kinds of vowels

Vowels (*Vokale*) are sounds in which there is no obstruction to the flow of air as it passes through the vocal tract. They are distinguished from each other by the way the vocal tract is modified by lips and tongue, which also modifies the sound produced.

In the following, we will first consider the parameters of phonetic description for vowels, i.e. dimensions along which different vowels differ from each other, to put it more bluntly, properties in which they may differ. Lists of examples given in this part are not exhaustive, but are only intended to give some rough indication as to what kinds of vowels are meant. After that, we will list all the vowels of British and American English systematically and with precise phonetic characterisations. In the last part of this section, certain problems in connection with English vowels are raised which are especially important for the learner.

- One important parameter for the description of vowels is **length** (*Vokallänge*). One basic distinction is that between long(er) and short(er) vowels:
  - **Short** vowels (*kurze Vokale*) are not additionally marked in our transcription; e.g. [e] as in *bed, bet, pen,* and *step*.
  - **Long** vowels (*lange Vokale*) are marked (in the transcription used here) by [ː] to indicate length; e.g. [iː] as in *meet, meat, reed, seem, Eve, etc.*

> ☞ Some phonetic descriptions of the English vowel system do not speak of vowel length, but of tenseness vs. laxness of vowels instead.
> Long vowels are regarded as **tense** (*gespannt*), short vowels as **lax** (*ungespannt*). The labels *tense* and *lax* are actually phonetically more appropriate in most cases as vowel length may vary considerably in the 'same' vowel depending on the phonetic environment. We will be able to understand this better in section →2.2.3.

- Another parameter for the description of vowels is vowel **height** (*Vokalhöhe*). Depending on the highest position of the tongue in each particular case we distinguish on the vertical axis:

  - **high** (*hoch*) (e.g. [ɪ], as in *bit, bid*; [uː], as in *spoon, youth*),
  - **mid** (*mittel*) (e.g. [e], as in *bed, leopard*; [ɔː], as in *core, saw*) and
  - **low** (*tief*) (e.g. [a] as in German *lachen, matt*; [æ] as in *axe, tan*, [ɑː] as in *park, calf*).

> ☞ Frequently, a four-way distinction is made on the parameter of vowel height. Many phoneticians use the terms
> - **close** (*geschlossener Vokal*) (e.g. [uː] as in *loop, rude, new*),
> - **half-close** (*halb geschlossener Vokal*) (e.g. [oː], as in German *ohne, schon*),
> - **half-open** (*halb geöffneter Vokal*) (e.g. [ɔː] as in *core, saw*), and
> - **open** (*geöffneter Vokal; offener Vokal*) (e.g. [ɒ] as in *off, because, what*; [a] as in German *lachen, matt*; [ɑː] as in *park, calf*).
>
> These terms refer to the opening of the jaw. There is of course a correlation between tongue height and jaw opening: When the tongue is high, the jaw is usually not lowered, but when the tongue is low, the jaw is also low and your mouth is wide open.
> Combining both classifications for vowel height, we get a five-way distinction: **close/high**, **half-close**, **mid**, **half-open**, **open/low**. So many distinctions are, however, hardly ever needed in phonetic decription.

- On the horizontal axis the following distinctions are made:
  - front vowel (palatal vowel, vorderer Vokal, Vorderzungenvokal) ([iː], [e], examples see above),
  - central vowel (zentraler Vokal) ([ə] as in again, another; [ɜː] as in err, curve, word, stir, [ʌ] as in us, enough, onion, [ɐ] as in Standard German Vater, ändern) and
  - back vowel (velar vowel, hinterer Vokal, Hinterzungenvokal) ([uː], [ɔː], [ɑː], examples see above).
- According to the **position** of the lips we distinguish
  - rounded (gerundeter Vokal) ([uː], [ɔː] (examples see above)) and
  - unrounded / spread (*ungerundeter Vokal / gespreizter Vokal*) vowels ([iː], [e], [a], [ɑː] [æ] (examples see above)).

- Depending on whether some of the air or no air passes through the **nasal** cavities, we distinguish

  - oral vowels (Oralvokale) in which no air passes through the nasal cavity (examples: all vowels mentioned so far) and

  - nasal vowels (*Nasalvokale*) (some of the air passes through nasal cavities; as in French **un bon vin blanc** [œ̃], [õ], [ɛ̃], [ɑ̃].

> △ English does not have nasal vowels, except (optionally) in two cases:
> - in 'posh' pronunciations of French loanwords (often of people trying to show off they know French): *genre* [ʒɑ̃rə] or [ʒɑ̃ŋrə],
> - in some cases when a nasal consonant follows a low vowel, as in *can* [kæ̃n]. (→ 2.2.3, 2.4.2).

Combinations of two vowels are called **diphthongs** (*Diphthonge*), as in *cow* [kaʊ], *lame* [leɪm] (→ 2.1.1.1.4). Simple, 'pure' vowels are called **monophthongs** (*Monophthonge*) (→ 2.1.1.1.2; 2.1.1.1.3).

2.1.1.1.2 The vowels of English

In this section you find a systematic description of all the monophthongs of English. There are certain differences between

- British **Received Pronunciation** (RP), that type of pronunciation widely regarded as a model in England and Wales, and

- **General American**, that variety spoken by the majority of Americans, namely those who do not have a noticeable eastern or southern accent, both in realisation (vowel quality) and in the system (vowel inventory). (For more on accents, see → 7.1.3). Fig. 24 and Fig. 25 only list the vowels of RP. For the vowels of General American, see Fig. 27.

Fig. 24: Short (lax) vowels of English (phonetic descriptions)

IPA	Precise phonetic description	Example words
[ɪ]	lowered-centralised close (high) front unrounded	*sit, bid*
[e]	mid front unrounded	*bed, bet*
[æ]	raised open front unrounded	*bad, bat*
[ə]	mid central unrounded, always unstressed (→2.3.3)	*about, information, mother*
[ʌ]	half-open central unrounded	*but, pub*
[ʊ]	lowered-centralised close (high) back rounded	*put, hood*
[ɒ]	open (low) back rounded	*pot, rob*

Fig. 25: Long (tense) vowels of British English (Received Pronunciation) (phonetic description)

IPA	Precise phonetic description	Example words
iː	close (high) front unrounded	*see, beat, bead*
ɜː	mid central unrounded	*nurse, stir, herd*
uː	close (high) back rounded	*food, root, shoe*
ɔː	half-open back rounded	*north, law, board*
ɑː	open back unrounded	*father, calm, tart*

The approximate position of the tongue in the formation of the vowels can be represented in a schematised diagram, the **vowel diagram** (vowel chart; *Vo-kalviereck, Vokaltrapez*) showing the approximate position of the tongue in articulating the different vowels.

The following charts (Fig. 26; Fig. 27) show all the short and long vowels of Received Pronunciation and General American in their approximate position in the vowel diagram.

Fig. 26: Vowels of English (Received Pronunciation)

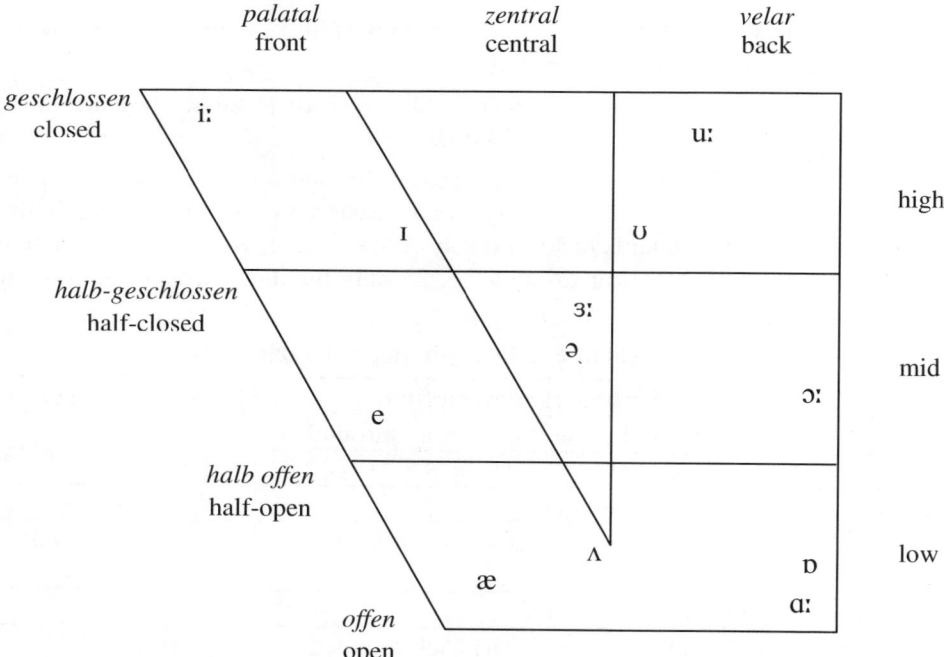

Fig. 27: Vowels of English (General American)

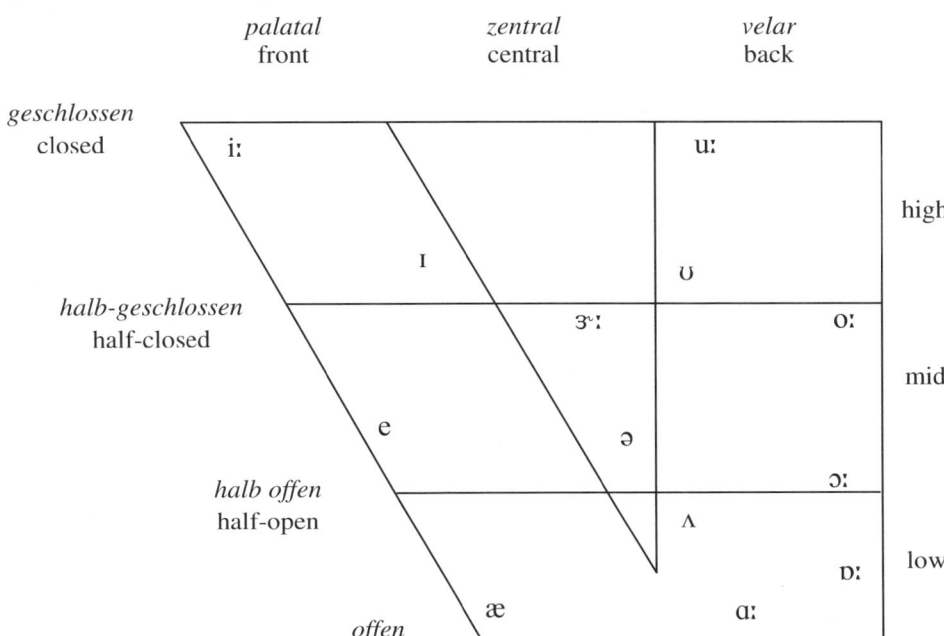

palatal   *zentral*   *velar*
front   central   back

geschlossen
closed

halb-geschlossen
half-closed

halb offen
half-open

offen
open

high

mid

low

2.1.1.1.3 Contrastive observations on the monophthongs

This section is intended to note differences between German and English vowels that present special problems for learners.

○ The following observations can be made on the **short vowels** of English:

–   Fig. 26 and Fig. 27 show that [ɪ] and [ʊ] are fairly low (much lower than their German counterparts in *Kitt* and *Butt*) and also more centralised (which gives them a somewhat 'muffled' sound quality).

–   The [æ] in *trap* is very low and has very little similarity to the stressed vowel in German *Treppe*, with which it is often identified by untrained learners. In fact, [æ] is far closer to the [a] sound in German *Trappe*, and learners are advised to try starting from this basis when learning the English [æ].

–   The German [a] is usually identified with British English [ʌ] as in *cup*, which is thus often pronounced like *Kap* by German learners. The vowel in *cup*, however, is more centralised than the German sound in *Kap*, and is, in fact, very similar to the unstressed vowel heard in the Northwest German pronunciation of *Mutter*, which, incidentally, is usually transcribed [ɐ] in German phonetics.

–   The [ɒ] sound in the British pronunciation of *lot* is also very low, much lower and less rounded than the German [ɔ] in *Lotte*, with which it is often identified. The two sounds should by no means be mixed up with each other.

–   Hence, the only short English vowel with an approximate equivalent in German is the vowel transcribed here as [e], as in *bed* [bed], or *wet* [wet], (sometimes also transcribed as [ɛ] as it is actually fairly low). This vowel, especially the one in [wet], is very close to the German stressed vowel in *Wette, Bett, Treppe*. (This German vowel is traditionally transcribed as [ɛ].)

O Contrastive observations on the **long vowels**:

— The long English [iː] in *fleece* is slightly different from, i.e. lower than, the vowel in German *Vlies*. In some varieties, it is even slightly diphthongised. This is sometimes transcribed [ɪi] or [ɪj].

— Analogous observations can be made on [uː]. English [uː] is also more fronted than its German counterpart.

— Comparison of Fig. 26 and Fig. 27 reveals some rather momentous differences between the vowel systems of Received Pronunciation and General American, especially among the long back vowels, which also have important consequences for the learner.

— The vowel in RP *start, father* [ɑː] is not only the vowel in the General American equivalents of these words, but also in General American *lot* and *odd*, and for some varieties even in *thought* and *law*.

This leads to a lot of confusion in German learners, who sometimes identify this vowel with the long German vowel in *Vater* (which is not quite as far back as English [ɑː]), sometimes, however, they also identify it with the sound in RP pronunciation of *cup* [ʌ], which is rather close to German [ɑː] or [a] in quality.

This, in connection with the spelling inconsistencies of English, often leads to confusion concerning the pronunciation of frequent words such as

- *body* which is
    - [ˈbɒdɪ] in Received Pronunciation but
    - [ˈbɑːdɪ] in General American, and
    - *[ˈbadɪ] in bad German learners' pronunciation, which to British ears makes it sound rather like
    - [ˈbʌdɪ] *buddy*, leading to gross misunderstandings, or

- *onion*, whose first vowel is actually [ʌ]:
    - [ˈʌnjən], though it is spelled <o> and which for this reason is often mispronounced
    - *[ˈɔnjən] by German learners.

> ✍ Note on the transcription: The apostrophe [ˈ] is used in the IPA to indicate that the <u>following</u> syllable is stressed (→ 2.3.3). Secondary, weaker stress in long words is indicated by [ˌ], as in *compensatory* [ˌkɒmpnˈseɪtrɪ]. Note the difference from the widely used informal notation of stress on the stressed vowel: *bódy, ónion, còmpensátory*.

To make the confusion perfect, both British English Received Pronunciation and General American have several long, more or less rounded back vowels which to German ears are all more or less vaguely identifiable with German versions of vowels between [ɑː] and [oː]. However, none of these vowels is identical or even similar to a German vowel. It might thus seem in order to explain them in more detail.

– Let us start from the RP vowel in *thought*, *law*, *north*, and *war*. The RP vowel [ɔː] is fairly high and very closely rounded, almost like German [oː] in *Kohl*. By most German learners, it is, however, regarded as a long-drawn version of the open rounded [ɔ] vowel in *Lotte* or *Ross*, as it occurs marginally in colloquial Standard German in the interjection of astonishment *Boah!* [bɔː] or as in *eh boah eh!* [eː bɔː eː]. The British English vowel in *thought*, *north*, etc. is, however, much closer and rounder.

– The General American vowel in *thought* and *law*, [ɒː], on the other hand, is less rounded and more open than the German [bɔː]. If, however, the sound [r] follows in General American, then the sound is somewhat closer, but still more open than British Received Pronunciation [ɔː], as in General American *north* [nɔːrθ] or *war* [wɔːr]. In some words it may be even higher than in Received Pronunciation, like in some varieties in *force* [foːrs] and *four* [foːr]. We may thus say that there are two or three variants in General American: [ɒː], [ɔː], and sometimes [oː], that correspond to RP [ɔː], but none of them remotely resembles a German sound, and none of them is identical with the RP sound.

It should also be noted that, in contrast to British Received Pronunciation, all the above vowels in General American, whenever the spelling indicates it, are followed by [r] or contain an [r]-like articulation.

– Accordingly, the American vowel [ɝː] as in *blur*, *stir* and *err* is also strikingly different from Received Pronunciation [ɜː]: Although it has roughly the same position as far as the back of the tongue is concerned, it contains an additional [r]-like articulation in that the tip of the tongue (which is usually at rest behind the lower teeth when vowels are articulated) is curled back into an alveolar position (i.e., behind the teeth).

✍ For simplicity's sake, this vowel is often notated as a sequence of [ɜː] and [r], viz., [ɜːr]. But since in American pronunciation [ɜː] never occurs without an [r] following, and there is no clear boundary to be heard between two articulatory gestures [ɜː] and [r], [ɝː] had better be regarded as one sound in that variety.

◉ A sound produced with the tongue curled back is usually called **retroflex**. Apart from the above American sound, English does not use retroflex sounds. Some languages, most notably in India, have a number of retroflex consonants.

The corresponding RP vowel [ɜː] (right in the centre of Fig. 26) is often mistaken for a long version of the German vowel [œ], as in *Hörner*, in particular in varieties which do not pronounce the <r> and monophthongise the remaining vowel sound: [hœːnɐ]. This German vowel, however, is a rounded front vowel, whereas [ɜː] is unrounded and central. The British English vowel is in fact very similar to a long-drawn [əː] (and is indeed transcribed like this in older dictionaries!), which is sometimes heard in both English and German as a hesitation phenomenon when people don't know what to say but don't want to give up the floor either. In terms of phonetic similarity it is advisable to take this sound as a model for [ɜː].

2.1.1.1.4 Observations on the English diphthongs

◉ The following observations can be made on the diphthongs ending in [ɪ].

– [eɪ] in *cake* does not exist in Standard German and should not be equated with the German monophthong [eː] in *Keks*. In some American varieties, though, [eɪ] approximates the German monophthong.

– The first element of the diphthong in English *shine* [ʃaɪn] is slightly further to the front than the first element of German [ae] as in *Schein* and does not occur on its own in English. The final element is much further up than its counterpart in Standard German.

– The first element in English [ɔɪ] in *noise* is slightly higher and more rounded than its counterpart in the Standard German pronunciation of *neu* [nɔø]. The second element of the German diphthong is a front rounded vowel, very much like the [ø] in the first vowel in *Ökonomie*, which does not exist in English. Instead, the second element in the English diphthong is higher and unrounded. German speakers should thus take care to spread their lips and raise their tongue towards the end of English [ɔɪ].

◉ Observations on the diphthongs ending in [ʊ]:
There is another interesting difference between British Received Pronunciation and General American pronunciation: It concerns the pronunciation of the diphthong in *goat*, *show*, and *cold*.

– RP has developed two rather different variants: in *goat* and *show*, the diphthong starts on the central vowel [ə]; in *cold* and similar words in which the diphthong precedes [l], along with the more traditional pronunciation [kəʊld], more and more people say [kɒʊld], where the diphthong almost sounds like the (Northern Standard) German diphthong in *Kaulquappe* or *Maul*. Students who wish to learn RP should note that [əʊ] and [ɒʊ] have absolutely nothing in common with German [oː] in *Kohl*, and should practice these diphthongs carefully.

– The pronunciation of this diphthong in General American (GA) is altogether different. It is transcribed [oʊ]. The starting point and the target point of the diphthong are not very far from each other, making the sound almost a monophthong, fairly close to German [oː] in *Kohl*.

◉ Observations on the centring diphthongs:
– The diphthongs [ɪə], [ʊə] and [eə] are called **centring diphthongs**, and are a typical feature of RP. In most varieties of American English, the *r* found in the spelling of these diphthongs is still pronounced, so that these diphthongs do not exist in General American pronunciation. In RP, the *r* is only pronounced as a so-called linking *r* or intrusive *r* (→ 2.4.3).

> ➤ Centring diphthongs historically arise from vowel + [r] combinations; they are the result of a sound change in Southern English English: a postvocalic [r] sound turned into [ə]. This counts as a major feature distinguishing different varieties of English from each other. Varieties that have kept the [r], like most varieties of American English, are called **rhotic** dialects.
>
> ◉ A similar phenomenon occurred to varying degrees in northern and Standard German, most extremely in the area around Dortmund [doɐtmʊnt] and Gelsenkirchen [gɛlznkiɐçn]. Note that the vowel arising in place of the vanishing *r* is not identical to [ə].

It should be noted that two of the centring diphthongs in RP are presently undergoing a **monophthongisation** which is part of a long-term historical tendency in Southern English English to eliminate all centring diphthongs (➔ 3.2.1.6):

– [ʊə] is giving way in favour of [ɔː], so that for increasingly many speakers nowadays, *poor*, *sure*, and *during* sound like [pɔː], [ʃɔː] and [djɔːrɪŋ], and *poor*, *pour, pore*, and *paw* are homophones (➔ 4.1.2.1). Furthermore, [ɔː] has been raised considerably over the last few decades to become almost [oː] so there is a marked difference in pronunciation between older and younger speakers.

– [eə] is increasingly being monophthongised, with a new long vowel [ɛː] (not notated in the charts) arising in its place, which is actually very close to (southern) Standard German [ɛː] in *spät, Mädchen* (the lips are slighty more spread in the new English monophthong), but clearly lower than [e] in *bed* and higher than [æ] in *bad*. One could say that the place of *bared* [bɛːd] is precisely between *bed* and *bad*.

2.1.1.1.5 Observations on the English vowel system

It will be noted that both the British and the American system look fairly unbalanced, especially when tense and lax vowels are considered separately. Without the new RP monophthong /ɛː/ (as in *fair*, *there*, and *bared*), there is a huge gap in the area of tense lower front vowels; given that the new monophthong catches on, there will be 'fierce competition', so to speak, for distinctive places of articulation between /e/, /ɛː/ and /æ/, like in *bed, bared* and *bad*, a veritable challenge to German-speaking learners to whom all these vowels sound the same! Among the lower back and central vowels, this competition, together with dialectal variety, has already led to utter confusion, in particular between /ʌ/ and /ɑː/ (with *love* and *laugh* becoming homophones!) or /ɒ/ and /ɔː/, and some of these vowels are very close to each other for German ears.

The Present-Day English vowel system seems extraordinarily complex: It has 12 to 14 different monophthongal phonemes (➔ 2.2.3), depending on the accent, which are not, like in other languages, often neatly ordered in pairs of tense/lax or front/back or rounded/unrounded. The 'normal' number of vowels in a language is five, or ten if short and long vowels are distinguished. The English system is, not surprisingly, fairly unbalanced, unstable and full of variation. All these are properties which make it especially difficult to learn. Most learner varieties, including the German ones, simplify it drastically.

> ➢ Historically, the Present-Day English vowel system is the result of many complex and partly chaotic sound changes which have never come to a rest since the beginnings of the English language (→ 3.2.1). The English vowel system is thus a challenge not only to learners, but also to historical linguists who believe that phonological changes are drifts towards more balanced, symmetric systems.
>
> ⊙ This is not to deny that a universal tendency exists towards such balanced systems, because an optimal distribution, e.g. of vowels in the oral cavity, makes it easier to keep all vowels apart from each other and thus facilitates listening comprehension. The most frequent vowel system in the languages of the world is, indeed, something along the lines of /a e i o u/ (on the transcription, → 2.2.2), five vowels optimally distant from each other and optimally exploiting the space in the oral cavity.

2.1.1.2 Consonants

[handwritten: Sounds in which obstruction occurs at various points in the vocal tract]

When consonants are produced, obstruction to the flow of air occurs at various points in the vocal tract (cf. Fig. 23 above). Consonants sound different from each other because this obstruction may be of different kinds and may be produced at different places in the vocal tract. This creates different noises and different resonance chambers in the vocal tract. We thus obtain two important parameters of description for consonants:

- **manner of articulation** (*Artikulationsart*) and
- **place of articulation** (*Artikulationsstelle*).
- Besides place and manner of articulation, **voice** is the third important parameter for distinguishing consonants from each other. Regarding the parameter of voice we draw a principal distinction between
  - **voiced** (*stimmhaft*) ([b d g] etc.) and
  - **voiceless** (*stimmlos*) ([p t k] etc.) consonants.

When we produce voiced sounds there is vibration of the **vocal folds** (vocal cords, glottis, *Stimmbänder*); in the case of voiceless sounds there is no vibration. You can test whether there is vibration or not by holding your fingers against your throat. Furthermore, there is an infallible test for the voicedness of a consonant (except for plosives; see above): You can sing, and thus change pitch height, only when producing a <u>voiced</u> consonant or vowel.

> ☞ The voiced / voiceless distinction varies in its precise phonetic characteristics from phonetic environment to environment, and from language to language, and its appropriate terminological designation is controversial among linguists. To avoid commitment to claims about voicedness or voicelessness of consonants (which may be subject to considerable variation), some linguists use the phonetically more neutral terms.

- **fortis** (for what is usually called "voiceless") and
- **lenis** (for what is usually called "voiced").

To give you a preliminary overview of the consonants discussed in this textbook, Fig. 28 below groups the consonants of English and German (and also some consonants used in other languages) according to the above parameters of place and manner of articulation. The upper consonants in a cell are voiceless, the lower consonants voiced. Included are also some variants (allophones → 2.2.3) which occur as a result of coarticulation (→ 2.4.2). The following tables (Fig. 29 to Fig. 32) will then give examples for the sounds presented in Fig. 28 to give you are more concrete impression of what sounds are meant. After that, the phonetic terminology used will be explained. The terminology used to describe places of articulation is summarised in Fig. 33. Meanwhile, some indication as to what consonant is meant can also be gathered from the letters used, and, by analogy, from the columns and lines in which they occur in Fig. 28, and from the examples given in Fig. 29 to Fig. 32.

Fig. 28: Transcription of sounds by place and manner of articulation in IPA

place⇨ ⇩manner	bilabial	labio-dental	dental	alveolar	post-alveolar	palato-alveolar	palatal	velar	uvular	glottal
plosive (stop)	p b		t̪ d̪	t d				k g	q	ʔ
frica-tive		f v	θ ð	s z		ʃ ʒ	ç	x ɣ	χ	h
affri-cate						tʃ dʒ				
nasal	m	ɱ	n̪	n			ɲ	ŋ		
liquid			l̪	l	ɹ (r)		ʎ		ʁ	
semi-vowel	w*						j	w*		

(left margin label: "obstruents" reading vertically for plosive/fricative/affricate rows; "sonorants" reading vertically for nasal/liquid/semivowel rows)

* [w] is a labiovelar, i.e. simultaneously articulated with the lips and at the velum, that is why it occurs both in the labial and the velar column.

📖 Try to work out the pronunciation of all the examples in the following tables and pronounce them aloud, paying attention to the pronunciation differences indicated by the differences in transcription.

Fig. 29: Examples for English obstruent consonants

(In the example words, the relevant letter (combination) is underlined.)

voiceless (fortis)				voiced (lenis)		
	initial	medial	final		initial	medial	final
[p]	pit	rapid	cap	[b]	bid	rabid	cab
[t]	town	metal	sat	[d]	down	medal	sad
[k]	cold	decree	back	[g]	gold	degree	bag
[f]	fine	hefty	proof	[v]	vine	heavy ·	prove
[θ]	think	earthy	oath	[ð]	this	worthy	with
[s]	sink	racer	place	[z]	zinc	razor	plays
[ʃ]	sheep	mission	dish	[ʒ]	genre	vision	garage
[h]	hot	behind		[dʒ]	gin	ridges	purge
[tʃ]	chin	riches	perch				

Fig. 30: Examples for English sonorants

voiced (lenis)		
	initial	medial	final
[m]	malt	simmer	sum
[n]	night	sinner	sun
[ŋ]		finger	sung
[l]	look	silly	milk
[r]	rag	mirror	(car)*
[j]	yes	view	
[w]	wet	away	

* in General American only

Fig. 31: Examples for the use of some variants

ŋ	invariable
t̪	that thing
d̪	that lad there
n̪	enthral
l̩	although
ɾ	latter, ladder in General American
q	cool

In South Eastern English colloquial pronunciation, e.g., in Cockney and Estuary English, the **glottal stop** ('*Knacklaut*') [ʔ] (see → Fig. 28) often replaces [t] after vowels:

  pity [pɪʔɪ], *what* [wɒʔ], *what a pity* [ˌwɒʔəˈpɪʔɪ]

For more examples, see → 7.1.1.

In many English varieties, the glottal stop can be used, for special emphatic effect, before any word beginning with a vowel, like, e.g.

  He's such an idiot!
  [hiːzˈsʌtʃənˈʔɪdjət].

◉ In Standard German, the glottal stop is obligatorily used at word boundaries when the second word starts with a vowel:

Er ist so ein Idiot!	*Iss auch ein Ei!*
[ʔeɐ ʔɪst ˈzo ʔaen ʔiˈdjoːt]	[ʔɪsˈʔɔɔχʔaenˌʔae]

Fig. 32: Examples of consonants not used in English

Sound	Language(s)	Example(s)
ɲ	French	*gnon, champignon, campagne*
	Spanish	*ñu, año*
	Italian	*gnocchi, Bologna*
ʎ	(Castilian) Spanish	*llamar, caballo*
	Italian	*tagliatelle*
ç	Standard German	*Licht, König*
ɣ	Spanish	*agua*
	North and West German dialects	*sagen, wagen*
ʁ	Standard German	*riesig, kehren, (Herr)**
x	German	*Loch, ach*
	Spanish	*ojo, hija*
χ	German	*trug, Frucht***

* in some areas only. In some variants, between vowels and also initially, this sound
may become very similar, even identical to the sound [ɣ], making *Waren* and
Wagen homophonous in North and West German dialectal pronunciation.
** variant both of German [ʁ] and [x]

➢ In contrast to the vowels, the consonants of English have not changed very
much since Old English. Only the sounds [ç], [ɣ], and [χ], i.e., all uvular, velar
and palatal fricatives which were still present in Old English, vanished during the
Middle English period (→ 3.2.1.7). Most of their instances were preserved to this
day in German. In English, spelling evidence shows in many cases in which
words they once occurred, cf. **night** (*Nacht*), **laugh** (*lachen*) and **where**. What has
changed considerably, however, is the system in which English consonants function. To understand this, we need some more knowledge of segmental phonology
(→ 2.2). We will deal with an example of such a change in section → 3.2.1.7.

Let us now discuss the parameters of manner and place of articulation in detail.

- Regarding the **manner of articulation** (*Artikulationsart*) (or the nature of the
  obstruction) in the vocal tract we distinguish mainly between plosives (often
  called *stops*), fricatives, affricates, nasals and liquids.

  - **Plosives** (stops; *Plosive, Verschlusslaute*) are produced by a complete lo-
    cal obstruction of the vocal tract (and its sudden release) such as in [p], [g],
    [t] etc. *(and its sudden release [b] [k] [d])*

☞ Strictly speaking, the categories 'plosive' and 'stop' are not identical.
Stops include nasal conconants (see below) as well: Usually the vocal tract
is completely closed at the place of articulation while nasals are produced.
What is missing in nasals is the sudden release characteristic of plosives. In
this textbook, we have no occasion to make use of this terminological distinction.

no final obstruent devoicing!

- **Fricatives** (*Frikative, Reibelaute*) are produced by a local narrowing of the vocal tract, such as in [s], [f], [θ] etc.

- **Affricates** (*Affrikaten*) are produced by an initial complete local obstruction of the vocal tract (as in the case of plosives) and its ensuing gradual release, which leaves the local tract narrowed and causes friction (as in the case of fricatives). [tʃ],[dʒ] are the only affricates in English.

- **Nasals** (*Nasale*) are produced by lowering the velum (soft palate) so that part of the air-stream passes through the nose: [m], [n] etc. The vocal tract is usually completely blocked as in plosives.

- When **liquids** (*Liquide*) are produced, there is obstruction of the vocal tract, but this obstruction is not complete.
  - Either the air escapes over the sides of the tongue, as in the case of the lateral [l];
  - or the obstruction is periodically opened, as in the case of 'rolled' [ʀ] in German, which is called a **trill**.

> ✎ Quite commonly, the English [ɹ], conventionally represented as [r] in the phonetic literature on English for simplicity's sake, is also included among the liquids although it is really an **approximant** (→ 2.1.1.3). Glides such as [j] and [w] (→ 2.1.1.3) in English are also approximants. English [r] however is a **frictionless continuant**, another kind of approximant.
> Strictly speaking, then, English [r] should not be counted among the liquids, because then the glides [j] and [w] would also have to be called liquids: They perfectly meet the above definition. But the classification of English [r] as a liquid is so entrenched that this is hardly ever questioned.
> In general, it must be said that terminology in this area of 'peripheral consonants' is variable and inconsistent. Often, phonetic characteristics and requirements of a systematic phonological (→ 2.2.1) description contradict each other: The phonetic facts tend to be fuzzy and form a continuum; phonology, however, distinguishes clear-cut discrete (→ Box 25) categories. It makes perfect sense to treat English [r] and [l] as one (phonological) class of sounds as they function similarly and have, in this respect, more in common with each other than with any other sound in English. But phonetically they have little in common.

- **Flaps** are sounds which are like one phase of a trill, and therefore often discussed along with them. The tongue as the lower articulator touches the upper articulator (→ 2.1.1.3), e.g. the alveoli, very lightly and briefly, and only once, so that no air pressure builds up behind the closure. Nevertheless, flaps are sometimes difficult to distinguish from either plosives or approximants. An alveolar flap [ɾ] occurs in most varieties of American and Canadian English in intervocalic position and replaces both [t] and [d], making word pairs like *ladder – latter* and *rider – writer* homophonous in some varieties (→ 4.1.2). A very similar flap occurs in some prestigious British English varieties in the pronunciation of *very* [verɪ] and the like.

⊙ A similar flap also exists in Spanish, which is spelled <r>.

- Depending on the **place of articulation** (*Artikulationsort*) (or the place of the obstruction) we distinguish many different types of consonants because languages may draw very fine distinctions here. The most important types of consonants are listed in Fig. 33 below. (You can compare the descriptions with Fig. 23 above):

Fig. 33: Terminology for places of articulation

Phonetic term	Description	Examples
bilabial	produced with both lips	[p], [b], [m]
labiodental	produced with front teeth and lower lip	[f], [v]
dental	produced at the upper front teeth	[t̪], [θ], [d̪], [ð]
alveolar	produced at the alveoli (teeth-ridge)	[t], [d], [s], [z]
palatal	produced at the hard palate	[tʃ], [dʒ], [ʃ], [ʒ]
velar	produced at the soft palate (velum)	[k], [g], [x]
uvular	produced at the uvula	[q], [χ]
glottal	produced at the glottis (vocal folds) in the larynx	[ʔ]

Alveolar and palatal fricatives are often subsumed under the label **sibilant** (*Zischlaut*). Thus, [s], [z], [ʃ], and [ʒ] are the sibilants of English.

📖 Explain the pronunciation of the *-s* suffix in English nouns and verbs using the notion of sibilant!

2.1.1.3 Approximants / Glides / Semi-vowels. The sonority continuum

Some sounds (which were already included in the above tables) take an intermediate position between vowels and consonants, the so-called **approximants** (*Approximanten*) which include the **semi-vowels** (*Halbvokale*) or **glides** (*Gleitlaute*). These, as the alternative name *semi-vowels* indicates, are sounds that have consonantal as well as vocalic properties. Phonetically some of them are very close to vowels, but they function like consonants.

Approximants in general are sounds where **lower** and **upper articulator**, usually the tongue and some part of the roof of the mouth, but in other cases lower and upper lip, e.g., are approximated but never actually make contact. English approximants are

- [j], as in yet [jet], pure [pjɔ:], and
- [w], as in web [web], aware [əwɛ:], and, strictly speaking, also
- [r], which is usually regarded as a liquid (→ 2.1.1.2, ☞ box).
- In French there is another glide, [ɥ], e.g. in *nuit* [nɥi].

> ✍ In some (especially older American) descriptions, the second part of diphthongs is also regarded as a glide, so that you may find transcriptions such as [kaw] for *cow* and [fajn] for *fine*. This is, depending on the variety described, not without phonetic justification.

But the quality of being intermediate between vowels and consonants is also the case, in some respects, for the **liquids** [l] and [r] and the **nasals** [m], [n] and [ŋ].

> ☞ Therefore, glides (semi-vowels), liquids and nasals are often subsumed under the term **sonorants** (*Sonoranten*); they are all voiced sounds in which there is no noise component.
>
> Terminology may vary, however. A slightly different basic classification of sounds is that between **obstruents** (*Obstruenten*) and **sonorants** (GIMSON [5]1994, 31):
>
> - **Obstruents** are those sounds in whose production the constriction impeding the airflow through the vocal tract is sufficient to cause noise; they include all plosives, fricatives and affricates.
> - **Sonorants** in this case include all glides / approximants, liquids, nasals, and the vowels.
>
> This alternative classification may have its merits when discussing syllable structure (→ 2.3.2, ☞ box).
>
> Some phonologists also take obstruents and sonorants as fuzzy categories and assume a sonorant – obstruent **continuum** extending from the vowels via semi-vowels, other approximants, liquids and nasals to fricatives and plosives. This continuum has also become known as the **sonority hierarchy**.

> 📖 The sonority hierarchy is often invoked in discussions of syllable structure (→ 2.3.2). You yourself can use it to find out about English syllable structure before even reading the relevant section. English is in fact fairly well-behaved in terms of predictions based on the sonority hierarchy concerning admissible syllable structures. Look at the following monosyllabic words and orthographic renderings of inadmissible sound sequences in English, try to transcribe them phonetically and consider how the sonority hierarchy as described above could be used to formulate generalisations.
>
> *tramp, gulp, kiln, duke, twin, golf, blast, *ptrapf, *ndrookw, *shkawp, *lfoiksh*

2.1.2 Acoustic phonetics

Acoustic phonetics describes the acoustic properties of speech sounds. The utterance of a speech sound produces – as any other noise – sound waves, which carry the information to the hearer's ear. These sound waves are very complex events:

They are vibrations of a certain carrier substance, in most cases the air, with different loudnesses and pitches at the same time.

The most important parameters in the description of acoustic phonetics are:

- the **fundamental frequency** (*Grundfrequenz*) of the waves, that is, the lowest frequency of a signal, which the hearer perceives as **pitch** (*Tonhöhe*);

- the **amplitude** (*Amplitude*), that is the intensity of the vibrations, whose effect is **loudness** (*Lautstärke*); and

- the **formants** (*Formanten, Obertöne*), which represent the non-fundamental frequencies of the signal, which are produced by the sound-specific form of the vocal tract, and which allow the hearer to distinguish different sound qualities. Differences in formants allow us, e.g., to distinguish different musical instruments from each other, and also different speech sounds.

The classical tool of acoustic phonetics is the **spectrograph** (*Spektrograph*). It makes possible a graphic representation of the above-mentioned parameters of a sound signal by 'translating' the distribution of energy (higher or lower amplitude) across the different frequencies (the spectrum) of sound waves into black marks on paper. The different frequencies of the signal (fundamental frequency and formants) are arranged vertically in the spectrogram, lower and higher amplitude is shown in different shades from grey to black.

The spectrograms in Fig. 34 below show the different fundamental frequencies and formants of three long English vowels and one diphthong. Each vowel has its characteristic pattern of formants which accounts for its sound quality.

Fig. 34: Spectrogram I
(GIMSON [5]1994, 21, Arnold)

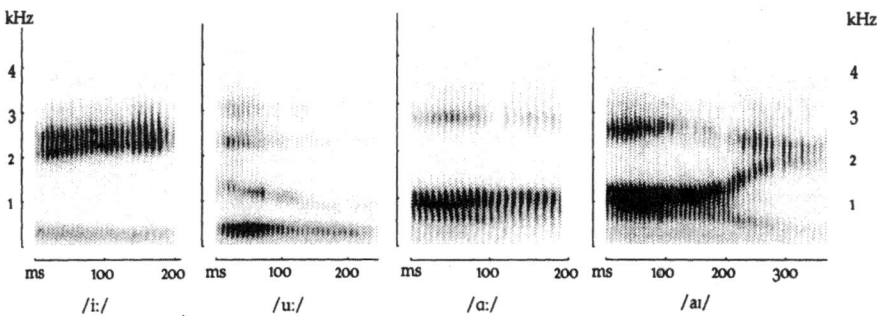

The spectrograms in Fig. 35 below show the distribution of energy across the spectrum in three English voiceless fricatives. The diffusion of energy over a wide range of frequency (as shown by extensive blackening in the spectrogram) is heard as a hissing noise.

118

Fig. 35: Spectrogram II
(GIMSON [5]1994, 21, Arnold)

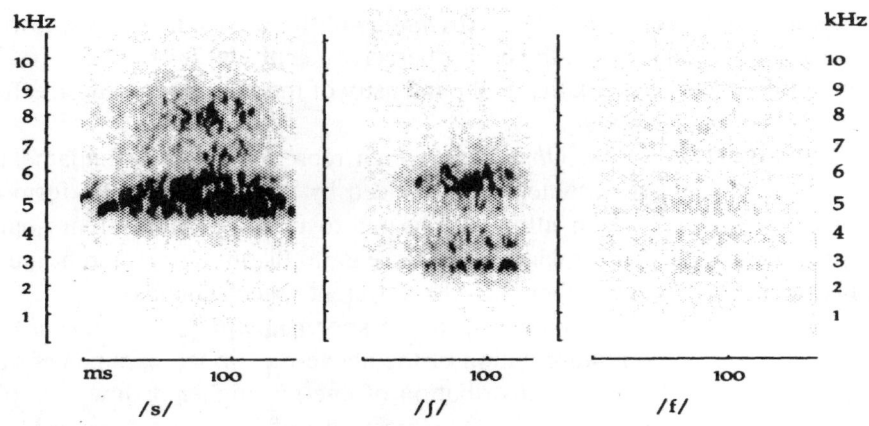

/s/ /ʃ/ /f/

Fig. 36: Spectrogram III
(GIMSON [5]1994, 21, Arnold)

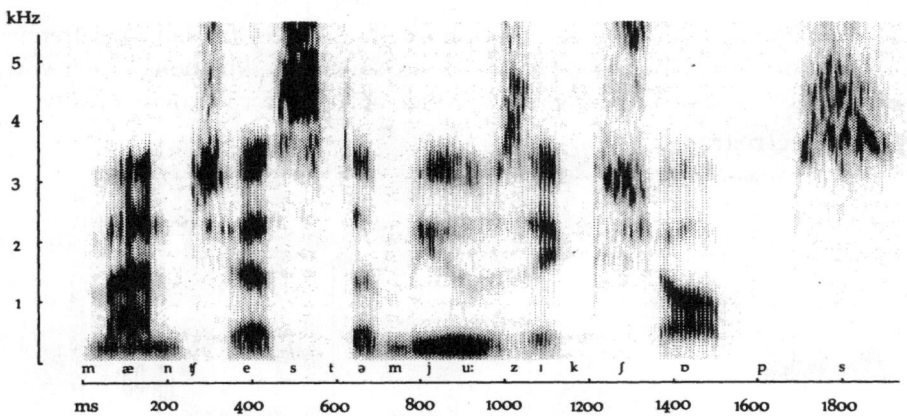

Fig. 36 above shows a spectrogram of a British speaker pronouncing the phrase *Manchester music shops*. It shows nicely

- that clear boundaries between successive sounds in performance as noted in a phonetic transcription are not always easy to draw,
- that within the articulation of one sound the acoustic properties are not necessarily stable (see, e.g. the first syllable "*Man ...*"),
- that what is 'the same sound' to us does not necessarily look the same on the spectrogram.

The [tʃ] in *Manchester* and the [ʃ] in *shop*, the two [m]'s in *Manchester* and *music*, and the two [s]'s in *Manchester* and *shops* are not as similar as one might expect; on the other hand, the three plosives [t], [k], and [p] look very much the same except for their length: The whiteness of the paper indicates the brief moment of silence while the vocal tract is completely closed for the articulation of the plosive.

Despite these difficulties, and supplemented by a host of other sophisticated techniques, spectrography has made a valuable contribution to our knowledge about acoustic properties of sounds and of the speech flow.

2.1.3 Auditory phonetics

Auditory phonetics examines the perception of speech sounds by the hearer by experimental methods. It is thus a branch of **psycholinguistics** (not dealt with in this volume, but see www.narr-studienbuecher.de). It examines, i.a., the way individual speech sounds are distinguished by the hearer.

Important findings of auditory phonetics, sometimes embarrassing to phonological theory (→ 2.2) are the following:
- It is a fact that speech sounds are perceived differently from other noises. Different parts of the brain are involved, and the processing of speech signals is different.
- Above all, speech sounds – as opposed to other noises – are categorised during the process of hearing itself in accordance with the sound system of the mother tongue (**categorial perception**; *kategoriale Wahrnehmung*).
- The parameters along which speech sounds are distinguished are often not properties of the particular sound itself but properties of adjacent sounds.

For example, the difference between a 'voiceless' and a 'voiced' final consonant in English is perceived more via the difference in length of the preceding vowel than via the acoustic properties of the consonant itself (e.g. the half-long vowel in *bid* [bɪ·d] vs. the short vowel in *bit* [bɪt]).

O This is most significant for learners who find it difficult to distinguish voiced and voiceless sounds in final position (→ 2.2.4 on German *Auslautverhärtung* (final obstruent devoicing)). A slight lengthening of the vowel not only helps pronounce the obstruent more lenis-like, but is also in accordance with English pronunciation habits anyway.

For German learners, in any case, vowel <u>length</u> is often the distinctive feature that distinguishes *bad* from *bat*. The latter, in turn, is often not distinguished from *bet* because vowel height is not distinctive at that point in German. So untrained Germans simply don't hear the difference, due to categorial perception.

2.2 Segmental phonology

2.2.1 Phonetics vs. phonology. The phoneme

While phonetics examines the physiological (articulatory phonetics), physical (acoustic phonetics) and psychological (auditory phonetics) properties of speech sounds, **phonology** (Phonemics, *Phonologie, Phonemik, Phonematik*) deals with the function of speech elements in the language system, i.e. in speakers' and hearers' competence.

One of the founder fathers of modern phonology, TRUBETZKOY from the influential and pioneering **Prague School** of linguistics between the world wars, wrote:

> Um einen treffenden Vergleich R. Jakobsons zu wiederholen, verhält sich die Phonologie zur Phonetik wie die Nationalökonomie zur Warenkunde oder die Finanzwissenschaft zur Numismatik. (TRUBETZKOY [1939] 1971, 14)

We may forgive a genius like Trubetzkoy for not giving any exact reference on JAKOBSON (another member of the Prague School). Presumably he wasn't even quoting a publication. The witticism has become common linguistic folklore since and is usually quoted in English as "Phonetics is to phonology as numismatics is to economics". Numismatics deals with the physical properties of coins and bank notes, not paying attention to their monetary value; economics, and *Finanzwissenschaft* in particular, with the function of money as an abstract entity in economy. However, while for economic theory the physical properties of the coins and bank notes is truly irrelevant, phonology cannot emancipate itself to such an extent as to completely ignore the phonetic properties of the speech segments (although attempts to this effect have been made).

On the contrary, it is an increasingly accepted fact that a phonological theory needs phonetic substantiation. In discussing phonology, we will of course have to use phonetic terminology, as no other terminology is available. Conversely, phonetics needs phonology in order to define its object of study. Who would tell a phonetician what sounds to study, if not phonologists? Phonetically, there is no big difference between, say, a raspberry and a speech sound. Both can be described accurately in phonetic terms.

There are two major branches of phonology,

- **segmental** and
- **suprasegmental** phonology.

Segmental phonology examines the function of the segments, the abstract individual sounds of a language, whereas suprasegmental phonology covers the phonological properties of larger chunks of speech, i.e. syllables, words, phrases and clauses (→ 2.3).

The most important segmental unit in classical 20th century phonology is the **phoneme** (*Phonem*). It can, first of all, be defined as the smallest distinctive segment in a language, that is: There are no smaller segmental distinctive units into which spoken language can be cut up.

The term **distinctiveness** (*Distinktivität*) of a phoneme means that these segments can distinguish words from one another: If in a given word we replace one phoneme with another, we produce a different word, or a meaningless combination of sounds, e.g. English /bɪt/ – /pɪt/ – */dɪt/. That's why it is said that phonemes **contrast** (*kontrastieren*) with each other, or that they are in **opposition**.

A phoneme is not a pronounceable unit, but an abstract segment that subsumes a set of non-contrastive, actually realised (or realisable) sounds, called **allophones** (*Allophone*) (phonetic variants), which – within a given language system – are regarded as the 'same' sound, although phonetically they may be subject to considerable variation.

Box 23: The notion of 'opposition' or 'contrast' in modern linguistics

This notion of **opposition** or **contrast** is of paramount importance in modern linguistics. It may be said to be one of its hallmarks that it is primarily concerned with oppositions or contrasts rather than with the substantive properties of linguistic units. SAUSSURE put it in this way:

"... dans la langue il n'y a que des différences." (SAUSSURE 1965, 166);

in English:

"... in language there are only differences." (SAUSSURE 1966, 120)

We should not be misled by SAUSSURE's use of the term *différence*. In present day linguistics, the terms *contrast* or *opposition* are the correct technical terms for what he means by *différence* here. It is not mere 'differences' that 'make a difference' in linguistics, but contrasts or oppositions in this technical sense. Thus, phonetics is 'less linguistic' than phonology: Phonetics is about subtle differences in pronunciation; but it is phonology that is concerned with the relevant contrasts and is part of the *langue*, whereas phonetics belongs to the *parole*.

The notion of opposition or contrast is not only used in phonology, but also in grammar and semantics. Values of morphological categories in particular (such as those described in → 1.1.3) may be said to contrast with each other, such as when the past tense contrasts with the present tense or the singular with the plural. Again, the expression substance and form of these categories may vary and they are less important for a characterisation of a given language than the fact that the language in question has a tense contrast or a number contrast of that kind, i.e. that it has such a contrast in its content form (→ Box 24).

Contrasts or oppositions are also important in lexical semantics, in particular in the description of sense relations (→4.2.2) and lexical fields (→ 4.2.1).

☛ The term *contrast* is also used in a more colloquial sense by linguists (as we repeatedly had occasion to do in this book), and it is also used in two more different technical senses in lexical semantics (→ 4.2.2.4) and textlinguistics (→ 6.1.4). Also note that there is no special affinity between *contrast* as discussed here and *contrastive linguistics* (→ Box 22).

2.2.2 Phonemic and phonetic transcription

Before we can discuss examples, we have to introduce a notational convention: The difference between phonemes and allophones, or, in other words, between phonology and phonetics, is so important for argumentation in linguistics that we also note this difference in transcription. In section → 2.1 we only used

- **phonetic** (or **narrow**) **transcription** (*phonetische, enge Transkription*), for which we use square brackets, e.g. [p]. Above we used

- **phonemic** (**phonological, broad**) **transcription** (*phonemische, phono-logische, weite Transkription*), for which we use slashes, e.g. /p/.

The difference between these transcriptions is as follows: When we are dealing with a specific sound phenomenon, it is important to be able to note this specific detail in transcription. This is when we use phonetic, narrow transcription, i.e. we transcribe allophones rather than phonemes.

For example, the British English phoneme /l/ has two major allophones which occur in different environments:

- so-called 'clear' [l] is used when a vowel or [j] follows, as in *lip* [lɪp] and *failure* [feɪljə];

- 'dark' [ɫ] is pronounced with the back of the tongue raised in the direction of the soft palate, so that a small cavity is formed between hard palate and tongue, the tip of the tongue being pressed against the teeth ridge. This cavity serves as an additional resonance chamber and gives this allophone its 'dark' sound quality. Dark [ɫ] is used whenever /l/ is not followed by a vowel or /j/, as in *pill* [pɪɫ] or *felt* [feɫt].

We say that [l] and [ɫ] in British English are **variants** or **allophones** of the phoneme /l /.

To take another example: The English phoneme /p/ has also got a number of allophones. We will discuss only three major ones here.

- When /p/ is realised word-initially before a vowel in an accented syllable, it is strongly **aspirated** (*aspiriert*). You can verify this by putting your hand close to the front of your lips while pronouncing *pen* or *pill*. You will notice a strong puff of air following the release of the lip closure in /p/. We transcribe this allophone as [pʰ], as in [pʰen], [pʰɪl].

- Aspiration of /p/ is much weaker when /p/ is not word-initial (as in *spill* [spɪl]) or when the following vowel is not in an accented syllable (as in *flipper* [flɪpə]).

- When /p/ precedes a plosive consonant, the lips briefly close to form the articulatory gesture for /p/, but this closure is never audibly released, so that strictly speaking this allophone of the plosive /p/ is not a plosive at all. This phonetic feature is transcribed in the IPA as [̚], so that this unreleased variant of /p/ is notated [p̚], as in *trapped* [træp̚t], *stepdance* [step̚dɑːns] and *clipboard* [klɪp̚bɔːd].

We thus say that the English phoneme /p/ has at least three major allophones: aspirated [pʰ], unaspirated [p] and unreleased [p̚].

✍ Note that in the examples above, we used the transcription [pɪɫ] for *pill* when we were discussing the allophones of [l]; we transcribed the same word as [pʰɪl] when we were discussing the allophones of /p/.

This may seem inaccurate and inconsistent, but is indeed very common in the phonetic literature. We always make our transcription as narrow as necessary for the current purposes of our discussion, and accordingly concentrate on one aspect of pronunciation while ignoring others.

This makes a lot of sense, as a maximally narrow transcription of a word, which notes all the potentially interesting details of pronunciation in all sounds, may be very cumbersome and tend to become illegible.

- Thus, if we wanted to produce such a transcription of the British English pronunciation of *pill*, we should also have to note that the vowel /ɪ/ in the middle is slightly longer than in other environments because a voiced consonant follows it. This can be expressed in the transcription as follows: [ɪˑ].

- And we might want to record the transition from [ɪˑ] to [ɫ], which is a kind of glide or velar approximant, a sort of unrounded [w], which we could transcribe as [ɰ] in accordance with IPA, and we might also wish to indicate that the articulation of this sound is very brief and transient.

An even **narrower** transcription of *pill* would thus have to look like

[pʰɪˑɰ̆ɫ].

More detail could be added almost *ad libitum*. Such a transcription, however, is hardly ever needed in linguistic description, as we usually concentrate on only one aspect of pronunciation at a time.

For many practical purposes, a phonemic (**broad**) transcription is sufficient which ignores all the detail of pronunciation

- that is predictable from the environment of each sound and
- that is not distinctive in the above sense.

Thus, in pronunciation dictionaries, and in most other discussions of pronunciation or phonology, you will find the word *pill* transcribed as

/pɪl/.

Using the slashes to indicate phonemic transcription, however, really means a commitment to a certain description of the phonemic system of the language in question. It means you subscribe to a certain phonological analysis that cuts up the sounds of the language in a certain way to assign them to phonemes. There may well be disagreement about this.

> ✍ To avoid commitment to a specific analysis, many linguists prefer to use [ ], i.e. square brackets, even in fairly broad transcriptions. On the other hand, / /, i.e. slashes, are often used in a loose way to indicate a broad transcription without any specific commitment to the correctness of a certain phonological analysis.

2.2.3   Phoneme vs. allophone

How do we recognise which sounds in a language can be grouped together as variants of one phoneme?

It is a general rule for allophones of a phoneme to be in **complementary distribution** (*komplementäre Distribution / Verteilung*). Complementary distribution of allophones means that each allophone can only occur in those environments where none of the other allophones of the same phoneme can occur. Thus, as described above, the two major allophones of /l/ in RP are in complementary distribution because 'clear' [l] only occurs in environments where 'dark' [ɫ] could never occur. Clear [l] only occurs before vowels or [j], dark [ɫ] never occurs before vowels or [j]. Clear [l] never occurs before consonants or word-finally, dark [ɫ] only occurs in these environments. That is, they show a complementary pattern of distribution. We therefore regard [l] and [ɫ] as allophones of one phoneme /l/. Our decision is further supported by the fact that [l] and [ɫ] are phonetically fairly similar (both are alveolar lateral liquids).

But note that **phonetic similarity** is <u>not</u> the decisive criterion that leads to the analysis of [l] and [ɫ] as allophones of /l/. Nor is it in any way relevant that the letters we happen to use for their description are similar, one looking just like a modification of the other. Our decision to regard [l] and [ɫ] as allophones of /l/ is solely based on their distribution and function in English; and it is a strictly language-specific decision.

> ⦿ Russian, for example, has two sounds that are fairly similar to English [l] and [ɫ]; but in Russian, these two sounds represent different phonemes which can distinguish Russian words from each other and are also, incidentally, spelled differently in Russian orthography.

This means: The fact that two sounds appear similar to us does not mean that they have to be allophones of the same phoneme.

To consolidate this, let us take two other allophone examples in English. The first is rather simple and straightforward, the second is more elaborate.

- The vowel phoneme /æ/, as was noted above (→ 2.1.1.1), is usually pronounced as an oral vowel, in accordance with its notation, but it has an occasional nasal allophone [æ̃] when it precedes a nasal that is not in turn followed by a vowel. We thus get the nasal allophone in spam *[spæ̃m]*, rang *[ræ̃ŋ]*, can *[kæ̃n]*, *and* can't *[kæ̃nt]* (*General American pronunciation*) but *not in* scanner *[skænə]*.

The origin of this allophone is easy to grasp. It is a result of what is called **coarticulation** which leads to an **assimilation** of the vowel to the following nasal (→ 2.4.2). Such processes, in particular as they remain on the subphonemic level, are so automatic to native speakers that they are usually not aware at all of allophones. Speakers of languages, however, where such a contrast matters will notice such differences, that is, in this case learners may be at an advantage over the native speakers because they 'hear more'.

> ○ Thus, the nasality of vowels is phonemic in French, and we get a contrast between
>
> > *quête* [kɛt] ('quest') and
> > *quinte* [kɛ̃t] ('musical interval of five tones').
>
> This sounds deceptively like the contrast between *cat* and *can't* in American English, but we should note that nasal vowels in English are always followed by a nasal consonant (which is no longer there after nasal vowels in French and not transcribed, accordingly). The presence of this consonant motivates the nasal vowel in English. Thus, the contrast between *cat* and *can't* in English does not lie in the vowel phoneme, but in the presence or absence of a nasal consonant. As long as this is the case, oral and nasal vowels do not contrast in English.

Coarticulation is also the background in the next example. The English phoneme /k/ has a fairly elaborate system of allophones that are, of course, determined by the different environments in which /k/ can occur. The phoneme /k/ in English can vary along several parameters that are dependent on certain features of the environment. We will discuss here the three most important ones:

- aspiration (just like we saw above with the phoneme /p/), and
- place of articulation
- release.

– Like all voiceless plosives in English, /k/ can be **aspirated** or non-aspirated. Thus, the word-initial allophone in *cull* [kʰʌl] and in *cat* [kʰæt] is strongly aspirated, whereas the allophone in *skull* [skʌl] and *scat* [skæt], which is not word-initial, is not.

– But also the place of articulation of the allophones of /k/ varies, depending on what follows it:

- – Before /l/, /r/, and open and half-open vowels (such as /ʌ/, /æ/, /ɒ/, /ɔː/ etc.) a 'neutral' place of articulation is chosen, which is describable as velar.
- – Before close and half-close vowels the place of articulation shifts to wherever the vowel is articulated:
  - – When a front close vowel or glide follows (/ɪ/, /iː/, /eɪ/, /j/), the /k/ allophone shifts to the front and becomes palatal, sounding as if followed by a short [j] sound: *kill* [kʲʰɪl], *key* [kʲʰiː], *queue* [kʲʰuː], *Kate* [kʲʰeɪt], *skill* [skʲɪl], *ski* [skʲiː], *skew* [skʲjuː], *skate* [skʲeɪt].

–   Before back close vowels and glides (/uː/, /ʊ/, /w/) the place of articulation for /k/ shifts back to become almost uvular, which we transcribe [q] in accordance with IPA. We thus get *cool* [qʰuːl], *could* [qʰʊd], *quick* [qwɪk], *school* [squːl], and *squib* [sqwɪb].

–   The third, less important parameter is release: The plosive /k/, like all other plosives, may be released or **unreleased**. Most realisations of the phoneme are released, i.e., the closure of the vocal tract is really opened in a kind of 'explosion' before the next sound is articulated. It is only when another plosive follows in rapid speech that the release of the closure is dropped: The tongue only briefly moves into the position for the articulation of /k/ and then, without actually releasing the closure and thereby making the plosive audible, the next consonant is articulated. Examples are *act* [æk̚t] or *crackpot* [kræk̚pɒt]. It is clear that an unreleased plosive can neither be aspirated nor unaspirated. The place of articulation for this allophone seems to be mostly neutral.

We thus get seven major allophones of /k/ depending on the context in which the phoneme occurs:

[k] [kʰ] [kʲ] [kʲʰ] [q] [qʰ] [k̚].

> ♦ Note that the allophones have nothing, we repeat: absolutely nothing, to do with the variation in spelling of the /k/ phoneme in Modern English orthography: /k/ can be spelled *k*, *c*, *ch* or *q*, but any of these spellings can in principle represent any of the allophones discussed (as can partly be gathered from the table below). Allophones are solely dependent on <u>phonetic</u> environment and not on spelling.

The following table (Fig. 37) shows the complementarity of their distribution in summary:

Fig. 37: The major allophones of English /k/ and their complementary distribution

	Before high and mid front (= palatal) vowels and glides	Before low and central vowels and /l/ and /r/	Before high and mid back (= velar) vowels and glides	Before plosives	Word-final
Syllable-initial	[kʲʰ] *queue*	[kʰ] *cull*	[qʰ] *cool*	-	-
Following /s-/ or vowels	[kʲ] *skew*	[k] *scull*	[q] *school*	[k̚] *asked*	[k] *ask*
Syllable-final	-	-	-	[k̚] *blackboard*	[k] *stock*

> ○   Although the variations of /k/ appear so natural to us that we hardly notice them, and become fully aware of them only with special phonetic training, they, too, are strictly language-specific and should not be expected to be found in all languages.

- Thus, in **Russian**, a /kʲ/ phoneme contrasts with a phoneme whose allophones are found further back, transcribed /k/.
- In classical **Arabic**, it is a back (in fact a uvular) plosive that is set apart as a separate phoneme, transcribed in IPA as /q/, so that the letter q in *Iraq* really makes phonological sense for Arabs. **Irak* with a [k] would be a non-word to a speaker of Arabic, just as **Deutschrand* would be to speakers of German. This means that /k/ and /q/ occur in minimal pairs in Arabic: /kalb/ means 'dog' in Classical Arabic, but /qalb/ means 'heart'.
- In **Hindi**, it is aspiration which is phonemically distinctive in plosives, so that /k/ and /kʰ/, but also /t/ and /tʰ/ and /p/ and /pʰ/, are separate phonemes which may distinguish Hindi words from each other. /tali/ means 'key' in Hindi, but /tʰali/ means 'dish'.

This means that theoretically two languages may share the same sound inventory, but have completely different phonological systems. As far as certain subparts of the phoneme system are concerned, this situation is by no means rare. In fact it often obtains between closely related dialects or accents of the same language or between different historical stages of the same language. An example will be discussed below, but before we can do this, we need another concept: '**minimal pair**'.

There is one almost fool-proof test for phonemic status of a sound difference, which is applicable in the vast majority of cases. If you are in doubt whether two sounds represent different phonemes or are allophones of one phoneme, try to find a minimal pair (*Minimalpaar*). A minimal pair is a word pair that is distinguished only by one phoneme, such as

- *beat – peat* /biːt/ – /piːt/,
- *sing – thing* /sɪŋ/ – /θɪŋ/,
- *singer – sinner* /sɪŋə/ – /sɪnə/
- *rapid – rabid* /ræpɪd/ – /ræbɪd/
- *bid – bit* /bɪd/ – /bɪt/
- *Kate – cake* /keɪt/– /keɪk/
- *house* (noun) – *house* (verb) /haʊs/ – / haʊz/.

The above examples show that /b/ and /p/, /s/ and /θ/, /n/ and /ŋ/, /d/ and /t/, /s/ and /z/, and, of course, /t/ and /k/ contrast in English, and are thus separate phonemes in this language.

The minimal pair test can also be used to decide whether a given phonetic feature is a separate phoneme, or just a feature of a neighbouring phoneme. Thus, it might be asked why the palatalisation [ʲ] in [kʲ], as in [kʲɪŋ], should not be analysed as a separate phoneme /j/. But as it is completely predictable, occurring only before front close vowels and glides, there are no minimal pairs in English of the kind *[kɪŋ] vs. [kʲɪŋ]. We just don't have a *king* without palatalisation in English. Therefore, the palatalisation is regarded as a feature of the phoneme /k/ that is realised before front close vowels. On the other hand, the [l] in [klɪŋ] is

128

counted as a separate phoneme because of the minimal pair /kɪŋ/ – /klɪŋ/: The [l] does make a difference here, the palatalisation [ʲ] doesn't.

○ Another example of this is the glottal stop in German. We saw above (→ 2.1.1.2) that it is used before vowels at the beginning of words, as in

Er ist so ein Idiot!
[ʔeɐʔɪst'zoʔaenʔɪ'djoːt]

Iss auch ein Ei!
[ʔɪsʔɔoxʔaenʔae]

This glottal stop, however is not regarded as a phoneme in German as it is an automatic onset for an initial vowel. German speakers are actually unable to start a word with a vowel that is not preceded by a glottal stop. (This is part of what often makes their accent sound 'harsh' to speakers of other languages). Thus, the glottal stop is simply a feature of certain vowel allophones.

In those varieties of English where the glottal stop also replaces a /t/ in certain environments (→ 2.1.1.2), as in

He got a lot of water bottles.
[ɪgɒʔəlɒʔəwɔːʔəbɒʔoz]

the situation is more complicated. Some instances of glottal stops must be regarded as accompanying features of initial vowels under certain conditions, as in

He's such an idiot!, which may be pronounced
[hiːz'sʌtʃən'ʔɪdjət].

In the cases in which it replaces a /t/, it may be regarded as an allophone of /t/. This is a true challenge for phonological descriptions in the classical phoneme / allophone framework because the same sounds should be uniquely assigned to the same phonemes wherever they occur. This cannot be discussed here any further.

➤ We can now turn to an example in which different historical stages of a language may have different phoneme systems even though the phonetic inventory has not changed much. Thus, Old English had much the same inventory of obstruent sounds as Modern English, as we noted above (→2.1.1.2). But the voiced fricatives were not phonemes of their own, but only allophones of a fricative phoneme specified only for place and manner of articulation but not for voice. This was a heritage from Proto-Germanic which also had no voice contrast in the fricatives. In Old English there was, e.g., the labiodental fricative phoneme conventionally transcribed /f/
- with a voiced allophone [v] (occurring only between vowels)
- and a voiceless allophone [f] (occurring in all other environments).
Later on, during the Middle English period, [v] also cropped up in environments which had been reserved for [f], in French loans, e.g. So suddenly there were minimal pairs such as *fine* vs. *vine* which had not existed in Old English.

Furthermore, a long /fː/ phoneme, spelled <ff>, had contrasted with /f/ between vowels in Old English. That was precisely the environment where /f/ had its voiced allophone [v]. Long /fː/ was shortened in the Middle English period and thus no longer distinguished from simple /f/. As a corollary, it suddenly also contrasted with [v] between vowels.

From then on, /f/ and /v/ had to be regarded as separate phonemes. (This case will be taken up again in section →3.2.1.2).

○ The Proto-Germanic heritage of the lacking voice contrast in fricatives has also led to repercussions in the German fricative system. /f/ and /v/, and /s/ and /z/, respectively, do not contrast in all environments to this day:

- /f/ and /v/ in fact only contrast word-initially, and that only because Proto-Germanic /w/ turned into /v/ at some point in the development of Standard German pronunciation, so that Middle High German /wiːn/ became /vaen/ in Present-Day Standard German, producing the minimal pair *Wein* vs. *fein*. Many dialects have not followed this development.
- /s/ and /z/ only contrast between a long vowel or diphthong and another, usually short vowel, with very few minimal pairs (*reisen – reißen*). In all other cases the occurrence of either /s/ or /z/ is predictable by rules: It is, basically, /z/ at the beginning of a syllable (/zɑːl/ '*Saal*') and /s/ at the end (/lɑːs/ '*las*').

It is such discrepancies in the way languages divide up the phonetic space into phonemes that lead to the greatest difficulties for learners, and not so much the sometimes unusual phonetic characteristics of sounds in the foreign language.

○ Thus, German learners of English usually do not find [w] difficult to pronounce (in fact it is an easy sound universally and a similar sound occurs in several dialects and regional varieties of German); what they do find difficult is to keep /w/ and /v/ apart as separate phonemes. It is thus a standard joke about Germans trying to speak English that they 'mix up' /v/ and /w/, as in *[pensɪlˈweɪnjə] (almost the 'rule' on German TV) or (very commonly heard) *[werɪˈvel].

It is thus crucial to understand the notion of phoneme and the functioning of a phonemic system when trying to study and teach the pronunciation of a language. This is not always easy to accomplish due to the largely unconscious character of these structures.

Box 24: Content vs. expression, form vs. substance

To understand fully the function of phonetics within linguistics, in particular how it differs from phonology, we need to understand a somewhat difficult distinction introduced by another classical founder father of modern linguistics, the 20th century Danish linguist HJELMSLEV (²1969 [¹1953] (Danish original ¹1943), 47-60). We introduce it here because, once understood, it really helps to clarify things.

HJELMSLEV first distinguishes two so-called **planes** (*Ebenen*) in language, superficially analogous to SAUSSURE's *signifiant* and *signifié*:

- the **expression** plane (*Ausdrucksebene*) which contains the means of expression of a language, that is, sounds or letters, combinations of these, and grammatical structures and
- the **content** plane (*Inhaltsebene*), which contains the 'meanings' that can be expressed by the means of expression in the language.

Any linguistic sign, any word, any sentence, any text must be analysed into these two planes before meaningful communication about them is possible. Failure to distinguish between content and expression planes when speaking about language leads to confusions similar to those caused by failure to distinguish between object language and metalanguage (→ Box 2).

What makes this distinction so difficult to maintain is that expression and content are like two sides of a coin: "An expression is expression only by virtue of being an expression of a content, and a content is content only by virtue of being a content of an expression" (HJELMSLEV ²1969, 48-49).

Note that this means that the distinction is not the same as that between object language and metalanguage; it is first of all a distinction drawn within metalanguage.

There is, however, a further source of confusion when speaking about linguistic expression and content: Both content and expression have a certain

- **form**, by virtue of being integrated into an abstract sign system, and they have a
- **substance** (*Substanz*), by virtue of being materialised or having a material substratum.
- On the **expression** plane this distinction corresponds to the difference between the abstract units of language: phonemes (→ 2.2.1), graphemes (→ 2.5), lexemes (→ 4.0) and the material realisations of these: sounds (allophones, → 2.2.3), sound sequences, letters, etc.
- On the **content** plane, again the formal side is the linguistic 'meaning' of the units of the expression plane; the 'substance' of the content plane is what corresponds to the meanings in the 'real world'.

Fig. 38 and Fig. 39 below show the relations between these concepts with a concrete example:

Fig. 38: Content / expression vs. form / substance (table)

content form: the meaning 'cup'	content substance: the actual cup you may be drinking from; whatever the word *cup* may refer to
expression form: the lexeme *cup* in English, the phonemes /k/, /ʌ/, /p/, the graphemes <c>, <u>, <p>	expression substance: - the sound sequence or syllable [kʌp] with its parts, the sounds [k], [ʌ], and [p]; - the letter sequence *c – u – p* with its parts, the letters *c*, *u*, or *p;*

Fig. 39: Content / expression vs. form / substance (graph)

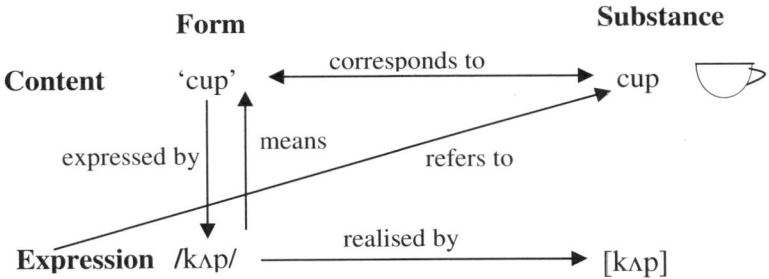

The diagram shows that the mediation between expression substance (the sounds in [kʌp]) and content substance (the 'real' cup in the 'real world') is only brought about via form, that is, via the linguistic system. The non-existence of a connection between content substance and expression substance, that is, between the real world and the sounds of language, shows the arbitrariness of language (→ Box 19; 8.1): It is only the linguistic system, the linguistic form in HJELMSLEV's terminology, that establishes this connection. The diagram is not valid for non-arbitrary signs, viz. icons (→ Box 26) and indices (→ Box 27).

✍ Note that HJELMSLEV uses the term *form* in a somewhat special sense. In many discussions on linguistics, HJELMSLEV's tetrachotomy ('four-way distinction') outlined above is reduced to a two-way distinction between **form** and **meaning** (especially in cognitive linguistics), or form and **function** (*Form / Funktion*). *Form* in this sense is roughly equivalent to HJELMSLEV's *expression form* whereas *meaning* or *function* are equivalent to *content form*.

> ☞ We prefer the HJELMSLEVian terminology here as it provides separate terminology to discuss substance and form separately, which are often confusingly mixed up. The distinction is extremely useful for succinctly characterising and discussing a lot of different phenomena and concepts in linguistics, and this usefulness shows that HJELMSLEV indeed laid important groundwork for 20ᵗʰ century linguistics and beyond. We will accordingly make use of it wherever suitable.
>
> Occasionally, will also use the simpler, more usual form / function terminology, especially when discussing approaches that do not follow HJELMSLEV in this distinction.

2.2.4 Neutralisation

Presumably every language has phonemes that do not contrast in all environments.

> ⭘ The German plosives /p/, /t/ and /k/, e.g., respectively contrast with /b/, /d/ and /g/ only at the beginning of a syllable. /b/, /d/ and /g/ do not occur as final consonants, but are replaced by /p/, /t/ and /k/ (e.g. /ɡɑːp/, /ʁɑːt/, /tɑːk/ for *gab, Rad, Tag*). The same applies to German fricatives like /v/ and /f/, /z/ and /s/. This phenomenon is called **final obstruent devoicing** (*Auslautverhärtung*). Linguists say that the opposition between voiced and voiceless obstruents is **neutralised** (*neutralisiert*) in final position in German.
> ➢ *Auslautverhärtung* is presumably originally a sound change in the history of Germanic and is still active in Present-Day German. But it is no longer applied in English, and most of its traces have vanished.
> 📖 What evidence is there in German that *Auslautverhärtung* is still active? (Think of how English words taken over into German are pronounced!)
> 📖 What traces of a former rule of final obstruent devoicing may be found in English? (Think of past tense forms ending in *-t*!).

Phonological neutralisations are not easy to find in English as they are not as straightforward as German final devoicing.

- Sometimes the rules are difficult to formulate. Thus, unstressed (→ 2.3.3) vowels diachronically underwent a large-scale neutralisation process in favour of /ə/ as can be seen in

> *information* /ˌɪnfəˈmeɪʃn/ vs. *inform* /ɪnˈfɔːm/
> *explanation* /ekspləˈneɪʃn/ vs. *explain* /ɪksˈpleɪn/
> *courageous* /kəˈreɪdʒəs/ vs. *courage* /ˈkʌrɪdʒ/
> *curious* /ˈkjʊərɪəs/ vs. *curiosity* /ˌkjʊərɪˈɒzɪtɪ/,

but only under certain conditions which are not easy to see through. It is however clear that /ə/ only contrasts with other vowels in unstressed position, and that not all vowels contrast with each other in that position.

- Sometimes a neutralisation only becomes evident when the phonological system is seen at large and at a rather abstract level. In the latter case, neutralisation does not necessarily go back to a diachronic sound change, but results from language-specific constraints on the combinability of phonemes. It will, therefore, be dealt with in the section on **phonotactics**, → 2.3.1.

2.2.5 Morphophonology

Morphophonology (morphonology, morphophonemics; *Morpho(pho)nologie*, *Morphophonemik*) is the study of phonemic variation which morphemes sometimes undergo in combination with one another (e.g. *hoof – hooves* in English; for a historical explanation of this particular example → 3.2.1.0). This includes the study of alternation series, e.g. recurrent alternations of phonemes before certain suffixes in English such as:

- electri[k]– electri[s]ity;
- preten[s] – preten[ʃ]ous.

Such alternations are from one phoneme to another, as [k], [s] and [ʃ] are certainly not allophones of the same phoneme. In many languages there are phonological rules which can only be described with reference to morphological structure. The problem of morphophonology arises from the fact that allomorphs are not generally arbitrary, but not always completely regular either. Morphophonemic allomorphs practically always arise from certain historical developments, like in the above examples, so that the rules formulating the relevant alternations often look or sound like rules describing historical changes. It should be noted, however, that morphophonemics is a strictly synchronic discipline and tries to establish the synchronically recoverable regularities. These in turn may sometimes be useful in reconstructing historical facts and developments.

Completely arbitrary allomorphs, such as English *went* (*go* + past tense), are relatively rare in the lexicon, and occur almost exclusively with a few very frequent words. This unpredictable kind of allomorphy is called **suppletion** (*Suppletion*). Completely regular allomorphs are not as rare; often they can be described by generally applicable morphological or phonological rules.

⊙ For example, in German the allomorphy of the morpheme *Bund*:

/bʊnt/ (as in *der Bund*) ~ /bʊnd/ (as in *des Bundes*)

is not an arbitrary phenomenon applying only to this particular word, but can be described by a general phonological rule of German (final obstruent devoicing, → 2.2.4). Things are different with the allomorph /bʏnd/ in *Bünde* (*Umlaut*, → 3.2.1.3). From a phonological viewpoint, a fairly simple rule applies here: German back vowels are turned into or, synchronically speaking, alternate with, the corresponding front vowels. Orthographically this rule has the corollary that <u> alternates with <ü>, <o> alternates with <ö> and <a> alternates with <ä>. But the conditions under which this rule applies can only be defined morphologically and lexically: It applies only when the plural of certain (but by no means all elegible) nouns is formed, and it applies in a number of other morphological processes (e.g. *groß – größer* and *Mann – männlich*).

A well-known example of a rather simple and inconspicuous morphophonemic rule from English is the phonologically determined allomorphy in the formation of regular plurals (→ 1.3.3):

Fig. 40: Allomorphs of plural -s in English

/ɪz/	after sibilants and affricates (/s, z, ʃ, ʒ, tʃ, dʒ/) as in *kisses buzzes, wishes, garages, batches, badges,* etc.
/s/	after voiceless consonants which are not sibilants or affricates, as in *cats, caps, cliffs, cloths*;
/z/	after voiced sounds which are not sibilants or affricates, i.e., also after vowels, as in *cabs, cads, doves, cans, manners, studios.* Note that this rule applies strictly according to phonological structure only, and ignores spelling altogether!

Such rules, which are to be formulated in phonological terms but have morphological conditions on their application, are called morphophonological rules.

What is typical of English is the great number of fairly complicated morphophonological rules in its derivational system, which have been much discussed over the last decades in connection with CHOMSKY / HALLE (1968). These rules are meant to explain alternations such as the following:

Fig. 41: Examples of morphophonological alternations in English*

/aɪ/ ~ /ɪ/, as in *derive – derivation*	/dɪˈraɪv – ˌderɪˈveɪʃn/
/eɪ/ ~ /æ/, as in *explain – explanatory*	/ɪksˈpleɪn – ɪksˈplænətrɪ/
/aʊ/ ~ /ʌ/, as in *pronounce – pronunciation*	/prəˈnaʊns – prəˌnʌnsɪˈeɪʃn/

* for further examples see also → 1.3.3.

CHOMSKY / HALLE try to formulate these rules as rules of Present-Day English, but in fact some of these rules bafflingly resemble some sound changes historical linguists have reconstructed for the development of English pronunciation. And indeed, the vowel alternations exemplified in Fig. 41 go back to a complicated series of sound changes.

> ➤ In early Middle English (→ 3.1.2), the alternating vowels in lexical items such as above did not alternate, but still had the same – non-diphthongised – quality. The Middle English Period, that is, the period in which the spelling of English was fixed, saw a major reshuffling of long and short vowels. Vowels in some positions were lengthened, in others, they were shortened or remained short. However, those vowels that were stressed (→ 2.3.3) and remained long or were lengthened for some reason, underwent, between the 15th and 18th century, a substantial change known as the **Great Vowel Shift** (*Große Vokalverschiebung*; → 3.2.1.5). Those vowels that were unstressed and short or had been shortened for some reason were not affected by this shift and remained short.

Completely unstressed short vowels were then even further weakened to /ɪ/ or /ə/. In *explanation* [ˌeksplə'neɪʃn], the secondary stress prevents weakening of [e] to [ɪ], whereas the completely unstressed <a> in the syllable *-pla-* is weakened to [ə], in contrast to *explain* and *explanatory*, where the *ex-* syllable is completely unstressed and weakened accordingly, whereas the *-pla-* syllable is stressed and receives a full vowel.

These developments have greatly contributed to the discrepancy perceived by speakers of other European languages between spelling and pronunciation in Present-Day English (➔ 2.5). Throughout all these sound changes, English spelling remained practically the same. Thus, from the result of all these developments, a set of pronunciation rules for English words, in particular those of Latin origin, has evolved which is also applied to words that didn't even exist in Middle English (s.a. ➔ 3.2.5). That is, new words formed from Latin or Greek roots, which are practically always first formed and learnt in the written form, are pronounced in English as if they had gone through all the sound changes since Middle English times.

⦿ Unfortunately for the non-native learners of English, this set of pronunciation rules is, due to the many sound changes that have occurred, and the many exceptions to them, rather complicated, and sometimes no regularity at all can be observed. What is more, the rules lead to pronunciations that differ grossly from the way speakers of other European languages are used to pronounce a given spelling so that even cognate words that we recognise in writing because our language has borrowed the same Latin word (e.g., *information*, *university*, *original* etc.) have a very different pronunciation in English (s.a. ➔ 2.5.2).

2.3 Suprasegmental phonology

Suprasegmental phonology (*Suprasegmentale Phonologie*) is concerned with those phonological properties of language that go beyond individual phonemes (segments). On the one hand it deals with the combination of segments (➔ 2.3.1) into larger units such as the syllable (➔ 2.3.2); on the other hand it deals with properties of speech that cannot be described in terms of segments at all, such as word stress, intonation (➔ 2.3.4), rhythm, etc. The latter properties are often subsumed under the label **prosody** (*Prosodie*).

2.3.1 Phonotactics

Phonology also concerns itself with the rules and restrictions regarding the combination of phonemes to form syllables, morphemes or words. This sub-area of phonology is called **phonotactics** (*Phonotaktik*). No language allows just any arbitrary combination of phonemes. The reasons for this are partly universal phonetic constraints on the pronounceability of sound sequences, partly they are language-specific.

English, for example, has fairly heavy constraints on combinations of phonemes at the beginning of a word or syllable. Although it is true that, except for /ŋ/, all single consonants may occur at the beginning of a word, combinations of two consonants have either to

- begin with an /s/ (/st/ /sp/ /sk/ /sm/ /sn/ /sl/ /sw/), or
- end with a liquid or a semi-vowel (/kr/, /kl/, /kw/, /kj/, /fr/, /fl/, /fj/ etc.).

There seem to be further constraints, as is suggested by the non-occurrence of /*fw/ or /*tl/.

Combinations of three consonants have to begin with an /s/, and the /s/ has to be followed by a 'legal' two-phoneme sequence including a plosive (/skr/, /skl/, /skw/, but not /*sfj/, /*sfr/, etc.).

The first constraint was already alluded to in → 2.2.4 as an example of neutralisation. Thus, it could be said, e.g., that all English consonants are neutralised in favour of /s/ at the beginning of a word when another consonant follows. In other words, the only consonant which may occur before another consonant at the beginning of an English word is /s/. But this does not mean that formerly other consonants were possible instead of /s/ and were then replaced by it.

> What is indeed the case, however, is that several consonants that did occur before other consonants at the beginning of words were deleted at some time in the history of English, thus reducing the inventory of initial consonant clusters in English and simplifying phonotactic rules. See, for example, *know* and *gnaw*, where the spelling, as in many cases, reflects an older pronunciation. The above rule for initial consonant clusters also asserts itself in loans such as *psychology* and *pneumonia*, which despite the spelling do <u>not</u> contain an initial consonant cluster.

2.3.2 Syllables

The syllable (*Silbe*) is an important phonological unit above phoneme level, which was – similarly to the word (→ 1.1.2) – neglected for a long time, because it was not definable in sufficiently unambiguous terms. However, many phonological rules are most elegantly described with reference to syllable structure, so that the phonological reality of the syllable is now undisputed.

When analysing syllable structure one usually distinguishes between **onset** (*Anlaut*) and **rhyme** (*Reim*). In the English syllable *string* (which happens to realise a word on its own), for example, /str-/ would be the onset, and /-ɪŋ/ would be the rhyme.

The rhyme is further divided into **peak** (nucleus), in our case /ɪ/ and **coda** (*Gipfel, Koda*), viz. /ŋ/. The peak is usually a vowel, but may also be a sonorant in English (see Fig. 42).

☞ This is where the alternative classification of sounds in which sonorants include vowels may be useful (→2.1.1.3, last ☞ box).

Onset and coda may be missing in English (→ Fig. 43 further down for an example).

Fig. 42: Syllable structure

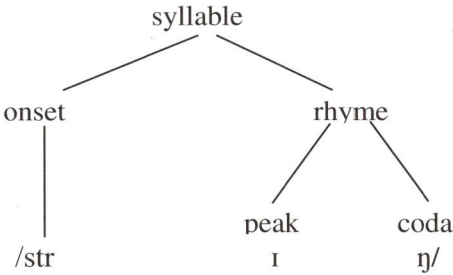

Note that syllable structure is completely independent of morphological structure (→ 1.3.1, 1.3.2) in English. A syllable may be the phonological realisation of just one morpheme or word, part of a morpheme or word, or contain several morphemes or fragments of morphemes. A morpheme or word may consist of just one syllable or several syllables, and a morpheme may also be just part of one syllable or even straddle across syllable boundaries. The following examples show some of this variety:

Fig. 43: Words with several syllables
W= phonological word; S= syllable; O= onset; R= rhyme; P= peak; C= coda

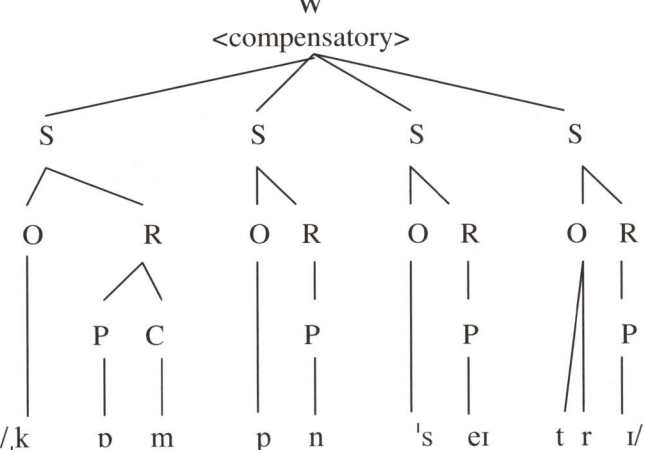

138

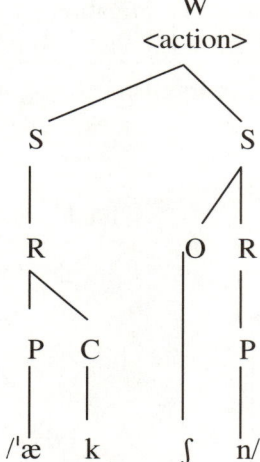

Given this minimal tool kit of syllable theory, we can describe the **allophones** of /l/ (→ 2.2.3) much more parsimoniously and elegantly than we did above. Instead of having to give a list of environments ("before vowels and /j/") for the 'clear' variant [l], we can simply state that [l] occurs before the syllable peak (as in [lɪp]), and [ɫ] never occurs before the syllable peak, that is, it occurs when /l/ either *is* the syllable peak (as in *able* [eɪbɫ]), or follows it (as in *pill* [pɪɫ]). In other words,

- the 'clear' allophone [l] only occurs in the onset of a syllable,
- 'dark' [ɫ] only in the rhyme.

It can thus be shown that introducing the notion of syllable as a structured unit into phonological theory really makes sense and helps us to improve phonetic and phonological descriptions.

2.3.3 Word stress

In most languages we observe the phenomenon that the different syllables of a word are not pronounced with equal intensity. We say that some syllables are
- **stressed** (betont),
- others are **unstressed** (unbetont).
In longer words we also have to distinguish
- **primary** (stronger) and
- **secondary** (weaker) stress.
Here are a few examples of English words with their stress patterns:

Fig. 44: Examples of stress patterns

compare	/kəmˈpeə/	summer	/ˈsʌmə/
comparable	/ˈkɒmprəbl/	temperate	/ˈtemprət/
darling	/ˈdɑːlɪŋ/	controversy	/ˈkɒntrəvəsɪ/ or /kənˈtrɒvəsɪ/
uncontrollable	/ˌʌnkənˈtrəʊləbl/	controversial	/ˌkɒntrəˈvɜːʃl/
particularly	/pəˈtɪkjʊləlɪ/	filibuster	/ˈfɪlɪbʌstə/

> ✍ Note on the transcription: The sign [ˈ] is used in the IPA to indicate that the following syllable is stressed. Secondary, weaker stress in long words is indicated by [ˌ], as in *compensatory* [ˌkɒmpnˈseɪtrɪ]. Note the difference from the widely used informal notation of stress on the stressed vowel: *bódy, ónion, còmpensátory*.

In most languages stress is a property of a particular word, that is, a word is always pronounced with the same **rhythm** (*Rhythmus*): The same syllables in a word are practically always stressed or unstressed, in whatever context the word may occur, except perhaps in a few cases when speakers vacillate between two stress patterns (as in *controversy* above).

> ⊙ Languages differ as to the principles of stress assignment to the syllables of a word, and also as to the prominence of the phenomenon.
> - In French, e.g., stress is comparatively weak and it is always the last syllable that is stressed, so that stress can be used as an indicator of word boundaries.
> - In Latin and Ancient Greek, complex stress rules apply which every student of classical languages has to learn, but they mean that stress is predictable in these languages (in Greek only partly).
> - In German, it is (in the native vocabulary) the root that is always stressed (rather strongly).
> This is in principle also true of English native Germanic vocabulary, but as it is much more difficult to distinguish between native vocabulary and loan words in English, this rule does not help very much.

It is thus more appropriate to say that in English, stress is more or less unpredictable and has to be learnt with each word, although linguists have tried to set up rules (CHOMSKY / HALLE 1968). Stress is even distinctive in some cases in English, such as in ˈimport (noun) vs. imˈport (verb). So it could be said that stress, in contrast to French, is phonemic in English, a suprasegmental phoneme, so to speak, as it forms minimal pairs.

The precise phonetic characteristics of stress are still controversial among linguists, but it seems that languages may differ in that respect as well. In English, it is **duration**, **pitch**, **loudness** (→ 2.1.2), and even the **quality** of the syllable nucleus that distinguish stressed from unstressed syllables (GUSSENHOVEN / JACOBS 1998, 206).

Stressed syllables are generally
- slightly longer,
- higher in pitch and
- louder than unstressed syllables.

Due to the strength of stress in English, interesting restrictions as to the vowel quality under stress apply. One English vowel, /ə/, which counts as weak, is not allowed as a nucleus in stressed syllables at all, and no liquid or nasal is allowed in that position either. Apart from vowels, only a limited number of sonorants is allowed as a nucleus in unstressed syllables: /ə ɪ ʊ l r m n ŋ/, and /iː/ only in some varieties and only in word-final position. These constraints lead to a number of interesting vowel alternations when stress shifts, as can be gathered from the above examples. The so-called weak forms (→ 2.4.1) of many function words (→ 1.1.3.1, ☞ box) are also the result of the peculiar strength of stress in English.

So much for the phenomenon of word stress. Stress also operates on higher levels, that is in phrases, clauses and sentences. In these domains, it interacts more strongly with pitch changes. That's why we discuss sentence stress in the following section → 2.3.4.

2.3.4 Intonation

2.3.4.1 Theoretical preliminaries: What is special about intonation?

A significant component of the phonological expression plane of language which, however, has often been neglected, is the variation and control of **pitch** (*Tonhöhe*). There are various reasons for the neglect which also tell us a lot about intonation itself.

One thing is that the relation between **expression** and **content** (→ Box 24) is not always very clear. There are many features of intonation which signal rather affective components of the meaning of an utterance and whose description is still problematic for many linguists. There are, on the other hand, also distinct relations between certain ways of expression and certain contents which are clearly delimited and linguistically definable, such as the intonation of questions or the use of intonation for marking sentence boundaries.

Moreover, intonation has some features which make it a marginal field within the system of language and which might represent a continuum from linguistic to non-verbal ways of expression. This gives us occasion to introduce a number of essential theoretical concepts of the theory of language. That's why this section consists almost entirely of boxes.

To be more precise: The principles of
- **discreteness** (→ Box 25 below), and of
- **arbitrariness** (→ Box 19), in particular, are not valid for all intonation phenomena.

Box 25: Discreteness

> **Discreteness** (*Diskretheit*) is another fundamental feature ascribed to linguistic signs: the fact that expressions on all levels are clearly set off from each other in the *langue* (→ Box 4).
>
> Thus, the sounds of a language do not vary infinitely, but are clearly distinguished from each other as a finite set of language-specific phonemes. There is no phoneme in English between /d/ and /t/, or between /ɪ/ and /e/, although in principle there are infinitely many sounds between the two. But whenever speakers of English hear such a sound, they will assign it to either /d/ or /t/, or to /ɪ/ or /e/ (→ 2.1.3). There might be languages that do have phonemes in between /t/ and /d/, or /ɪ/ and /e/. But even then it would still be a finite number, never infinitely many significant contrasts.
>
> That is, the space between phonemes is never used to signal additional meaning distinctions: i.e., phonemes are always discrete units.
>
> The same argument holds for morphemes. Although there are infinitely many meanings to be expressed, there is only a finite number of morphemes in a language to express these meanings, and each of these morphemes is clearly distinct from all the others (except in the case of homonymy → 4.1.2.1, but in this case the two expression forms are absolutely identical). Expression forms (→ Box 24) are either identical or they contrast; just as you can't be 'a little pregnant', there can't be 'a little bit of contrast' or 'a little bit of identity' between expression forms.
>
> Temperatures vary infinitely, but natural languages have only a finite number of lexical morphemes to express degrees of temperature, such English *hot – warm – lukewarm – cool – cold*, and you have to use one or another of these words to describe temperature (unless you resort to an artificial system like the numerical scales of Fahrenheit or Celsius, but even these are practically discrete unless you accept numerical expressions of infinite length).

As regards arbitrariness and discreteness in suprasegmental phonology and intonation,

> "[i]t would be generally agreed [...] that the correlation of increasing loudness of voice and rising pitch with increasing anger or excitement is iconic; and moreover that it is biologically, rather than culturally, determined" (LYONS 1977, 71).

That is, intonation features are not always arbitrary nor are they always discrete: The principle of arbitrariness does not hold for certain intonation phenomena which are **iconic** (→ Box 26) or even **indexical** (→ Box 27).

Box 26: Iconicity

An **icon** is one kind of non-arbitrary sign. In icons, there is a correspondence of properties (**isomorphism**; *Isomorphismus*), a natural or functional resemblance, or some kind of analogy of forms, between the expression substance and what it signifies, the content substance (→ Box 24 and Fig. 39). Note that the graphic representation in Fig. 39, which was meant to show the properties of <u>arbitrary</u> language signs, denied just that kind of relationship.

This means that most kinds of pictorial representations of objects will be **iconic** (*ikonisch, objektähnlich*). But also more schematic representations have this property. Part of a floor plan can signify a room because of the configuration of the lines in it. A graphic representation of some complex concept or network such as → Fig. 1 in this book may be iconic in that it shows important components of the concept and interrelations between them, in other words: It is isomorphic to this concept.

In language, the example of **iconicity** (*Ikonizität*) that is most often adduced is **onomatopoeia** (*Onomatopöie*), an apparent exception to the principle of arbitrariness. Words like *cuckoo* in English, *Kuckuck* in German, and *coucou* in French are, in their spoken form, naturally representative (at least to a certain degree) of the characteristic cry of the species of birds that they signify.

But the very fact that these 'iconic' language signs are not phonetically identical and sometimes not even particularly similar across different languages shows that they, too, are arbitrary to some extent (see also section → 8.1).

Iconicity does play an certain part in **syntax**, a fact which is taken into account both by cognitive grammar and by generative grammar.

- One indication of iconicity in syntax is that what belongs together functionally also tends to be locally close. This is sometimes called the **adjacency principle**, particularly in Generative Grammar (RADFORD [1988] 1998, 350-351). Thus, for example, determiner (where such exist) and noun are typically adjacent (*the dinosaur*) or as close as possible (*the cheerful dinosaur*), as are nouns and associated adjectives, verbs and objects (*saw the cheerful dinosaur*), prepositions and their complement (→ Box 11) (*under the dinosaur*), etc.

- A rather trivial corollary of this is

△ the relative <u>infrequency</u> of **discontinuous constituents** (*diskontinuierliche Konstituenten*), i.e. constituents that functionally belong together but are separated by other elements, as in the case of the German **brace construction** (*Satzklammer*):

> *Sie **hat** die schlimme Nachricht erst gestern über lange Umwege **erfahren*** (separation of auxiliary and past participle, and of subject and main verb),

> or in the French negation construction *ne ... pas*, e.g.

> *Il **n'**est toujours **pas** venu.*

- Another iconic link between form and function, or to be more precise, between expression substance and content substance, can often be observed in **grammaticalisation** (→ 3.2.3.3): When lexical items acquire a grammatical function, they typically lose content substance, becoming more abstract and less distinct semantically. At the same time, they often also lose expression substance, becoming shorter and less distinct phonetically. The relationship between *going to* and *gonna* may suffice as a brief example here: *gonna* only has grammatical function, no lexical meaning like *going to*. But this does not mean that *gonna* is an iconic sign. What is iconic is its formal and functional relation to *going to*. We are dealing with a kind of meta-iconicity here.

- In **lexicalisation** (→ 3.2.5.3), the loss of semantic transparency of the lexicalising unit is often accompanied, if not triggered, by a loss of phonological transparency: The phonic expression substance, i.e., the pronunciation, of *cupboard* does not involve the pronunciation of *cup* and *board* any longer; neither does the content substance of this lexicalised word contain the content substance of *cup* or *board*. Again, to forestall misunderstandings: It is not the lexicalising word that is iconic, but the relation between phonological and semantic transparency, or between phonological and semantic opacity, that is, a rather abstract semiotic relationship.

Cognitive linguists, who believe in the arbitrariness even of syntax, may rightly point out here that for all the iconic properties of syntax, the precise syntactic function of items in constructions and the precise meaning of such syntactic functions remains arbitrary, i.e. a matter of convention. Adjacency does indicate constituency, but not in all cases. And if it does, we have not gained very much. Adjacency may signal attribute – head relations, but also preposition – complement, verb – object, or object – predicative relations. In the ditransitive construction, as we saw in section → 1.2.3.2, it even signals the beneficiary – theme relation, and the order of elements in this construction is even counter-iconic: After all, the theme goes from the agent to the beneficiary; so the iconic order should be agent – theme – beneficiary. Note that the ditransitive construction is very specific to one language, English. It is even ambiguous, as a sequence of two NPs may also be an object predicative construction (Note the ambiguity of *She found him a good friend*). This also argues for an arbitrary character of this construction.

📖 In what other English construction denoting change of possession do we find the iconic order of elements?

Box 27: Indexicality

Let us also look at the third term in Peirce's classification, **index** (see also section → 8.1). Let us read the above quotation from LYONS more closely. He says that certain aspects of intonation are iconic, and then goes on to say that they are "biologically … determined". If they are biologically determined, then they are actually, pace LYONS, more likely to be **indexical**.

Indices (or indexes) (*Indizes, Indexe*), like icons, are non-arbitrary. An **index** is a sign in which a direct, natural, situational, typically causal relation exists between **content substance** and **expression substance**, but not a relation of similarity.

If you take a look at → Fig. 39 once again, you will notice that such a direct relation does not normally exist in a language sign. This simply indicates that language signs are normally arbitrary; icons and indices are not.

Thus, a mercury thermometer provides an <u>index</u> of the temperature in a room because changes in the temperature immediately cause the mercury in the thermometer to expand or contract.

In the same way, the cat's arched back may be said to be indexically, i.e. causally, related to its propensity to pounce, as this posture constitutes a preparation and prerequisite for pouncing.

And, to come back to the above example and to intonation, it could also be said that "the correlation of increasing loudness of voice and rising pitch with increasing anger or excitement" (LYONS 1977, 71) is not only iconic, but perhaps also indexical: Increasing anger may be said to increase the loudness of people's voices in a more direct way than it causes them, e.g., to say nasty things.

It may be said that these features of intonation are not linguistic; very likely they are prelinguistic. But intonation has also become integrated into linguistic systems, acquiring typical linguistic properties.

A simple example showing that intonation, too, can be discrete, is when the choice between a fall-rise tone and a rise-fall tone correlates with a difference in meaning. Thus, an utterance like *She's gone* is interpreted as a statement when the tone is a rise-fall, but as a question when the tone is a fall-rise. PIERREHUMBERT / HIRSCHBERG (1990) have shown that intonation in American English possesses a small number of discrete patterns which may be analysed compositionally, that is, each of these patterns is composed of meaningful components whose meanings combine to form the meaning of the pattern as a whole (→ Box 16).

On the other hand, an utterance like *Really?* with a rise-fall tone conveys an expressive meaning, which may be characterised as 'surprise'. This tone can be varied at will for pitch level while retaining its contour.

Any such change constitutes a change on the expression plane, whilst on the content plane the meaning 'surprise' remains constant, but varies in degree. In such a case, intonation lacks discreteness: Both the pitch level on the expression plane and the degree of surprise vary in infinitely small steps and are correlated with each other iconically and indexically: The greater the difference in pitch level, the greater the surprise. And great surprise naturally increases the differences in pitch level in people's utterances.

Last but not least, it needs to be mentioned that on the one hand, our alphabetic writing is in principle able to represent the phonological segments of our language quite accurately, but that on the other hand an appropriate notation system to represent supra-segmental phenomena is still missing.

Punctuation (*Zeichensetzung*) is the only element of our writing system which transports intonatory information, yet it does so vaguely rather than approximately. It is therefore much more difficult to mark intonation in a linguistic description without producing misunderstandings, and so far linguists have still not managed to agree either on a uniform notation or on a uniform canon of analytic categories. This shows that many linguists are still fixated on the use of alphabetical writing to a high degree.

To give you an idea of how intonation may be described, we will take a look at ARNOLD / HANSEN's ([8]1992) notation. Intonation is represented graphically by using the following symbols: (●) standing for unstressed syllables, (–) representing stressed syllables with a relatively constant pitch and (\ ) or (⌡) for stressed syllables with a falling or rising tone. In this manner the utterance *It's been a very enjoyable evening for all of us* could be transcribed as

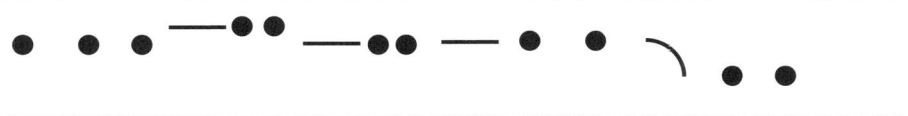

/ɪts   bɪn   ə   've   rɪ   ɪn   'dʒɔɪ   ə   bl   'iːv   nɪŋ   fər   'ɔːl   əv   ʌs/

For practical purposes, however, linguists make use of capital letters and slashes, too. Thus a word written in capital letters bears the main sentence stress, and / represents a rising, \ a falling tone:

> *It's been a /very enjoyable evening for ALL\ of us.*
> */DAS hat mich noch NIE\ interessiert.*

This simplified transcription is sufficient in many cases where precise detail is not crucial.

2.3.4.2 The function of intonation in language systems

Keeping these limitations in mind we would now like to present some results of research on intonation. To exemplify one clearly linguistic function of intonation, we start on a somewhat exotic note.

Box 28: Tone languages

❍ Pitch has a central linguistic, arbitrary and discrete function in those languages where it is lexically distinctive in a direct way: There are languages in which the pitch or the tone-curves by themselves are able to distinguish different words from each other. Such languages are called **tone languages** (*Tonsprachen*).

Especially well known tone languages are Chinese, Vietnamese and Thai, where 4 to 6 different tones are used as a means of distinguishing words. Thus, the Thai syllable /naa/ means either a nick-name, 'rice-field', a degree of kinship, 'face' or 'fat' depending on the tone it is pronounced with. Note that we have to do with small number of discrete tone patterns, not with infinite variations of pitch. So this is clearly a linguistic feature.

This might seem exotic to us, but there are similar phenomena even in European languages, as e.g. in Swedish or in certain Central-Rhenish, i.e. Ripuarian (*Ripuarisch*), Moselle Franconian (*Moselfränkisch*), and south-eastern Dutch dialects (*Limburgs*) (GUSSENHOVEN 2000). In Central Rhenish vernacular speech e.g., *rein* 'clean' is distinguished from *rein* 'in (to)' by the pitch curve on this word (Central Rhenish lexical tone, *Rheinische Akzentuierung*). The name of the river *Rhein*, by the way, is not pronounced like *rein* 'clean', but like *rein* 'in (to)' (maybe due to a realistic assessment of its water quality).

The main functions of intonation in English (and for the most part also in German) are:

- the marking of constituents of a sentence according to their felt **information content**. What a speaker regards as new in his or her utterance is stressed by intonation, what is assumed to be known moves into the background. Thus,

  /HEUTE so und MOR\GEN so

means something completely different from

  Heute /SO und morgen SO\

In the first sentence the unstressed *so* refers to something that is given, that is, known to the hearer, whereas in the second sentence it is stressed to signal that it refers to something new and different on each occurrence. Intonation is thus an important marker of **information structure** in English (see also → Box 39).

– The second function of intonation in English is the marking of certain **interactive meanings** such as question, order, request etc. Thus, in German and in English it is possible to turn each statement into a question by only changing the intonation:

  He didn't go to WORK \ today.
  He didn't go to WORK / today?

– A third function is the marking of the **completeness** or incompleteness of an utterance. A falling intonation expresses a stronger determination or the completion of an utterance, whereas a rising intonation signals uncertainty and makes the hearer understand that the utterance is not yet complete, compare the following two examples:

One/, two/, three/, four/ ...
One/, two/, three/, four

— Last but not least, the marking of special intentions and attitudes such as irony, helplessness, triumph, anger, impatience a.o. is an important function of intonation. Here it is difficult to find linguistic rules and there is a fluid transition to non-verbal forms of expression.

It is also worth mentioning that there are differences in intonation within languages. There are differences that depend on upbringing, social class, age, sex, and even, in the case of trained speakers, personal choice. Differences hold particularly between different dialects of the English language. In British English e.g., as compared to American English, a greater proportion of high initial pitches for both questions and statements can be found:

Have you been there ?

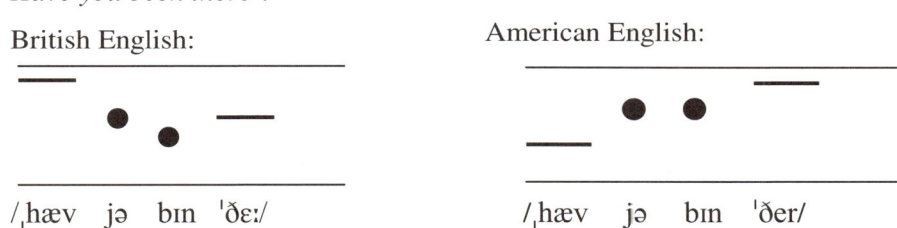

British English:

/ˌhæv jə bɪn ˈðɛː/

American English:

/ˌhæv jə bɪn ˈðer/

Apart from this, an increase in the proportion of terminal rises in British English expressing greater considerateness has been noted. Thus, a command such as

is normal when addressed to a dog, but

would be preferred for a person.

This degree of solicitude is found less in American English, where the second version may suggest that the speaker is protesting too much, exerting himself to mask the opposite feeling. Moreover, there is a tendency in today's British English intonation to have a rise of the tone not only at the end of a question but also at the end of a statement which might sound quite odd to non-native speakers.

2.4   The phonetics and phonology of connected speech

A normal phonological representation of speech, even if it keeps close to the actual pronunciation, is always an idealisation. The words are usually represented in such a way as they would be pronounced in isolation or in careful, fairly slow speech.

If however, words are connected to form larger units, then a whole series of phonetic rules comes into force, which may drastically change the phonetic shape of a word.

2.4.1   Weak forms

In connected speech, <u>lexical</u> words have roughly the same pronunciation as when they are pronounced on their own. Many <u>function</u> words (→ 1.1.3.1, ☞ box), however, change in pronunciation according to whether they are unaccented (as is usual) or accented (in special situations or when said in isolation).

As compared with the accented realisations of these words (the **strong forms;** *Starktonformen*), the unaccented **weak forms** (*Schwachtonformen*) of these words are **cliticised** (→ 1.3.2, last paragraph), that is,

-   they phonologically behave like affixes of the preceding or following word and consequently
-   show reductions in the length of sounds, obscuration of vowels towards /ə, ɪ, ʊ/, and the **elision** (complete omission of a sound that would otherwise be present) of vowels and consonants.

> ➢   This is why **phonetic attrition** or **erosion**, as this is called (→ 3.2.1.8), counts as a symptom of **grammaticalisation** in historical linguistics (→ 3.2.3.3). It is certainly one of the most powerful and omnipresent mechanisms of sound change.

The following list of examples presents the most common of these words, first in their unaccented (normal) weak form and secondly in their (less usual) accented strong form. Where the former has a standard spelling of its own, this is indicated in angled brackets < >:

Fig. 45: Weak forms (clitics) in British English
(GIMSON [5]1994, 228f., Arnold)

Auxiliary verbs	Unaccented (cliticised)	Accented
am	<'m> /m, əm/	/æm/
are	<'re> /ə/ before consonants /ər, r/ before vowels	/ɑː/ /ɑːr/
be	/bɪ/ ([bi])	/biː/
been	/bɪn, bɪŋ, bɪm/	/biːn/ (also /bɪn/ for some speakers)
can	/kən, kn, kŋ/	/kæn/
could	/kəd, kd/	/kʊd/
do	/dʊ, də, d/ ([du])	/duː/
does	/dəz, z, s/ e.g. <When's (= does) he ar- rive?> /wenz iː ə`raɪv/	/dʌz/
had	<'d> /həd, əd, d/	/hæd/
has	<'s> /həz, əz, z, s/	/hæz/
have	<'ve> /həv, əv, v/	/hæv/
is	<'s> /s, z/	/ɪz/
must	/məst/	/mʌst/
shall	<'ll> /ʃəl, ʃl, l/	/ʃæl/
should	/ʃəd/ ([ʃd])	/ʃʊd/
was	/wəz/	/wɒz/
were	/wə/ before consonants /wər/ before vowels	/wɜː/ /wɜːr/
will	<'ll> /l/	/wɪl/
would	<'d> /wəd, əd, d/	/wʊd/

Prepositions and conjunctions	Unaccented	Accented
and	(in fixed expressions) /ənd, nd, ən, n/	/ænd/
as	/əz/	/æz/
at	/ət/	/æt/
but	/bət/	/bʌt/
for	/fə/ before consonants /fər, fr/ before vowels	/fɔː(r)/
from	/frəm, frm/	/frɒm/
of	/əv, v, ə/	/ɒv/
than	/ðən, ðn/	/ðæn/
that	/ðət/	/ðæt/
to	/tə/ before consonants /tʊ/ before vowels	/tuː/

Pronouns and determiners	Unaccented	Accented
a	/ə/	/eɪ/
an	/n, ən/	/æn/
he	/hɪ, iː, ɪ/ ([hi])	/hiː/
her	/hə, ɜː, ə/	/hɜː/
him	/ɪm/	/hɪm/
his	/ɪz, ɪs/	/hɪz/
me	/mɪ/ ([mi])	/miː/
she	/ʃɪ/ ([ʃi])	/ʃiː/
some	/səm, sm/	/sʌm/
that	/ðət/	/ðæt/
the	/ðɪ/, [ði] before vowels /ðə/ before consonants	/ðiː/
them	/ðəm/ also /əm, m/	/ðem/
us	/əs, s/	/ʌs/
we	/wɪ/ ([wi])	/wiː/
who	/hu, uː, ʊ/ ([hu])	/huː/
you	/jʊ/ ([ju])	/juː/

Other	Unaccented	Accented
not	/nt, n/	/nɒt/
Saint	/sənt, snt, sən, sn/	/seɪnt/
Sir	/sə/ before consonants /sər/ before vowels	/sɜː/ /sɜːr/
there	/ðə/ before consonants /ðər/ before vowels	/ðeə/ /ðeər/

2.4.2 Assimilation

Assimilation is a phenomenon of (especially rapid) connected speech by which adjacent sounds are altered to make them more similar to each other (**partial assimilation** (*partielle Assimilation*),
–   *width* [wɪd̪θ], *eighth* [eɪt̪θ], *tenth* [ten̪θ] show alternation on the allophonic level: The usually alveolar /t/ and /d/ and /n/ are realised as <u>dental</u> allophones, i.e. the tongue makes contact with the front teeth in anticipation of the place of articulation of the following fricative.
–   *ten bikes* /tem'baɪks/ shows alternation on the phonological level, that is, one that actually leads to another phoneme being pronounced. The usually alveolar nasal in *ten* becomes a bilabial nasal in rapid or careless speech because of the following bilabial /b/ in *bikes*.
–   or even, in extreme cases, identical: **total assimilation** (*totale Assimilation*), e.g. *spaceship* /'speɪʃʃɪp/, *ten mice* /ˌtem'maɪs/, *bad guys* ˌbæg'gaɪz/). In *spaceship* the preceding sound, which would usually be /s/, becomes completely identical with the following sound /ʃ/ in casual speech. Something analogous happens in the other cases.

> 📖   Note that, e.g., /d/ may be assimilated to /g/ but never vice versa: No
> */ˌveɪddɪ'skrɪpʃnz/ *vague descriptions* are ever heard! The same applies to /t/
> and /n/. Any idea why this could be the case? Hint: It has to do with the notion
> of markedness (→ Box 10).

All the examples given are characteristic of assimilation in English in so far as assimilation is, in most cases, **regressive** (*regressive Assimilation*), i.e. the articulation of a phoneme influences that of the preceding phoneme. Alternatively this is called **anticipatory assimilation** (*antizipatorische Assimilation*) because the articulation organs, in forming the preceding sound, anticipate the articulation of the following sound.

In addition to regressive assimilation there is also
–   **progressive assimilation** (*progressive Assimilation*) (one phoneme influences the following phoneme), which is much rarer (e.g. if /s/ becomes /ʃ/ in *lunch score* /'lʌntʃˌʃkɔː/), and
–   **coalescent assimilation** (*reziproke Assimilation*) (the phonemes in question fuse into a third phoneme, e.g. /t/ and /j/ become /tʃ/ in *don't you* /dəʊntʃə/ or /s/ and /j/ become /ʃ/ in *kiss you* /kɪʃʊ/.

All types of assimilation involve **coarticulation** (*Koartikulation*), i.e. the retention of a phonetic feature that was present in preceding sound, or the anticipation of a feature that will be needed for a following sound (or a combination of both). Coarticulation is the cause for assimilation and for most cases of allophony.

Rapid connected speech sometimes creates combinations of sounds which otherwise go against the phonotactic rules of the language in question, e.g.

English *you can go* /jʊkŋ'gəʊ/, or

Berlin underground station attendants' German *Einsteigen!* /ˈaenˌʃtaeŋ/ (closer to Standard German) or /ˈaenˌʃtaeɲ/ (closer to Berlin dialect).

It sometimes even produces sounds that otherwise do not occur at all in the language in question, e.g. the occasional pronunciation in English of *the difficulty* as [d̪ːɪfxltɪ], where the definite article *the* completely fuses with the following sound, leaving a trace in the dental rather than alveolar articulation and in an audible lengthening of this sound [d̪ː], and the plosive consonant /k/ develops an allophone [x], otherwise unheard-of in Modern English. It is rather diffult to describe such pronunciations in terms of classical phonology, which is why phonologists usually restrict their scope of description to a so-called careful speech style.

> ➢ Assimilation is a powerful, though not the only, motor of sound change. Once two clearly distinct allophones have developed through assimilation, they sometimes develop into separate phonemes (**phoneme split**). Examples will be discussed in section ➔ 3.2.1.0.

2.4.3   Linking /r/ and intrusive /r/

In connected speech an /r/ phoneme is often added in British English, which would not occur if the word(s) in question were pronounced in their isolated forms. They prevent the vowels of two immediately adjacent syllables to directly succeed one another.

Fig. 46: Examples of linking /r/ and 'intrusive' /r/

Linking /r/	Intrusive /r/
My car is gone /maɪˈkɑːrɪzgɒn/	*China and Japan* /ˈtʃaɪnərəndʒəˈpæn/
They're at home /ðeərətˈhəʊm/	*We saw him* /wɪˈsɔːrɪm

The difference between intrusive /r/ and linking /r/ is that in the case of intrusive /r/ the addition of this phoneme is neither historically nor orthographically justified. While linking /r/ is a normal feature of educated fluent British speech, intrusive /r/ is sometimes frowned upon by normative purists.

> ➢ The introduction of 'intrusive' /r/ constitutes a textbook example of a phonological change by rule simplification. As long as /r/ is only inserted after words which historically contained an /r/, the rule was, for speakers without knowledge of dialects that had kept the old /r/, lexically conditioned: Speakers had to remember which words allowed /r/-linking and which didn't. The use of 'intrusive' /r/ means that speakers have turned the rule into a purely phonological rule: An /r/ is inserted in word-final position after certain vowel phonemes if the next word begins with a vowel. These '/r-/inducing' vowels are:

- all instances of /ə/ (including the centring diphthongs),
- /ɑː/, /ɔː/, /ɜː/,
- and the new monophthong /ɛː/ (→ 2.1.1.1.4).

It is clear that a phonological rule is easier to learn than a lexically conditioned rule. This change was to be expected since most centring diphthongs, the results of /r/-vocalisation, had merged (→ 3.2.1.6) with tense vowels that were not originally the result of such a vocalisation.

2.5 Writing

2.5.1 Graphemics and spelling

Modern linguistics has had a somewhat problematic relationship to topics related to writing and written language. Writing is a relatively late invention in the development of the human race (see below). Human beings have lived and used language without writing for a much longer time, many millennia before writing came into being. Even today, some cultures make do without writing, and the majority of the world's languages is still unwritten. Modern theoretical linguists' interest in language has mainly been focused on universal properties of human language. Writing is obviously not among those properties and was, in consequence, not looked into very thoroughly. It was regarded as a mere way of representing spoken language without any interesting properties of its own.

Linguistic interest in written language only awoke in the mid 1980s when a number of pioneering publications appeared. Today it is generally acknowledged that the written forms of the languages are systems of their own which cannot be described by simply referring to phonological properties. The fact that often lexicon and syntax and particularly the structure of texts in written language are completely different from those in spoken language will be dealt with in section → 6.3.1. In this section, we are interested in the smallest units of writing, which obviously have nothing in common with the smallest units of spoken language: Phonemes are based on hearing and acoustic properties, letters and other written signs are visible marks on paper or other material.

We will first look at **alphabetic writing** (*Alphabetschrift*), which is used by practically all European languages, most commonly in the form of the **Roman alphabet**. In a first linguistic approach, we can say that the letters of an alphabet in their physical properties are a special kind of **expression substance** which of course differs completely from sounds.

💣 For this reason alone, it is nonsense to say that a language "is spoken as it is written". What is usually meant by such rather unprofessional statements is, at best, that the correspondence between sound units (such as phonemes) and letters happens to be fairly regular or transparent in a certain language, more often that the sound – letter correspondences in the language in question are the same as in the mother tongue of the person making this statement.

Such ethnocentrism has of course no rational basis. There is no 'natural' relation between certain sounds and certain letters. Finding a spelling system for a given language always involves a system of arbitrary rules relating letter and sound to each other. When dealing linguistically with letters and sounds, the two should be dealt with separately, each in their own right, and should by no means be confused with each other, which is one the most frequent fallacies which lay people talking about language fall prey to.

To talk professionally about writing systems, we use a linguistic terminology which is analogous to that of phonology. The smallest unit in writing is called **grapheme** (*Graphem*) (which corresponds as a rule to a letter of an alphabet as a systematic unit in the writing system) and its variants are called **allographs** (*Allographe*). To distinguish them from phonemes and from allophones, graphemes are written in angle brackets < > . Consequently, small and capital letters, such as *s* and *S* e.g., would be allographs of the grapheme <s> in Latin writing. In Gothic script the grapheme <s> had one allograph more than today, due to the difference of 'round' and 'sharp' *s*.

A combination of two graphemes which stands for one phoneme in a language, such as <ch>, <ea> etc., is called a **digraph** (*Digraph*). Note that <ch> is a digraph both in English and German, but with different sound value, whereas <ea> is a digraph in English only, as it usually stands for one phoneme in that language, but not in German, where it is not very common at all and normally pronounced as two phonemes, such as in <kreativ> /kʁeatiːf/. The linguistic study of grapheme systems is called **graphemics** (*Graphemik*) (<u>not</u> graphology!).

➤ Especially in the research on extinct languages which are available only in written form, the examination of grapheme systems is of high importance. Strictly speaking, one ought not to do phonology here, but only graphemics. The phonology of such languages can be inferred only indirectly from their graphemics, by comparison with other grapheme systems or from other sources.

Today, most of the grapheme systems by far are officially fixed and their use is settled by strict norms which have been created expressly for that purpose. Such an official writing norm is called **orthography** or **spelling** (*Orthographie*; *Rechtschreibung*). For the most part, an offence against this norm is less accepted from a social point of view than an offence against pronunciation norms, since to the minds of many, especially of educated people, orthography is simply <u>the</u> rule-system of language.

Of course, the relation between the phoneme and grapheme systems of a language is also quite interesting. Here, languages differ immensely. Originally most alphabets matched more or less exactly the phoneme system of the languages for which they were used.

For most languages the optimal orthography would be an orthography in which one and only one grapheme corresponds to each phoneme, and in which each grapheme represents one and only one phoneme. Such a spelling is called **phonemic spelling** (*phonemische Schreibung*).

☛ It is nonsensical to call such a spelling "*phonetic spelling*", as often happens in the semi-professional literature. As we saw in section → 2.2.2, a <u>phonetic</u> spelling would have to (unnecessarily and confusingly for the native speaker) distinguish all allophones, if not record all minute detail of pronunciation, which none of the people who use this term would be able to do.

◉ Modern languages rarely use ideal phonemic spellings. Even Latin spelling is not optimally phonemic because it is a stupid adoption of an alphabet that was not designed for the Latin language. Some of the congenital defects of the Latin alphabet plague users of many European languages to this day, e.g. the use of three (!) different letters, <c>, <k> and <q>, for <u>one</u> /k/ phoneme. Apart from problems arising from the adoption of an unsuitable alphabet, the older the writing tradition of a language becomes, the more other factors are added so that there is often only a very inconsistent relation between phoneme and grapheme. Extreme examples of this are provided by English and French.

➢ One reason for the chaotic use of certain graphemes in English spelling is the fact that spelling became fixed very early in time. It had become fixed e.g. before certain important sound changes took place (→ next ➢ box below and 3.2.1.5). Another reason was the influence of French on the English language after the Norman Conquest in 1066. In British English spellings like *colour* or *theatre*, for example, were a result of the French influence.

2.5.2 English spelling

➢ The history of English spelling is comparable to that of other European languages, except that Old English was among the very first vernacular languages (→ 7.1.3, ☞ box) to be written at all. Very few very early documents are extant written in **Runic** script (*Runenschrift*), an alphabet ultimately and on mysterious paths derived from the Greek alphabet and occasionally used by some pre-Christian Germanic tribes. Along with Christianisation (from the late 6th century onwards), Old English began to be written (mainly by monks) in a Latin-based script supplemented by some letters borrowed from Runic. We find them in words such as *þæt* ('that') or *ōðer* ('other'). Incidentally: The macron (the line above vowels to indicate length) is not originally part of Old English spelling, but was added by modern scholars to facilitate pronunciation.

> The letters <þ> ('*thorn*'), <ð> ('*edh*'), and <æ> ('*ash*') disappeared until the end of Middle English. Their function was taken over by already existing letters (of Latin origin), and combinations of these respectively, which rendered the spelling less phonemic, i.e. less transparent. Spelling partly came under the influence of French spelling habits. Thus, the good Old English <hus> was suddenly spelled <house>, even though the pronunciation hadn't changed! Spelling was more or less fixed in the 14th to 15th century, mainly due to the influence of the printing press and did not adapt to later changes in pronunciation, although a lot of variation persisted ($\rightarrow$ 3.1.2; 3.1.3).

It is presumably undisputed among learners of English, and also among most of its native speakers, that English spelling is extremely difficult. This is because the correspondences between graphemes and phonemes in this spelling system seem extremely inconsistent and unreliable. Mismatches in the relations between phonemes and graphemes can be found all over the English vocabulary. Thus, the phoneme /ɔː/ can be represented by a large number of different graphemes or grapheme combinations such as

-    <o> (*glory*),
-    <a> (*all*),
-    <oor> (*door*), etc.,

and the digraph <ou> can represent several phonemes such as

-    /aʊ/ (*stout*),
-    /əʊ/ (*soul*),
-    /ɔː/ (*bought*),
-    /uː/ (*youth*) or
-    /ʌ/ (*young*).

The inconsistency between sound and writing also becomes obvious if you look at words like *name, fate, behave* and compare them to the word *have*. Another inconsistency is created by the fact that many words contain letters which do not seem to have any counterpart in the pronunciation. A linguistic joke says that actually all letters are silent letters in English, referring to the following list:

Fig. 47: 'Silent letters' in English

<a>	as in	*bread*	<m>	as in	*mnemonic*
<b>	as in	*debt*	<n>	as in	*autumn*
<c>	as in	*victuals*	<o>	as in	*people*
<d>	as in	*handkerchief*	<p>	as in	*psychology*
<e>	as in	*give*	<r>	as in	*iron*
<f>	as in	*halfpenny*	<s>	as in	*island*
<g>	as in	*gnaw*	<t>	as in	*castle*
<h>	as in	*hour*	<u>	as in	*guard*
<i>	as in	*friend*	<w>	as in	*wrong*
<k>	as in	*know*	<x>	as in	*grand prix*
<l>	as in	*calm*	<z>	as in	*pince-nez*

Nevertheless, one should not overlook that there are also many **pronunciation rules** which point at regularities of relations between graphemes and phonemes. Many regularities can be explained by the type of (written) 'syllable' of which a vowel in a word is part. Thus the vowels in *bite* [baɪt] and *bit* [bɪt], or in *fate* [feɪt] and *fat* [fæt] are pronounced differently; *bite* and *fate* have a diphthong in pronunciation because the vowel letters are followed in writing by one consonant letter plus <e> ('open syllable'). In *bit* and *fat* the vowel is short because no <e> follows the final consonant letter ('closed syllable').

> ➢ This is the result of sound changes which took place in Middle and Early Modern English. In Middle English, vowels in open syllables (which were phonologically open syllables at that time because the final <e> was still pronounced) were lengthened under certain conditions. These lengthened vowel then underwent the Great Vowel Shift which eventually led to the present-day pronunciation (➔ 3.2.1.5). The spelling was not changed accordingly.
>
> ❍ As a rule, languages with younger writing traditions have a grapheme system which corresponds more consistently to the phonemic system (e.g., Turkish and Finnish). Occasionally there are also spelling reforms (*Rechtschreibreformen*) with the aim of restoring or achieving precisely these correspondences (as e.g. in Russian in 1917, in Dutch and in Hungarian).
>
> The recent reform of German orthography did not react to sound changes that had obscured sound-letter correspondences, but to complaints about some inconsistencies and difficulties that German writers had lived with ever since DUDEN.

2.5.3   Non-alphabetic writing systems

❍   Alphabetic writing is not the sole possible way for a language to take on a written form, though.

- The oldest writing systems were systems in which each morpheme is represented by one sign. Today this kind of writing is still used for Chinese. It is called **logography** (*Ideographie, Logographie*). It has to be pointed out, however, that this kind of writing is as arbitrary as any other writing system. It is not to be equated with **pictograms** (*Piktogramme*), that is, signs directly representing meanings, such as found in airports etc.
- Many ancient logographies developed into **syllabographies** (*Silbenschrift, Syllabographie*), like the famous cuneiform writing (*Keilschrift*) of the ancient Middle East, one of the oldest writing systems in the world, or into mixed systems of logography and syllabography, especially when they were taken over by other languages. Today the best known mixed system is Japanese writing, perhaps the most elaborate and puzzling writing system in the world.

3 The history of English

Box 29: Diachrony vs. synchrony. Historical linguistics

One can approach all different aspects of language, such as grammar, vocabulary, semantics, phonology, etc., from two different points of view:
- **Diachronic linguistics** (*diachrone Linguistik*) studies language in its development across time (this is what the term *diachronic* means).
- **Synchronic linguistics** (*synchrone Linguistik*) tries to understand the functioning of language through the study of language at a single point of time, without reference to earlier or later stages.

Originally, the dichotomy **diachrony / synchrony** (*Diachronie / Synchronie*) was introduced into linguistics by Ferdinand de SAUSSURE ([[1]1916] 1965, 117), in reaction to the then traditional overemphasis on historical approaches and the failure to recognise the significance of synchronic data, and synchronic explanations repectively.

For most practical purposes, diachronic linguistics is largely identical with what is called **historical linguistics** (*historische Linguistik*) – after all, it always means going back into history. However, the two should not be completely equated. Historical linguistics is the study of earlier stages of languages, and this can, in principle, be done from a synchronic or a diachronic perspective. The term *historical* thus refers to the point in time at which a certain language under study is situated, whereas the term *diachronic* refers to a perspective, irrespective of whether we look at present-day language or at a historical stage. In practice, however, historical linguists for the most part take a diachronic perspective, and present-day language is almost exclusively studied from a synchronic perspective.

In this chapter, we try to present a very concise **diachronic** overview of the English language. We will also take a diachronic perspective on some fairly recent or ongoing developments. We will take a closer look at both the external and internal history of English, the latter with special reference to different levels of language change and respective methods of analysis, focusing on such developments as can throw light on certain interesting or puzzling properties of the present-day language and on differences between English and German.

3.1 External history

English did not fall from heaven. Its origin and development up to now reflect the cultural history of its speakers. In fact, what we label "English" today has been shaped by sixty (!) generations and more. (You may want to try to imagine this time span.) A lot can and actually did happen in the meantime, historically and, thus, linguistically. First of all, we will deal with particularly those historical or sociopolitically relevant facts that had an impact on the course of English. This is usually called the **external history** or outer history of a language (*äußere Sprachgeschichte*). From our ex post perspective, this course was occasionally non-linear and hardly predictable, which shows all the more that history and language must be regarded as irrevocably intertwined matters.

In the following, for the sake of convenience, we will distinguish five phases and group the language-external events according to the approximate start/end dates given below.

Old English	450-1150
Middle English	1150-1500
Early Modern English	1500-1800
Late Modern English	1800-2000
Present-Day English	2000-

☞ It should be clear that the dates given reflect arbitrary divisions which are not really matched by real sudden changes. They are, however, motivated by momentous events in external history and the onset or completion of certain important developments in internal history. Accordingly, there may be disagreement among historical linguists about the precise delimitation of the periods.

3.1.1 The onset: the formation of Old English

English is a Germanic language which was imported from continental Europe to the British isle. Before, there were only Celtic tribes and some speakers of Latin whose languages were both very different in nature to the 'oldest' English (→ 3.2.1.0 below). Thus, the pre-invasive (linguistic) events in Britain, i.e. the time before the arrival of the first Germanic settlers in the 5th century, could not affect English (as it did not exist yet). Let us have a look at how it came into existence.

The pre-history of the English language does not start until the beginning of the 5th century A.D. The Roman Empire, which had included most of what is now England, was about to collapse. All of Britain was inhabited by Celtic speaking tribes, among them Picts and Scots in the north. As the Romans withdrew, they left a power vacuum in the south of the island, and the northern tribes began to raid the former province. Local Celtic tribes did a hard job against them and, reportedly, called for assistance. They found it among certain Germanic tribes on the neighbouring continent. This development gave way to the subsequent Germanic invasions and thus, to the 'birth' of the English language.

For more than a hundred years from the mid-5th century onwards, there was an influx of several Germanic tribes of the North Sea shores (i.e. today's coastal area of Germany and Denmark). The **Jutes** (*Jüten*) and some of the **Frisians** (*Friesen*) constituted the first wave; **Angles** and **Saxons** (*Angeln und Sachsen*) followed. Together with their armed forces, settlers came in considerable num-

160

bers and soon felt at home from Northumbria to what is now Wessex and Kent. In the event, the Celtic-speaking peoples were repelled to the rims of the island, namely to today's Scotland, Wales, Cornwall, and beyond.

> ○ Celtic languages are spoken as minority languages to this day in Ireland (Irish), Scotland (Gaelic (*Gälisch*)) and Wales (Welsh (*Walisisch*)); the Celtic language of Cornwall, Cornish (*Kornisch*), survived until the late 18th century.

Seven unstable Germanic kingdoms were established side by side (i.e. the so-called Anglo-Saxon heptarchy). In terms of language, we can distinguish four main, yet intelligible dialect areas (→ 7.1.1) in these territories. Henceforth, these Northumbrian, Mercian, West Saxon and Kentish dialects constitute the first stage of English – conventionally named **Old English** (*Altenglisch*).

> ○ To begin with, it must have been closely related to the Saxon dialects that continued to be spoken on the continent, to begin with in an area stretching from what is now Westfalia to the Elbe and Saale rivers. These dialects developed into what later became known as **Old Saxon** (*Altsächsisch*), of which written documents from around 800 A.D. are extant. It was to become more or less the ancestor language of **Low German** (*Niederdeutsch, Plattdeutsch*). To this day, German dialectologists identify a 'Saxon' dialect area in Germany, extending from Westfalia in the West via Lower Saxony and Saxony-Anhalt to the Free State of Saxony in the East.
> ☞ The term *englisc* ('English'), originally denoting the language of the Angles, soon in the Old English period referred unanimously to all Anglo-Saxon-Jute dialects, as these were perceived as mutually intelligible.

Fig. 48: Dialects of Old English (BAUGH / CABLE [4]1993, 52)

In the 9th century, Wessex became the most influential of the above-mentioned kingdoms. The reign of King Alfred (871-889) can be seen as the first heyday in the history of English. He beat invaders from Scandinavia who had raided the coastline time and again. Further, the economy and cultural life prospered, leading to a substantial amount of literature, e.g. a translation of the New Testament in Old English. Most sources today are thus in West Saxon which established as a quasi-standard (→ 7.1.3). Its prestige lasted until the Norman Conquest.

However, Alfred could not prevent that wide parts in the east of the isle remained under Scandinavian rule, which became known as the **Danelaw**. Dane kings even seized the English throne for a short period in the 11th century.

Why is this important? In terms of language, English borrowed several elements, both lexical and grammatical, from **Old Norse** (*Altnordisch*) which the Danes spoke. The close relatedness of the Germanic languages Old Norse and Old English might have eased the intermingling.

With the help of the following example from *Beowulf*, an all-famous epic, we may obtain a first impression what the Old English language, in this case manifested in poetry, was like. It may seem foreign for many reasons; apparently, the language, including its orthographic representation, has changed considerably since. However, it might be closer to Present-Day English or even German than expected – you may want to check whether you can recognise some elements:

> … *þæt wæs gōd cyning! Ðǣm eafera wæs æfter cenned*
> *geong in geardum, þone God sende folce tō frōfre;* … (ll. 11-14)

'…that was a good king! Afterwards, a son was born to him
a young boy in his yard, whom God sent as a comfort to the people; …'

The earliest English records, though, date from approximately 700. These rare instances are mostly fragments in Runic script (→ 2.5) emblazing e.g. the Franks Casket, the monumental Ruthwell Cross, or individual jewelry items.

3.1.2 The transformation: Middle English

The battle near Hastings in 1066 and the Norman Conquest respectively, as we may recall from our school days, represents a milestone in the history of the English civilization. In a period that saw several claimants to the English throne, William, the Duke of Normandy, later to become known as William the Conqueror, was finally crowned as his mastery was uncontested soon after the battle. Yet, years of social disorder followed; in the event, the executive forces, including the aristocracy and clergy, were thoroughly replaced. Subsequently, many Normans settled in England by the end of the 12th century. These and the new upper class, although they originally were of Scandinavian origin, spoke a northern French dialect exclusively, known as **Norman French**. A fact which had far-reaching consequences with respect to language development. A Romance language now took over all official and elitist functions, including the prestigious domain of literature. English was thus demoted to a locally used, albeit majoritarian, substandard (→ 7.1.3).

The coexistence of French and what we from now on call **Middle English** (*Mittelenglisch*) mirrored, before all, the social distinction of their speakers. Nevertheless, language contact became more and more inevitable; the social layers became permeable (e.g. by intermarriages) and gradually fused. At the same time, the mastery of French was on the wane and a more positive attitude towards English, and its exclusive use respectively, spread. English reclaimed its formerly lost functions as a spoken and written medium (→ Box 40) and even gained new domains traditionally reserved to Latin (which had been conservatively cultivated in monasteries since the christianisation and as the language of records). Peasants, guildsmen, school teachers, barristers, members of parliament – all were gradually united by English, which gave considerable momentum to a growing sense of English, i.e. national, identity. This was the time when a political rivalry with France culminated in the Hundred Years' War (1337-1453), which ultimately led to the loss of influence of the English on the continent and thus to a dissociation from continental affairs, including the French language. The general adoption of English was followed and backed by the triumph of the printing press which was introduced by William Caxton in 1476. The impact of this innovation on the development of the English language can hardly be overstated. A new, modern era could set in (→ 3.1.3).

By the end of the 15th century, the French influence in particular had left its marks on the English language, with immense consequences for grammatical structure in general, lexical quantity, and semantic specification. In fact, these marks formed an integral part of an utterly remodelled form of English that was used in all conceivable domains, i.e. from vulgar speech to exalted writing. Interestingly, at the same time, the dialectal diversity throughout England increased.

During this Middle English period, more and more individual authors began to use English confidently and artistically. The Bible translation by John Wycliffe, the secular works of John Gower, William Langland and, particularly, Geoffrey Chaucer laid the new foundation for the use of English as a literary language. An example from Chaucer's (end-14th century) *Canterbury Tales* may provide a first glimpse at the character of Middle English:

> *Have pitee of my bitter teeris smerte, and taak myn humble preyere at thyn herte... I ne have no langage to telle th'effectes, ne the tormentz of myn helle.* (*The Knight's Tale*, ll. 1367-1370)
> 'Have pity on the pain of my bitter tears, and take my humble prayer to your heart... I do not have words to tell the effects and the torments of my hell.'

3.1.3 The eve of modernity: Early Modern English

Modern English encompasses five centuries up to the turn of the millennium. Being aware of fuzzy boundaries, we may distinguish between an early and a late phase.

The 16th and 17th centuries saw, among other culturally relevant events, the promotion of mass literacy, Protestant Reformation movements, civil wars, revolutions, diversified scientific progress, overseas discoveries and settlements, and the so-called English Renaissance with its manifold artistic achievements. Named after the Tudor queen Elizabeth I. (1533-1603), this Elizabethan Age gave rise to the future role of England – and the English language accordingly – as a veritable global player.

With respect to literature, William Shakespeare, as you might have expected, is the chief representative of this period. His skilful linguistic performance is, and this is a sign of the times, characterised by a liberal and creative use of words, including extensive borrowing (→ 3.2.5.1) and neologisms (→ 3.2.5.2). Shakespeare and contemporaries such as Bacon, Marlowe or Spenser have significantly contributed to the English language, thus enforcing its ever-developing character. Let us consider some original lines from *Julius Caesar* (1599) to get an impression of what linguists call **Early Modern English** (*Frühneuenglisch*):

> *He hath brought many Captiues home to Rome,*
> *Whose Ransomes, did the generall Coffers fill:*
> *Did this in Cæsar seeme Ambitious?*
> *When that the poore haue cry'de, Cæsar hath wept* (III.2,92-95)

You may note that a present-day translation is less and less imperative to grasp the meaning of the words. More recent versions of the play, for example your school copy, are nevertheless linguistically modernised (except for, perhaps, some ostensibly old-fashioned elements).

Reflecting an increasing awareness of 'things English', the 17th and 18th centuries were characterised by a general societal quest for identity and stability. One of the major playgrounds was language.

With the growing economic importance of London in the Early Modern English period, the local dialect was more and more felt to meet the speakers' demands of (supraregional) prestige. The choice of the metropolitan dialect soon became a marker of social class and represented the impetus for the promotion of a **standardisation**, the effects of which last until today (→ 7.1.3).

In consequence, a lasting set of rules in terms of grammar and orthography was wanted which should be adhered to by all, particularly in the growing number of print media (including translations of classical Greek and Latin originals). In this regard, first authoritative grammars and dictionaries were published, with Samuel Johnson's *Dictionary of the English Language* (1755) and Noah Webster's *A Grammatical Institute of the English Language* (1784) being prescriptive models in Britain and the young United States for the years to come. Therein, consistent and normative principles for the use of English were provided in order to enhance it and to totally emancipate it from French or Latin. At the end of the day, however, the attempts to level out the lot of exceptions were not successful. Thus, orthography, e.g., has remained, more often than not, deceptive for learners of English.

3.1.4 Becoming global: Late Modern English

☛**Late Modern English** is occasionally (and confusingly) termed *Later Modern English*, *Modern English*, or *Present-Day English*. As always, terminology is a matter of convention.

The imperialist British Empire, which had expanded ever since the union with Wales, Scotland, and Ireland, reached its height in the 19th century. The decline of the colonial era in followed. Former colonies from Australia to Jamaica became successively independent; the US itself rose to a world power, which gave another boost to English and the sheer quantity of its speakers. This **Late Modern English** (*Spätneuenglisch*) period was further characterised by the breakthrough of democracy, mass mobility and telecommunication, all of which reflecting cultural and technological quantum leaps.

These events, accompanied by scientific progress in new fields from psychology to space travel, led in total to an enrichment of the vocabulary ($\rightarrow$ 3.2.5.1). The English language became, due to its additional global spread, progressively more cosmopolitan in nature. The becoming a world-wide means of communication showed, among other things, in the recognition of English as an official, if not *the* official language of the United Nations.

In terms of **language planning** ($\rightarrow$ 7.2.3), continued (yet on the whole, vain) attempts to modernise the spelling were made. The huge undertaking to compile and revise the *Oxford English Dictionary* (*OED*) since the end of the 19th century, however, is invaluable in terms of a public historical awareness of the language, and its vocabulary respectively. This comprehensive dictionary, now available online, also pays tribute to the increasing influence of non-standard usage, e.g. slang, in speech or the ever-growing bulk of literature. Authors influential to the English language became legion and more and more non-British in this period.

3.1.5 New communicative modes: Present-Day English

It is expedient to establish a separate period in our third millennium which has only just begun. There are several main reasons to do so.

English has become a must in the vast majority of international transactions; domains such as tourism or academic discourse draw upon English today, though it may not be the first (or even the second) language of its users. Moreover, the status quo of English includes the more and more distinctive postcolonial (national) varieties, i.e. the so-called new Englishes, e.g. in Africa of South Asia ($\rightarrow$ 7.3). There, language contact is the key factor that contributes to a reshaping of the diversity of English.

The utilitarian use of **Present-Day English** (*Heutiges Englisch*) is particularly promoted by the information revolution that is currently going on (JUCKER 2000). English has become the primary medium ($\rightarrow$ Box 40) of electronic publication forms across national boundaries with the help of computer technology. Multimedia platforms on the WorldWideWeb, for example, are just a click away; there, new modes of communication can be performed, such as e-mail, interactive chat or hypertextual linking. In this regard, the quantity and the acceleration of knowledge exchange is not only beyond historical compare, but was also unthinkable to generations before us. Yet, we may always beware: What is English today can be contested by another language tomorrow.

Indeed, these are catchy examples of English a-changin' presently due to external factors. They show that the language has come a long way since its origins more than 1500 years ago. Now, to complete the diachronic outline, we need to throw some light on the details of change from a language-internal perspective. This is done in the following subchapter. The order if treatment will not be chronological, however, but systematic. The focus will be on changes which have left lasting traces in the structure of English or which account for differences between German and English.

3.2 Internal history and types of language change

Language change is inevitable – it may be seen as the essence of language itself. Only usage tells whether changes are a blind alley, short-lived, or significant thoughout generations and thus for further possible change. As a consequence, speakers of earliest English, time-warped into the here and now, would rather not be understood by today's users (besides other problems, of course). Still, they are united under the umbrella of a common language.

For the sake of a synopsis, the following verse from the Gospel of Matthew (8, 20) allows an ad hoc comparison of the phases, and important linguistic characteristics respectively.

Old English	*Foxas habbað holu and heofenan fuglas nest;* *sōþlice mannes sunu næfð hwǣr he hys hēafod āhylde.*
Middle English	*Foxis han dennes, and briddis of heuene han nestis,* *but mannus sone hath not where he shal reste his heed.*
Early Modern English	*The foxes have holes, and the bryddes of the ayer have nestes,* *but the sonne of the man hath not wheron to rest his heede.*
Late Modern English	*Foxes have their holes, and birds their roosts,* *but the Son of Man has nowhere to lay his head.*

As not all changes can be pointed out in detail here, only some features and methods of analysis will be highlighted. Yet, these hint at the multi-facetedness and dynamism of language change that we may discover step by step according to the interacting domains phonetics and phonology, morphology, syntax, vocabulary and semantics. Some cases of semantic change which can only be fully understood against the background of pragmatic theories, will be taken up in section → 5.4. Other or more specialised changes, such as pragmatic or sociolinguistic change, will be discussed in the respective chapters of this book.

3.2.1 Sound change

3.2.1.0 Comparative reconstruction. The Indo-European language family

Many sound changes have occurred and left their traces since and even before Old English. With the help of certain methods, several instances of sound change, and their morphological conditioning respectively, can be elucidated.

A glorious, extremely seminal method of diachronic linguistics is **comparative reconstruction** (*vergleichende Rekonstruktion*). The basis of this reconstructional type is the assumption of languages being **genetically related**, just like family members in a family tree. It is assumed that in passing on languages from generation to generation, mother languages split up into several daughter languages which in turn become mother languages for further daughter languages, etc.

There is, e.g., good historical evidence that a late variety of Latin split up into the different Romance languages, and that some version of Ancient Greek is the mother (if not grandmother) language of Modern Greek. The same is assumed for other older and modern European languages, too. A tree in which ancestors and their descendants are visualised can, therefore, be put up for most of the European languages, showing that most of them belong to one huge language family, ultimately going back to a reconstructed language called **Proto-Indo-European** (*Indoeuropäisch*, *Indogermanisch*). Fig. 49 on the next page represents one attempt in this respect. It tries to show all important branches of the family, but in detail only those that had an influence on the development of English.

By involving and comparing different, yet genetically related languages, we might now be enabled to trace back the expression form of words in so-called proto-languages, i.e. languages that existed way before Old English and of which we have no written traces whatsoever. The farther we can go back in time with this method, the more do we know about the oldest possible ancestor. This reconstruction is commonly conceived of as the progenitor of a vast range of languages from Icelandic in the north-west to Bengali in the south-east.

> ✎ Extinct, but attested languages are marked †.
> Unattested, reconstructed languages are marked *.
> Note that the 'branches' in the tree exclusively mark 'genetic' relationships, that is relations assumed to have been established by intergenerational transmission. Borrowing (→ 3.2.5.1) or other influence is not noted in this way.
> The languages that have been mainly influential in the shaping of English, e.g. via loanwords, are represented in **bold** print in the diagram.

Fig. 49: The family tree of English

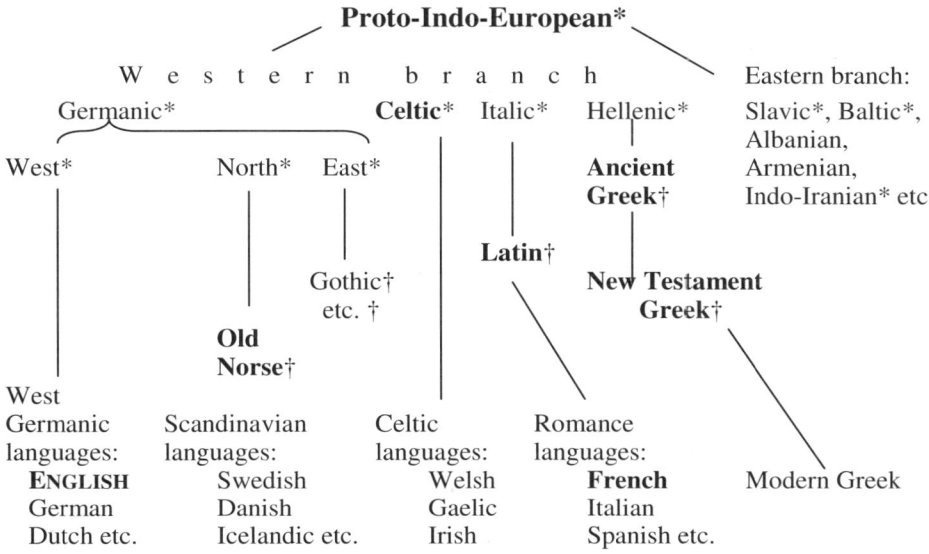

The most obvious application of methods of reconstruction is **etymology**, tracing the origin of the words of a language back to words in ancestor languages, or to a donor language in a contact that led to borrowing (→ 3.2.5.1).

Box 30: Etymology

> The term **etymology** (*Etymologie*) originally refers to the <u>study</u> of the origin of words, i.e., the question: What is the oldest form in which this word occurs, called the **etymon**, or what are its original components, and from which language does it or do they originate? What kind of changes did the word undergo to yield its present form? The term *etymology* is then also used to denote the origin of words itself. Etymology used to be a major preoccupation of diachronic linguistics and is probably its oldest branch. It concentrates on the expression form (→ Box 24) and is firmly anchored in methods of phonological reconstruction (→ 3.2.1.0). But of course it must also be able to argue with plausible semantic changes (→ 3.2.4) and, if necessary, with plausible assumptions about language contact in the relevant period (→ 3.2.5.1).

3.2.1.1 What Grimm's Laws tell us

Let us have a look at a famous example of comparative reconstruction. If we detect sets of words which are systematically similar in terms of meaning and form in two languages, we can assume that these languages are related. What is more, we may analyse the sets on the basis of their pronunciation to trace their form in a common ancestor language. In Present-Day English and German, we can identify, e.g., a definite connection on the basis of the words *tame, ten, toll* and their corresponding equivalents *zahm, zehn, Zoll*. The main systematic difference, apparently, is the realisation of the initial consonant(s) – /t/ in English, /ts/ in German. Let us, thus, go as far back as written sources allow; there, we find a similiar pattern:

Fig. 50: Cognates in Old English and Old High German

Old English	Old High German
tam	*zam*
tēn	*zehan*
toll	*zol*

> ☞ Pairs of words in different languages that can be traced back to the same etymological (→ Box 30) origin, such as the ones in the table above, are called **cognates** or cognate words in the terminology of historical linguistics. Note that pairs of cognates are not only found in cognate, i.e., genetically related (→ 3.2.1.0) languages, but may also arise from borrowing (→ 3.2.5.1). This always has to be considered in comparative reconstruction as it messes up the neat chronological patterns of sound changes. This is why we exemplify German-English cognates in the earliest available forms of these languages, because loan relations can be excluded at that early stage.

> ☐ Find further examples of regular sound correspondences between English and German cognates, involving other sounds as well!

We want to reconstruct the initial sound(s) in the common ancestor language, say, Proto-Germanic. Was it /t/, /ts/, or even something else? Help might be found in sister languages such as Gothic which is now extinct. In Gothic sources, older than Old English, we can find *taíhun* ('ten') and *tunþus* ('*tooth*') – this is a hint to the fact that it was probably /t/ even before. This provisional result eventually led to the detection of an underlying pattern, namely that /t/ as well as other word-initial plosives underwent a change in High (= southern) German. Particularly there, certain affricates developed out of earlier /t, p, k/, viz., /ts, pf, kx/ (the last is found in Swiss German only). Yet, this development did not take place in Old English nor in Low German.

> ☙ Note that the terms *High* and *Low German* do <u>not</u> allude to the social status of their speakers. This is a common misconception among German speakers who (erroneously) use the term *Hochdeutsch* with such social implications. High German is called 'High' because the term refers to language varieties which happened to be spoken in the geographically higher regions of Germany, which included most of what is now Bavaria and Baden-Württemberg, German-speaking Switzerland, Austria and South Tyrol. Low German, accordingly, was and is still spoken in the lower, northern regions of Germany as a dialect. Standard German was associated or even equated with High German because it happens to be based on mostly High German language varieties.

> 📖 How come that paradoxically, the 'best' High German is now believed to be spoken in northern Germany, in the Low German area, stereotypically in Hanover? Consult histories of the German language.

Once several reconstructions of this kind have been achieved, certain patterns begin to emerge, and phonological typologists may also form hypotheses about sound changes that are likely or less likely. Such hypotheses are also increasingly being informed by a growing body of theoretical knowledge about articulatory, acoustic and auditive phonetics: Which sounds are more difficult to pronounce universally than others? Which sounds are easily dropped or inserted in certain environments for articulatory reasons? Which sounds have similar acoustic and auditive properties even if they aren't close to each other in articulatory terms? (Remember the example of *enough*, which must have gone through a sound change from /χ/ to /f/, which can hardly have been brought about by slight shifts of articulation.) These considerations may in turn be used to test reconstructions. These tests in turn may corroborate or falsify typological generalisations etc. Thus, it can now be assumed that a sound change from [t] to [ts] or to [s] (both changes must have happened, according to comparative reconstruction, in the early history of High German) is more likely as a natural sound change than vice versa, so [t] must be the older sound, irrespective of the Gothic evidence.

Comparative reconstruction led, thus, to the formulation of general sound 'laws' by grammarians of the 19th century. Back then, sound change was preferably considered as being strictly and inherently logical in nature and, what is more, 'at work' without exceptions. One of the representatives was Jacob Grimm (yes, one of the fairy tale brothers). **Grimm's Law** (*Grimmsches Gesetz*) refers to certain changes with respect to plosive sounds.

> ⭘ The sound shifts we mentioned above ('Grimm II'), are incidentally called *Hochdeutsche Lautverschiebung* in German historical linguistics, as they separated the High German from the Low German dialects. Their results can still be observed in many differences between traditional dialects of northern and southern Germany (cf. *dat* vs. *das*, *Appel* vs. *Apfel*, *ick* vs. *ich*, *doll* vs. *toll*). As Standard German is mostly based on High German dialects, and Low German is largely based on Old Saxon anyway, Low German word forms are thus often much closer to English than High and Standard German ones.

Grimm also reconstructed much earlier changes separating Proto-Germanic from the other Indo-European languages ('Grimm I'), which, i.a. account for differences between cognates (→ 3.2.1.0, ☞ box) in Germanic and, say, Latin.

As a result, Old English (and, *mutatis mutandis*, German) shows regular characteristics of the following kind: Mainly, Indo-European voiceless plosives were realised as voiceless fricatives (maintaining the place of articulation), e.g. */p/ > /f/ as in Old English *fæðer*, German *Vater* compared to Latin *pater* ('father'). In fact, this is also the way /θ/ came about; compare in this regard Old English *þrēo* to Latin *tres* ('three'). In Proto-Old High German, /θ/ was abandoned as a result of 'Grimm II' or never arose so tat Proto-Indo-European /t/ appears as /d/ in Present-Day German. In both examples, Latin happened to keep the presumed, i.e. reconstructed Proto-Germanic consonant. Grimm's Law also includes former voiced aspirated plosives becoming voiceless, which explains instances such as Old English *cnēo*, German *Knie* with initial velar /k/ in contrast to Latin *genu* ('knee') with initial velar /g/.

3.2.1.2 Internal reconstruction of a phoneme split

Another powerful method of diachronic analysis is **internal reconstruction** (*interne Rekonstruktion*), which enables us to reconstruct former regular patterns from present-day irregularities. Thus, what appears to be exceptional in terms of deviating from a paradigm today may be traceable to some ordinary norm in past stages of English.

In → 2.2.5, we learnt about the allomorphs (or the sound-variational pattern) of the nowadays productive plural -s. A rule was set up, so we know when to apply either /s/, /z/ or /ɪz/. Yet, as a matter of fact, when forming some plurals such as /wʊlvz/ or /pɑːðz/ (*wolves, paths*), speakers seem to disobey this rule with respect to the singular forms that end in unvoiced fricatives: /wʊlf/, /pɑːθ/. How come? Shouldn't there be */wʊlfs/ and */pɑːθs/? Indeed, the irregularity is due to a diachronic change. In Old English, fricatives such as /f/ and /θ/ had two allophones:

Fig. 51: Some fricative phonemes and their allophones in Old English

Phonemes	Allophones	Examples (in Old English spelling)
/f/	[f]	*wulf* (nom.sg.) 'wolf'
	[v]	*wulfas* (nom.pl.) 'wolves'
/θ/	[θ]	*pæþ* (nom.sg.) 'path'
	[ð]	*pæðas* (nom.pl.)'paths'

📖 Do you remember the rule for the distribution of the allophones? (It was given in section 2.2.3).
Furthermore, what observations can you make on Old English spelling? Was it strictly phonemic?

Thus, we may assume that it was only after Old English that voiced [v] and [ð] acquired full phoneme status. Such a development is called **phoneme split** (*Phonemspaltung*). The exceptional plurals today are, consequently, a remainder of a former complementary distribution. Their original realisations have survived until today.

○ To give you a more vivid idea how phoneme splits might be accomplished: German is presently undergoing one. In strict Standard German, [x] and [ç] are still in complementary distribution. [x] only occurs after back and low vowels (*Kuchen doch machen*), [ç] in all other environments (*ich tüchtig Pech möchte Milch Chemie*). The phoneme is conventionally transcribed as /x/. In several varieties of colloquial Standard German, however, the two allophones have begun to form (sometimes marginal) minimal pairs: northern German [kuːxn] *Kuchen* vs. [kuːçn] *Kuhchen*, [loːx] *log* vs. [loːç] *Lurch*, [ɑːxn] *Aachen* vs. [ɑːçn] *Archen*; Rhenish Standard German [vɪxt] *Wirt* vs. [vɪçt] *Wicht*. Hence, in large areas of the German-speaking territory, [x] and [ç] no longer contrast in all environments in all current varieties.

📖 Describe the varieties of your own speech. Try to find out which of the above descriptions applies to it. Are /x/ and /ç/ already two phonemes for you?

3.2.1.3 Umlaut

Grimm's Law referred primarily to unconditioned sound changes, i.e. to changes the cause of which is obscure. Let us now exemplify a conditioned one, i.e. a change the cause of which is much more clearly identifiable. You have already come across the term **umlaut** (*Umlaut*) (→ 1.3.2, 2.2.5). Here, it relates to a diachronically relevant process which is occasionally also called **i-mutation**. During this process which took place in pre-Old English times, several stem vowels (including some diphthongs) were affected by a fronting or fronting and raising 'in the direction' of /i/ (→ Fig. 52), the effects of which can be witnessed in Old English as well as in German.

Fig. 52 The Old English umlaut pattern
(adapted from BRINTON / ARNOVICK 2006)

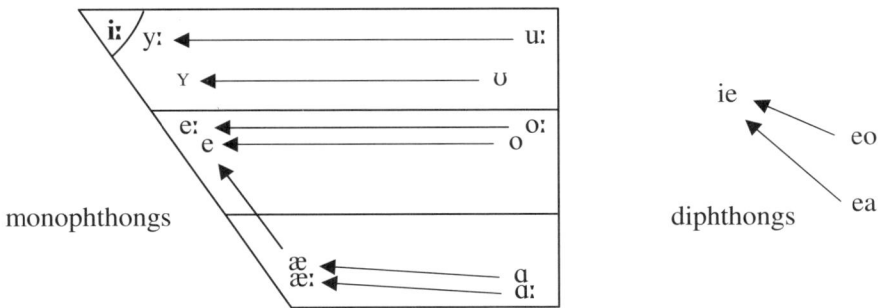

Umlaut affected those vowels which preceded a syllable containing /i/ or /j/. These triggering, conditioning elements are – in the frequent event of the process of suffix attrition (→ 3.2.1.8; 3.2.2) – mostly lost, which can render a straightforward reconstruction of the Proto-Germanic origin complicated at times. Yet, the results can still be seen in today's English (or German) throughout the major word classes. Take a look at, e.g., the plurals of the following Old English nouns *fōt* /foːt/ ('*foot*') and *mūs* /muːs/ ('*mouse*'):

pre-Old English reconstruction **foti*   > Old English *fēt*   /feːt/   '*feet*'

*musiz > Old English *mȳs* /myːs/   '*mice*'

(Suffixes are lost after triggering stem vowel umlaut)

✍ Note that in the literature on <u>historical</u> linguistics, the asterisk is used to mark reconstructed, non-attested sounds, forms or words.

⊙ In German, **umlaut** resulted in the typical umlauted vowels [y, ʏ] and [ø, œ] which are spelled <ü> and <ö>. It is still pervasive in its inflectional and derivational morphology, and even productive: It is highly unlikely that an etymon of *Generäle* existed in Proto-Germanic!

Box 31: Areal typology: Sprachbünde

⊙ From a phonological angle, it can be said that front rounded vowels are a rare phenomenon cross-linguistically. They do, however, form a kind of areal cluster on the European continent. Apart from German, front rounded vowels are found in French, in Northern Italian dialects, in the Scandinavian languages, in Finnish, Hungarian and Turkish. This is practically a geographically contiguous area. Apart from that, they are found hardly anywhere in the world. This can hardly be a coincidence. Areal typologists assume that language contact over centuries leads to such phenomena which have been designated by the nice German technical term **sprachbund**.

The best-studied sprachbund is the Balkan sprachbund which consists of Turkish, Modern Greek, Bulgarian, Serbian, Roumanian and Albanian. These languages, most of them genetically (→ 3.2.1.0) only distantly related at best, share a surprising number of sometimes unique or unusual grammatical features. This can only be due to the close contact among those languages within the Ottoman empire, which lasted many centuries.

In Old English, which obviously showed little to no inclination to join the European sprachbund, a process of unrounding had already begun: [øː] had become unrounded to [eː], etc. This process was later completed so that Present-Day English umlauted vowels are 'normal' front vowels such as [iː] (as in *feet*) and [e] (as in *length*).

3.2.1.4 Ablaut

Still, we can detect other interesting, yet very complex systematic patterns of vowel alternation in (pre-)Old English. One of the prominent Germanic patterns is definitely **ablaut** (*Ablaut*), also called **vowel gradation**.

In present-day Germanic languages, certain types of verbs show this vowel alternation in their inflection to mark past tense and past participle. It is also occasionally found in derivation (*brechen – Bruch*). Once more, many traces of this strategy, though not being productive any more (just as umlaut), have survived until today:

Present-Day English	*see*	–	*saw*	–	*seen*
	sing	–	*sang*	–	*sung*
	drive	–	*drove*	–	*driven*

You may want to compare these strategies with ablaut in the corresponding German verbs *sehen, singen, treiben*. Now, you are surely reminded of long lists of 'irregular' verbs which you had to learn in your school days. Yet, again, these verb forms relate to former regular ablaut patterns.

> ○ Ablaut is also found, with precisely the same functions, and sometimes in directly cognate forms, in Indo-European languages outside the Germanic branch, notably in Ancient Greek. E.g., the Ancient Greek word form meaning 'I know' (*oîda*) is an exact cognate of German *(ich) weiß*. The phonetic similarity has been thoroughly obscured by (completely regular and accountable) sound changes, including Grimm I and II. But the paradigm of *oîda* shows precisely the same ablaut patterns which in German are evinced by the vowel alternation between *weiß* and *wissen*. Incidentally, *wissen* is originally the past tense (in Greek, the perfect) of a verb meaning 'to see', thus instantiating a widespread pattern of semantic development from verbs of seeing to verbs of cognition (→ 3.2.4).

These patterns were a characteristic of so-called **strong verbs** (*starke Verben*) which in Old English can be classified into seven groups. For the sake of simplification, an orthographic representation is chosen in the following Old English examples. Note that most of these verbs also have cognates in German which are strong verbs! Some of these verbs also have cognates in German which are strong verbs!

Fig. 53: Old English ablauting verbs

strong class	infinitive	3rd p.sg. pres.ind.	1st p.sg. past ind.	pl. past ind.	past part.	
I	*drīfan*	*drīfþ*	*drāf*	*drifon*	*(ge)drīfen*	'drive'
II	*crēopan*	*crīepþ*	*crēap*	*crupon*	*(ge)cropen*	'creep'
III	*helpan*	*hilpþ*	*healp*	*hulpon*	*(ge)holpen*	'help'
IV	*beran*	*birþ*	*bær*	*bǣron*	*(ge)boren*	'bear'
V	*sprecan*	*spricþ*	*spræc*	*sprǣcon*	*(ge)sprecen*	'speak'
VI	*faran*	*færþ*	*fōr*	*fōron*	*(ge)faren*	'go'
VII	*feallan*	*fielþ*	*fēoll*	*fēollon*	*(ge)feallen*	'fall'

> 📖 Find the German cognates and see how many of them are still going 'strong'!

You may have noticed the interesting fact that the second column often features the umlauted stem vowels of the first column, e.g. /ea/ > /ie/ in *feallan* > *fielþ* (*'he falls'*). In general, the groups themselves allow for exceptions and are thus not entirely consistent. What is more, several verbs changed their class member-ship throughout the Old English period; some even defected to the so-called **weak verbs** (*schwache Verben*) (→ 3.2.2.4).

🖋 The notions 'strong' and 'weak' in terms of verb (but also noun and adjec-tive) categorisation, however established they may be, occasionally cause con-fusion. The metaphor (→ Box 34; 4.1.2.2) on which this 19th century designa-tion was based is enigmatic to 21st century scholars. It would make much more sense to speak of 'ablauting verbs'. Nowadays, 'strong' verb forms are minor-ity forms and, synchronically speaking, unproductive or anomalous. So why not call these 'weak', if at all?

What makes things worse is that "strong" and "weak" patterns are not only distinguished in verb inflection, but also in noun <u>and</u> adjective inflection, re-ferring to two yet completely different phenomena, respectively, which are not even remotely analogous. It would lead too far to explain all this here. But be prepared for some confusion.

3.2.1.5 The Great Vowel Shift

As regards the phoneme inventory, a universal tendency towards a quantitative symmetry e.g. with respect to front and back or tense and lax vowels has been claimed to prevail. The changes throughout the stages of English have, however, repeatedly brought about new imbalances. This leads us to the most prominent sound change of all, namely the **Great Vowel Shift** (*große Vokalverschiebung*). This unconditioned change began in Middle English and lasted until the end of the Early Modern English period. As it happened in that very era, it is also called the **Tudor Vowel Shift**. It affected all and only the long stressed vowels, took several centuries to be completed and eventually led to a radical rearrangement of the whole system. Fig. 54 shows the primary changes involved. All long stressed vowels were raised by one step; the high vowels /iː/ and /uː/ which, naturally, could not be raised any further, were diphthongised.

The incipience of the development as shown in the figure is by no means clear. On one view, the lowest Middle English front and back vowels became eventually raised to the next position 'up', thus pushing the vowels that were in this position further up until the highest positions are reached. The highest vow-els themselves, /iː/ and /uː/ were, as a consequence, expelled from the mo-nophthongal system; where these occurred, diphthongs were used instead by the end of Early Modern English.

According to the other view, we must not necessarily assume such a 'push chain', but a 'pull chain' might also have been diachronically at work, as it were. The latter view implies that the highest vowels turned into diphthongs first; the resulting gap was filled by the vowel in lower position, etc, etc. The outcome is the same – either the diphthongs pull or the lowest vowels push all others into their new place. Fig. 55 retraces the development with the help of some 'real-life' examples.

Fig. 54: The Great Vowel Shift

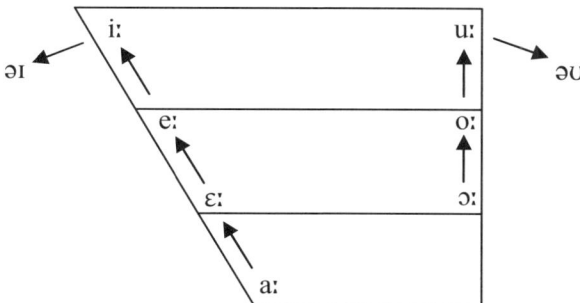

Fig. 55: The Great Vowel Shift ff.: examples

	Middle English	Early Modern English	Present-Day English	
front vowels	/maːk/ >	/mɛːk/ > /meːk/ >	/meɪk/	'make'
	/mɛːt/ >	/meːt/ > /miːt/ >	/miːt/	'meat'
	/meːt/ >	/miːt/	>	/miːt/	'meet'
back vowels	/tiːm/ >	/təɪm/ >	/taɪm/	'time'
	/bɔːt/ >	/boːt/	>	/bəʊt/	'boat'
	/foːd/ >	/fuːd/	>	/fuːd/	'food'
	/huːs/ >	/həʊs/	>	/haʊs/	'house'

The Great Vowel Shift

3.2.1.6 Phoneme merger

In some cases, the shift resulted in homophonous (→ 4.1.2.1) words, e.g. *meat* and *meet*. There, only the orthography may hint at the fact that the words used to be a minimal pair in Middle English. This kind of development is usually referred to as **phoneme merger** (*Phonemverschmelzung*) (which could also be described as complete **neutralisation**, → 2.2.4).

> ☙ Note that we call it phon<u>eme</u> merger. This means the merger takes place in the <u>system</u>, i.e. in *langue*, in a paradigmatic relationship. Two former phonemes in the system are no longer distinct. 'Merger' of sounds in *parole*, in a syntagmatic relationship, is something altogether different and was described in section → 2.4.2 as "coalescent assimilation".

> The two notions are sometimes confused because untrained people tend to think about language in terms of *parole* rather than *langue*.
> This remark is meant to show that distinctions such as above are no end in themselves, but are useful in linguistic reasoning and may be used to make our thinking and speaking about language more precise.

Other instances of phoneme merger are supplied by the development of centring diphthongs in RP since Late Modern English, another long-term phonological shift. As hinted at in → 2.1.1.1.4 (comments on centring diphthongs), there is a monophthongisation tendency of the system of centring diphthongs in RP, which after the loss of syllable-final /r/ had consisted of /ɑə/, /ɔə/, /ʊə/, /eə/, and /ɪə/. While /ɑə/ had already fully merged with /ɑː/ by the beginning of the 20th century, e.g. in *farther*, creating a homophony (→ 4.1.2.1) with *father*, the merger of /ɔə/ and /ɔː/ in favour of the monophthong was not completed before the second half of the 20th century, making *saw* and *sore* homonyms. As soon as this had been accomplished, /ʊə/ began the join the club, merging with /ɔː/, and /ɔː/ (maybe in consequence of this?) began to rise and become more closed and rounded. In today's young people's pronunciation, the three former phonemes have merged or (among the elderly) are about to merge to a relatively high mid, that is almost half-closed, /ɔː/ (e.g. in *poor*, creating a four-way homophony with *pour*, *pore*, and *paw*).

Over the last three decades, an analogous development of the diphthong /eə/ is to be observed, in order to re-establish the former balance, as it were. The result is the current monophthongisation of /eə/ to /ɛː/ (e.g. in *hair*) which incidentally fills a previously existing gap in the system of low front tense monophthongs (→ 2.1.1.1), although it creates disturbing near-homophonies for German learners. In the near future, we can expect /ɪə/ (e.g. in *beer*), being the last of the Mohicans, to change, too. This may, in analogy to the back diphthongs, also result in a merger with /ɛː/, or create another new front high tense monophthong, as has been reported from Australian English.

3.2.1.7 Phoneme loss

If a language can acquire new phonemes, it will also have to part with one now and then. The history of English provides at least one rather striking example of **phoneme loss** (*Phonemverlust*), which also happens to touch upon German – English contrasts and affinities. Historical linguists reconstruct for Old English a phoneme /χ/, usually spelled <h> in Old English manuscripts, with three realisations in complementary distribution, namely [χ], [ɣ], and [ç]. During Middle English,

- /χ/ was either vocalised and thus formed a diphthong together with the preceding vowel, which, however did not survive later sound changes (in words such as *draw*, *night* and *brought*),
- or was substituted by /f/, e.g. in /inʊχ/ ('*enough*'),
- or was dropped, such as in /χluːd/ '*loud*' or /χwan/ '*when*'.

The latter kind of instance, however, seems to have survived as an allophone of /h/ in some American varieties (/hwen/ 'when'); but this may also be the result of a **spelling pronunciation** inculcated by schoolteachers who desperately clung to the belief that English spelling somehow must represent the 'correct' pronunciation and thus pronunciation should be adjusted to the spelling.

> What conclusion may we draw from the fact that the former presence of /χ/ is still reflected in the spelling of words like *when*, but not in *loud*? Also consider the <w> in *draw*, a word which once contained the allophone [ɣ]. Could this have to do with a difference in the time at which the sound ceased to be pronounced in the respective words?

- In any case, during the Middle English period, a period less worried about correctness of spelling and pronunciation, /χ/ gradually made its way out of the core phoneme inventory of English until it was ultimately lost. Interestingly, modern spelling, conservative as it is, occasionally reflects the existence of a former /χ/ in many words, such as <gh> in *enough* or *night*. However, if you ever wondered why there is [χ] in today's German but not in Standard English, you are on the right way to become a diachronic linguist.

3.2.1.8 Phonetic attrition

Another widespread type of sound change, which has had drastic consequences in the history of English, is called **phonetic attrition** or **erosion**. This has repeatedly been referred to already, as it is responsible for the emergence of weak forms (→ 2.4.1) and the catastrophic loss of inflection in the history of English (→ 3.2.2), and is a typical concomitant of grammaticalisation processes (→ 3.2.3.3).

The precise scope of this phenomenon is debatable. What certainly has to be regarded as attrition is a tendency of unstressed vowels to be shortened, to centralise and thereby converge on something like [ə]. This is usually referred to as **vowel weakening** (*Vokalschwächung*). Consonants may also be weakened: from tense to lax, from lax plosive to lax fricative, from fricative to approximant, etc. (for the terminology, → 2.1.1.2). The complete **elision** of unstressed vowels, preferably [ə], and also consonants, especially in clusters (/lɪsn/ for *listen*!), is certainly another case in point.

> ⦿ These tendencies are typical of Germanic languages, i.e. languages with an extra strong stress (→ 2.3.3). They are not found in all languages.
>
> - Among the Romance languages, French was most affected, cf. Latin *amicum* 'friend_ACC' with its cognates in French (*ami*), Italian (*amico*) and Spanish (*amigo*). From these data, one might establish a 'hierarchy of attrition' French > Spanish > Italian. The weakening of Latin /k/ to Present-Day Spanish [ɣ] is what distinguishes Spanish from Italian, in which only the last Latin sound fell prey to attrition. French did not merely weaken the last syllable, but shed it altogether.

> - Modern Greek preserves the full strength of all the vowels of Ancient Greek, stressed or unstressed, although extensive mergers (→ 3.2.1.6) have taken place, reducing the number of vowel phonemes to five and with the result, e.g., that in the largely historical orthography of Modern Greek, there are six different spellings for the vowel /i/. But Greek does not have and never had a vowel that one could call 'weak'. Stress has hardly had any influence on the development of vowels in that language.

What is controversial, however, is to what extent other sound changes may be attributed to attrition. But this shall not concern us here.

3.2.2 Morphological change

3.2.2.0 Mechanisms of morphological change

Morphological change may have several reasons. On the one hand, there is the relentless process of phonetic attrition (→ 3.2.1.8) which is a normal part of grammaticalisation processes (→ 3.2.3.3) and which in the history of English mainly affected the unstressed endings of words containing inflectional morphemes. It is obvious that the system of inflections cannot remain unaffected by such changes. Thus sound change triggered morphological change.

On the other hand, morphological change comprises more than just the consequences of sound change. There seems to be a constant pressure on morphological systems to maintain important distinctions, to weed out irregularities and to make the system more transparent. Thus, certain morphological procedures are changed, whole paradigms reshuffled. These tendencies can also be observed to be working in the history of English morphology. Here, the principle of **analogy** must be mentioned as a crucial factor.

Box 32: Analogy

> **Analogy** (*Analogie*), a high-ranking feature of human cognition at large (GENTNER et al. 2001), is defined in Webster as "an inference that if things agree in some respects they probably agree in others". Apart from its role in reorganising inflectional paradigms, it is also the principle underlying the creation of metaphors (→ Box 34; 4.1.2.2; 4.3.2) as well as the development of schematic syntactic constructions (→ 1.2.3.2). It is also at work in the spread of sound changes and sound shifts (→ 3.2.1). Its relevance was clearly seen by traditional historical linguists and has especially been noted recently by cognitive linguists. For linguistic uses of the concept cf. ITKONEN 1975; LANGACKER 1987, 409-447; SKOUSEN et al. 2002.

Old English was a highly inflected language (for the implications of this → 1.4.2). For example, inflections marked five cases (nominative, genitive, dative, accusative, instrumental), three numbers (singular, dual, plural), and three genders (masculine, feminine, neuter), let alone additional verb marking (→ 1.1.3.4.4). Further, two declensions for both nouns and adjectives and diversified verb classifications can render Old English very strange indeed for today's speakers of English. In fact, looking at the declension and conjugation tables of an Old English grammar, one is more reminded of German than of English. But let us consider the major word classes of Old English one by one.

3.2.2.1 Declension of nouns

Fig. 56: Old English noun declension: examples

strong class	masculine		feminine		neuter	
	sg.	pl.	sg.	pl.	sg.	pl.
nom.	*stān*	*stānas*	*giefu*	*giefa, giefe*	*word*	*word*
gen.	*stānes*	*stāna*	*giefe*	*giefa, giefena*	*wordes*	*worda*
dat.	*stāne*	*stānum*	*giefe*	*giefum*	*worde*	*wordum*
acc.	*stān*	*stānas*	*giefe*	*giefa, giefe*	*word*	*word*
	'stone'		'gift'		'word'	

weak class	masculine		feminine		neuter	
	sg.	pl.	sg.	pl.	sg.	pl.
nom.	*nama*	*naman*	*sunne*	*sunnan*	*ēage*	*ēagan*
gen.	*naman*	*namena*	*sunnan*	*sunnena*	*ēagan*	*ēagena*
dat.	*naman*	*namum*	*sunnan*	*sunnum*	*ēagan*	*ēagum*
acc.	*naman*	*naman*	*sunnan*	*sunnan*	*ēage*	*ēagan*
	'name'		'sun'		'eye'	

Note: The instrumental case is not mentioned in the above table because it is always identical to the dative in nouns.

> 📖 Compare the paradigms in Fig. 56 with those of the German cognates! How many endings are still similar? What has changed in German? Does German still distinguish different paradigms of declension?

After Old English, inflections disappeared gradually, but radically. With respect to nouns, grammatical gender was given up, while a simplified regular expression of number distinctions was kept: Present-Day English regular pluralisation with the help of suffixation by *-s* (→ 2.2.5 on allomorphs) is a remainder of the 'strong' masculine paradigm:

Old English *stānas* > Middle English *stones* > Present-Day English *stones*

The strategy of the 'weak' paradigm, thus, lost its productivity after Old English. Nevertheless, some formerly weak formations of plurals we might call irregular or lexically conditioned (→ 1.3.3) today are still around, e.g. *brethren* or *oxen*. Other morphologically minority, yet frequent forms such as *eyen* ('eyes') or *schoon* ('shoes') changed the paradigm completely as late as in Early Modern English. On the basis of such a process of **analogical levelling** (*analogische Angleichung*), most weak plurals were reformed according to the model of the strong masculine declension. Thus, the Present-Day English results *books*, *names*, *gifts* or *words* level out different pluralisation stategies such as Pre-Old English **umlaut** (cf. Old English *bēc*; → 3.2.1.3), and other masculine (*naman*), feminine (*giefa*), or neuter forms (*word*).

Case endings, if present, became reduced to /ə/ in Middle English before they were dropped entirely. Entirely? In fact, we still have an overt genitive (*stone's, stones'*) vs. non-genitive (*stone, stones*) marking today, once again stemming from the strong masculine paradigm. You can rightly argue that we can avoid even this distinction by using a preposition (*of the stone(s)*). However, the genitive marking (with the apostrophe being an Early Modern English invention) is a common strategy particularly with nouns denoting animate beings (*Snoopy's, teachers'*). Yet, we can detect its increasing functioning in non-nouns (*today's*).

In this context, it must however be pointed out that the 'genitive' in Present-Day English is no longer a case marking because it attaches to noun phrases rather than nouns, e.g.:

> *The Queen of England's family problems.*

In other words, it is no longer inflectional, but a clitic (→ 1.3.2, 2.4.1), which is also hinted at by the apostrophe spelling. Diachronically, though, this construction is clearly in a continuity with the genitive usage in Old English, so that we can say that the genitive *-s* of Old English 'strong' masculine nouns was not lost, but degrammaticalised (→ 3.2.3.3). (Is that why they're called "strong"?)

3.2.2.2 Declension of adjectives

Old English adjective declension shares with German a Germanic heritage, not to say burden, in that it not only distinguishes three genders, two numbers, and four cases but also uses two separate paradigms depending on the presence of a definite article (yielding 3*2*4*2 =48 forms to be learnt). The latter paradigms are confusingly called (guess what) 'strong' and 'weak' (→ 3.2.1.4, ☙ box). In contrast to the residual traces we found in nouns, and to the relief of today's learners of English, all those redundant distinctions have disappeared totally in adjectives already by the beginning of Middle English. From then on, one form serves all the purposes mentioned above.

> 📖 Compare the complicated situation in Present-Day German: It was Mark Twain who remarked that he would rather decline two drinks than one German adjective. How many different declension forms does German distinguish in the adjective? Does it 'out-decline' Old English? Note forms like: *guter Wein, der gute Wein, ein guter Wein, mit gutem Wein, mit einem guten Wein, mit dem guten Wein.*

3.2.2.3 The pronoun system

Let us turn to pronouns. Here, it is interesting to take a closer look at the Old English personal pronouns. They all had a full paradigm of four cases like the nouns; today, only two are left, a subject case (*I, he, we* etc.) and an object case (*me, him, us* etc.). The genitive forms developed into today's possessive pronouns (*my, his, our* etc.). The distinction between dative and accusative was abandoned, like in Low German, so that it could be said that English speakers confuse *mir* and *mich*: They use only one form for both.

It is more interesting, however, to scrutinise the development of the pronoun system as a whole. Fig. 57 shows part of the Old English system of personal pronouns, viz. all nominative forms.

Fig. 57: Old English personal pronouns (nominative forms)

	1st	2nd	3rd masc.	3rd fem.	3rd neut.
singular	*ic*	*þū*	*hē*	*hēo*	*hit*
dual	*wit*	*git*	*hī(e)* in all three genders,		
plural	*wē*	*gē*	in dual and plural		

Comparing this to the present-day system, the first notable change is the loss of the number category **dual** after Old English, resulting in today's binary singular / plural distinction.

> ◐ The dual as a separate inflectional number category for mentioning two persons or things is not exactly frequent cross-linguistically, but it seems a feature of ancient Indo-European languages. Ancient Greek had a well-developed dual in both verbal and nominal morphology. Accordingly, its presence in Old English is not over-surprising.

Further, if you look at some of the forms, like *hēo* for present-day *she*, or *hī(e)* for present-day *they*, you will find it difficult to imagine how they could have developed into the present-day forms. And indeed, they didn't. It is an astonishing and unparalleled fact in the history of the English language that loanwords managed to enter this closed class (→ Fig. 19) of personal pronouns and replaced several former elements.

> 📖 To assess the outrage this development constitutes, imagine this would happen in German. For all the borrowing taking place from English into German (→ 3.2.5.1), German has not borrowed a single pronoun or any other grammatical morpheme from English. (Maybe *-ing* will one day be a German suffix). Borrowing pronouns, for that matter, would even make a lot of sense, as German has a disturbing plethora of homophonies (→ 4.1.2.1) in its pronoun system. How many functions do the pronoun forms *sie / Sie* and *ihr / Ihr* have in German? Don't forget the case distinctions! So why don't we use the wonderfully unambiguous *she, her, you, your, they, them* and *their* instead?

What happened in English? In the Danelaw era (→ 3.1.1), loans from Old Norse were incorporated into Northern dialects of Old English – among them the 3rd person plural forms *þei* and *þæm* (for subjective and objective uses) and *þæra* (for possessive use). These forms (and variants) established in Middle English at the expense of the formerly functional plural forms *hī(e)*, *him* and *hira* and gave rise to Present-Day English *they, them*, and *their*. Additionally, *sche*, a dialectal counterpart of *hēo*, served as the source of the modern form *she*. Homophonies that had developed seem to have supplied the motivation for this.

The pronoun system underwent further modification in Middle and Early Modern English, for example a redistribution of the usage of the 2nd person personal pronouns (i.e. Old English *þū* and *gē*) that resulted in the multifunctional Present-Day English form *you* for both singular and plural, as well as for subject and object case. As this development is mainly socially motivated, it will be discussed in more detail in section → 7.6.

3.2.2.4 Verb inflection

While Old English can be seen as a 'full inflection period', Middle English is the period of drastic morphological reduction and levelling (BAUGH / CABLE [4]1993, 50). Old English verb inflections distinguished three persons, two numbers, two tenses and two moods, plus two imperative forms, one infinitive and two participles, yielding 3*2*2*2 + 2 + 1 + 2 = 29 conjugation forms. For precision's sake it must be said, however, that some of these forms had already become levelled before the Old English period (as can be gathered from Fig. 58 below), so that actually only 20 different forms had to be distinguished; a very common phenomenon in paradigms, called **syncretism** (*Synkretismus*).

From early on, an inflectional loss runs more or less systematically rampant in English until the Present-Day system had established itself during the Early Modern English period. Of course, verbs were not spared in the course of events which was, moreover, closely connected to fundamental syntactic changes (→ 3.2.3.1). For the sake of an overview, the present tense conjugation of the (hopefully well-known) verb '*love*' throughout the periods of English may serve as an example of inflectional loss.

Fig. 58: The fate of English verbal inflection, present tense

		Old English	Middle English	Early Modern English	Present-Day English
	infinitive	*lufian*	*love(n)*	*love*	*love*
indi-cative	sg.(1st p.)	*lufie*	*love*	*love*	*love*
	sg.(2nd p.)	*lufast*	*lovest*	*lovest*	*love*
	sg.(3rd p.)	*lufaþ*	*loveth*	*loveth*	*loves*
	pl.	*lufiaþ*	*love(n)*	*love*	*love*
sub-junctive	sg.	*lufie*	*love*	*love*	*love*
	pl.	*lufien*	*love(n)*	*love*	*love*
impe-rative	sg.	*lufa*	*love*	*love*	*love*
	pl.	*lufiaþ*	*loveth*	*love*	*love*
	pres.part.	*lufiende*	*lovynge*	*loving*	*loving*

As for the past tense, in Old English most verbs followed either a 'strong' (tense-ablauting, → 3.2.1.4) or a 'weak' (tense-suffixing) paradigm. Not only the 'strong', but also the weak' verbs were divided in several subclasses. There is no need to go into further detail here. Suffice it to state that weak verbs were characterised by a suffix containing a so-called 'dental' element (e.g. /d/) in their past forms, which is absent in 'strong' verbs. This 'dental element' surfaces in most cases as the well-known regular <-ed> past tense suffix in written Present-Day English, sometimes as <-t> (*sent, slept*).

> ➤ The 'dental element' presumably goes back to a very early, obviously Proto-Germanic **periphrasis** (on the term see section ➜ 3.2.3.2) involving forms of the reduplicating past tense of the predecessor of *do* (➜ 1.3.5.4), which were obviously turned into inflectional suffixes in a process of grammaticalisation (➜ 3.2.3.3) before written documentation of Germanic languages set in. Note that if the *did*-forms turned into suffixes, we must assume a different order of elements than today. Indeed, Proto-Germanic has been reconstructed to have been a verb-final language, i.e., every clause was ordered like a German subordinate clause.
> In a gross but elucidating simplification, we may imagine that the starting-point was a clause like **weil sie das sagen taten*, which was, *nota bene*, formed because no other past tense of *sagen* seemed available. Indeed, speakers of some German dialects use precisely this kind of periphrasis because the 'weak' preterite has been lost or become unusual in their varieties. This kind of form must then have been slurred together into something like **weil sie das sagen taten → weil sie das sagten*.

<-ed> (though sometimes under a different spelling) became the regular, productive past tense suffix after Old English and was adopted in a process of analogical levelling (➜ 3.2.2.1) by most strong class verbs (cf. *helped* vs. German *half, geholfen*!). Thus, if a new verb enters the English language now, e.g. *blog* in the 1990s, its past tense is most likely to be formed with the help of *-ed*:

*I've blog**ged** the results on my website.*

> 📖 Describe the phonologically conditioned spoken allomorphs of <-ed> evinced, e.g. in *stabbed, starved, killed, erred, wooed, walked, kissed, wanted, ended*, which are quite analogous to the allomorphs of the plural *-s* (and, incidentally, the verbal *-s* suffix) (➜ Fig. 40).

3.2.2.5 Changes in word formation

Word formation (➜ 1.3.4, 1.3.5), especially seen from a diachronic perspective, is a topic that can fill (and has filled) books (e.g.; MARCHAND [2]1969, SAUER 1992), if not libraries. We will pick out a few raisins only.

The Germanic word formation pattern of **compounding** by juxtaposition (➜ 1.3.5.2) was as productive in Old English as it is today. A semantically special type of compounds which is worth mentioning here have become known as **kenningar**. These served as a poetic device particularly in Old English and show par excellence not only the word-forging possibilities in (early) English, but also the creative use of figurative language by its speakers:

banhus (literally: '*bone-house*') → *body*
sweordplega (literally '*sword-play*') → *battle*

> 💣 It must be emphasised that kenningar are <u>not</u> a special type of word formation. They are compounds and nothing but compounds. What distinguishes them and makes them unusual to sober and austere modern Western minds, is the extensive exploitation of poetic metaphor (→ Box 34; 4.1.2.2; 4.3.2) for naming trivial objects, so that their meaning is rather opaque. One could say they are lexicalised (→ 3.2.5.3) from the beginning. Kenningar may begin to appear less exotic if we look at non-Western varieties of English, Pidgins for example (→ 7.4.1), and also phenomena like Cockney rhyming slang (→ 7.1.1).

With respect to 'normal' word formation, different (types of) **suffixes** which were productive in the past fell out of use again as their function merged with others or was taken over otherwise. Some originated from nouns such as Old English *dōm* (*state*, *quality*, *domain*), became bound morphemes and gave rise to modern derivations like *stardom*. Many more by far were imported into English from French or Latin because many words had been borrowed that contained them with a recognisable function, like *-ity*, *-ment*, *-al*, *-ous*, *-(a)tion*, *-ise* and many others (→ 1.3.2). These were soon freely used, even with Germanic roots, to form new derivations.

Most **prefixes** that once existed in Old English were lost on the way, so that very few Germanic prefixes made it into Present-Day English, *mis-* and *un-* being the most common ones. As if in compensation, many prefixes were borrowed from Greek, Latin and French, such as *pre-*, *post-*, *super-*, *sub-*, *hyper-*, *anti-* and many others.

Thus, the quantity and the use of affixes has always been liable to change in English. Today, we may use the suffixes *-ity* or *-ness*, e.g., to derive abstract nouns with the additional meaning 'state, condition or quality of' from adjectives. *-ity* was made possible via French loans in Middle English and gained 'popularity' in Early Modern English with the revival of Latin as a donor language. *-ness* (see also → 3.2.5.3 on *business*), however, is more likely to derive words of Germanic origin, though its usage has been extended to originally foreign words such as *absoluteness* or *tenderness*. With the help of this brief example, we could state that English speakers allow themselves the luxury to have many formally different, but functionally equivalent word formation devices. Besides *-ity* and *-ness*, we also find words such as *champion**ship***, *likeli**hood***, *normal**cy*** and *star**dom***.

3.2.3 Syntactic change

3.2.3.1 Word order changes

Generally speaking, we can say that the English of past periods was characterised by more syntactic variation. Today, SVO word order is dominant and proves to be effective. Yet, from Early Modern English back to Old English, clauses could be organised differently. A main reason for this was, as we may deduce from the preceding chapter on morphological change, detailed inflection which rendered, e.g., the overt realisation of a subject redundant; it was not obligatory. Such subject omission can be found until Early Modern English. There, the verb form only (particularly in 2nd p.sg. contexts) allows an unambiguous inference of the unexpressed subject, here *thou* ('you') in Shakespeare's *Henry IV*:

> *Canst not heare…? …hast no faith in thee?*　　　　(Part I, II.1,26.28)

A 'proper' grammatical translation into Present-Day English, yet, requires to express the subject ('*Can you not hear?*'). In Old English, the subject could be easily identified from its case marking. Thus, we can find all word orders imaginable, though not with equal frequency:

SVO	*he hæfde an swīðe ǣnlic wīf*	'he had a very beautiful wife'
SOV	*se cyning þās word gehīerde*	'the king heard these words'
VSO	*ne sende se dēofol þā fȳr*	'the devil did not send fire'
VOS	*slōh þone cyning se man*	'the man slew the king'
OSV	*micelne gelēafan hē hæfde*	'he had great faith'
OVS	*dēman gedafenað setl*	'a seat suits a judge'

You have recognised that all the Present-Day English translations show an SVO syntax. Indeed, SVO began its breakthrough in connection with the subsequent loss of inflections after Old English. Thus, the respective function within the clause becomes clear on the basis of its fixed syntactic position, and not on the basis of morphology. Due to this, an OVS word order (compare '*a judge suits a seat*') would be impossible today.

With regard to the relative order of direct and indirect objects, the syntactic choice was optional in Old English. The type of object could be clearly deduced from the case marking, e.g. accusative in *legan* or dative in *mannum* (see below). Compare the following instances with their Present-Day English equivalents that may make use of the syntactically disambiguating device to employ prepositions, here *to*:

SVO$_{indir}$O$_{dir}$	*hī gesealdon him seofon legan*	'they gave him seven legions'
SVO$_{dir}$O$_{indir}$	*hē forgēaf eorðlīce þing mannum*	'he gave earthly things to men'

3.2.3.2 Developments in the verbal syntagm

An interesting detail, among so very many, are changes in the linear combinability within syntactic slots after Old English. E.g., the verbal syntagm increased more and more in complexity with respect to the combination of modality, tense /

orientation, aspect, and voice marking. In principle, most of the elements of to-day's complex verbal syntagms were available in Old English: the modal verbs, the *have*-perfect, *be* + participle in a kind of progressive meaning, *be* + participle to form a passive. But they were rare, and mostly used to translate analogous Latin constructions. They were not really part of Old English grammar. And they could not be combined freely.

The last combination to become acceptable was the combination of progressive and passive (*The house is being built*), which was still being castigated by language purists in the early 19th century. Thus it is only since Late Modern English that a combination of four verbal categories in one syntagm is possible, i.e. is felt as being grammatically 'okay'. For your convenience we repeat the authentic 'maximalist' example given in section →1.1.3.4.5:

He might have been being captured by the Iraqis but he wasn't.

This development is all the more remarkable as the last-mentioned innovation certainly didn't come from colloquial language. It can thus be seen that educated language can also serve as a laboratory for linguistic innovation. In any case, the combinability of passive and progressive made the whole system of English auxiliary complexes complete, symmetric, regular and also fairly compositional (→ Box 16); analogy (→ Box 32) had finally prevailed. The next new auxiliary on the waiting list, *be gonna*, is now about to mess up this symmetry again and has to find its place in the system yet (cf. → Fig. 9). We are going to wait and see how far it gets.

You have certainly noted that the verbal syntagm in the above example consists of five verb units, which is quite complex, isn't it? As implied above, the explicit combination of passive voice and progressive aspect was by no means common in Shakespeare's time. Rather, the meaning of the modern sentence *The house is being built* was expressed by a sequence such as *The house is building*.

Furthermore, simple and progressive aspect had still been in so-called **free variation** (*freie Variation*) in Early Modern English. In the event of enriching the verbal system by developing new grammatical categories, it seems that English speakers took the good, i.e. grammatical precision and consistency, always with the bad, i.e. an increasing complexity of the verbal syntagm. In general, the progressive is much more frequent today than it was in former times, and its range of application is still increasing (→ 3.2.3.3).

Box 33: Free variation

The notion of 'free variation' is sometimes invoked by linguists to describe situations in which language usage seems to allow several expression forms for the same content substance without any immediately apparent conditioning factor. 'Free variation' is not only observed in syntax, but on all levels of linguistic description: phonetics, phonology, morphology, syntax, lexicon and pragmatics. Free variation in the lexicon is called synonymy (→ 4.2.2.1).

The notion of free variation is highly problematic, however. Many linguists cannot believe in 'free variation' given their theoretical tenets.

If you believe that all constructions qua constructions are meaningful (→ 1.2.3.2), like a cognitive linguist, then you must look for differences in meaning when encountering 'free variation'.

If you believe that linguistic competence is rule-governed (like a generative linguist, → 1.2.2), then you must keep looking for rules explaining the variation, or relegate it to performance, thus manoeuvring it outside the scope of linguistics.

The specialists for linguistic variation, the sociolinguists (→ 7.6), do not like free variation either; it is, on the contrary, a favourite preoccupation of sociolinguists to find the conditioning factors of variation which, in contrast to the other branches of linguistics, are always sought in social differences between language users and in societal influence. Indeed it is sociolinguists that have developed the most sophisticated and at the same time realistic models of linguistic variation.

Statistical corpus-based text analysis à la BIBER (→ 6.3.1) investigates variation as conditioned by the existence of different text genres. What has become clear through textlinguistic (BIBER 1988) as well as sociolinguistic research (LABOV 1966, → 7.1.2) is that the conditioning factors are not conditioning in the strict sense, but operate in a **probabilistic** manner. This means: The conditioning factors influence the probability of occurrence of a given linguistic form rather than completely determine its use. The **usage-based approach** in cognitive linguistics (→ 1.2.3.1) is also increasingly following this assumption.

In plain English, the use of the notion of 'free variation' by linguists usually means: "We don't know why."

⌂ Speaking of 'free variation', we will discuss two more interesting features of English.

Negative concord, also known as **double** or **multiple negation** (*mehrfache Verneinung*), was a commonly accepted syntactic device to reinforce negation from Old to Early Modern English. Thus, we should still find it in Shakespeare, and there it is:

> *I haue one heart... / And that no woman has,*
> <u>*nor neuer none*</u>*/ Shall mistris be of it (Twelfth Night III.1, 148-150)*

Such instances were abhorred by normative grammarians when first attempting to standardise the language at the end of Early Modern English. According to their logic, such usage has to be avoided at any cost. Double or multiple negation survived, however, in present-day non-standard usage – you can witness it as an everyday informal feature of many native speakers of English (and German).

💣 Although "double" or "multiple negation" seems to be the most common term for the phenomenon in question even among well-meaning, linguistically unprejudiced linguists, we prefer the term *negative concord* for the simple reason that it analyses the phenomenon more appropriately and draws attention to the fact that users of this construction are not dumb or incapable of logical thinking.

The latter is, unfortunately, suggested by the term *double negation*. In a true double negation, the two negations logically cancel each other out. True double negations are not infrequent in English. Did you discover one in the last sentence? Of course this sentence means that true double negations are fairly frequent, not that they are rare. True double negation is a common rhetorical figure and known as **litotes**.

Quite different is the case of negative concord. It strengthens and emphasises the negation by giving every negatable word in the sentence its negative form, i.e., all indefinite pronouns such as *ever*, *one*, or *any* become *never*, *none* and *no*, and often the auxiliary verb is negated as well, as in the following examples from **Black English** (➔ 7.1.2):

Nobody ain't gonna spend no time going to no doctor.
Nobody around here ain't never heard of him. (MUFWENE et al. 1998, 19)

The phenomenon is called concord (that is, agreement, ➔ Box 7) for precisely this reason: All words in the sentence capable of negative agreement agree in negation with the first negative element.

🅾 Negative concord is possibly more common cross-linguistically than true double negation. It is ironic that Ancient Greek, of all languages, a language admired by language purists for its "logical structure" (in fact, Greek or Latin are not more logical than any other language in the world!), and the language in which formal logic was first formulated (this is, for once, not a myth!), also has – *horribile dictu* – rules of negative concord in its grammar.

🖑 *do*-**periphrasis** (do-*Periphrase*, do-*Umschreibung*) is attested in Middle English as a syntactically optional construction.

> ➤ In fact something like it must have existed in Proto-Germanic already as the 'weak' *-ed* preterite obviously goes back to such a periphrasis (➔ 3.2.2.4).

Until Early Modern English, the Middle English periphrasis existed in 'free variation' with constructions without lexically emptied *do*, be it in positive or negative statements and questions. Shakespeare shows us examples that differ in this respect from present-day usage:

...thou dost meet good hap;	(*The Two Gentlemen of Verona* I.1,16)
...nay, give me not the boots.	(ibd. I.1,28)
...gavest thou my letter to Julia?	(ibd. I.1,95)

While the author was free to choose either a *do*-periphrasis or not in these instances, a specified, complementary distribution was established by the beginning of Late Modern English. Thus, we have to use lexically functionless *do* in negative statements and questions (except with *be*, *have*, and modal verbs), whereas the opposite holds for positive statements (except emphatic usages). Accordingly, if Shakespeare wanted to publish his play including the above-mentioned constructions today, the editors would have reprehended him for using incorrect grammar!

☞ The term *periphrasis* is not very technical as it refers to several functionally quite different phenomena. Colloquially it refers to 'a roundabout way of speaking' (Webster). In the examples given in → 3.2.2.4, ➢ box, however, periphrasis seems to fulfil a genuine need of language users to fill a glaring gap in the system (no past tense forms for the 'weak' verbs available). There apparently <u>was</u> no less roundabout way of expressing the past tense.

❍ Indeed, this is not infrequent cross-linguistically as paradigms do occasionally develop gaps. Latin, e.g., uses a periphrastic construction for the perfect passive (*dictum est* 'it was said, it has been said') because no person-number suffixes are available for this tense-voice combination.

In other cases, *periphrasis* refers to a grammatical problem solution that is indeed unnecessarily roundabout, e.g. the above-mentioned Present-Day English obligatory *do*-periphrasis, which does not fill a gap, but rather seems a result of analogy (→ Box 32).

For the Early Modern English period, this 'periphrasis' is said to be in free variation with a less 'roundabout' way of forming a verbal syntagm, i.e., it neither fills a gap nor is it obligatory.

This free variation in the meanings of terminology makes it difficult to define *periphrasis*.

3.2.3.3 Grammaticalisation

What we just called 'lexically functionless' *do* is in fact a syntactic operator, an auxiliary that developed from an Old English full verb (*dōn*). We can still employ it as a full verb meaning *to act* or *to perform* – yes, we can *do* that. Yet, more important here is its losing lexical meaning and acquiring a purely grammatical, thus lexically empty function. Such a process is called **grammaticalisation** (*Grammatikalisierung*, *Grammatisierung*).

Grammaticalisation is a powerful agent of language change. It acts as a repairing device via the speakers and is omnipresent throughout the periods of English. Grammaticalisation explains how grammatical structures arise, e.g. by (former) lexical units gradually turning into grammatically functional morphemes (→ 1.3.2). Thus, this mechanism fills gaps flexibly wherever there is a felt need. (This does not explain all instances of grammaticalisation, though).

The **be-passive**, the **have-perfect** and the **-ing-progressive** have historically developed through processes of grammaticalisation. Even if *be*-passive and *have*-perfect are borrowings (→ 3.2.5.1) from Late Latin or French that already occur occasionally in Old English, they arose through grammaticalisation processes in the donor languages and sometimes English had to re-enact this grammaticalisation process.

The *ing*-progressive, at least, is a home-made English development, but reflects universal tendencies for progressive aspect forms and its history shows typical characteristics of grammaticalisation processes: **phonetic attrition**, grammatical **reanalysis**, **semantic bleaching**, and **obligatorification**. The following account will illustrate what this means.

The precise details of the course of the English progressive's development are still controversial because the evidence is slim, complicated and contradictory. On the one hand, there are indications that originally, at least one source of the English progressive is even more similar to the colloquial German progressive *Er ist am Arbeiten*: -*ing* was originally a purely nominal ending (like German -*ung*) and there was a construction containing the preposition *on*, like in:

> *On huntyng he was in Ingleswod,*
> *With alle his bold knyghtes good...*
> (from: *The Wedding of Sir Gawain and Dame Ragnelle*, l. 16-17, early 15th century)

The preposition was eroded to the prefix *a*-, which still survives in some archaisms (*"The times, they are a-changing!"*). On the other hand, both preposition and prefix must have been disappearing from this construction already as early as the Middle English period; in Chaucer (who died around 1400) we find forms like *syngynge he was*. Around that time, the -*ing*-form must have been being reanalysed as a participle.

To complicate the matter further, we find constructions of the type *be* + present participle with aspectual meaning in Old English already (*he wæs lærende* 'he was teaching'); but as can be gathered from the example, the participle in Old English had an -*nd* ending, just like in German. At some point in the somewhat chaotic history of Middle English, the construction based on the -*ing* form and the one based on the -*nd* form must have been conflated, presumably facilitated by a transitional homophony (➔ 4.1.2.1) of the two forms: To this day, substandard varieties of English use an -*in* suffix for the present participle, which could have come both from -*ing* and from -*nd*.

> ♠ The latter form, when it is used in writing, is usually spelled -*in'* (as in *goin'*, *havin'* etc.) to indicate that it should "really" be -*ing*, and the phenomenon is often very unprofessionally called "g-dropping". It is by no means clear that it ever contained a /g/ that could have been dropped. In Present-Day English, there is simply a variation between two different nasals, /ŋ/ and /n/; nothing is being dropped.

What is more interesting from a grammaticalisation perspective is that the use of the progressive has been expanding continually over the last centuries, which means, of course, that semantic bleaching took place: The more frequent a certain form, the less distinctive its meaning. Presently a well-known fast food provider is doing its best to foster this tendency: *I'm loving it* is a form that until not long ago was regarded as ungrammatical; and not even native speakers are able to tell what the progressive is meant to mean in this slogan.

Another strong indication of its grammaticalisation is that the progressive, along with other grammatical features of Modern English, has clearly become obligatory in the relevant contexts in which there was free variation 400 years ago. Shakespeare could still write

"What dost thou with thy best apparel on?";

today, we would have to ask in an analogous situation:

"What are you doing with your ...?".

> What other grammatical changes from Early Modern to Present-Day English do you observe on this example?

Grammaticalisation can be seen as a counterbalance to the tendency that has become apparent in the preceding subchapters, namely that the grammar of English as a whole loses the complexity it once was characterised by (→ 3.2.2.4 for the loss of verb inflections, etc.). But the time scale of this 'repair' mechanism is millennia rather than centuries: Over the last 15 centuries, English has gradually developed a new tense-aspect-voice system which is about as complex and differentiated as the ancient Indo-European one more than 3,000 years ago (though in other respects the two systems are quite different). The Indo-European system, known to us only by reconstruction from languages such as Sanskrit, Ancient Greek, or Latin, had been drastically reduced in Proto-Germanic, the common ancestor of both English and German.

Another prototypical and fairly recent example of grammaticalisation within the verbal syntagm is the so-called ***going-to*-future**. It meant the development of an entirely new grammatical category of English. The grammaticalisation of *going to* is shown syntactically and also phonologically, in that a contracted, more economical unstressed form *gonna* [gənə] has developed in colloquial usage. Thus, a contrast is emerging that had not been there before:

I'm going to the cinema indicates an active movement; *go* is the main verb.
I'm going to work is ambiguous: movement or intention.
I'm gonna have fun is unambiguous: intention; *gonna* is an auxiliary.

The intentional future meaning draws on the full verb *go* (plus *to*) which is emptied lexically and loaded grammatically to provide an alternative to the *will/shall*-future (→ 1.1.3.4.3). In other words, the construction *be going* (plus a prepositional phrase including *to*) developed into *be going to* (plus main verb) and was 'routinised' in the exclusive use of *gonna* as an auxiliary.

Once lexical morphemes have turned into grammatical morphemes, the process of grammaticalisation often goes further than that, given enough time. Free grammatical morphemes change so that they become more and more bound to a lexical morpheme next to them. In this way, new inflectional categories may arise.

The French future tense, e.g. (like that of most other Romance languages), arose from a combination of the infinitive of a verb with the successor of Latin *habere* ('have') as an auxiliary verb with the meaning 'have to'. Thus, a late Latin expression *cantare habeo* ('I have to sing') developed into French *chanterai* ('I'll sing').

There is no commonly accepted example of this kind from Present-Day English. Some linguists (ZWICKY / PULLUM 1983) have argued, though, that the 'weak form' of *not*, the clitic *n't*, has actually developed into an inflectional suffix now (which is restricted in its attachability to auxiliary verbs, of course; but all affixes are restricted to being used with one syntactic category or other).

The presumable development of past tense forms of the Proto-Germanic predecessor of Present-Day English *do* into the present past tense suffix *-ed* (as well as the German past tense suffix *-te*) would also be a case in point, but this grammaticalisation process lies so far back in history that we cannot reconstruct details (for the little we <u>can</u> reconstruct see → 3.2.2.4, ➢ box), and commonly historical linguists are very hesitant in this case to fill the huge gap in the evidence by speculation.

At present English grammar, it seems, is still recovering from the almost complete loss of inflectional morphology from Old to Early Modern English (→ 3.2.2) through trivial phonetic attrition (→ 3.2.1.8). The centuries since then have been spent in the repair shop, so to speak, of grammaticalisation within the verbal syntagm: Auxiliary after auxiliary emerged and expanded its combinability to accomplish the potentially complex verbal syntagm English boasts today (see above and also → 1.1.3.4). And it is in the verbal syntagm that possibly new inflectional categories are or will be emerging. We have already mentioned *n't*. In addition, the personal pronouns *me*, *him*, *them* etc. have already become clitics (→ 1.3.2; Fig. 45) and might some day be inflectional suffixes in, say, colloquial American English. Speaking of the latter, note oral 'conjugation paradigms' like

/wɒrəmaɪ/   /wɒrəjə/   /wɒtsɪ/ /wɒtʃɪ/ /wɒtsɪt/
/wɒrəwɪ/   /wɒrəjə/   /wɒrəðeɪ/

📖 Can you decipher what these forms are? Try to pronounce them from the transcription! All the phonetic letters used are contained in → Fig. 26 to Fig. 31. Try to 'translate' the forms into Standard English forms! Formulate sentences in which they are used! Then try to transcribe the non-standard forms in Standard English orthography!

The latter is something that is often done by novelists if they want to indicate that someone is speaking non-standard. (This technique of representing spoken language in writing, by the way, is called **eye dialect**.) So you might actually find spellings for the above forms in the novel you are presently reading.

> ⦿ Indicating the object (and also the subject) of the verb by an affix gram-
> maticalised out of personal pronouns is very common cross-linguistically; sev-
> eral European languages are presently undergoing grammaticalisation pro-
> cesses in that direction, including casual Standard German (quoted here in eye
> dialect):
>
> *Kommter an un fragt mich: Hastema'n Euro? 'chabbem eing gegeben.*

◈   We can now solve the puzzle why **mood** should be more **grammaticalised**
than modality (➔ 1.1.3.4.6). Mood is, as we said, by definition expressed by
bound morphology. This can be observed in the subjunctive moods of languages
like Ancient Greek, Latin, the Romance languages, and German (which by no
means all have identical functions and uses). In English, the subjunctive is almost
exclusively signalled by the <u>absence</u> of any inflectional suffixes. The formulaic
exclamation *Long live the Queen!* contains a subjunctive form, which is quite
rare nowadays. Yet, until the end of Early Modern English, the marking for subjunctive was much commoner in order to express a purpose, a hypothesis, or a
state of doubt. How about some Shakespearean examples (from *Richard III*)?

> *What if it come to thee againe?*
> *Thy selfe …Out-live thy glory…*
> *For Edward our Sonne…Dye in his youth, by like vntimely violence.*

The *if*-clause would be rendered in indicative mood today, the subjunctives in the
main clauses have 'optative' meaning, which would be expressed by a modal
auxiliary like inverted *may* today: 'May you outlive your glory…', 'May Edward
… die in his youth'.

The high degree of phonetic erosion in the subjunctive indicates a long history
of grammaticalisation. But also the meaning of the subjunctive has eroded. It
could be said that the subjunctive, in Present-Day English, but also in most of the
other languages mentioned, rarely has a 'meaning' of its own. In the Shakespeare
examples above, it could still be said to signal 'hypotheticality' or 'optative' and
contrasts (➔ Box 23) with an indicative form that does not have these meanings.
It is only in frozen, isolated formulaic expressions of the *God save the Queen*
kind that the present-day subjunctive truly contrasts semantically with the indicative mood (though, admittedly, we don't see many occasions on which one would
actually say *"God saves the Queen"*). In all other cases, the subjunctive, if it is
used at all, is automatically triggered by the lexico-grammatical context. There is
a certain semantically defined group of predicates which in a very formal register
of American English require the use of the subjunctive in their *that*-complement
clause (for the forms, ➔ 1.1.3.4.6, for the term *complement*, ➔ Box 11):

> *I **demand** that the committee reconsider its decision.*
> *It is very **important** that he come.*
> *I **insist** that you not insult my parents.*

A higher degree of obligatoriness is hardly conceivable. The use of the subjunctive in English is not motivated by any speaker's intention to express a specific

meaning shade by using it. Its use is completely automatised. This holds to an even higher extent for the subjunctives in French, Ancient and Modern Greek or German.

The subjunctive in many European languages represents an excellent example of a moribund grammatical category that has reached the end of its career. Phonetically eroded to a point where most of its forms have become indistinguishable from indicative forms, semantically emptied to a point where no semantic contrast can be expressed by it, and almost totally automatised in its use, it shows the final, lethal stage of grammaticalisation. If grammaticalisation continues to proceed to the extreme, the grammatical category involved commits suicide, as it were. It is a striking feature of grammaticalisation that phonetic and semantic decay often go hand in hand, demonstrating the inseparability of content and expression (→ Box 24) and the ultimate iconicity (→ Box 19) of grammar on the level of substance.

This is, as we saw, the point where modal verbs step in. They are in a more initial stage of grammaticalisation. They can express different shades of meaning and contrast with each other as well as with their own absence. They are not completely bound yet, although cliticisation has set in. For the next centuries, they will presumably do the job once done by mood in English.

So far we have been giving the impression as if grammaticalisation was a relentless, irreversible process. And indeed, this seems to be largely true. Language change appears as a gigantic funnel-shaped word grinder. Linguistic units seem to be constantly sliding down the lexicality – grammaticality scale, gradually being worn off in the process: Free lexemes persistently turn into clitics, clitics into bound morphemes, and bound morphemes erode until no phonetic substance is left. The language users, if they still feel the need, then have to find new ways to express the grammatical meaning whose means of expression they have just lost.

The phenomenon of grammaticalisation again shows the **fuzziness**, or rather: permeability of category boundaries in language. It is – this is what we can learn from the grammaticalisation debate – virtually a prerequisite for language change. If the boundary between lexical and grammatical morphemes (or between free, clitic, and bound morphemes) (→ 1.3.2) was fixed once and for all, nothing would ever change in grammar, and no grammar as complex as we find it today in all languages in the world could ever have developed.

3.2.4 Semantic change

Semantic changes are changes with respect to the meaning of, e.g., individual words vis-à-vis other words, and what they refer to respectively (see Chapter → 4 for a detailed account). On the basis of some diachronic examples, we may identify different dimensions of semantic change (JUCKER 2000, 118-120):

The Old English term *dogca* (or Middle English *dogge*) is reported to have been used by the respective speakers to refer to a particular variety of dogs (cf.

German *Dogge*). Later, the term was semantically generalised and could be used as a generic term to refer to all dogs. In this function *dog* is still used nowadays. This process is one of **broadening** (*semantische Erweiterung*). Another example from the animal kingdom is Old English *brid*, which was used to describe a young bird or nestling exclusively before the meaning became broadened to all members of the feathered tribe, as it were.

Fig. 59: Examples of broadening and narrowing

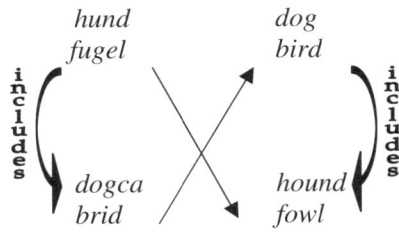

You now may rightfully ask: What were the equivalents of today's generic terms *dog* and *bird* back in Old English, then? What if speakers wanted to refer to all dogs and all birds? (You may think of German *Hund* and *Vogel* right now.) Indeed, they used *hund* and *fugel* to do so. The semantic fate of these words, in the contrasting light of the broadening described above, was to undergo a **narrowing** (*semantische Verengung*), i.e. a specialisation. Here, Elvis Presley comes to mind: *You ain't nothing but a hound dog...* Indeed, in Present-Day English, *hound* refers primarily to a hunting dog only, while *fowl* is used to describe a subcategory of birds, namely a special domestic type. This particular change involved, thus, a change of meaning hierarchies (→ 4.2.2.2).

If the meaning of a word changes in order to reflect general social or attitudinal changes, we may call it either **amelioration** (**elevation**, *semantische Melioration*) or **pejoration** (**degeneration**, *semantische Pejoration*). These can be seen as special types of narrowing or broadening. Take, e.g., the Old English word *cniht* which was used to describe a boy and/or a servant (similarly to '*boy*' in Late Modern English). Later on, as the position of the military servants of the king acquired prestige, the meaning of *knight* underwent amelioration, leaving behind the connotation of low social rank. And, who would think of this original meaning today when we think of a *knight* in shining armor? The corresponding cognate in German, *Knecht*, underwent pejoration and narrowing to the agricultural sphere to obtain its present-day, somewhat old-fashioned meaning.

A parallel semantic process of amelioration affected *minister*, which was used to refer to an executive servant in Middle English. Today, it has several meanings of executive persons of somewhat higher rank.

> 📖 Find out how many meanings *minister* has today and delineate the development of these meanings (by means of the *OED*, e.g.).

Pejoration, however, can be witnessed in the semantic 'career' of words such as Old English *cnapa* ('*knave*'). Originally referring (neutrally) to a male child (cf. German '*Knabe*'), *cnapa* acquired the semantic position and thus the low social rank of *cniht* when the latter was elevated to the more modern meaning of *knight*.

Such changes do not happen out of the blue. Speakers negotiate and alter the semantic range of words as they see fit and/or as external events (e.g. conquests, inventions) induce new communicative needs. If such meaning adaptations are conventionalised over time, the change is complete until a new one may be initiated. Resources for innovation are manifold. As mentioned above, social change has an influential say in this matter. After the Norman Conquest, when many lexemes of French origin were incorporated into English (→ 3.2.5.1), there occasionally was an open competition with words of Germanic origin that described the same entity in the real world, as it were. The results of this 'semantic rivalry' are, e.g., today's restricted, i.e. narrowed usages of *pork* vs. *pig* or *mutton* vs. *sheep* – the first elements of the pairs (of French origin) refer to meat, while the latter (of Germanic origin) refer to living animals exclusively (→ 4.2.2.1).

📖 Why should the distribution of meanings in *pork* vs. *pig* be the way it is in Present-Day English and not vice versa?

Further resources for semantic innovation are, amongst others:
- **metaphorical** (see below and also → 4.1.2.2; 4.3.2) and
- **metonymic** uses of language (see below), and last but not least,
- utterance **implicature** (→ 5.4).

Metaphor is a ubiquitous meachanism for the creation of new designations for new or old concepts. In classical rhetoric it was regarded, like metonymy, as a **figure of speech**, that is the use of a word in a sense deviating from its 'original' or 'proper' sense.

Box 34: Metaphor

The traditional view of metaphor is that it is something like a comparison, called **simile** in classical rhetoric, in which the marker of comparison, an expression such as *like*, or *similar to*, is simply left out. Thus, when people looked for a word for the a new invention like the electric lamp and called it *bulb*, they did so because they felt: "This is like a bulb of a tulip or the like". They thus extended the traditional meaning of bulb to cover further objects. Similarity is thus a decisive criterion for calling a semantic change metaphorical. Tons of ink have been spilt in classical rhetoric, literary studies, philosophy, linguistics, and, recently, cognitive psychology to define and explain the phenomenon of metaphor (MOOIJ 1976; see DIRVEN / PÖRINGS 2002 for a recent overview). The traditional theory has increasingly been attacked.

This textbook cannot even remotely do justice to this controversial discussion. Metaphor is a particularly crucial topic in cognitive semantics (LAKOFF / JOHNSON 1980). It will therefore be taken up again in section → 4.3.2.

Technological progress is another interesting motor of semantic change. To quote a somewhat dated example, technological development has influenced, for example, the semantic shift of *pen* as a writing tool. Nowadays, it is, apparently, not necessarily a bird feather any more which you dip in ink – yet, from a diachronic perspective, it was clearly derived from Norman French *penne* ('*feather*').

In most cases, language users are well aware of technological changes, but less aware of the gradual semantic shifts that accompany them. Everybody knows that watchmakers don't make watches anymore. They sell them, and if you are lucky, they repair them. But the technological change leading to that situation was so gradual that language users did not adapt their vocabulary to it. We still say *watchmaker* and not *watchseller. This means that the word *watchmaker* did not only change its meaning, but also its status: It became less motivated and more arbitrary (➜ Box 19).

In general, diachronic semantics is complex and elusive; changes appear impossible to predict. Yet, in retrospect, semantic changes often are not random needfillers, but follow an internal logic that encompasses many related languages. This logic is actually the 'logic of conversation', i.e., pragmatics (GRICE 1975; HORN 1984). Hence, we will return to questions of semantic change in section ➜ 5.4.

⚭ One more example shall be discussed here, illustrating SWEETSER's (1990) observations on systematic, recurring patterns of semantic change. Leaving theoretical underpinnings aside, part of the gist of her argument is as follows: Cognitive processes are not visible and difficult to conceptualise. A frequent strategy of gaining vocabulary to express abstract cognitive meanings is **metaphorisation** (Box 34) of suitable physical processes and entities (see also ➜ 4.3.2). Verbs of physical abilities and perception play a central role here. We will briefly look at verbs of perception.

Fig. 60: Meaning development of verbs of perception

physical perception	non-physical perception
see	*realise, know*
hear	*obey*
grasp	*understand*
taste	*prefer*
feel	*perceive*

⚭ The vocabulary of the semantic field of physical perception in English is systematically linked via metaphor to the vocabulary of internal, i.e. non-physical sensations (➜ 4.1.2.2; 4.3.1). Even more interesting, other languages have gone through a similar change. Compare the 'new' non-physical meanings of English *interview*, German *Einsicht*, French *clairvoyance*, Spanish *inspección* or Latin *supervidere* – all of these units are semantically linked to the physical action of 'seeing' (see also ➜ 3.2.1.4 on the ancient connection between seeing and knowing). Hence, there appears to be a coherent set of changes yielding a whole system of expressions for cognitive states and processes.

3.2.5   Lexical change

The lexical inventory of a language is constantly changing, too. Indeed, the vocabulary is probably the domain of language where the pace of change is fastest. We can witness lexical change even synchronically. You may just want to compare the words that were considered fashionable, i.e. 'hip', thirty years ago to those which you have fancied in your youth. You may face some difficulties of understanding when using these in a conversation with your grandparents, or even with your younger sister today.

It is not always clear where the new words come from. In this subchapter, we will primarily look at two strategies available to the speakers of a language to enrich its vocabulary: borrowing (→ 3.2.5.1) and neologism (→ 3.2.5.2). We will then turn to certain interesting changes that take place in new words once they have been formed (→ 3.2.5.3) and finally take a look at how and why words might disappear from the lexicon (→ 3.2.5.4).

3.2.5.1 Borrowing

As far as we can look back in the history of languages, there has always been contact between speakers of different languages. If there is contact, there is cultural exchange in the course of which people get to know new items, ideas, concepts. And often they take over the words with the things. Or the other culture is felt to be so superior in some way that it becomes fashionable to use words from the language associated with it.

☞Such a process of taking over words from another language is called **borrowing** (*Entlehnung*). The words that are borrowed are called **loans** (*Lehnwörter, Fremdwörter*). The language from which the loans are borrowed is called the **donor language**.

The metaphor involved in the terms *borrowing* and *loan* is actually a bit odd if you think twice about it. If you borrow a book from a library, you are expected to return it. How could a language return a loan to the donor language? It might be said that English is now returning some of its French loans to the French language in the form of so-called anglicisms, but they are not as welcome as your borrowed books are at the library...

❍ German linguists make a subtle distinction between *Lehnwort* and *Fremdwort*.

Lehnwörter are words of foreign origin that are completely integrated into the native vocabulary so that naïve speakers don't recognise they are loans, e.g. German *Mauer* from Latin *murus*.

Fremdwörter are words that still bear traces of their foreign origin, either in pronunciation, spelling or inflection: *Aktion* has 'un-German' stress; *Chanson* contains nasal vowels, even in some German speakers' pronunciation, which don't normally occur in German; *Aperçu* contains a strange letter, *Desideratum / Desiderata* is still inflected the Latin way.

For English, this distinction is never made and would in any case be much more difficult to draw. Let's hope the distinction made in German is not a token of German xenophobia.

As far as its lexicon is concerned, the English language can by no means be called xenophobic. It is probably the language in Europe that has integrated the

most loanwords from other languages, most of them from or via French. This accounts for some peculiar, unique properties of English vocabulary. It is
- unique by its sheer size (→ below),
- contains, as a direct corollary of this, unusually many synonyms (→ 4.2.2.1) or near-synonyms, and
- is extremely **opaque**.

Let us start with the last point first. It can only be hinted at by a few examples. As a result of extensive borrowing mainly from Greek, Latin, and French, English often uses words that are closely related in meaning, but completely unrelated morphologically, where other languages tend to use words derived from the same root, cf.

heart – cordial – cardiac	vs. German *Herz – herzlich – Herz-*
king – queen – royal	vs. German *König – Königin – königlich*
sun – sunny – solar	vs. German *Sonne – sonnig – Sonnen-*

As for synonyms or near-synonyms, lexical change is closely linked to semantic change; these particularly often go hand in hand. Thus, semantic differentiation processes as pointed out in the preceding subchapter (→ 3.2.4) allow for a reorganisation of the lexical stock when e.g. the usefulness and acceptability of new loanwords is negotiated by the speakers.

Hence, a word such as Old English *hærfest* survived as a lexeme next to the Middle English loan *autumpne*, resulting in today's (semantically specialised) *harvest* and (the more general) *autumn*. The function of lexemes such as Old English *feoh*, *here*, or the compound *wundorweorc*, however, have been more or less entirely replaced by other lexemes mostly from a foreign source. (Compare German *Vieh*, *Heer*, and *Wunderwerk* in this respect.) Today, we use *cattle*, *army*, and *miracle* as if they had always been genuine, i.e. 'native' English words.

Diachronically speaking, we can identify several waves of reshaping and enrichment that resulted in the lexical inventory of Present-Day English which is actually a melting pot of non-English influences. Reading an Old English text, we will find only approximately half of its words in today's English, even allowing for sound and meaning changes. What is more, you may consider, the sheer number of lexemes which has grown from less than 25,000 to way more than 500,000 today. Contemporary German dictionaries contain up to 250,000 words only, even though German is said to be so much more compound-friendly than English (→ 1.3.5.2).

How do we account for such an impressive number? The first donors to contribute significantly to the lexical stock were, as early as in Old English, Latin and Celtic languages. The traces we can identify still today reflect the nature of the contact between the respective speakers on the British isle more than a thousand years ago.

However trendy Celtic heritage may have become recently, Celtic elements are extremely and surprisingly rare in English. Thus, some elements the etymology of which can be traced back to Celtic have survived in placenames. The first Latin loans often referred to household articles, trading goods, or warfare (→ Fig. 61). Beware that many of these early words of Latin origin were already integrated while the Angles and Saxons still lived on the continent, and this is the only path of borrowing Latin at that early time that we may be sure of. It was only several centuries later, with the growing impact of christianity and monasterial life by the end of the Old English period, that new words from Greek and Latin related to religion and schooling were borrowed, i.e. incorporated into the language to become used as 'regular' English vocabulary items.

Fig. 61: Celtic and early Latin loans in English

Celtic	Latin	Old English	Present-Day English
broc		*broc*	*brock* (*'badger'*)
Canti(on)		*Cant-*	*Kent*
cumb		*cumb*	*-combe* (*'valley'*, e.g. in *Salcombe*)
	candela	*candel*	*candle*
	catillus	*cytel*	*kettle*
	vinum	*wīn*	*wine*
	vallum	*weall*	*wall*
	discipulus	*discipul*	*disciple*
	schola*	*scole*	*school*

*Originally from Greek

A next wave of loans was a consequence of the hegemony of the Danes in England (→ 3.1.1). Their Old Norse contributed many everyday words, several of which have survived until today as very basic lexical items such as *egg*, *knife*, *sister*, *window*, or *sky*. Word-initial /sk/ is often mentioned as indicating Late Old English Scandinavian loans. Originally, all initial Germanic /sk/-sequences had become /ʃ/ in Old English, but not in Old Norse. When Old English borrowed an Old Norse /sk/-word, of which a cognate (→ 3.2.1.1, ☞ box) pronounced with /ʃ/ already existed, this resulted in occasional pairs of **etymological doublets** such as *shirt* vs. *skirt*.

Box 35: Etymological doublets

Etymological doublets are a typical phenomenon in languages with long-standing loan relations to other languages, typically genetically related (→ 3.2.1.0) to the receiving language and / or among each other. In this respect, English provides ideal conditions for this phenomenon. Greek, Latin and French influence have persisted from the end of antiquity to this day. Old Norse, another important donor language, is genetically closely related. In consequence, many words were borrowed several times via different paths in different phonological shapes and with different meanings. Thus, *hostel*, *hospital*, and *hotel* all go back to the same Latin etymon *hospitale* and were borrowed from or via French at different periods.

The Old Norse words *by* (*'village'*) or *þveit* (*'piece of land'*) became productive in placenames such as *Derby* or *Applethwaite*. The most interesting loans, however, are those that entered the pronominal paradigm to form today's *they*, *them*, and *their* (→ 3.2.2.3).

> One group of etymologically related words, an 'etymological quadruplet' in English, was generated by the already polysemous Latin adjective *gentilis*: *gentle*, *gentile*, *genteel*, and, yes, *jaunty* all ultimately go back to this productive Latin adjective. Find out when, on what path, and in what meaning they were borrowed and try to explain the differences in meaning, phonological shape and spelling. We recommend using the *OED Online*.

While we leave the Old English period, we have to cope with a new donor language, French. The influence of this language is unparalleled in the history of English, indeed, almost unparalleled in the loan relations between any two languages in Europe (Italian influence on Maltese might come close to it, though). Traces of French ancestry can be found in almost every modern English sentence. (Even the last sentence contained four: *trace*, *ancestry*, *modern*, and *sentence*.) During Middle English, French-based loans were integrated in virtually all domains of life on a large scale. As examples that have survived until today are omnipresent, the following list can only provide a glimpse:

Fig. 62: Norman French loans

Norman French	Middle English	Present-Day English
assemblee	*assemble*	*assembly*
corune	*croune*	*crown*
justise	*iustise*	*justice*
preere	*preiere*	*prayer*
gramaire	*gramer*	*grammar / glamour**
remede	*remedie*	*remedy*
poete	*poyet*	*poet*
saussiche	*sausige*	*sausage*

*via Scots

The table illustrates that according to the societal reorganisation, 'high-brow' domains, such as government, law, church or education (including medicine and art), were chiefly affected.

> Find three words of French origin that were borrowed in the 13th century. You may want to use the *OED Online* or etymological dictionaries for this task.

Remember that the Middle English period is characterised by a considerable increase of dialectal diversity. Thus, the Middle English examples mentioned each represent one of several realisations of spelling (and presumably of pronunciation, too).

The Early Modern English period saw first efforts to take stock with respect to the language and, in the event, to standardise it (→ 3.1.3). Meanwhile, there was a general revival of classical languages such as Ancient Greek and Latin which led to the integration of loans such as *anonymous*, *catastrophe*, *species* and *virus*. Additionally, French served (again) as a prestigious model for the language, i.e. particularly lexical, behaviour of an educated elite. The desire of some to enrich the lexicon radically on these bases culminated in a heated public debate which became henceforth known as the **inkhorn controversy**. In the event, some advocated a filling of subjectively felt vocabulary gaps or pursued a boosting of their ego with the help of lexemes of the above-mentioned source languages in order to embellish English on the one hand, and to make it internationally 'competitive' on the other. One of the more extreme text examples containing so-called inkhorn terms is criticized in Thomas Wilson's *Arte of Rhetorique* (1553). For a better overview, the words that were newly introduced are in italics. Note that the function words, i.e. the words with a definite grammatical function such as auxiliaries or conjunctions (→ 1.1.3.1, ☞ box), are left untouched.

> … *expendyng*, and *reuolutyng* with my selfe, your *ingent affabilitee*, and *ingenious capacitee* for *mundane* affaires: I cannot but *celebrate*, & *extolle* your *magnificall dexteritee*, aboue all other. For how could you haue *adepted* such *illustrate* prerogatiue, and *dominicall superioritee*, if the fecunditee of your *ingenie* had not been so *fertile*…

Do you understand the passage ad hoc? Think of how most readers (let alone speakers) of Early Modern English, educated on average, might have reacted. As you will have recognised, some of the inkhorn terms made their way into everyday usage (e.g. *capacity*, *celebrate*). Most terms, however, were ephemeral and vanished soon. The contemporary, more purist opponents of this lexical movement campaigned acrimoniously against such artificial and wholesale borrowing, which ultimately led to the felt necessity to compile lists of genuinely English words, thus dictionaries. The controversy is, in retrospect, a mirror of the quest for 'English' identity that shaped the whole Elisabethan era. It shows all the more the prevalent ambitions to 'tune' the language to pay homage to it as a carrier of (national) grandeur and pride.

In Late Modern English, the lexical inventory experienced a next boost due to the worldwide expansion of the British Empire and, subsequently, the increasing globalisation of English. Thus, due to diversified language contacts, speakers of English have been exposed to new, also extra-European, language influences. Quite expectedly, there has been extensive borrowing into English from all continents ever since. (You may deduce where *voodoo* or *kangaroo* come from).

A specific role of the British Empire should not be overstated, though. Looking at Fig. 63 below more closely, you will no doubt notice two things: Quite a few languages are represented in it which were never spoken natively in the British Empire, and many of the words in it are true **internationalisms** (*Internationalismen*), i.e., they are found in practically every modern language.

Fig. 63: Loans from all over the world

Source language	Late Modern English
Afrikaans	*apartheid*
Algonquian	*racoon*
Arabic	*jihad*
Czech	*robot*
Dutch	*cookie*
German	*schadenfreude*
Hindi	*shampoo*
Italian	*lottery*
Spanish	*embargo*
Turkish	*yogurt*

English has simply been taking part, and serving as a powerful relay station, in a general globalisation which is turning the whole world into one sprachbund (→ Box 31). For this development, US-American dominance after 1945 was probably more decisive than the decaying British Empire.

But French and Latin have not lost their role as the main quarries for new lexical material. Large numbers of new words were and are constantly being borrowed from these languages or formed with splinters derived from their roots and affixes (→ 1.3.4, 1.3.5).

Since many European languages did the same, it is sometimes difficult to tell where exactly a word comes from, i.e., in which language it was first formed. Would you have guessed, e.g., that *informatics*, whose morphological raw material is clearly Latin and/or French, was coined on the model of a Russian word (which in turn, of course, was formed using Latin material)?

Nowadays, English is more known (if not notorious) as a donor rather than a receiver of loanwords. Languages all over the world, and German is among them, now use English as a seemingly inexhaustible lexical quarry whenever needed. In this view, it is replacing formerly prestigious resources such as like Latin or French (→ 7.3).

In German, borrowing from English has come to be taken so much for granted that the language, in some areas at least, seems to have suspended its creative potential for the formation of new words, a situation ironically reminiscent of the Middle English period (→ 3.1.2; 3.2.2.5).

In this situation, where borrowing seems to be overwhelmingly preferable to using native word-formation strategies, mysteriously, English **pseudo-loans** (*Pseudoentlehnungen*) are sometimes created, i.e. words which give the appearance of being English loans as they are formed from English morphemic material, but which are unknown to speakers of English. Are they the inkhorn terms of the 20th century? An early example of this kind is *Quizmaster* ['kvɪsˌmaːstɐ] (from the 1950s), two more recent ones the presently trendy and omnipresent *Handy* ['hɛndiː] and *Mobbing* ['mɔbɪŋ].

3.2.5.2 Neologisms

Lexical (or lexico-semantic) change, however, is not limited to borrowing as an innovation strategy. Innovation as the most conspicuous phenomenon of language change in general is diversified also in terms of twists and turns along the never-ending road of development of the lexical inventory. Thus, an additional possibility are **neologisms** (*Neologismen*, *Wortneuschöpfungen*). In this case, especially the mechanisms of word-formation mentioned in sections → 1.3.4 and → 1.3.5 make themselves felt. Neologisms are mostly formed from existing material in order to name new (kinds of) entities that have been created, be it in technology, industry, politics, science, advertising or elsewhere.

Neologisms are construed via e.g. compounding (*'database'*), derivation (*'zeitgeisty'*), blending (*'edutainment'*), abbreviation (*'3D'*), acronymy (*'snafu'*) or eponymy (*'Kleenex'*), reflecting modern eclecticism and thus language creativity. It seems that blending and secretion have recently increased in comparison to 'classical' types of word formation.

Users of jargons as specialised, job-specific language varieties (e.g. computer specialists) may obscure the communicative access for non-members of the group by coining and employing neologisms such as *software* or *to debug*. These may catch on and enter general usage, just as words originally restricted to regionally or socially based language varieties. E.g., some slang terms like *nerd* (*'foolish or technically obsessed, socially inept person'*), *to hit pay dirt* (*'to achieve profit or success'*) or *hippie* made it and crossed social borders.

> ✒ Beware that the term **jargon** is used differently in sociolinguistics, especially in pidgin/creole research (→ 7.4).

Occasionally it also happens that a word or morpheme is a pure (artificial) **invention**, such as the famous *googol*, which is a fanciful, colloquial name for ten raised to the hundredth power (10^{100}). Could you think of a better word for it? Maybe *gazillion*?

An interesting problem for neologism research and lexicography is the question of how to distinguish between ephemeral spontaneous word creations, so called **nonce-formations** and genuine neologisms that actually lastingly make it into the lexicon in some (however small) speech community (HOHENHAUS 1998; → 1.1.1.2, ☞ box). Many 'new words' that are found in the literature on neologisms were actually only coined on one occasion, e.g. as a proper name for an event, for a business of some kind, or a product, and forgotten when the occasion was over, the business closed down, or the product out of fashion. Here, the methods of corpus linguistics (→ Box 3) again prove useful (FISCHER 1998).

3.2.5.3 Lexicalisation

Neologisms very often undergo a complex process called **lexicalisation** (also → 1.3.4), usually manifested in a semantic change. In the long run, even the pronunciation of the lexicalised derivation may change, the former identity of its components thus becoming blurred. Some older lexicalisations have become so opaque that language users without historical linguistic knowledge are not aware that they have to do with a former compound or derivation.

⚱ If it wasn't for the conservative spelling of *cupboard*, no one would surmise today that a cup-board was once a board to place cups on. The Early Modern English period actually saw spellings such as <cubbard>, but then language purists came along and claimed that a cubbard was 'really' a cup-board (which was nonsense in Shakespeare's time already; *cupboard* is used in a meaning coming close to the present-day one at least from the early 16th century on!). Presumably, they also tried to introduce a spelling pronunciation, but obviously failed. They managed, however, to add another item to the oddities that ruined the reputation of the English spelling system (→ 2.5).

⌗ A fairly recent, well documented example of lexicalisation is the noun *business* (derived from *busy*) which has changed its meaning considerably since it was formed in Middle English. Its derivational history would suggest that it denotes 'the state of being busy', but this meaning is obsolete today. However, among many other senses that it developed and lost again over the centuries, those that are prevalent today also cropped up very early. Interestingly, a new word was formed in Late Modern English to cover the original meaning which, contradicting English spelling rules, was cautiously spelled *busy-ness* (with a hyphen) at first, later *busyness*. This new word shows that the process of lexicalisation of the derivation *business* has been completed: It is no longer felt to be related to the adjective *busy*, and that is why the need arose to form a new derivation to cover the original meaning. Note that also the pronunciation differs between *business* [bɪznɪs] (some people even start spelling it <biznis>) and *busyness* [bɪzɪnɪs].

> ♠ The term **lexicalisation** is used in a different sense in lexicology and semantics (→ 4.2.3).

3.2.5.4 Other lexical changes

Further, words may become gradually **obsolete** (*veraltet*) as the object they denote is not in use any more (e.g. *gamash, phonograph, postilion; telegram*) due to fashion or technological progress, e.g.

Another powerful reason for words disappearing or at least changing the stylistic level is culture-specific **taboo** (*Sprachtabu*) connotations. With respect to the latter, a short compilation of examples includes

- **euphemism** (*Euphemismus*), i.e. the replacement by a 'sugarcoating' expression which is less embarrassing for both speaker and listener:

    to die vs. *to decease, to pass away, to pay the debt of nature, to go to the house of the father.*

- Its opposite, **dysphemism** (*Dysphemismus*), however, conveys a less positive or harsher meaning than the corresponding neutral word.

    to die vs. *to croak, to flatline, to kick the bucket, to peg out.*

> 📖 Taboo indeed is a creative field of innovation. Just check how many expressions you know, e.g., to describe the facts of 'going to the toilet' (or the place itself), 'vomiting', or 'having (homo)sexual intercourse'.

Euphemism, and even less so dysphemism, nor any other of the reasons adduced in the literature, <u>necessarily</u> lead to word obsolescence, nor are they the decisive reasons. Sometimes words disappear simply because they are no longer fashionable in a certain sense. As most words are polysemous (→ 4.1.2.1), however, even this does not usually end the career of the word. In any case, obsolescence may be a very subjective category. Some people may regard a certain word as obsolete because they don't remember encountering it, others may carry on using it. It should also be remembered that old texts (Shakespeare, 18th century novels, etc.) are being read by some people, so that their vocabulary may continue to influence educated contemporaries' speech.

§   Occasionally, euphemism can start a whole chain of replacements, viz. in cases in which the new euphemism immediately starts undergoing a process of **pejoration** (→ 3.2.4) because the social causes of the taboo haven't changed. For example, people of African origin used to be called *negroes* or *moors*, but these words are now old-fashioned. Especially *negro* is usually considered politically incorrect and offensive, hence taboo. Instead, the more recent term *coloured* came to be used, which, however, is now considered to be unacceptable, too. The most widely and quasi-neutrally employed term today is *black*, in place of which *African-American* is also sometimes used. (The term *nigger*, by the way, an insult of the highest degree, may even be positively used as an in-group identifier – it all matters who says it to whom in what context; see Chapter → 7 for matters of sociolinguistics.)

§   The gay community and its use of the word *gay*, by the way, is a good example of how the above-mentioned pejoration trap can be escaped. *gay*, when referring to sexual behaviour, started out as a slang euphemism with clearly pejorative connotations (contradictory as this may seem). In the 19th century, it could also refer to prostitutes. It was then simply taken up by gay people as a proud self-designation and has clearly not only undergone semantic amelioration, but has also risen sociolinguistically: It is no longer considered a slang word.

3.3   Why do languages change?

Phenomena of language change are so dynamic and complex that the attempt to describe them must result in a somewhat sketchy account. The lexical stock represents a perpetuum mobile of obsolescence and creative innovation. Further, the phenomenon of grammaticalisation (→ 3.2.3.3) gives the lie to language purists who claim that language change is to be identified with language decay (e.g. AITCHISON [2]1994). Language change in general is a process operating on a huge time-scale – one particular development can take centuries and millennia to become completed, without necessarily coming to an end. Why all this?

Generations of linguists have asked this question again and again. Some have held the prescriptive view that language would not change if it were taught properly at school.

> ⊙ A surprisingly good example of the relative success of this view is the history of the Greek language, where the model of Ancient Greek was so overpowering and culturally important as a token of Greek national identity that it managed to delay and even reverse language change over many centuries.

This challenging view notwithstanding, we can only analyse *a posteriori* when and why a certain change took place. Then, it may be possible to find generalisable reasons for the fact that languages do never come to a rest, as it were. In most cases, the reasons lie in the process of communication itself, which is marked by incongruent or even contradictory intentions and interests of the participants (→ 5.4). Moreover, on the basis of what we learnt in section → 3.2, we can state that the necessity for language change results, above all, from cultural changes, both evolutionary and revolutionary. In a nutshell: Languages are constantly changing because they are being used.

Language change thus often reflects social change (→ 7.6 for a sociolinguistic example of change). E.g., a certain feature of pronunciation, lexicon or grammar at one point in time may be regarded as a **stigmatised** deviation, that is, a deviation that is not well received by influential people and that marks (that's what the term *stigmatise* means) the speaker using it as socially hopelessly inferior. It may later, given the suitable societal developments, turn into a norm or at least into an accepted possibility.

Some of the most interesting approaches to the question how linguistic innovations spread within and across speech communities come from sociolinguistics. In his famous Martha's Vineyard study, LABOV (1972) found that inhabitants of an island off the American East Coast reacted to an influx of tourists from the mainland by variation and changes in their pronunciation that asserted their identity as true islanders against the 'invaders'. Hereby he "showed that synchronic variation (…) is often the root of diachronic change (….)" (MEYERHOFF 2006, 22; see there for further detail). MILROY / MILROY (1978), in a study conducted in Belfast, have shown that the degree to which individuals approximate to a vernacular speech norm correlated to the extent to which (the individual) participated in close-knit networks of people living and working together.

Apart from that, further explanations for language change seem necessary. There appear to be some general principles underlying the communication process, be it in Old or Present-Day English, in Latin or High German. On the one hand, there is the principle of optimal **comprehensibility** of linguistic utterances: Most people want to be understood while communicating. On the other hand, there is the principle of **economy** which is 'active' at the same time: Most people try to express themselves as briefly and effortlessly as possible. This may, i.a., result in a number of natural sound changes some of which we have discussed in → 3.2.1. These sound changes might, however, mess up neat patterns on the morphological level (➔ 3.2.2), which in turn may trigger changes on the syntactic level (➔ 3.2.3).

| 📖 Find an example for the latter development in English language history! |

The two principles, comprehensibility and economy, are weighed against each other whenever people speak. A momentous outcome of this constant balancing act is that frequent words tend to be shorter than less frequent words. Phonetic attrition and clipping do their job most effectively in frequent words. This effect became known as **ZIPF's Law** (*Zipfsches Gesetz*; see ZIPF 1929). Consequentially, as soon as a (long) word increases in frequency, it will be liable to eventual shortening, e.g. by clipping (➔ 1.3.5). However, an economising sound change which has gone 'too far', i.e. which causes misunderstanding, has to be compensated for by other processes in order not to impair intelligibility. Hence, an endless and mostly irreversible cycle of language change keeps revolving in all languages, e.g. from Proto-Indo-European to Present-Day English and beyond.

⊙ A prototypical instance of such shortening preceding a clarifying **expansion** (*Expansion*) process is Latin *hodie* ('today', really a transparent phrase literally meaning 'on_this-day'), which was eroded in French into the phonologically shorter and opaque form *hui* /ɥi/. Later, this sound sequence was felt not to be distinct or transparent enough and was replaced by a much more complicated but transparent expression, *au jour d'hui*, literally 'at the day of today', which then coalesced (lexicalised) into one word which is still transparent, i.e. modern French *aujourd'hui*. So in Present-Day French we surprisingly have a form that is longer and more complicated than the Latin form 2000 years ago. Again, this word might become reduced and obscured in the future due to a process of attrition.

The Romance languages afford better examples of such long-drawn processes than English or German because developments can be traced much further back into the past, thanks to the written documentation of Latin, which dates back to the 6th century B.C.

Economy and comprehensibility do not explain everything yet. KELLER (1990; [2]1994) convincingly shows how language change comes about as the result of many different decisions of people, none of whom in fact *wants* to change language, but pursues other goals, goals beyond economy and comprehensibility, such as to draw attention to oneself, to present oneself as ingenious and eloquent, or to simply differ from others. Thereby, conflicts of communication arise again and again and can become reasons for language change.

Further explanations for language change will be given in section ➔ 5.4.

4 Semantics

4.0 What is semantics?

Semantics (*Semantik*) is concerned with the **meaning** of linguistic units, especially with the form of the content plane of language (→ Box 24).

It can be subdivided into **word semantics** (*Wortsemantik*) and **sentence semantics** (*Satzsemantik*). Sentence semantics in most linguistic schools has a strong affinity to formal logic and is therefore often called **formal semantics** (*formale Semantik*) (→ 4.4). In cognitive linguistics, it is dealt with in close association with syntactic questions, however (→1.2.3, 4.3.1).

In section → 1.1.2 we already tried a definition of *word*. Following that definition, we may say that in the sentence

I was late again and so were you,

there are eight words. That definition of *word* relates to actually pronounced or written words, i.e. to the substance plane of language (→ Box 24), or, it may be said, to the *parole* (→ Box 4). It is, however, equally true to say that the above sentence consists of only seven words, if we assume that *was* and *were* are really one and the same word, used in different forms. This is, then, a notion of word seen on the level of the *langue*.

When we want to refer to the unit (in the above example, *be*) that underlies formally different instantiations we use the term **lexeme** (*Lexem*). We might thus say that *was* and *were* are different forms of the lexeme *be*. Lexemes are abstract units; they combine a (simple or complex) expression with a more or less consistent meaning (a word might be polysemous (→ 4.1.2.1), having a number of meanings that are closely related to each other).

The term *word* can be used when talking about expression form (e.g. the expression form /kʌp/, representing an abstract sound image), or expression substance (e.g. the expression substance [kʌp], representing an actual utterance), or the combination of these. We might thus also say that the term *word* may refer to a unit of the lexicon as part of the *langue* or to an occurrence of that unit in an utterance as part of the *parole*.

A further complication in the use of the term *word* arises from the fact that in both these cases the content associated with the expression (i.e. the meaning of the word) may also be meant along with the expression itself. For example, when we say that "*cup* is a word" we mean that *cup* is an expression in the lexicon, or an occurrence of that expression in an utterance, or both at the same time. In many cases, we also mean that *cup* is an expression in the lexicon, or an occurrence of that expression in an utterance, associated with the meaning 'cup'.

We will continue to use the term *word* when we don't want to restrict our-selves to one of these meanings.

In linguistic terminology, the **lexicon** (*Lexikon*) of a language is the sum of all the words, more precisely, lexemes, of this language. The sum of all the lexemes that an individual speaker has in his/her mind is often referred to as the **mental lexicon** (AITCHISON 2004, see also → www.narr-studienbuecher.de on psycho-linguistics). It is not just a list of words, but also includes that information about words that is not predictable by general grammatical rules, e.g., grammatical peculiarities such as irregular past tense forms, the valency of a verb (→ 1.2.1.1), or the use of prepositions, etc. This means that words have a grammar of their own, a 'word grammar', which has to be learnt specially.

When we want to refer only to the words of a language, excluding grammati-cal or other information, we talk of the **vocabulary** (*Wortschatz, Vokabular*) of this language. A **dictionary** (*Wörterbuch, Lexikon*) is an actual book constituting an attempt to list the lexicon of a language.

Lexicology (*Lexikologie*) is concerned with the lexicon of a language and the description and delimitation of each individual word meaning. It also tries to clarify theoretically which properties of a word belong in the lexicon. It is thus that discipline on which **lexicography** (*Lexikographie*), the writing of dictionar-ies, is based. Lexicology needs a well-founded theory of word meaning and meaning relations.

The term **meaning** (*Bedeutung*) is a term frequently used in everyday speech and also in linguistics, as in this book. It is, however, often not precise enough for linguistic study. In order to get a clearer idea of the nature of meaning we need to make some basic distinctions and know some basic terminology that will be introduced in the following sections (For yet another meaning of *meaning*, see Chapter → 5.)

4.1   General key concepts of semantics

4.1.1   Reference vs. sense and related dichotomies

The distinction between reference and sense as different aspects of the meaning of a word or string of words is an important one for a precise discussion of se-mantic questions.

- The **reference** (*Referenz*) of an expression is its direct relation with the extra-linguistic world. When we say that an expression refers to something, we mean that it picks out an actual or imagined entity or state of affairs from the world. Identical expressions may have different reference in different contexts and at different times, e.g.

   the Pope; my neighbour; I, you; here, there; now, tomorrow.

Reference is concerned with content substance (→ Box 24).

- The **sense** (*Sinn*) of an expression is its content without reference, those features and properties which define it. It is what we are able to understand when we hear a word, without picking out a specific entity or state of affairs from the world, e.g.

> *rhino; president; city; walking stick; year; lovesickness*

Hence, *sense* is concerned with content form (→ Box 24).

To take another example: The expressions

> *morning star,*
> *evening star,*
> *planet Venus*

actually all happen to refer to the same object; they have the same reference. Their sense, however, is different, since they do not have the same defining properties. Thus,

- *Venus* could be defined as 'the planet second in order from the sun and nearest to the Earth';
- *morning star* as 'bright planet seen in the eastern sky when the sun rises'; and
- *evening star* as 'bright planet seen in the western sky when the sun sets'.

Semantic terminology is neither standardised nor uncontroversial. Apart from *reference* and *sense*, the following terms are often used for the description of (similar aspects of) meaning:

- The **extension** (*Extension*) of an expression is the class of actual or imagined objects or states of affairs it may be used to refer to. For example, I can use the expression *rhino* to make reference to the animal I keep in my garden pond. But when I am using it without any specific reference, I am including all the rhinos in the world; this is the extension of *rhino*. Similarly, the expression *lovesickness* may make reference to one particular instance of this emotional state or to the phenomenon in general.

  Thus, when we are not focussing on one specific instance but rather referring to all such states, past and present, we are talking about the extension of this term. *Extension*, then, like *reference*, relates to the substance of the content plane of language (→ Box 24). It could also be said that the extension of an expression is its **reference potential** (*Referenzpotential*).

- The **intension** (*Intension*) of an expression is those properties which define it, its mental content independent of context. It may roughly be equated with *sense*.
- The term **denotation** (*Denotation*) is used in several different meanings. It may signify reference, extension, sense/intension, or both extension and intension, depending on terminological context. Most importantly, however, the denotation of an expression is its context-independent, 'objective' basic meaning, also called descriptive meaning (*deskriptive Bedeutung*) and contrasts with *connotation*.

- The **connotation** (*Konnotation*) of an expression is the variable, subjective, often emotive part of its meaning. For example, the denotation of the expression *night* would be something like 'the dark part of each 24-hour period, when the sun cannot be seen'; but its connotations may be, e.g., 'lonely', 'uncanny', or 'romantic'.

Another distinction relevant to the description of meaning is that between

- **paradigmatic** relations (*paradigmatische Beziehungen*) and
- **syntagmatic** relations (*syntagmatische Beziehungen*).

When we speak of paradigmatic relations we are interested in what expressions can be potentially <u>substituted</u> for others. In the sentence *She was very sad*, for example, *sad* may be replaced by *unhappy* (→ 4.2.2.1) or by *happy* (→ 4.2.2.4). *Sad, happy* and *unhappy* are thus said to be in a paradigmatic relation to each other. It is also said that they belong to the same **semantic field** (*semantisches Feld*; → 4.2.1). Networks of paradigmatic relations define semantic fields.

When we speak of syntagmatic relations we are interested in the linear combinability of expressions. For example, we can say *That's a tall rock*, but not **That's an intelligent rock*, as *intelligent* and *rock* are not combinable expressions. It is then said that "*tall*" and "*rock*" are in a syntagmatic relationship because they co-occur in the same clause or even phrase. We could also say that *tall rock* is a possible **collocation** (*Kollokation*). The study of collocations has become an important feature of corpus-based cognitive semantics (→ 4.3).

> ☞ The notions of *paradigmatic* and *syntagmatic* are also used in phonology and morphology, for the exchangeability and combinability of phonemes and morphemes, and in syntax, where the exchangeability and combinability of words, constructions and other expressions plays an important role, as we have seen.

4.1.2 Ambiguity, homonymy and polysemy; metonymy and metaphor; vagueness

4.1.2.1 Two kinds of ambiguity: homonymy and polysemy

We speak of **ambiguity** (*Ambiguität*) if a word or sentence may be assigned more than one interpretation.

We saw in section → 1.2.2.5 that some sentences are ambiguous by virtue of their structure alone. Other sentences are ambiguous because they contain ambiguous words. For example, the sentence *She watched the ball* is ambiguous because the word *ball* is ambiguous as illustrated below. An ambiguous word, then, is a word whose form on the expression plane corresponds to more than one form on the content plane (→ Box 24).

There are two different kinds of word-based ambiguity: homonymy and polysemy. It is not always easy to distinguish between them.

- We speak of **homonymy** (*Homonymie*) if different words happen to be identical in expression (form and) substance, i.e. if they happen to have the same spelling and pronunciation. In other words, homonymous words are different lexemes with different content, but with the same expression (form and) substance (Fig. 64).

Fig. 64: Examples of homonymy	
expression form	**content form**
ball	'round object'
	'dancing event'
bank	'financial institution'
	'sloping side of a river'
trunk	'elephant's nose'
	'suitcase'

In most cases people do not even notice the ambiguity of a sentence, since most contexts only allow one interpretation. And ambiguous words, too, more often than not appear in contexts that preclude misunderstanding. In dictionaries, homonymy is often indicated by separate entries.

- Depending on the **modality** of communication (→ Box 40), ambiguity may also arise in speaking (homophony) or alternatively in writing alone (homography).

Fig. 65: Example of homophony		
expression form		**content form**
phonological	**orthographic**	
/θruː/	<through>	(spatial preposition)
	<threw>	(past tense of *throw*)

We speak of **homophony** (*Homophonie*) if words happen to have only the same pronunciation, but are spelled differently (Fig. 65).

Fig. 66: Example of homography		
expression form		**content form**
phonological	**orthographic**	
/wɪnd/		'air movement'
/waɪnd/	<wind>	'turn round and round'

We speak of **homography** (*Homographie*) if words happen to have only the same spelling (Fig. 66).

- The other kind of word-based ambiguity is **polysemy** (*Polysemie*). In contrast to homonymy, where two different lexemes are involved, polysemy is a property of individual lexemes in which there is a close and often systematic relationship between different senses of this word.

In particular, the reference of polysemous lexemes often includes quite heterogeneous classes of things which are nevertheless systematically and predictably related.

For example, words like *school, church, university*, etc., may designate a building, an institution, or a group of people, as can be seen in the following examples from the BNC:

Building:	*... Ireland's smallest **church**, measuring 12ft by 6ft ...* A5X 293
Institution:	*You cannot, in isolation from **church** doctrine, ... say that Jesus said this thing or that thing.* A7C 1280
Group of people:	*Until the practice was banned, the **church** used this image to signify the Holy Trinity.* A7D 1098

Because of the close relatedness of the senses of a polysemous word, we do not treat them as distinct lexemes, and often we do not even notice the polysemy or may not be able to tell precisely which of the senses is actually meant, and do not realise that quite different things may actually be referred to by such a word. In a dictionary polysemous words are usually given sub-entries under the same head entry. Note, however, that most dictionaries are historically oriented in this respect, and give unitary entries for all lexemes that happen to share the same etymological origin.

    📖   What kind of ambiguity is illustrated and exploited in the cartoon below?

"I'm sorry, the professor is tied up at the moment. Can you ring again a little later?"   (Cartoon by Annette Freund)

Sometimes, when the differences between the different senses become too large or unpredictable, a polysemous word may split up into several homonyms, which is not always noted by dictionaries. This happened, e.g., in the case of *key*, which has developed many different senses, e.g.:

1.   a small metal instrument specially cut to fit into a lock and move its bolt.
4.   something that affords a means of access.
10.   one of a set of marked parts, designated areas, or levers pressed in operating a typewriter, computer terminal, calculator, etc.
12   **a.** (in a keyboard instrument) one of the levers that when depressed by the performer sets in motion the playing mechanism.
    ... (*Random House Dictionary*, online)

It is clear that some of these meanings are closely related (such as 1. and 4. or 10 and 12). The relationship between 1 and 4 on the one hand and 10 and 12 on the other, however, are rather obscure synchronically. It might thus be justified to postulate a split into at least two homophones. But it is also clear that this is a point which invites disagreement among linguists.

4.1.2.2 Metonymy and metaphor

As we saw above, ambiguity caused by polysemy is not accidental; rather, the different meanings are derived from each other. Such derivation frequently takes place by way of **metonymy** (*Metonymie*) or **metaphor** (*Metapher*).

- **Metonymy** (*Metonymie*) is the replacement of an expression by a factually related term. The semantic connection can be of a causal, spatial, or temporal nature, e.g., *the bench* 'the judiciary' (who traditionally sit on a bench). We are so familiar with the phenomenon of metonymy that the polysemy of words like *school* (→ 4.1.2.1) hardly ever strikes us as unusual.

- **Metaphors** (*Metaphern*), as already mentioned (→ Box 34), are additional meanings of lexemes that are based on a relationship of similarity, i.e., an **iconic** (→ Box 26) relationship, between two objects or concepts, e.g.

bulb ⌐ 'thick rounded underground stem of certain plants' (e.g. the lily, onion, tulip), but also
'light bulb', due to the similarity in shape.

grasp ⌐ 'seize sb./sth. firmly with one's hands',
'understand sth. fully'.

In a process of semantic change (→ 3.2.4), 'transferred' meaning is either added to the original meaning or displaces the old meaning partially or completely: In many cases, originally metaphorical denotations are no longer perceived as such; e.g.

ride ⌐ 'ride on horse-back'; but nowadays mostly
'go for a ride in a car'.

Metaphor and metonymy used to be an embarrassment to feature-oriented (→ 4.2.3) and logically oriented (→ 4.4) approaches in semantics, because these common semantic processes mess up the featural and logical properties of the reference of expressions. What may hold logically of a 'school' in one sense (e.g., being a physical object), need not hold for other senses of this word. In the same way, what is true of a vegetable or flower bulb, need by no means be true of electric bulbs. These approaches to semantics, in consequence, find it difficult to distinguish between homonymy and polysemy. Cognitive semantics, on the other hand, happily embraces metaphor as a crucial cognitive mechanism not only in language, but also in thinking. (→ 4.3.2).

4.1.2.3 Vagueness

A polysemous word often has another characteristic, namely that of creating **vagueness** (*Vagheit*). Take the adjective *good*. A *good student* describes either someone who behaves well, or someone who works well, or someone who shows a high level of ability, or any combination of these properties. A *good* film is either one which gives enjoyment, or one which is thought to be of lasting value, or both. The important point is that there is no one single context that can disambiguate these possible meanings, i.e. impose one interpretation rather than the others.

True homonymy, on the other hand, tends to create ambiguity, as in the sentence

John and Bill went to the bank.

It has been suggested that one test of ambiguity is the "*do-so*" co-ordination test. We cannot say, e.g.,

John went to the bank and so did Bill

with the two meanings of *bank* (that is, if John went to a 'financial institution' and Bill to a 'sloping side of a river'). You may very well say, however

John is a good student and so is Bill

and mean that John and Bill are both good students, each of them in their own way, so that *good* may actually have two slightly different meanings when referring to John or to Bill. The vagueness of *good* allows this.

4.2   Structural semantics: semantic fields, sense relations and componential analysis

Box 36: Structuralism in 20th century linguistics

Structuralism is an approach to language which developed during the early 20th century under the major influence of the Swiss linguist Ferdinand de Saussure (→ Box 4; Box 19; Box 23; Box 29). It contrasts strikingly with earlier approaches in several important ways. Structuralism continues to have a major influence on current linguistic schools.

-   Unlike historical linguistics in the 19th century, which studied and compared the historical development of languages (→ chapter 3), structuralism focusses its attention on the language system at a certain point in time, that is, it favours a synchronic approach to language.

-   In sharp contrast to the norm-orientated, prescriptive earlier schools, structuralism puts special emphasis on a descriptive approach to language, i.e. on describing language as it is actually used by its native speakers (→ 1.1.1.4).

- Unlike the largely atomistic approach to language pursued in 19th-century linguistics, in which a language was seen primarily as a collection of individual elements, such as words, syntactic patterns, etc., structuralism views language as a system of relations between interdependent elements:

[...] every language is a unique relational structure, or system, and [...] the units which we identify, or postulate as theoretical constructs, in analysing the sentence of a particular language (sounds, words, meanings, etc.) derive both their essence and their existence from their relationships with other units in the same language-system. We cannot first identify the units and then, at a subsequent stage of the analysis, enquire what combinatorial or other relations hold between them: we simultaneously identify both the units and their interrelations. Linguistic units are but points in a system, or network, of relations; they are the terminals of these relations, and they have no prior and independent existence (LYONS 1977, 231-232).

4.2.1   Semantic fields

Semantic field theory (*Wortfeldtheorie*), which most notably goes back to TRIER (1934), applies structuralist ideas to the study of the lexicon of languages. It provides the important insight that the meaning (or rather: the **sense**) of a word does not exist as an isolated unit, but rather clusters together with semantically related words, forming a semantic field, also called **lexical field** (*lexikalisches Feld*). Such fields could consist, for example, of words for cooking, plants, colours, kinship, temperatures, motion, etc.

☞ Some approaches make a distinction between *lexical field* and *semantic field*, but we will not go into this here.

Semantic field theory is based on several premises.

–   First of all, the meaning of an individual word is dependent on the meaning of the other words of the same semantic field; in others words, the crucial semantic fact about a word is that it **contrasts** with other words (→ Box 23).

–   Secondly, a lexical field is conceived of as a mosaic with no spaces in between.

–   Thirdly, the totality of the semantic fields of a language represents a unified picture of reality.

–   Finally, if a particular word undergoes semantic change, then the structure of the entire field changes.

Field theory offers a fruitful way of comparing languages. Every language carves up the world in different ways; for example Arabic has a large number of words for different types of camel to cover the semantic (sub-)field 'camel', as English or German have for different types of dog to cover the (sub-)field 'dog', not to mention the often-cited and often grossly overstated case of the Eskimo snow vocabulary (PULLUM 1991, 159ff.).

What makes things more complicated is that the meaning of the words covering a semantic field in one language is unlikely to correspond precisely to the meaning of the words covering the same field in another language, even when the speakers share similar cultures. In all such cases we may also say that languages differ in the semantic contrasts they make.

⌁ Let us consider some relatively simple examples.

Fig. 67: English and Welsh colour adjectives

English	Welsh
green	gwyrdd
blue	glas
grey	llwyd

Colour terminology is a popular object of study among linguists because here the content substance (→ Box 24) seems undebatably objective. The colour terminology in English and Welsh is only one case in point (AITCHISON [4]1995, 82). English and Welsh speakers have in the past led fairly similar lives, yet Welsh *glas* traditionally covers not only the area that English speakers would call *blue*, but also part of what they would call *green* and *grey*, as shown in Fig. 67. This example shows that languages may differ even in apparently quite basic areas.

Fig. 68: 'cousin' in English and German

English	German
cousin	Cousine
cousin	Cousin /Vetter

Another example regards kinship relations, which are also often studied not only by linguists but also by ethnologists because interesting differences between languages in content form concerning identical content substance can sometimes be observed. Within this lexical field, e.g., the semantic area that covers cousinhood is carved up differently in English and German (Fig. 68). In German it is necessary to specify the biological gender of the cousin, a male cousin being a *Cousin* or *Vetter* and a female cousin a *Cousine*; there is no term that covers both male and female cousins. Naïve English speakers indeed find it bizarre that "German doesn't have a word for 'cousin'". In English, the word *cousin* covers both genders. But of course, the distinction between 'male cousin' and 'female cousin' can be expressed in English. We've just done so. As JAKOBSON, a famous 20th century linguist from the Prague School (→ Box 39) who emigrated (guess when) to the USA, once put it:

> "Languages differ essentially in what they <u>must</u> convey, and not in what they <u>may</u> convey." ([1959] 1966, 236)

Other relatively simple examples of lexical fields being structured differently in different languages are parts of the body and divisions of the animal and vegetable worlds.

Fig. 69: *neck* **in English and** *Hals* **in German**

English	German
neck	Hals
	Nacken
throat	Kehle

Thus, *neck* in English refers to the connection between the head and the rest of the body, but also, more specifically, to its back part, whereas *throat* refers to the front part of the neck as well as to its interior.

German has *Hals* for the whole body part, *Kehle* for the front and the interior, and *Nacken* for the back of the neck, for which English happens to lack a specific word (Fig. 69).

It should be clear that such divergences in the way languages structure reality or conceptualise concepts become all the more difficult to analyse when abstract concepts such as values, emotions (WIERZBICKA 1992; 1999), or human character traits are concerned. It is simplistic to assume that any two languages have exactly the same network of meanings, the only difference being the labels (the words) attached to the nodes in the network.

 📖 Use thesauri to collect as many English and German words (nouns, adjectives, and verbs) referring to 'anger' or '*Wut*'-like emotions. Try to determine the differences in meaning between all of them and compare the two emerging semantic fields.

It is another question whether such divergences really inexorably determine the way speakers of different languages see the world, a hypothesis indirectly suggested by semantic field theory and internationally associated with the names of two early American linguists who studied Native American languages, SAPIR (1921) and WHORF (1956). This is the famous and much-debated **SAPIR-WHORF hypothesis**, or the theory of **linguistic determinism**, also preposterously called the **linguistic relativity theory**. A major problem with this hypothesis is that it has never been formulated clearly and rigorously enough to be empirically tested and proved or falsified; in other words, it seems very difficult to say which facts would prove or disprove the theory. This is because it is not clear what predictions concerning verbal and non-verbal behaviour the theory would make. This is probably why the SAPIR-WHORF hypothesis has met with considerable scepticism among linguists.

Empirical evidence, however, does seem to suggest that the availability of a ready-made concept in our native language helps us to remember things more easily. On the other hand, new concepts are learnt very quickly. This is abundantly borne out by the fact that new words, or at least concepts, from other languages have been and are constantly being integrated at an incredible rate and in large numbers whenever there was contact between two cultures (→ 3.2.5.1).

4.2.2   Sense relations

One of the basic assumptions of semantic field theory was that the meaning of an individual word is dependent on the meaning of the other words of the same semantic field, in faithful observance of Saussure's dictum that language (or rather: langue) consists of contrasts only (→ Box 23). **Sense relations** (meaning relations; *Sinnrelationen*) represent a very old attempt to classify possible relations between the senses of different words and, i.a., allow us to describe how the individual words of a semantic field are related to one another in terms of their meaning, although many relations between senses in lexical fields are not accounted for by the classical sense relations.

We have seen (→ 4.1.1) that words can refer to classes of objects or situations (extension) and, less frequently, to individual objects (*the moon, the Pope*). Between these classes various logical relations can hold, which are the basis for different sense relations. The most important ones are describes in the following sections.

4.2.2.1 Synonymy

Synonymy (*Synonymie*) is the relation between words having the same meaning.

Some people say that there is no true synonymy. This is correct in so far as there are probably no two words in any language which are identical in meaning in all contexts. For many pairs of synonyms, however, there are a number of contexts where it makes no difference whether one or the other is used. For example, in

> *I'll be glad to come*
> *I'll be happy to come*

replacing one adjective by the other does not make a big difference. On the other hand, in

> *He's happy as a clam*

glad would not fit. Hence, we would certainly not consider *glad* and *happy* to be absolutely synonymous.

There is a tendency in everyday language to avoid true and absolute synonymy by differentiating the meaning of synonymous words: **differentiation of meaning** (*Bedeutungsdifferenzierung*).

➢ Today's meaning distinction between *pig* and *pork*, *calf* and *veal*, *ox* and *beef*, where the Germanic term is used for the live animal and the French term for the meat, is a historical instance of this tendency: In the wake of the Norman invasion many French loan words came into English (→ 3.1.2), so that frequently there were synonymous terms for the same thing (in our example above, one word each for the animal and its meat). Since this is uneconomical, the meaning of such words was often differentiated, each undergoing a restriction (narrowing) of meaning (→ 3.2.4).

Fig. 70 presents a contemporary example of meaning differentiation.

Fig. 70: English loans in German and their synonyms

❖ Meaning differentiation is also found these days in the substantial number of German fashion words taken over from English, e.g.:	The aspect of meaning that differentiates these words from well-established German words is often connotational rather than denotational. (→ 4.1.1), cf.
Jogging	*Dauerlauf / Langstreckenlauf*
Store	*Kaufhaus*
shoppen	*einkaufen*
Kids	*Kinder / Jugendliche*
Event	*Ereignis / Veranstaltung*
walken	*gehen*

📖Find more word pairs of this kind and try to describe the differences in meaning!

Differentiation of meaning is also often a question of style and register. E.g., there are many synonyms for *die*:

> *decease, depart, pass away, return to the house of the Father, perish, expire, snuff it, kick the bucket, bite the dust*

which all belong to different levels of style or are appropriate (or inappropriate) in different situations.

4.2.2.2 Hyponymy

Hyponymy (*Hyponymie*) denotes the fact that the meaning of a word is included in that of another (**entailment**; *Implikation*; see also section → 4.4.3.1). That means if A is an X, then it is also a Y.

Fig. 71: Hyponymy / hyperonymy

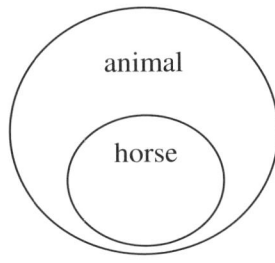

For example, if A is a horse, then it is also an animal. We can then also say:

A horse is a kind of animal

so *horse* is a **hyponym** of *animal*, and *animal* is a **hyper(o)nym** (*Hyperonym*) of, i.e. a superordinate term for, *horse*.

4.2.2.3 Partitive relations

Fig. 72: Meronymy

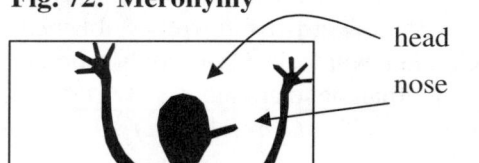

head

nose

arm

body

leg

Partitive relations (part-whole relations, meronymy, partonymy; *partitive Beziehungen, Teil-Ganzes-Beziehungen, Meronymie*) are to be strictly distinguished from hyponymy. For example, a head, arm or leg is a part of the body, not a kind of body. Therefore, *head*, *arm*, *leg* etc. are meronyms of *body*. Also cf. → Fig. 69: English and German differ in precisely the way they delimit meronyms of *neck*.

☞ Note the logical difference between the diagrams in Fig. 71 and Fig. 72:
Fig. 71 is an abstract representation of sets of objects and shows the set inclusion between the set of horses and the set of animals. The 'part-whole relation', so to speak, is between the sets, but not between real objects. But this is precisely what we called a hyponymy – hyperonymy relation above.
Fig. 72 is a drawing of a tangible object and shows tangible parts of that object. The part-whole relation is thus between real objects. And this is precisely what we call a meronymy relation.
This precisely constitutes the logical difference between hyponymy and meronymy and the difficulty of keeping them apart: Hyponymy may also be seen as a sort of 'part-whole relation', viz., between <u>sets</u> of objects and their subsets, meronymy represents a relation between <u>individual</u> objects and their parts. Distinguishing between hyponymy and meronymy thus presupposes the important insight that sets of objects are abstract entities and have entirely different logical properties from individual objects; in other words: It imposes on you to understand that the set of all red objects itself is not red.
To give you another, more real-life example of this issue: A family is a set of persons. Not everything that can be said about a family can be said about a given individual from that family.

4.2.2.4 Antonymy

Antonymy (*Antonymie*) is a meaning contrast, i.e. a meaning relation that can be loosely paraphrased by '...is the opposite of...'.

❦ Note that the terms *opposition* (see below) and *contrast* are used in a different, narrower sense here from their technical uses in linguistics at large (→ Box 23). Strictly speaking, all lexical items in a lexical field that differ in meaning contrast with each other, or form an opposition, as we saw above.

Antonymy, under this perspective, is just a special kind of lexical contrast or opposition. But in this passage, the terms are used synonymously with *antonymy*.

Logically, however, we have to distinguish various kinds of antonymy:

- In a **contradictory** contrast (*kontradiktorischer Gegensatz*) the meanings of two expressions exclude one another absolutely, that is, they are in complementary opposition.

Fig. 73: Contradictory contrast

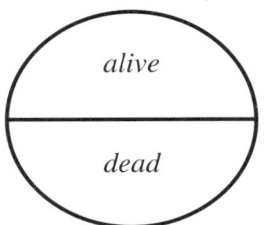

It is invariably either one or the other expression which is accurate. Examples: *man – man, alive – dead*, etc. Thus, it is normally assumed that a person is either alive or dead, and that an adult person is either a man or a woman. There is hardly anything in between.

- **Polarity** (*Polarität*) means that two expressions stand in a polar contrast with one another (**gradable antonymy,** contraries; *gradierbare / konträre Antonymie*) i.e. they designate the endpoints on a scale of 'more or less'. This is where contrasts such as shown in Fig. 74 belong. Thus, if an object is not large, it is not necessarily small, and someone who is not young is not necessarily old, etc.

Fig. 74: Polarity

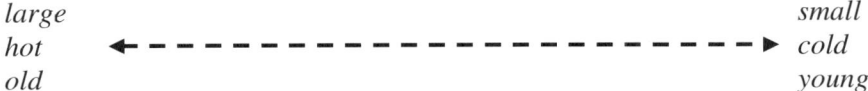

- **Converses** (*Konverse*) are expressions which represent the same event or the same relation from contrasting perspectives: If A is the teacher of B, then B is the pupil of A; if A gives something to B, then B gets something from A.

Fig. 75: Converses

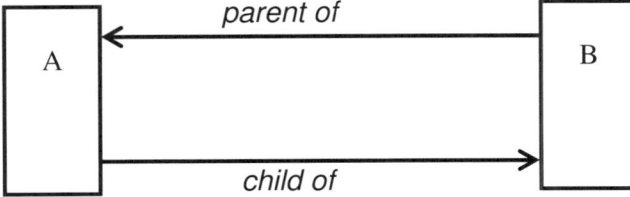

- Yet another kind of contrast, called **directional opposition** (*direktionale Opposition*), exists between pairs like *come* and *go*, *up* and *down*, *marriage* and *divorce*, *learn* and *forget*. It designates a relation between meanings which, as it were, cancel each other out.

4.2.3 Componential analysis: the semantic feature approach

The meaning of lexemes and their relations with each other may often be represented by using a linguistic framework called **componential analysis** (CA, feature analysis, *Komponentenanalyse*). In fact there are different kinds of componential analysis. In this textbook, we will only deal with one kind. This approach to meaning rests upon the thesis that the sense of every lexeme can be analysed in terms of a set of more general or basic sense components or **semantic features** (semantic components; *semantische Merkmale, semantische Komponenten*), some or all of which will be shared by several different lexemes.

Thus, the meanings of the eight lexical units in Fig. 76 below can be described by means of only three semantic features which are combined in different ways in the different word meanings. The difference of meaning between the words *human being, man, woman, child, boy, girl, animal*, may be unambiguously described by means of a small number of such components. They all share the feature ANIMATE, which constitutes a semantic field (A zero indicates that the feature is not specifiable for the lexeme in question):

Fig. 76: Semantic feature analysis

	human being	*man*	*woman*	*child*	*kid*	*boy*	*girl*	*animal*
HUMAN	+	+	+	+	+	+	+	–
FEMALE	0	–	+	0	0	–	+	0
ADULT	0	+	+	–	–	–	–	0

📖 Substituting HUMAN by BOVINE, try to construct an analogous semantic feature analysis for *cow*, *ox* etc.! What other feature(s) do you need for that?

These common features will also identify a word as belonging to the same semantic field. Semantic components, frequently written with small capitals to distinguish them from ordinary lexemes, may be thought of as universal atomic concepts. They may or may not be **lexicalised**, i.e. expressed by a single word, in a particular language.

👁 This use of the term *lexicalisation* differs from that in sections → 1.3.4 and → 3.2.5.3.

Apart from identifying semantic fields semantic features may also serve to precisely distinguish the sense of a given word from the sense of another word. In most approaches features are binary, which means that in a particular lexeme they are either present or not present; this is indicated by putting a plus or a minus sign before the feature in question.

E.g., the lexeme *bear* has the feature +ANIMATE, and the lexeme *teddy bear* has the feature –ANIMATE; sometimes the plus sign can also be omitted, which means that the component indicated is present. With other features, numerical values (such as –1, 0, and +1) are sometimes used.

Within this framework, two lexemes may be described as synonymous if they share exactly the same features, such as *child* and *kid* in table Fig. 76. And a lexeme X may be described as lexeme Y's hyponym if X has all the features of Y plus at least one more. Thus *man, woman, child*, etc. are all hyponyms of *human being*: They all share the feature +HUMAN but more features than this are specified for *man, woman*, and *child*, respectively, whereas for *human being*, only one feature is specified.

This type of componential analysis thus assumes that lexeme extensions (→ 4.0) are intersections of those sets that are extensions of their semantic feature. Thus, the extension of *boy* is the intersection of the three sets that are characterised by the features +HUMAN, −FEMALE, −ADULT:

Fig. 77: The extension of English *boy* as intersection of three sets

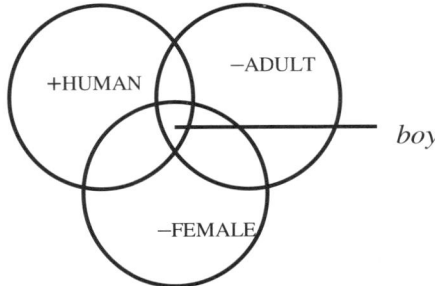

4.3   Cognitive semantics

4.3.1   Central tenets of cognitive semantics

This section introduces some of the guiding principles of cognitive semantics. Within the **cognitive semantics** framework, meaning is analysed in terms of conceptual structures. This strongly contrasts with the other approaches to the description of meaning discussed in this book, i.e. formal **truth-conditional** (→ 4.4) and **structuralist** (→ 4.2) approaches:

− Traditional truth-conditional approaches to semantics assume that the meaning of lexical units rests on the notion of **reference** to the 'real' world (**language-world approach**),

− This idea was rejected by structuralist semantics, which tried to describe lexical meaning by means of a set of sense relations such as hyponymy, antonymy etc. (→ 4.2.2) and to discover lexical field structures (→ 4.2.1). Words are understood in their semantic relation to other words, so this approach can be labelled a **language-internal approach.**

− In contrast to these, cognitive semantics takes it for granted that meaning is clearly in the heads of language users (**conceptualist approach**) (TAYLOR

2002, 187). This is what it has in common with the semantic primitives approach (WIERZBICKA 1996).

Categorisation and **conceptualisation** are considered to be the essential principles in cognitive semantics. Human beings are involved in a constant process of making sense of the phenomena perceived around them by grouping them into categories (→ 4.3.2), and forming concepts from these categories.

These conceptualisations are realised by means of choices made available by meaning structures of a particular language and they form the basis for understanding, modelling and describing the meaning of linguistic units. The construction of a conceptualisation is not so much based on the 'real' properties of a phenomenon in the world (this would be a language-world approach), but on the language user's ability to conceptualise or construe the same scene in multiple ways, e.g. in terms of different figure / ground alignments (→ 1.2.3.2). Figure / ground alignment is just one facet of this complex phenomenon, but lack of space precludes a further detailed discussion.

Conceptualisations can often be represented in the form of image-schemas. **Image-schemas** are structured representations of specific bodily experience in our mind. This experience is not necessarily visual, although most of the conceptualisations discussed in the literature so far are represented as based on visual experience. LAKOFF (1987) and JOHNSON (1987) argue that abstract notions such as time or causation are based on concrete experience such as moving or overcoming obstacles. Schemas such as 'container', 'source-path-goal' etc. are examples of widespread basic meaning units. The image schema for *through*, e.g., can be described as follows:

> An entity (called the **trajector**, **TR**) moves through a container (called the **landmark**, **LM**). The trajector's **path** begins at the point of entry, then extends from the point of entry to a point on the opposite side of the landmark, and ends at this point, the point of exit. (LEE 2001, 39).

Fig. 78: Image schema for *through*

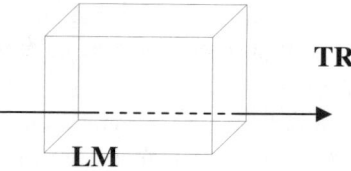

Box 37: Trajector vs. landmark

> **The trajector / landmark alignment** is similar to the already discussed figure / ground alignment (→ 1.2.3.2). The term *trajector* is used to refer to a more prominent, i.e. figure element in a relational structure, while the term *landmark* refers to the other entity in a relation. Whether the concepts are used in syntax or semantics, doesn't make any difference. This underscores the fundamental tenet of cognitive linguistics that the two levels of description are really inseparable.

In the following example, the train is the trajector and is syntactically realised as the subject, while the Channel Tunnel is the landmark and fulfils a syntactic function of a complement (in the sense of → Box 11) to the preposition *through*:

> The train rushed **through** the Channel Tunnel.

The trajector's path and its landmark may also be metaphorically conceptualised, as in:

> The Inspector manages to fumble his way **through** the craziest cases in criminal history.

In this example, criminal investigation cases are conceptualised as landmarks, with the inspector as the trajector. The path conceptualised here, of course, is not a real path, but a metaphorical mapping of cognitive processes into physical processes. Within other approaches to the study of meaning (language-internal and language-world approach), **metaphor** and **metonymy** have been considered as deviant phenomena, disturbing the logic of truth conditions and semantic features, and have thus been largely ignored. Within the cognitive semantics framework they cannot only be easily handled, but are crucial evidence of conceptual structure (→ 4.3.2).

The above examples also show that spatial configurations figure prominently in conceptualisations as described by Cognitive Linguistics. In contrast to classical componential analysis, the 'components' of meaning are not related via abstract set intersections (→ 4.2.3), but are found in concrete spatial arrangements. This explains why spatial prepositions such as *through, in, under* etc. are among the pet examples of cognitive semantics.

A further crucial characteristic of cognitive semantics is that it adopts the encyclopaedic view of meaning. In structuralist semantics, one basic assumption is that we have a strict separation of **encyclopaedic knowledge** (world knowledge, *Enzyklopädisches Wissen, Weltwissen*) from linguistic knowledge. Linguistic knowledge, in this conception, is what is absolutely necessary to distinguish the meaning of a word from that of other words and can be described by a relatively small set of distinctive features.

Thus, the linguistic meaning of *woman* is exhaustively described by the set of features [+ HUMAN], [+ FEMALE], [+ ADULT]. Everything else that people associate with the word *woman*, or know about women, is part of encyclopaedic knowledge. Cognitive linguists reject this separation because bits and pieces of encyclopaedic knowledge may well be relevant for an adequate description of the use of a lexeme.

Thus, the expression *a real woman* cannot be interpreted on the basis of structuralist distinctive features. This means that words trigger an access to vast repositories of knowledge, or rather: beliefs concerning a particular concept.

Thus, when describing the meaning potentials of certain lexemes we also have to take into account a network of shared, conventionalised and to a certain extent idealised knowledge embedded in a pattern of cultural beliefs and practices. This network results from physical experiences as well as from social interactions within a speech community (→ 1.1.1.2, ☞ box).

Furthermore, cognitive semantics assumes that

"concepts show **prototype** effects (instead of following the Aristotelian paradigm based on necessary and sufficient conditions)" (GÄRDENFORS 1999, 25).

This assumption will be discussed in more detail in the following section.

4.3.2 Prototypes. Metaphors

Classical structuralist semantics, as we have seen, assumes that word meanings can be clearly and exhaustively defined and related to one another in a neat and precise way by means of distinctive features. This view, however, does not seem to be in line with psychological reality. In fact, the way we categorise and structure the world is subject to varying degrees of flexibility, and this in turn is reflected in the **fuzziness** and **indeterminacy** (*Unbestimmtheit*) of the corresponding lexical meanings. People may often find it difficult to decide whether some referent actually belongs to a class or category or not. We may ask ourselves, for example, what makes the thing we are drinking tea from a mug as opposed to a cup (LABOV 1973), in what way an American football is a ball, where precisely the cut-off point between the colours green and blue is located, and how 'catty' the drawing of a cat has to be to be identified as a cat.

The closer something is to the *typical* or *ideal* representative of a category, its **prototype** (*Prototyp*), the easier we find it to classify our referent, and to distinguish it from members of rivalling categories. This was first empirically investigated by ROSCH (1973). The assumption of a prototypical rather than set-theoretical structure (as in componential analysis, → 4.2.3) of natural-language categories has the following corollaries which distinguish cognitive semantics from other approaches:

– One difference between **feature semantics** and **prototype semantics**, then, is that only the latter assumes different degrees of representativity of members of a category, with the prototype as its centre.
– Another difference is that prototype theory recognises the fact that the boundaries of a category are often not clear-cut, but **fuzzy**, so that a referent may be put into different categories, depending on context and also on personal judgement.
– Last but not least, a prototype approach allows us to see connections between the 'literal' meaning of an expression and its **metaphorical** uses.

Very often, what is called **metaphor** is an abstraction: disregarding some of the physical properties of an entity, and focussing on some essential relational properties. This also makes metaphor a frequent mechanism in grammaticalisation (→ 3.2.3.3). These more abstract relational properties can then be found in other domains for which no separate elaborate conceptual system exists.

    Hence, when we speak of the 'foot' of a hill, we just disregard all the physical properties of an ordinary human foot and concentrate on one essential relational property of feet: being the lowest part of a body when in default position, and in consequence, that part on which the rest of the body rests. There is thus a connection between the 'literal' meaning of *foot* and its metaphorical meaning(s) that prototype theory allows us to work out. LAKOFF / JOHNSON (1980) would say that in the expression *foot of the hill*, we understand the hill in terms of the human body.

    This is, according to them, what always happens in metaphors: We sometimes need to conceptualise certain rather abstract or complex domains of our experience. As our language cannot provide separate conceptual and lexical systems for all potential domains of experience, we turn to a simple, well-known domain of tangible objects and real spatial relations from our everyday life in which we perceive, by the principle of analogy (→ Box 32), certain abstract similarities to the domain we want to structure. This domain, we take as the **source domain** for new conceptualisations in the **target domain**.

    The most common source domains are the space around us, with its basic directions ('up', 'down' etc.) and movements in it. Another common source domain for metaphors is the human body, as we saw in the above example. Thus, we conceptualise life as a journey, love as war, being happy as being 'up' etc. Metaphor is thus more than just a 'figure of speech' (→ Box 34), it is a tool that pervades and influences our thinking.

  Find examples from English for the just mentioned metaphorical conceptualisations.

In a conventional feature approach, it would be more difficult to find enough common features, say, for the different referential meanings of *foot* or to formulate general truth conditions for the use of that lexical unit.

    Metaphorical meanings of lexical items are often so much taken for granted, especially in very old, so-called **'dead' metaphors**, that indeed, it is often very difficult to draw a line between 'literal' and metaphorical meanings.

    What, e.g., is the 'literal meaning' of *indicate*? This is a word borrowed from Latin with a ready-made set of physical and abstract meanings. The metaphorisations had already taken place in Latin, centuries ago. The scholars first borrowing the term into English didn't realise nor care that they were borrowing a polysemous item with a whole range of meanings. To them, these meanings were all instantiations of one abstract concept. The word is morphologically opaque to an English language user. So nobody can tell what it meant 'originally'. Is it a gesture performed with a finger (normally with an index finger) or is it some more abstract semiotic relationship (→ Box 27)?

    Rather than distinguishing 'literal' and 'metaphorical' meanings, it might be more useful in this case to make a difference.

– between concrete and abstract relationships:

*She sat down on the armchair that Mrs. Jones **indicated**.*
*He has already **indicated** the outlines of his plan to the police.*

– between persons as agents and abstract entities as pseudo-agents:

*The reader has to **indicate** the correct answer with a tick.*
*Evidence **indicates** that the experiments were unsuccessful.*

– between real physical objects and imagined hypothetical objects:

*'The car's just down there' she said, **indicating** it with a nod of her head.*
*An erect tail on a cat **indicates** aggression.*

> 📖 On the basis of Lakoff / Johnson's assumptions, which meanings of *indicate* would you say are the oldest? Is this borne out by the historical evidence? Check the *OED*!

4.3.3   Frames

As we have seen, the **structuralist approach** to the study of meaning assumes that the meaning of a lexical unit can be determined by "a checklist of conditions that have to be satisfied in order for the form to be appropriately or truthfully used" (PETRUCK 1996, 4).

The meaning of a given lexical unit within a frame semantics approach is elucidated in terms of structured schematisations of human knowledge concerning recurring social and cultural practices.

For these schematic configurations, which are usually centred around the meaning of a verb, FILLMORE introduced the notion of **frame** in the middle of the 1970s. The verb describes a typical situation that everybody knows or an entrenched social or cultural practice, involving various participants (the so-called **frame elements**) which are associated with the meaning potentials of the verb in question.

The notion of **frame** can best be explained by way of the frequently discussed Commercial Transaction Frame. *FrameNet*, which is an online lexical resource based on the guiding principles of frame semantics, defines the Commercial Transaction frame as follows:

> "These are words that describe basic commercial transactions involving a Buyer and a Seller who exchange Money and Goods. The individual words vary in the frame element realization patterns. For example, the typical patterns for the verbs *buy* and *sell* are: BUYER buys GOODS from the SELLER for MONEY, SELLER sells GOODS to the buyer for MONEY" (FRAMENET online).

This same frame underlies all the following examples, featuring different verbs taking different perspectives on the transaction:

*(a) She   always **bought** new hats.* FEE 3170
     BUYER   GOODS

(b) *The UK group has **sold** its 86.5 per cent stake ...*
    Seller   Goods

    to FICG   for C$54m (£28.3m). A37 317
    Buyer   Money

(c) *Mr Sawar ... **charged** the sum of £300,000...to BCCI. CBV 3355*
    Seller   Money   Buyer

(d) *... Mr Lamont **paid** him   £18.36 for 3 bottles of wine and ...*
    Buyer   Seller Money Goods

(e) *A pack of four funnels **costs** about £4. AHK 1843*
    Goods   Money
    (References at the end of lines are to the BNC.)

The following graph illustrates the commercial transaction frame, with the different verbs (in bold type), roles (in bold capitals), and the prepositions (in bold italics) used in English to express different figure / ground alignments (→ 1.2.3.2). Identical arrows symbolise one kind of perspective on a transaction, centred around one verb. The direction of the arrows indicates standard word order.

Fig. 79: The commercial transaction frame with its lexical realisations

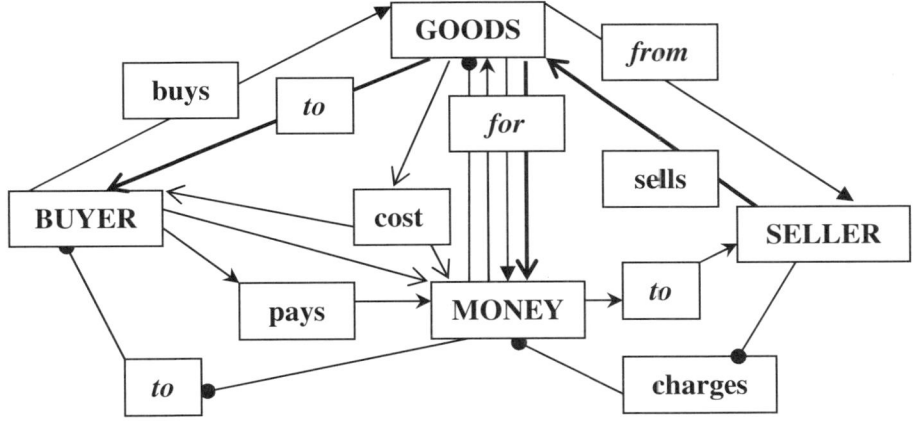

Among the verbs which may evoke the commercial transaction frame are: *buy, sell, pay, charge* and *cost*. The use of any of these lexical units evokes the entire frame, but the choice of one of these verbs highlights certain facets of it. Example (b) above, e.g., uses the verb *sell* which codes a commercial event from the perspective of the seller (serving as the subject of *sell*). Focus is also placed on the goods, which are syntactically realised as direct object, while the buyer and the money are backgrounded because they function as optional adjuncts only (→ 1.2.1.2). In (c), the verb *charge* puts focus on the seller and money (subject and object), backgrounding the goods and the buyer. It is an integral part of the semantics of the above verbs that they place a certain perspective on a situation.

Thus, the corollary of the selection of certain lexical units within one frame is the shift of perspective on the same situation.

> 📖 Try to develop a frame representation similar to Fig. 79 for teaching and learning!

The above discussion also shows how syntax and semantics are inextricably interwoven in cognitive approaches. The meaning of a verb, e.g., determines the different case roles that may be associated with it, and thereby the syntax of the whole clause in which the verb figures. This makes the description of syntactic frames an important part of verb semantics.

To summarise, in order to elucidate the meaning of a certain lexical unit we have to look at a complex network of relations and properties within which this particular meaning will be placed. These relations and properties evoked by a lexeme constitute a frame.

The similarity between semantic field theory and frame semantics consists in the fact that in both theories lexical units that are associated in experience are organised in groups.

But the difference between the structuralist theories of semantic fields and frame semantics is that the former specifies the meaning of lexical units in terms of lexical relations to other lexical units constituting the same field, whereas within the latter framework the meaning of a lexical unit is characterised by its relation to a background frame, and not by its relation to other units (→ 4.2.1). Within a semantic field the relations between lexical units are based on different types of lexical relations such as hyponymy or antonymy. In frame semantics, we cannot trace the relations between certain lexical units to structural semantic relations, but we can trace the association between such lexical units to ordinary human experience (as noted above, for example, the commercial transaction frame is associated with a number of concepts such as BUYER, SELLER or MONEY).

Semantic approaches advocating frames draw attention to the fact that word meanings function in a cultural framework in which they make sense, an aspect which feature analysis tends to neglect.

To give a much quoted example: The meaning of the English word *bachelor*, in its most common sense, is usually analysed in terms of semantic features in something like the following way: [+ADULT, −FEMALE, −MARRIED], meaning that an adult male unmarried person is called a bachelor. This description seems very plausible at first sight, but it is only plausible because it is based on a sort of prototypical 'career' of a man in our type of culture: A man grows up, lives through a certain (preferably short) time as a 'bachelor', and then gets married.

In this framework, a term like *bachelor* makes sense. In it *bachelor* is a 'marked' category (→ Box 10), referring to someone who does not conform to this prototypical course of life. The older an unmarried young man becomes, remaining unmarried, the more likely he is to be called a bachelor. If this framework changes or is not applicable, this is no longer true. Catholic priests, men living with a woman without being married to her, homosexual men, widowers, divorced men, all these don't fit into the prototypical picture, and thus, although they meet the above definition of *bachelor*, they will hardly ever be called *bachelors*. The above feature analysis of *bachelor* is thus both correct and incorrect. It is correct in the framework of a prototype approach, where it can be said to describe a prototype; it is incorrect if taken as a strict logical characterisation of the defining properties of a *bachelor*.

Prototype and frame theory have the advantage of presenting a more realistic account of meaning in real-world terms. Feature semantics is still, however, an invaluable tool in the description of semantic fields and relations. It should, however, be noted that in many cases feature descriptions typically describe a prototype and are not to be taken as a mere checklist.

4.4   Formal semantics

Formal semantics (*formale Semantik*) is an influential and interesting branch of linguistics that approaches meaning using the notion of truth, which has been inherited from the study of logic. It attempts to formalise the meaning of words and sentences and the relations that hold between them, such as the sense relations already discussed (→ 4.2.2), entailment (4.4.3.1), paraphrase (→ 4.4.3.2), presupposition (→ 4.4.3.3), contradiction (→ 4.4.4.1), tautology (→ 4.4.4.2), and anomaly (→ 4.4.4.3). Formal semanticists firmly believe in the **compositionality** principle (→ Box 16) and hope to devise a formal language to account for all ways in which meanings of simple expressions may be combined to yield the meaning of complex expressions, e.g., how the meaning of sentences is composed of the meaning of its words. For lack of space, we cannot deal with formal semantics in much detail. It is however, necessary for the linguist to possess at least some elementary knowledge of the basic terminology of formal semantics as most of it is common core of linguistic vocabulary across all schools of linguistics, even among the non-believers. We will only briefly point out the most important concepts and would like to refer the reader to the available specialised literature, such as SAEED 1997 and CANN 1993.

4.4.1   Truth values and truth conditions

A sentence can be either true or false, that is, it has a **truth value** (*Wahrheitswert*). The conditions that have to obtain in a specific situation or state of the world for a sentence to be true or false are called its **truth conditions** (*Wahrheitsbedingungen*). For formal semanticists, to know the meaning of a sentence, is to know the truth conditions of this sentence.

If we have a sentence

  (a) *He is an Englishman*

adding the negation *not*, as in

(b) *He is not an Englishman*

will reverse its truth value; if (a) is true, then (b) is false, and vice versa. To show that such a negation process works for any sentence, semanticists use a formalised notation schema called the **logical form** (*logische Form*), where a letter (p, q etc.) stands for a sentence and a symbol (~) stands for negation. We can say that negation is a **logical operator** (*logischer Operator*) that in ordinary English may be expressed by *not*. The logical form for the above sentences, as for numerous other pairs of sentences and their negation, would then be

(a) *p*
(b) *~p.*

Hence, if p is true, then ~p is false; and if p is false, then ~p is true.

It should be noted that *p* is only an abbreviation for other possible notations of the same proposition. These notations would specify the internal logical form of this proposition, dealt with in predicate logic ($\rightarrow$ 4.4.5).

Logical forms represent a universal semantic metalanguage, a formalised language into which formal semanticists hope the meaning of any sentence of any language can ultimately be translated.

4.4.2 Logical connectives

There are other operators corresponding to certain linguistic elements that are studied in the same way (SAEED 1997, 81ff.), especially the **logical connectives** (*logische Konnektive*) symbolised by the symbols in Fig. 80:

Fig. 80: Logical connectives and their names

Logical symbol	English paraphrase	Name of logical relation
&	'and'	conjunction
v	'or'	disjunction
→	'if...then'	material implication
≡	'if and only if'	equivalence

☞ Note that other notations are also used in the literature, such as

∧ instead of &,
⊃ instead of → and
↔ instead of ≡.

Logical connectives are especially important to formal semanticists because they have a predictable effect on the truth conditions of compound and complex sentences ($\rightarrow$ 1.2.1.3), that is, they describe an important aspect of the meaning of sentence connections.

It should however be pointed out that logical connectives are not semantically identical to natural-language connectors. Thus, the notation for *and* in the above explanation does not mean 'and', but stands for a rather abstract, purely logical relationship. Natural-language *and* usually carries additional meanings, at least it carries the 'presumption of relevance' ($\rightarrow$ 5.3) of the connected sentences for each other:

The lonely cowboy mounted his horse and rode off into the sunset.
The journalist criticised the Chinese government and was arrested.
Aspect is only found in English and not in German.
?I ate a banana yesterday and six people can fit into the back seat of my car.

In the first three examples, we give the sentence connection relevance by giving the *and* some additional temporal, causal, or comparative interpretation. The last example is questionable or of marginal acceptability because we find it difficult to imagine a context in which the two sentences connected by *and* would show any relevance for each other. In formal logic, this doesn't matter at all. *and* has certain logical properties, and they alone are analysed by formal semantics. All these sentences can be represented in a logical formula, and the semantic contribution of *and* is simply that both sentences must be true for the whole sentence connection to be true.

On the other hand, natural language knows many connectors that are logically equivalent to logical 'and', 'or' or 'if' alright; but they contribute important other aspects of meaning:

*Aspect is only found in English **but** not in German.*

but makes an important contribution to sentence meaning which is necessarily ignored by formal propositional logic. It does not change the truth value of the sentence. Thus, *but* could be logically represented by '&'.

The relationships between the simple sentences and the compound sentence are often shown by way of a **truth table** (*Wahrheitstafel*). An upper case T stands for 'true' and an upper case F for 'false'). Fig. 81 shows an example:

Fig. 81: Truth table for '&'

p	q	p & q
T	T	T
T	F	F
F	T	F
F	F	F

We can see that the compound sentence is only true if both p and q are true. This logical relation is called **conjunction** (*Konjunktion*).

💣 Note that the term *conjunction* is used in at least two other quite different senses in syntax (→ 1.2.1.3) and textlinguistics (→ 6.1.2).

The other logical connectors shown in Fig. 80 can also be described in this way. There are two logical connectives corresponding to the meaning of *or*. The first one is called **disjunction** (*Disjunktion*) or **inclusive *or*** (*inklusives* oder), is symbolised as v and is read as 'and/or'. A compound linked by this operator is true if one or both of the constituent sentences (disjuncts) are true.

E.g., the sentence

I'll phone him today or tomorrow

is true if either *I'll phone him today* or *I'll phone him tomorrow* is true, or if both are true.

The second connective that can correspond to the meaning of *or* is called **exclusive *or*** (*exklusives* oder), has the symbol v_e, and is read as '(p) or (q) but not both'. A compound sentence linked by this operator is only true if just one of its disjuncts is true, but not if both are true, as in the sentence

You will pay the fine or you will go to jail.

The connective → symbolises **material implication** (*materiale Implikation*), and is read as 'if...then'. Here, the truth of the antecedent p is a **sufficient condition** (*hinreichende Bedingung*) for the consequent q, as in the sentence

If the sun comes out, I'll go canoeing.

It is not, however, a **necessary condition** (*notwendige Bedingung*): If the sun doesn't come out, I might still go canoeing. Consequently, the conditional sentence can only be false if p is true and q is false, that is, in our example, if the sun comes out and I still don't go canoeing. This also means that a material implication is always true when the antecedent is false, and indeed this is borne out by at least some colloquial uses of *if*:

If the moon is made of green cheese, I'm the Empress of China.

Medieval philosophers expressed this in the Latin sentence *Ex falso quodlibet* ('From false premises, anything may follow'). Nevertheless, logical material implication should not be uncritically equated with colloquial *if – then* constructions.

A further connective, the **biconditional** (*Bikonditional*) ≡, symbolises **equivalence** (*Äquivalenz*) and is read as 'if and only if' (often abbreviated as 'iff'). Here, a compound sentence is only true if both disjuncts have the same truth value, as in

I will leave if and only if I am forced to.

> 📖   Try to draw up truth tables for all the connectives in Fig. 80. Find examples of colloquial uses of *and*, *or*, and *if*. See if they diverge in meaning from the logical connectives. Can false premises only be used sarcastically, as in the above example?

The area of formal semantics that deals with the truth value and logical representation of compound sentences, i.e. sentences related by conjunction (&), disjunction (v), and material implication (→) is called **propositional logic** (*propositionale Logik*). The **proposition** (*Proposition*) or **propositional content** (*propositionaler Gehalt*) of a sentence is that part of its meaning which can be said to be either true or false. Hence sentences have the same propositional content if and only if they have exactly the same truth conditions. For example, the two sentences

Shakespeare wrote the play "Hamlet"
The play "Hamlet" was written by Shakespeare

have the same truth conditions (it is not conceivable that one of them could turn out to be false and the other remain true) and thus the same propositional content, which could be stated as even though they may differ in other respects. Propositional logic tries to find ways to 'translate' such natural-language formulations into logical formulae.

> ☙ In accordance with SAEED (1997, 14) we try to distinguish our notations for sentences and propositions. We use *italics* when actual sentences in a specific wording are referred to, and we use CAPITALS when a proposition, regardless of its formulation in sentences, is to be represented in everyday language.

The logical connectives we have looked at are important for the establishment of valid arguments and correct inductive reasoning.

4.4.3 Logical relations between propositions

4.4.3.1 Entailment

While the truth value of the sentences described so far depends on empirical facts in the world, there are also fixed truth relations between propositions, and, thereby, between sentences, which hold regardless of the empirical truth of the sentences (cf. SAEED 1997, 90ff.).

> ☞ It is not always easy to decide whether a certain logical statement refers to a sentence or to a proposition, and in many cases, both may be meant. Thus, in much of what follows, *sentence* and *proposition* may be used interchangeably, although we try to apply the terminology as precisely as possible.

One such relation is **entailment** (implication, *Implikation*). It can be defined as a relation between propositions such that the truth of the second proposition, e.g. FIDO IS AN ANIMAL, necessarily follows from the truth of the first proposition, e.g. FIDO IS A DOG, and the same holds for the corresponding sentences. But the falsity of the second proposition does not necessarily follow from the falsity of the first proposition:

FIDO IS A DOG	**entails**	FIDO IS AN ANIMAL.
FIDO IS NOT A DOG	**does not entail**	FIDO IS NOT AN ANIMAL.

> ☞ **Entailments** are often also called **implications** as the logical relation is the same as described above as "material implication". The term *entailment* is preferably used for relations between isolated propositions, whereas *material implication* is used for the same relation if it is found between sentences connected in a complex sentence, typically by *if ... then*.
> ☙ There is the danger of confusing *implication* with *implicature* as defined in pragmatics. The difference is that entailment and implication are logically cogent, as described above.
> **Implicatures**, on the other hand, are based on plausibility considerations; they are assumptions that every rational person would make given the circumstances, but they do not follow in a strict logical manner from what was said. See → 5.2 for more explanation on implicatures.

> The verb that forms the base of the nominalisation *implication* is *imply*, which is also often used in a loose meaning in colloquial language:
>
> > *Politicians* **implied** *there was a clear link between Saddam Hussein, al-Qaida, and terrorists ...*
>
> The meaning of *imply* in this sentence comes close to what is called *implicate* in linguistic pragmatics (→ 5.2). It certainly does not refer to a relation of logical entailment. When discussing logic, the use of the term *imply* should be restricted to logical entailment.

In terms of the notions developed in the last section (→ 4.4.2), it could be said that entailment is a stable relation of material implication between two propositions that is based on their meaning alone, and not on any empirical facts. If Fido is a dog, then Fido is an animal. In whatever way the empirical world changes, this will remain true unless the meaning of *dog* or of *animal* changes.

The logical relationship between sentences that mutually entail each other is of course one of equivalence or paraphrase (→ 4.4.3.2): Such sentences always have identical truth conditions and have the same underlying proposition.

4.4.3.2 Paraphrase

Entailment allows us to define the relationship of **paraphrase**. It is the relation between two or more sentences that have the same truth conditions and hence mutually entail one another.

> 💣 This logical definition is to be distinguished from the everyday use of *paraphrase* as 'meaning more or less the same thing'.

Many relations of paraphrase can be explained by regular syntactic transformations such as the passive (→ 1.1.3.4.5; 1.1.3.4.7; Box 14; 1.2.3.2). Others can be produced by exchanging synonymous expressions (→ 4.2.2.1) or by a combination of syntactic transformations and exchanging an expression by its converse (→ 4.2.2.4). Many relations of paraphrase cannot, however, be as easily explained and are not always uncontroversial. They do nonetheless play an important role in semantic theory and linguistic methodology in general.

> 📖 Find or construct examples of paraphrases based on the methods mentioned above.

4.4.3.3 Presupposition

Presupposition (*Präsupposition, Voraussetzung*) is defined as a relation between two propositions or sentences A and B.

Fig. 82: Examples of presuppositions

Utterance A	**presupposes**	presupposition B
The King of France is bald	**presupposes**	THERE IS A KING OF FRANCE.
The King of France is not bald	(also) **presupposes**	THERE IS A KING OF FRANCE.
I regret going to the party	**presupposes**	I WENT TO THE PARTY.
I don't regret going to the party	(also) **presupposes**	I WENT TO THE PARTY.
My secretary is very nice	**presupposes**	I HAVE A SECRETARY.
My secretary isn't very nice	(also) **presupposes**	I HAVE A SECRETARY.

The first proposition, A, is actually uttered in a sentence, the presupposing sentence. The second proposition, B (the presupposed proposition), is usually not uttered, but its truth is implied by the truth <u>and by the falsity</u> of the first sentence. This is what we mean by a statement of the form *A presupposes B*. Presupposition thus often appears as a relation between an (uttered) sentence and a (non-uttered) proposition.

If the presupposed proposition B is not true, the corresponding sentence in the first column in Fig. 82 below does not make sense at all. A speaker who utters a sentence whose presupposition is not true, will often meet with puzzlement.

Thus, if someone told us

The King of France is bald

even though we know that France has no king, our reaction would be one of bewilderment. Similarly, if a friend told you

I regret going to the party,

and you knew full well that he or she never went to the party in question, you would feel you were being lied to. In the same vein, if somebody who you knew doesn't have a secretary said

My secretary is very efficient

you would think of that person as a boaster or a liar.

Presuppositions are usually triggered by certain linguistic expressions (called **presupposition triggers**). Among these are definite articles, possessive determiners and other definite expressions, certain verbs like *regret*, *know* and *remember*, and, under certain conditions, subordinating conjunctions such as *because*.

Presupposition is often used in situations where people are being manipulated, especially in advertising. Consider, for example, the following sentence (Cook 1992, 154), which was used in an ad encouraging people to use seat belts:

Because you know it makes sense.

The presupposition here is

IT MAKES SENSE

which, on its own, would be a mere claim. If this claim were presented in such a blunt, straightforward fashion, people's spontaneous reaction might be one of questioning reserve or caution. This is not, of course, what's intended by the creators of such an advertisement, who consequently try to disguise the fact that they are really only making a claim.

This is achieved by turning the claim into a presupposition. In our example, the words *"you know..."* presuppose the truth of what follows. Just as

I remember seeing him

presupposes

I SAW HIM,

You know it makes sense

presupposes

IT MAKES SENSE.

The choice of the verb *know* is a clever gambit for another reason as well: It is fairly difficult to contradict somebody who assumes some kind of knowledge on your part; it would be like putting yourself down.

Moreover, the use of the conjunction *because* at the beginning of the sentence covers up the lack of evidence for the claim even more, and makes it appear even more natural to use seat belts (or other products, for that matter).

This example illustrates, then, that presupposition is a clever rhetorical device often used to manipulate people. Since presuppositions are a kind of hidden meaning, they are often dealt with under the heading of pragmatics. Here they are usually regarded as part of the **background** of an utterance ($\rightarrow$ chapter 5.5).

> ☝ Presuppositions should not, however, be confused with **implicatures** as defined in pragmatics ($\rightarrow$ 5.2): Presuppositions are strict logical **implications** of, i.e., they are truly entailed ($\rightarrow$ 4.4.3.1) by what is said.

> 📖   There is an important difference between entailment and presupposition. A presupposing sentence always entails its presupposition. An enailing sentence also entails its entailed sentence. Comparing what is said in $\rightarrow$ Fig. 82 and in $\rightarrow$ 4.4.3.1, find out where the difference lies!

4.4.4   Logical properties of propositions

4.4.4.1 Contradiction

Sentences that are false purely on the basis of their denotative meaning are called **contradictions** (*Kontradiktion, logischer Widerspruch*). They violate principles of our experience of the world as well as of logic; they are logically not possible, i.e. necessarily false:

> *John is here and John is not here.*
> *My mother is married to a bachelor.*

The fact that a sentence is contradictory by no means implies that it is meaningless. Contradictions may be used in deliberate violation of semantic rules in order to signal specific meanings.

4.4.4.2 Tautology

Individual sentences that are true purely on the basis of their meaning are called **tautologies** (*Tautologie*). There are different kinds of tautologies, as can be seen from the following examples:

> *A rose is a rose.*
> *Bachelors are unmarried.*
> *My mother is either here or not here.*

It should again be pointed out that tautologies are not meaningless, but often have some communicative value, depending on the context in which they are used. They may be used, e.g., to rule out alternative interpretations or connotations of an expression, to define the meaning of an expression (as in dictionaries), or to achieve a special effect.

4.4.4.3 Anomaly

Sentences that are not contradictory (necessarily false), but semantically not acceptable on the basis of the meaning of the words they contain, are called **anomalous** (*anomal*). It is our real-world experience and our knowledge of the sense of words that tells us that a sentence is anomalous. Anomaly cannot be grasped by truth value statements. Examples:

> *My brother is pregnant.*
> *Yesterday a red atom came running up here.*
> *My frying pan is neurotic.*
> *The car is sleeping the sleep of the just.*

Sentences like these violate semantic rules of combinability of words, which we call **selectional restrictions** (*Selektionsbeschränkungen*). Of course selectional restrictions may be deliberately violated to produce a special effect. Some selectional restrictions merely concern the use of an almost synonymous expression;

violating these does not produce incomprehensible, but simply 'odd' sentences, as might be used by a non-native speaker:

Fig. 83: Examples of selection restrictions in English

odd	correct
She threw the letter in the box.	*She posted the letter.*
It was becoming dark.	*It was getting dark.*
My head is turning.	*My head is spinning.*
He was standing in the door.	*He was standing in the doorway.*

4.4.5 Predicate logic

While propositional logic deals with the formalisation of relationships between clauses within compound or complex sentences, in **predicate logic** (*Prädikatenlogik*) it is the internal **meaning structure** or **logical structure** of simple sentences that is assigned a **logical form**.

4.4.5.1 Simple statements

Simple propositions are composed of two types of expression, a **predicate** and a varying number of **arguments**. Predicates correspond to sentence elements, usually verbs, that require the presence of other elements to form a meaningful proposition.

> You will have noticed that the sense in which the term *predicate* is used in predicate logic differs from the one in traditional syntax (→ 1.2.1.1). In traditional syntax, it corresponds to the whole VP, whereas in predicate logic, a *predicate* is a component in a logical structure which usually corresponds only to a part, usually the verb, of what would be a predicate in syntax. This corresponds closely to the use of *predicate* in valency theory (→ 1.2.1.1).
> On the term *argument*, see → 1.2.1.1, 🖋 box.

For example, the verb *pluck* cannot form a sentence on its own or with only one argument:

> **Plucked.*
> **Plucked the apple*
> **Eve plucked.*

Thus, predicates can be said to open up semantic places that must be filled by arguments. This is what we already said about verbs in the syntax section (→ 1.2.1.1). Depending on the number of places, we distinguish one-place predicates, two-place predicates, and three-place predicates, taking one, two, or three arguments respectively. In the following examples the predicate is in bold face:

> *Sally$_1$ is **asleep**.*
> *Grandpa$_1$ **prepared** lunch$_2$.*
> *Vivien$_1$ **gave** Donald$_2$ the parcel$_3$.*

In one widespread notation of logical structure, the predicate is represented by a capital letter, the arguments by small letters, following the predicate in brackets, separated from each other by commas. The sentence "Sally is asleep", then, would be simply represented as *A(s)* and the other sentences, respectively, as *P(g, l)* and *G(v, d, p)*

> ✍ SAEED (1997) uses another very widespread notation which simply leaves out the brackets and commas. In this edition, we adopt the notation given above because it seems more legible and transparent.

If we want to leave the identity of the arguments unspecified, we use **variables** (*Variablen*) (w,x,y,z) like in mathematics, e.g.

x is asleep:	*A(x)*
x prepared y:	*P(x, y)*
x gave y z:	*G(x, y, z).*

> ☀ The term *variable* is used in quite a different sense in sociolinguistics (→ 7.1.2).

In this way, it is possible to talk about the logical argument frames of predicates without having to mention concrete arguments, and without committing oneself to specific syntactic constructions in which the predicates occur.

4.4.5.2 Quantification

An important topic that predicate logic deals with is quantification (cf. SAEED 1997, 274-279). All languages have words like *some, all, every, many,* which are used to specify quantities. This means they allow general statements about sets of individuals, for example,

> *Every student has to enrol.*
> *All children like sweets.*
> *Some professor will be helpful.*
> *Many people found this movie unpleasant.*

The simple logical representation developed so far is not able to reflect this capacity to make general quantitative statements about sets of individuals. To do this, specific logical operators called **quantifiers** (*Quantoren*) are introduced into the logical form of such sentences. We will concentrate here on the **universal quantifier** (*Allquantor, Alloperator*), symbolised as ∀, and the **existential quantifier** (*Existenzquantor, Existenzoperator*), symbolised as ∃. The universal quantifier represents the logical meaning of the English expressions *all, every,* and *each* (and the corresponding expressions in other languages). The phrase *every student* is represented in logical form (using the notation introduced in the last section) as ∀x: S(x) and is read as 'Every x such that x is a student'.

The logical representation of the sentence *Every student enrols* is

> *(∀x: S(x)) E(x),*
> to be read as 'For every x such that x is a student, x enrols'.

Another important quantifier is the existential quantifier, which symbolises English *some, a,* or *(at least) one* (and the corresponding expressions in other languages). The noun phrase *some professor* is given the logical form

$\exists x: P(x)$,

which is read as '(There exists) some x such that x is a professor'.

The sentence *Some professor will be helpful* has the logical form

$(\exists x: P(x)) H(x)$,

to be read as 'For some x such that x is a professor, x will be helpful'.

There are several advantages to representing sentences in terms of predicate logic. First of all, logical representations help us to see why there is a difference between sentences which at first sight may appear to have the same propositional content, such as

Everyone loves someone.
Someone is loved by everyone.

The logical forms of these sentences are, respectively,

$(\forall x\ \exists y)\ L(x, y)$ 'For every x there exists some y such that x loves y', and

$(\exists y\ \forall x)\ L(x, y)$ 'There exists some y such that for every x it is the case that x loves y'.

The difference is one of **quantifier scope**. We say that one quantifier takes scope over the other ($\rightarrow$ Box 5). Natural language sometimes finds it difficult to express scope differences clearly.

Logical representations are also very useful in disambiguating sentences with scope ambiguity. In this way, predicate logic tries to provide solutions to various problems of semantic description.

⌥ Let us provide as one further example a problem that is rather complex in nature, but has the advantage of being based on an authentic utterance overheard on the radio and can in principle be solved in terms of predicate logic. Look at the following sentence:

Beckham missed his third penalty.

This sentence has at least two different readings: It could mean that Beckham, *horribile dictu*, actually missed three penalties, or it could mean that Beckham shot three penalties and (only) missed the third one. It is clear that the sentence is not syntactically ambiguous and does not contain an ambiguous word. The ambiguity is in the logical structure, and existential quantification plays a central role in explaining it. To spare the reader complex technical detail that cannot be introduced here, let us just try to paraphrase informally the two logical structures that would explain the ambiguity of the sentence:

(1) 'There are three penalties such that Beckham missed them.'
(2) 'There are three penalties and there is one penalty among them such that Beckham missed it and this is the third penalty.'

5   Pragmatics: the context of language use

5.0   What is pragmatics?

Both semantics and **pragmatics** (*Pragmatik*) are somehow concerned with the **meaning** of 'sentences'. So their respective objects of study cannot easily be separated. Therefore, many introductions to semantics also treat some of the problems discussed here. There is considerable disagreement among linguists as to the precise borderline between semantics and pragmatics. We want to attempt the following delimitation here: All questions connected with the **truth conditions** of sentences ($\rightarrow$ 4.4) appertain to semantics. All further questions appertain to pragmatics.

A further help in distinguishing these two linguistics fields is to look at semantics as concerned with the **meaning of sentences** (*Bedeutung von Sätzen*, *Satzbedeutung*) or rather, with their propositional content ($\rightarrow$ 4.4.2) and pragmatics as dealing with the **meaning of utterances** (*Äußerungsbedeutung*), or with **speaker's meaning**, i.e. what speakers mean when they utter sentences (*'Was der Sprecher meint'*).

The following anecdote illustrates the point that the truth conditions are not everything that can be said about the meaning of a sentence:

> *Every day a captain gets annoyed about a sailor who is constantly drunk. Therefore, he makes a daily entry in the ship's log: "Sailor X. drunk today". The sailor in turn is angry about the captain's records. One day he happens to have unobserved access to the log and records: "The Captain is sober today".*

This last sentence is undoubtedly true but extremely misleading under its conditions of use since it implies that the sobriety of the captain is so exceptional an event that it must be recorded in the log-book. Thus, what the sailor wrote was indeed the truth; however, in writing it he offended against pragmatic rules which are at least as important as the truth claim of an utterance. One could say he lied by telling the truth.

Among other things, pragmatics deals with these conditions for the use of sentences, which do not follow from the truth claim but from other rules of communication. Linguistic pragmatics today is a vast area of research which cannot be dealt with exhaustively in this introduction. We will concentrate on a few concepts and issues that seem to be most widely used, discussed and applied in present-day linguistics. Chapter 6 will then continue the discussion of performance / *parole* phenomena under the heading of "textlinguistics".

Box 38: Pragmatics vs. semantics, competence vs. performance, *langue* vs. *parole*

Although notions of 'communicative competence' or 'pragmatic competence' have been discussed in the literature, it should be noted that this kind of competence is totally different from a Chomskyan-type linguistic competence (→ Box 4). The latter is supposed to be equal for all native speakers of a language, whereas communicative competence, as we all know, may vary considerably across different people, and is quite independent of grammatical competence.

Good communicators may communicate successfully in a foreign language in which they have very little grammatical competence. Thus, seen from the perspective of this Chomskyan dichotomy, pragmatics is certainly more a question of performance than of competence.

Similarly, although pragmatics certainly has an influence on *langue* (in Saussure's sense), it is difficult to see what a pragmatic component of *langue* could be like (→Box 4).

It thus seems more appropriate to assign pragmatics to the *parole* side of the classical dichotomy. We might then also say that semantics is concerned with meaning with regard to both

– semantic performance (the way the use of words in context determines their meaning) and

– semantic competence (knowledge about the meaning of words and their combinability to form interpretable linguistic entities).

Phrased in Saussurean terms, one could say that semantics has both a *langue* and a *parole* side.

– Semantic *parole* again has to do with the use of meanings and the way they influence each other in context.

– Semantic *langue* is, e.g., laid down in the lexicon (→ 4.0) of a language as the system of lexical meanings of that language.

Pragmatics, however, is mainly, if not solely, situated on the parole – performance side of the coin:

It deals with the use of sentences in context, and with the meanings of these utterances as they arise in performance, as an element of parole.

It should be noted that the above remarks are only meant as a rough indication as to where semantics and pragmatics belong in the description of language, and as to which notions are most typically associated with them. The following table was drawn up to show these approximate associations:

Fig. 84: The domains of semantics and pragmatics: some antitheses

Semantics	Pragmatics
Truth conditions	Conditions of use
Meaning of sentences	Meaning of utterances
Propositional content	Speaker's meaning
Context-free meaning	Meaning in context

5.1 Illocution

Let's have a look at the following example:

There's a piece of fish on the table.

The meaning of this sentence seems to be simple and straightforward. We could check the truth conditions of this sentence with our eyes, hands, mouth and nose. But is the meaning of this sentence when uttered really limited to the succinct information that there is a piece of fish on the table? If we imagine situations in which this sentence could be uttered, it can take on a variety of meanings:

Fig. 85: Illocutions

Utterance	Understood meaning	Illocutionary force
There's a piece of fish on the table	*(so don't let the cat in the kitchen)*	Warning
There's a piece of fish on the table	*(so could you please clear the table properly before I sit down)*	Complaint (addressed to a waiter)
There's a piece of fish on the table	*(so if you're hungry please help yourself)*	Offer
There's a piece of fish on the table	*(and you know I hate the smell of fish, so please don't ask me to come in)*	Apology
There's a piece of fish on the table	*(and you know I hate the smell of fish, so please take it away)*	Request (order to a butler)

It could be said that the speaker <u>does</u> different things in the different situations. The utterance of one single sentence can thus be used to perform diverse **speech acts** (*Sprechakte*), to be more precise: different **illocutionary acts**.

> The term *speech act* is also used for the same kind of act when performed in writing. It is often applied in a loose manner when illocutionary acts are meant, as illocutionary acts are the most salient speech acts.

We call this function of an utterance in a given situation its **illocutionary force** or **illocutionary role** (*illokutionäre / illokutive Kraft / Rolle / Funktion*). The illocutionary force of an utterance is an all-important part of its meaning – NB the meaning of the utterance, or speaker's meaning, not of the sentence.

According to SEARLE (1969, 31) the meaning of an utterance consists of its **illocutionary force** F and its **propositional content** (→ 4.4.2) (*propositionaler Inhalt*) p. It can thus be formally represented by

F(p).

To understand what an illocutionary force is you may look at the rightmost column of the above table: All the descriptions there given of the speech acts are descriptions in forms of illocutionary force. This means, these speech-act descriptions (*warning, complaint, offer* etc.) are examples of illocutionary forces.

Lists of examples of illocutionary forces are the nearest thing to a definition that is found in the literature on speech-act theory.

Another way of trying to understand the notion of illocutionary force is to ask what kinds of illocutionary force there are. Following SEARLE (1975a) we distinguish the following kinds of **illocutionary acts** (*illokutionäre / illokutive Akte*):

- **assertives**: a statement (with truth claim) is made.

  Today will be mostly dry and sunny. (in the weather report)
  Goethe died in 1832. (in a textbook)
  The capital of the USA is Washington. (in a geography book)

- **commissives**: the speaker commits him / herself to future action.

  I'll drive the children to school tomorrow. (father to mother)
  I promise to pay you the money. (to a blackmailer)
  I vow to get revenge. (after the blackmailer has left)

- **directives**: the speaker tries to tell the hearer to do something.

  Passengers are kindly requested to proceed to Gate 15. (in an airport)
  I order you to blow up this bridge. (in the army)

- **expressives**: the speaker's attitude towards a situation (congratulating, condoling, thanking etc.) is expressed.

  Happy birthday! (at a birthday party)
  Sorry for stepping on your toe. (on a crowded bus)
  Thank you for the nice present. (at a birthday party)

- **declarations**: the state they describe (baptising, naming, appointing / designating etc.) is induced by the very act of making the declaration.

  I pass. (in a card game)
  I now pronounce you man and wife. (in a wedding ceremony)
  The meeting is now open. (in a formal meeting)

> ♦ Not everything that is called a declaration colloquially is truly a declaration in SEARLE's sense, and vice versa. The models from which he took this term are declarations of war or declarations of independence. Furthermore, to avoid confusion with the sentence type 'declarative' in traditional grammar, which is set off against 'interrogative' and 'exclamatory' sentences, and which is used to make a lot of different speech acts (typically: assertives), SEARLE chose the term *declarations* rather than *declaratives*. The term *declaration* is a good example of a technical term in linguistics which is used in a strictly defined sense diverging from colloquial use.

Each illocutionary function has clearly defined conditions that must be fulfilled to make the speech act valid, i.e. meaningful and appropriate. We call them **felicity conditions** (*Gelingensbedingungen*) (SEARLE 1969, 54-71).

For example, it is meaningless and inappropriate:

- to solemnly promise something one would do anyway or in which the hearer is not at all interested,

- to ask for something the hearer would do anyway or is not able to do at all,
- to offer something the hearer has already got,
- to thank the hearer for something that was to be taken for granted.

A specific kind of felicity conditions are the **sincerity conditions** (*Aufrichtig-keitsbedingungen*) for speech acts (SEARLE 1969, 60). For example it is insincere:

- to assert something one does not believe oneself,
- to promise something one cannot or does not want to put into practice,
- to offer something one does not oneself have control of,
- to thank somebody for something one did not like.

All illocutionary acts have what SEARLE (1969, 60) calls the **essential condition** (*wesentliche Bedingung*) or **illocutionary point**. The illocutionary point of a speech act describes a certain relation between the speaker, the hearer, and the propositional content of that speech act. It is best described in terms of commitments the speaker enters into by uttering the speech act. The illocutionary point depends on the type of illocutionary act the speech act belongs to.

- Thus, the illocutionary point of an **assertive** speech act (a claim, a statement, etc.) is to commit the speaker to the truth of the assertion (of its propositional content).
- The point of a **commissive** is to commit the speaker to performing the action described in the propositional content of the speech act.
- The point of a **directive** is that it counts as an attempt by the speaker to get the hearer to do whatever is laid down in the propositional content.
- The point of an **expressive** is to express a certain attitude of the speaker to the propositional content of a speech act.
- The point of a **declaration** is to bring about the state of affairs described in the propositional content of an utterance.

The illocutionary force of a speech act is often signalled by its linguistic form. When speakers want to make the illocutionary force of their utterance abundantly clear, they sometimes use the appropriate **illocutionary verb** (**speech-act verb**, *illokutives Verb*, *Sprechaktverb*). A speech-act verb that can be used to perform the very speech act it describes is also called a **performative verb** (*performatives Verb*), and an utterance in which this is done is called a **performative utterance** (*performative Äußerung*).

However, performative utterances are actually much less common than is sometimes suggested in the literature on speech acts. Illocutionary verbs are much more often used to <u>discuss</u> or <u>invoke</u> speech acts than to perform them:

> *But you promised!*
> *Was that a warning or a threat?*

In our above examples only the following are performative:

Fig. 86: Performative utterances and their illocutionary force

Utterance:	Illocutionary force:
I promise to pay you the money	Promise (commissive)
I vow to get revenge	Vow (commissive)
I pass	Pass (declaration)

Thank you might be called an abbreviated performative, in which the personal pronoun *I* is left out.

If you are in doubt whether a given utterance is performative or not, you can apply the *hereby*-insertion test: In sentences used performatively, usually the adverb *hereby* can be inserted between the first-person pronoun *I* (or *we*) and the performative verb. This test works with the above examples, but it is not foolproof. Even the use of a performative verb does not necessarily mean that the illocutionary force which it denotes is intended, as the following example shows:

I promise that you will regret this.

The speech act performed in uttering such a sentence is very unlikely to be a promise. It is more likely to be a threat, which is also a commissive, but of a somewhat different kind (the difference being that the propositional content of a threat is not welcomed by the hearer and not meant to be).

There is a large group of speech acts in which linguistic form systematically and consistently does not express directly the illocutionary force intended. These speech-acts are called **indirect speech acts** (*indirekte Sprechakte*) (SEARLE 1975b).

Many requests are for example put as questions.

Why don't you shut up?

is usually not a question as to the reasons for noisemaking, but a request to stop it.

I can do the washing-up tomorrow.

is not a statement about my domestic abilities, but an offer to wash the dishes.

Some indirect speech acts are so conventionalised in their linguistic form that they are hardly perceived as such and their formulation can hardly be used to perform the speech act literally expressed by it.

Could you open the window?

thus has the linguistic form of a question, but it is hardly ever understood as a question (which according to SEARLE is a directive with the purpose of obtaining information from the hearer), but as a request (another directive which is a polite attempt to get the hearer to make the propositional content of the speech act true). **Politeness** is the most common reason for using indirect speech acts. For reasons of space, we are not dealing with politeness in much detail here (see, however, next section → 5.2).

> ● German learners should be aware that (in particular) British speakers tend to use more indirect speech acts than they might be accustomed to (HOUSE / KASPAR 1981). Perhaps, this is an instance of the much-quoted 'British understatement'

5.2 Conversational maxims

5.2.1 Speakers' maxims: GRICE

Indirect speech acts rely on the **cooperativeness** of the hearer. Taking such speech acts literally and answering, e.g., the above request

> *Could you open the window?*

by simply saying

> *Yes, I could.*

and doing nothing, is regarded as the violation of a **conversational maxim** (conversational postulate; *Konversationsmaxime, Konversationspostulat*).

Conversational maxims are basic principles we expect to be observed by others. Their non-observance signals that some special meaning is being expressed. They are general principles of communication and many philosophers and linguists believe them to be indispensable for the functioning of communication. The philosopher H. P. GRICE is regarded as the discoverer of those principles. He formulated the following maxims:

Fig. 87: Conversational maxims
(GRICE 1975, 45-46)

Quantity 1:	Make your contribution as informative as is required.
Quantity 2:	Do not make your contribution more informative than is required.
Quality 1:	Do not say what you believe to be false.
Quality 2:	Do not say that for which you lack adequate evidence.
Relation (also called relevance):	Be relevant.
Manner:	Avoid obscurity of expression. Avoid ambiguity. Be brief. Be orderly.

♠ Note that *manner* in GRICE has nothing to do with 'good manners', i.e. politeness. What is meant is the <u>way</u> in which the information is delivered, as indicated in the above table.

GRICE used the following examples, showing that the above maxims are valid not only for the use of language but also for other domains of human action:

"1. **Quantity:** If you are assisting me to mend a car, I expect your contribution to be neither more nor less than is required; if, for example, at a particular stage I need four screws, I expect you to hand me four, rather than two or six.

2. **Quality:** I expect your contributions to be genuine and not spurious. If I need sugar as an ingredient in the cake you are assisting me to make, I do not expect you to hand me salt; if I need a spoon, I do not expect a trick spoon made of rubber.

3. **Relation**: I expect a partner's contribution to be appropriate to immediate needs at each stage of the transaction; if I am mixing ingredients for a cake, I do not expect to be handed a good <sic> book, or even an oven cloth (though this might be an appropriate contribution at a later stage).

4. **Manner:** I expect a partner to make it clear what contribution he is making, and to execute his performance with reasonable dispatch." (1975, 47)

This could be taken as a confirmation from pragmatics that language behaviour is based on general cognitive principles and not on a specialised language module (➔ 1.2.3.6). It is certainly no coincidence that generative grammarians never became really interested in pragmatics.

Some pragmatic approaches postulate other important, yet not completely indispensable maxims for the functioning of communication which have to do with **politeness** (*Höflichkeit*):

Avoid embarrassing or insulting the hearer

(ROBIN LAKOFF 1973).

Politeness is the major disruptive factor in the application of the other maxims. The topic cannot be done justice to in this textbook. For further theories of politeness, we would like to refer the reader to LEECH (1983), BROWN / LEVINSON (1988) and WATTS (2003).

Indirect speech acts often violate conversational maxims. For example they superficially seem to ask for things which are self-evident or obviously irrelevant to the speaker. However, since hearers are usually cooperative, they will assume us to have meant something other than the literal meaning. Such assumptions we call **conversational implicatures** (*Konversationsimplikaturen*). We then say that a certain utterance **implicates** a certain speaker's meaning that was presumably meant, but not explicitly said. Hearers' implicatures are thus based on a deliberate and open violation (called "flouting" by GRICE) of maxims by the speaker.

> ☛ The notion of implicature should not be confused with the notion of **implication** as used in propositional logic. The verb forming the base of *implicature* is *implicate*, not to be confused with *imply* (➔ 4.4.3.1, ☛ box).

Thus, in the above example, a question as to a person's ability to open the window is very likely to be irrelevant, as most people are able to do this. The hearer, therefore, concludes that something else must have been meant. As it happens, the hearer's ability to open the window is a felicity condition (➔ 5.1) on the request to open the window. It seems plausible that if speakers want to be polite they want to play down the imposition that a speech act may mean for the hearer. This, in turn, often means that instead of making a request directly, speakers will pretend to be probing into the situation and ask whether the most important felicity condition of the request, that is, the hearer's ability to comply with it, is given. The hearer, also being polite and co-operative, will comply with the request before it has even been explicitly uttered, simply because the speaker has thematised a felicity condition of that request.

Eventually this leads to a conventionalisation of the question concerning the felicity condition of a request (*Could you open the window?*) as meaning the request itself. This conventionalisation is shown by the fact that conventionalised indirect request formulae like this can be combined with the interjection *please*, which clearly signals a polite request and does not normally go with genuine questions (which arise from curiosity).

> *Could you open the window, please?*
> **How did you like the film you saw yesterday, please?*

5.2.2   Hearers' heuristics: LEVINSON

LEVINSON (2000) tries to explain so-called generalised conversational implicatures, of which the above is an example. One could say he reformulates some of the GRICEan maxims, which are maxims for the speaker, from a hearer's perspective. According to this approach, the hearer, in interpreting the speaker's utterances, makes use of certain **heuristics** which help him or her to make sense of otherwise puzzling utterances. LEVINSON manages to reduce the GRICEan speaker-oriented maxims to three hearer-oriented heuristic principles which are immediately evident and find a wide range of applications:

The First (Q-) Heuristic:
"What isn't said, isn't." (LEVINSON 2000, 35.)

This principle, LEVINSON says,

> "... is more or less transparently related to Grice's first Maxim of Quantity, Q1: Make your contribution as informative as is required."

And he continues (p. 36):

> " ... the first heuristic depends crucially on a restriction to a set of salient alternates. For example, there is a scalar contrast set <*all, some*>, such that saying (15a) implicates the rationale being that the speaker would have chosen the stronger alternate if he was in a position to do so."

Thus (this is LEVINSON'S example (15a)),

> *Some of the boys came*

implicates in most cases

> NOT ALL OF THE BOYS CAME

because the speaker would have said

> *All of the boys came*

if he or she had been in a position to do so.

The Second (I-) Heuristic:
"What is expressed simply is stereotypically exemplified"
(LEVINSON 2000, 37)

LEVINSON explains that this principle

> "... may be related directly to Grice's second Maxim of Quantity, Q2: Do not make your contribution *more* informative than is required. The underlying idea is, of course, that one need not say what can be taken for granted." (LEVINSON 2000, 37)

It means that

> "minimal specifications get maximally informative or stereotypical interpretations" (ibd.)

LEVINSON gives the following elucidating examples:

- *bread knife* means 'knife stereotypically used to cut bread', not 'knife made of bread' or 'knife hidden in a bread'
- *kitchen knife* means 'knife stereotypically intended for use in a kitchen', not 'knife used to cut kitchens'
- *steel knife* means 'knife made of steel' not 'knife used to cut steel' or 'knife stored among steel'.

LEVINSON thus shows the usefulness of pragmatic theory in other branches of linguistics. The second heuristic can explain certain puzzles in word formation that have kept morphologists busy for decades, e.g., why compounds (→ 1.3.5.2) receive a certain interpretation and not another and why compounds formed in the same way may receive different interpretations.

The Third (M-) Heuristic:
"What's said in an abnormal way isn't normal" (LEVINSON 2000, 38)

Again Levinson gives a few interesting examples: Suppose somebody said

> *It's not impossible that the plane will be late.*

This is a somewhat abnormal way of talking about possibility. More normal ways would be, e.g.:

> *It is possible that the plane will be late.*
> *The plane may be late.*

This means that the formulation the speaker chose conveys a special additional meaning, irony perhaps or extreme caution. Similarly, in

> *Bill caused the car to stop*

the hearer immediately assumes that the speaker had a special reason not to use a more normal formulation such as

> *Bill stopped the car.*

Thus, the utterance could mean that Bill stopped the car in an abnormal way.

LEVINSON's theory is thus a useful supplement to GRICE's conversational maxims and goes a long way towards explaining implicatures.

5.3   Relevance theory

Relevance theory is, so to speak, another simplification and radicalisation of Gricean pragmatic theory and currently for many the prevailing paradigm in linguistic pragmatics. Relevance theorists claim that in order to understand implicatures, not four different Gricean maxims with submaxims are necessary but only one principle, the principle of **Relevance**. (We spell *Relevance* with a capital *R* here to show that it is different from the Gricean maxim of relevance.) According to SPERBER / WILSON, the founders of relevance theory,

> "a phenomenon is relevant to an individual to the extent that the contextual effects achieved when it is optimally processed are large" (SPERBER / WILSON 1986, 153).

This is more or less in line with our intuitive understanding of *relevance*. But SPERBER / WILSON add a second criterion for Relevance, counterbalancing the first:

> "a phenomenon is relevant to an individual to the extent that the effort required to process it is small." (ibd.)

This means, an utterance becomes less Relevant in SPERBER / WILSON's sense if it is difficult to process. Relevance R of an utterance can thus be 'measured' by a mathematical fraction with its contextual effects c in the numerator and the processing effort p in the denominator:

$$R = c/p$$

According to SPERBER / WILSON, there are three ways in which an utterance can achieve a contextual effect:

–   it can create new assumptions in the hearer,
–   it can contradict existing assumptions of the hearer,
–   it can strengthen existing assumptions.

This would explain why we regard some utterances as irrelevant: They simply do not have any effect or bearing whatever on our assumptions.

Note that this is a far cry from GRICE's (1975) relevance maxim which is primarily based on a notion of discourse coherence (➔ 6.1.3; 6.1.4). According to SPERBER / WILSON, an utterance can also be Relevant if it is completely incoherent in its context:

> A: *What did Susan say?*
> B: *You've dropped your purse.*

Of course, speaker B did not mean that Susan said "You've dropped your purse". B wanted to point out to A that he or she has dropped his or her purse. This remark may be extremely Relevant to A, more Relevant than an answer to the question, but it is certainly not coherent with the previous discourse (cf. BLASS 1990, 22). It does not attend "to the immediate needs at" this "stage of the transaction" (GRICE 1975, 47), but only to the immediate private needs of A (and, possibly, B).

5.4   Pragmatic inferencing and language change

In this section, we will discuss a few applications of pragmatic theory in historical linguistics.

Speakers of English have changed their language use again and again throughout the centuries – such instances of language change have been treated in detail in Chapter → 3. In fact, they do change their output particularly because they want to render it as efficient as possible, both in terms of quantity of linguistic units and of effectively conveying the message. According to this, the main underlying principles of our utterances (and their understanding respectively) are **informativeness** and **simplicity** which are, in turn, relying on the **cooperativeness** (→ 5.2) of speaker and hearer in order to establish a 'successful' communication. In other words, we want to be understood (and to understand) with the least possible effort.

These principles, which we could also term '**comprehensibility**' and '**economy**', are thus reported to have guided our communicative interactions at all times. Yet, they are conflicting principles which lead us to express ourselves in different ways or to infer a meaning that might not have been intended by the speaker in the first place.

> ☞ We would like to point out that these notions can be directly associated with some of GRICE's **maxims** (→ 5.2) and also correspond closely to the two sides of **relevance** in SPERBER / WILSON's (→ 5.3) approach. Informativeness and comprehensibility are the pursuit of GRICE's maxim of 'quantity 1' and also of 'relation', and can be equated with 'contextual effects' in SPERBER /WILSON's model. Simplicity and economy of course have to do with GRICE's 'quantity 2' and SPERBER /WILSON's 'processing costs'.

Hence, communication is the continuous negotiation of the principles informativeness and simplicity by both speaker and hearer. The outcome of this are gradually conventionalised lexical and grammatical changes including meaning shifts. Thus, we have established a pragmatic reason why languages do not stay as they are, but are in a constant state of flux.

Let us have a look at some examples: The creative reduction of phonetic substance can be witnessed in instances such as *gonna* (vs. *going to*; → 3.2.3.3) or *'d* (vs. *had* or *would* ; → 1.3.7). Here, Zipf's Law (→ 3.3) appears to be at work: The older a lexical item, the more does its size correlate inversely with its frequency. This means that *had* or *would*, which are rather old English words, are likely to be reduced if they occur often. And, in fact, they did and still do. Thus, *'d* is a highly economical result which may, however, lead to ambiguity and impede the principle of informativeness. Here, more sound information would increase ad hoc accessibility. Yet, as *'d* is routinised in everyday speech, language creativity in terms of a change of an expanding type is once again at hand. Parallely, abbreviations of frequent words may result in disturbing homophony: *'d* can mean 'had' or 'would', [əv] can mean 'of' or 'have', and *'s* can mean 'is', 'has' or 'genitive'. Which in turn triggers avoidance strategies.

But frequency alone doesn't seem to be the point. Phonetic erosion seems to be particularly associated with **grammaticalisation** (→ 3.2.3.3). Along with the highly grammaticalised *gonna*, we still find *going to* which has retained its lexical meaning.

The point here is that such grammaticalisation has always been pragmatically motivated by a goal-directed speaker/hearer interaction (HOPPER / TRAUGOTT 1993, 66). From their interaction, meaning is deduced beyond the structure of the utterance, creating a new construction (→ 1.2.3.2). In this view, it is not the abstract lexical item that acquires grammatical function in the event of grammaticalisation, but rather the use of the lexical item in discourse gives rise to new grammatical items. The context of an utterance and, hence, ensuing conversational inferences are decisive in changing form and function of items. Consequently, *going to* could have developed its grammaticalised function as a tense marker by the following inferences:

- *going to* indicates a spatial direction, so why not a temporal one?
- *going to* further refers to a process which has not come to an end yet, so it might indicate futurity!

To take another example, modal verbs such as *can* or *could* have become particularly functional in indirect speech acts (→ 5.1). A question introduced by *could you* seldom asks for an ability. It is automatically understood as a request. In any case, the 'weakness' of words such as *can* or *could* along with their frequent use gives rise to the counterbalancing creation of longer, yet semantically restricted constructions *be able* or *be capable* in order to grasp the notions that could be expressed by *can* in former times, i.e. before it was completely grammaticalised as an auxiliary.

Speakers / hearers may see old things from a new angle due to **pragmatic inferencing** (*pragmatische Inferenz*) (and change language on the battleground of simplicity and informativeness). In the event, associative transfer or metonymy may be involved – it allows to explain why the Old English lexeme *gebēd* ('*prayer*') is semantically related to Present-Day English *bead* as in the expression *to tell one's beads* (→ 4.1.2.2).

With respect to pragmatic inferencing, HORN (1984) takes up GRICEan theory (→ 5.2) and, as it were, prepares its modifications by SPERBER / WILSON (→ 5.3). He identifies an ideal, equilibrated division of the pragmatic labour between two diametrically opposed principles: the hearer-based, or **Q(uantity)-based** principle (called **informativeness** above) and the speaker-based, or **R(elevance)-based** principle (called the **simplicity** principle above), which are the only principles needed and constrain each other. In this framework, the hearer lays emphasis on the maxim of quantity (to obtain sufficient information), while the speaker rather aims at observing principally the maxims of quality, relation, and manner (to minimise effort). This division enables inferencing to happen easily in a conversation. However, as the system is dynamic and unstable, language change can take shape.

HORN (1984, 32) convincingly explains an example of **narrowing** of meaning (→ 3.2.4) by his theory of inferencing: We try to reconstruct his argumentation here, which is sometimes slightly over-implicit for beginners: Starting point is the inference of '(high) temperature' when hearing *fever* as part of an utterance, thus enabling the possibly confusing usage of *temperature* with the meaning 'fever' in instances like *The baby has a temperature*. For the speaker, this wording is relevant and economic, for whatever reason:

- *fever* is more specific than *temperature* and may be more difficult to process;
- *fever* may be regarded as exaggerated, or too blunt; after all, *fever* occurs in the names of some very serious diseases; this also means heightened processing effort; *temperature* could thus be a **euphemism** (→ 3.2.5.4);
- *temperature* provides sufficient information as any other interpretation of *temperature* ('normal temperature', 'low temperature') would not make sense, would not be relevant.

This leads the speaker to use *temperature* instead of *fever*. The hearer goes through one or several of the above reasoning steps in opposite direction; in particular, his reasoning probably ends: "If what he says is at all relevant, he must mean 'The baby has fever'".

If this happens often enough, and speakers have less occasion to use *temperature* in its normal meaning than in the inferrable meaning 'fever', the meaning of *temperature* will gradually begin to shift; *temperature* will become polysemous (→ 4.1.2.1). In the end, the original meaning may become obsolete (→ 3.2.5.4).

5.5   The notion of context

When sentences are uttered, they are always uttered in a concrete **context** (*Kontext*). We have repeatedly had occasion already to mention context. But what exactly is to be understood by that term, has been somewhat neglected in recent pragmatic theorising. But it should be obvious that the speaker's meaning can only be determined in such a context and that the use that is made of maxims of conversation is dependent on it.

It is generally agreed among linguists that we have to distinguish three spheres of context:

• First, each utterance is surrounded by other utterances, the speaker's own or other speakers', to which it relates and responds. Also, written utterances are usually part of a text which provides this kind of context for them. This context is what we call the verbal context (*verbaler Kontext*) or the textual context (*textueller Kontext, Ko-Text*).

> Note that the term *verbal* as used here has nothing to do with the word class called *verbs* (→ 1.1.3.1). It goes back to a wider definition of the Latin term which includes <u>all</u> words. To avoid confusion, we prefer the term *textual context*.

• Second, many utterances take place in a rich concrete situation: The speaker is in a particular room with particular co-present objects, at a particular time, with particular people present, some of whom will be hearers, others perhaps not. All this may be relevant to the meaning of an utterance. This context is called the context of situation (*Situationskontext*) (LUX 1981).

• Third, all utterances, written or spoken, are performed against a wider background of cultural and other knowledge (SEARLE 1980) and presuppositions (CLARK / CARLSON 1982). There's always something that writers or speakers take for granted that they expect their hearers to understand without realising their expectations. No utterance can be made totally free of presuppositions. This background is usually completely inconspicuous and only becomes evident if something goes wrong or communication breaks down. (The cartoon at the end of this chapter is meant to show this.)

The following graph (Fig. 88) illustrates these three spheres of the context around the speaker and his / her utterance.

Fig. 88: The three spheres of the context of an utterance

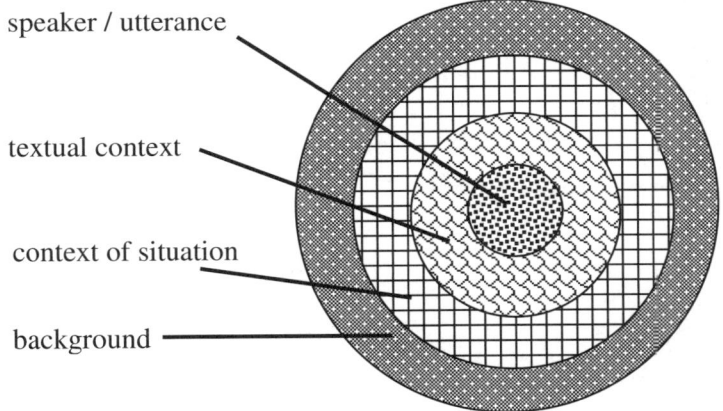

"Next time you reserve a table
think about getting some chairs."

6 Textlinguistics. Conversation analysis. Discourse analysis

Textlinguistics (*Textlinguistik*) is, under that name, a relatively new discipline in linguistics. It arose from the observation that the sentence is not a sufficient domain to describe everything that goes on in an utterance. There were felt to be regularities that called for an explanation above sentence level. Also, the question as to what properties there are in a text that make it a text, was felt to be a linguistic question. **Text constitution** (*Textkonstitution*) and **text coherence** (*Textkohärenz*) became important topics of linguistic discussion. The question was raised how texts are produced (**text production,** *Textproduktion*), received (**text reception,** *Textrezeption*), and understood (**text comprehension,** *Textverständnis*) (→ www.narr-studienbuecher.de).

Methods of linguistic text analysis have been developed, depending on varying theoretical interests.

> ☞ Unfortunately the terms **text analysis** (*Textanalyse*), **conversation analysis** (*Gesprächsanalyse, Konversationsanalyse*), and **discourse analysis** (*Diskursanalyse, Textanalyse, Gesprächsanalyse*) are used with very different and partly overlapping scopes and contents, by different people who all claim that their way of doing text analysis, or discourse analysis, or conversation analysis, is the real thing, to the exclusion of any other approach. In actual fact, the terms can be used for, and indeed, cover, a wide variety of different approaches. We will mention only a few here. We will not go further into possible differentiations in terminology between **text** and **discourse** here. We will use the term *discourse* when emphasising the process character of language use, and we will use the term *text* when emphasising the object or product character of linguistic utterances.

6.1   Textlinguistic approaches to text analysis

The term **text analysis** is usually reserved for the analysis of written texts. Analysing a text in some way or other can be of interest to a variety of different disciplines, not only to textlinguistics. Literary scholars, theologians, historians, lawyers, information scientists, psychologists, sociologists, journalists, media experts, documentalists, editors and many others all have their specific interest in texts and are increasingly beginning to realise that they need (text)linguistic expertise to deal with their text-related problems professionally. The Dutch textlinguist Teun A. VAN DIJK, more than twenty years ago (1980), introduced the term *Tekstwetenschap* (*Textwissenschaft*) into the debate, to draw attention to the fact that many different branches of knowledge relate themselves to texts in a professional way, and argued for an integration of all these approaches. Today, textlinguistics is an expanding branch of linguistics, seeking applications and interdisciplinary cooperation in all directions.

What is presented in this section is only a small portion of the research and practice of today's textlinguistics. We are going to present two classical approaches of textlinguistics:

– the analysis of **cohesion**, and
– the study of **coherence relations**.

6.1.1 Grammar beyond the sentence: cohesion phenomena

An important starting-point for textlinguistics was the observation that certain grammatical phenomena (called **cohesion** phenomena (*Kohäsion*) by HALLIDAY / HASAN 1976) can only be described and explained if larger units than the sentence are taken into account. The phenomena mentioned most often are the following:

- **Anaphora** (*Rekurrenz, Anapher*) is brought about by using an expression in one sentence that is coreferent with, i.e. has the same reference as, an expression in a preceding sentence:

  Lady Helen Clyde was surrounded by the trappings of death ... Yet despite the macabre nature of the environment Lady Helen's thoughts kept drifting to food. (Elizabeth George, *A Suitable Vengeance*, p. 23)

In the above example, Lady Helen is mentioned (**referred to**) twice: in the first sentence as "*Lady Helen Clyde*", in the second as "*Lady Helen*". The second mention is an example of anaphora.

It is the usual case that the second mention of a person or thing in a text is in an abbreviated form of some kind. The most common way of doing this is using a pronoun: **pronominalisation** (*Pronominalisierung*):

  Tina Cogin knew how to make the most of what little she had. She liked to believe it was a natural talent. (Elizabeth George, *A Suitable Vengeance*, p. 13)

In this example, "Tina Cogin" is twice referred to again by a personal pronoun, *she*, first in the same sentence, then in the next sentence.

- We also find a phenomenon called **ellipsis** (*Ellipse*), i.e. leaving out an element that can be supplied from the context:

  Not that Lee Chong was avaricious. He wasn't ø, but if one wanted to spend money, he was available. (John Steinbeck, *Cannery Row*, Mandarin Edition, p. 3)

Apart from two further examples of pronominalisation (Lee Chong is referred to again by *he* twice), the second sentence also contains an ellipsis: "*He wasn't ø* (= **avaricious**)". (ø stands for the 'gap' left by the ellipsis here). The adjective *ava-*

ricious is 'needed' once again in the second sentence but does not have to be explicitly used because a rule of ellipsis applies.

Ellipsis is also often used if the same <u>kind of things</u> must be referred to again in the next clause or sentence, but not exactly the <u>same things</u>.

> *Here are my two white silk scarves. I used to have three ø.*
> (HALLIDAY / HASAN 1976, 142ff.)

Note that in the above example, several fill-ins for the ellipsis are possible. The second sentence is most likely to mean

> *I used to have three **white silk scarves**.*

But it could also mean

> *I used to have three **silk scarves**.*

Or even

> *I used to have three **scarves**.*

In any case, however, the scarves mentioned in the first sentence are not completely identical with the scarves meant by ellipsis in the second: The first sentence refers to two scarves, the second to three, so the referent of the two phrases "*my two white silk scarves*" and "*three*" is not identical.

Further examples of ellipsis are:

> *Joan brought some carnations, and Catherine ø some sweet peas.*
> *Would you like to hear another verse? I know twelve more ø.*
> *'And how many hours a day did you do lessons?' said Alice, in a hurry to change the subject. 'Ten hours the first day,' said the Mock Turtle: 'nine ø the next ø, and so on.'*

Note that in the last example, two ellipses occur that require the reader to insert two different nouns (*hours* and *day*) from the preceding sentence.

- Another strategy, very closely related to ellipsis, is called **substitution** by HALLIDAY / HASAN:

> *My axe is too blunt. I must get a sharper **one**.*
> *You think Joan already knows ? – I think everybody **does**.*
> *Has Barbara left ? – I think **so**.*
> *Ah, but you should have seen the **one** that got away.*
> *These biscuits are stale. – Get some fresh **ones**.*

For nouns, the pronoun *one* is the most common substitution form. The rules for the use of substitution or ellipsis are actually quite intricate, and sometimes the two compete, see the following example:

> *Here are my two white silk scarves. Can you see any black (**ø / ones**)?*

The most common substitution verb is *do*. It usually substitutes for a whole verb phrase (minus auxiliaries):

> *He never really succeeded in his ambitions. He might have **done**, ..., had it not been for the restlessness of his nature.*

- Another grammatical regularity that operates across sentence boundaries is called **consecutio temporum** in Latin grammar (sequence of tenses, *Zeiten-folge*). It leads to the use of perfect and so-called conditional forms in English if the point of reference is in the past, and the time of the narrated event before (perfect) or after ('conditional') the point of reference:

  *As McLoughlin returned thankfully to the house, Inspector Walsh took a pipe from his pocket, filled it and lit it thoughtfully, then began a careful examination of the ground and the brambles around the door and pathway. The ground itself told him little. The summer **had been** an exceptional one and the last four weeks of almost perpetual sunshine **had baked** it hard.*
  (Minette Walters, *The Ice House*, p. 22)

In the above example, the summer is obviously over for the most part, so that the relevant part of it was before the point of reference, that is the time when the Inspector is investigating. If the summer had been after the point of reference, Inspector Walsh would have had a prophetic gift, and a different tense form would have been used :

  *The summer **would** be an exceptional one.*

The above-mentioned phenomena have been discussed thoroughly by textlinguists and taken as proof that grammar does not stop at sentence boundaries.

Other linguists, critical or sceptical of textlinguistics, have argued that all these phenomena are not only observable across sentence boundaries, but also between clauses within the same sentence, and have thus regarded this as proof that anaphora, ellipsis, substitution, and sequence of tenses could be handled in a sentence grammar, cross-sentence phenomena being only special cases of the within-sentence ones.

6.1.2 Cohesion as text constitution

These arguments, however, did not stop early textlinguists from believing that the cross-sentence phenomena mentioned above, were the true text-creating properties, so that cohesion seemed the answer to the question of text constitution. It was said that cohesion created a connection between the sentences in a text. HALLIDAY / HASAN also added a few other phenomena to the list of cohesion devices (that had already been mentioned by HARWEG, 1968):

- Sometimes, neighbouring sentences are not only connected by common reference (as in anaphora) or common phrases that are then left out or substituted (ellipsis and substitution). There is also what is called **lexical cohesion** (*lexikalische Kohäsion*), that is, a looser connection between neighbouring sentences through lexical elements that have certain semantic features in common without being coreferent. (HALLIDAY / HASAN 1976, 284ff). Look at the following example:

*A **season** of growth*

***Flowers** in the **spring**, swaying in the wind; from a distance, a wash of **red**; up close, stains of **blue**, flashes of **yellow** and **purple** and **white**; **hundreds** of species, **millions** of **plants**: nature's **commonplace** diversity. So **commonplace**, indeed, that it is matched many **billions** of times within your **body**. Each **cell** of the immune system has such a **meadow** on its surface: **millions** of proteins of **hundreds** of types. (Economist, 24.2.1995)*

This passage abounds in lexical cohesion, to mention the most striking examples:

- There's a hyponymy – hyperonymy relation between "*season*" in the headline and "*spring*" in the first sentence, and between "*flower*" and "*plant*" in the first.

- Different colours are mentioned (*red, blue, yellow*, etc.) and also numbers (*hundred, million, billion*); both of these lexical fields are strongly associated with the noun *diversity*.

- Then there's the lexical repetition "*commonplace*",

- the part-whole relation between *cell* and *body*,

- and of course *flower* and *meadow* are also somehow semantically related.

- Finally, HALLIDAY / HASAN regard the use of **conjunctions** (*Konjunktionen*) as important cohesive devices. They distinguish four major classes of conjunction (1976, 226ff.). The four types of conjunction distinguished by them are reminiscent of coherence relations (cf. → 6.1.4):

  For the whole day he climbed up the steep mountainside, almost without stopping.
  ***And** in all this time he met no one.* (additive)
  ***Yet** he was hardly aware of being tired.* (adversative)
  ***So** by night time the valley was far below him.* (causal)
  ***Then**, as dusk fell, he sat down to rest.* (temporal)

> In a somewhat looser sense, the term **connector** (*Konnektor*) is also used to refer to such explicit linking devices between clauses.

- For oral texts, **intonation** is also said to play a role in cohesion. Thus, the fall-rise pattern (\ /) seems to carry a meaning of contrast, even if there is no other cohesive device to that effect (HALLIDAY / HASAN 1976, 271ff.).

  People used to dress up to go to the theatre. \ Now / they wear any old thing. (→ 2.3.4)

> The sense in which *contrast* is used here is again different from that in linguistics at large. It will be explained in → 6.1.4.

Critics of textlinguistics remained sceptical. They pointed out that all these cohesion devices constitute rather a mixed bag, and are neither sufficient nor necessary to make a text. It is rather difficult, though, to find a text lacking any kind of cohesion device. The following passage comes close to it.

There are hardly any cohesive links between the sentences, although the passage forms part of a (much) larger text which is clearly coherent:

> *Destitutes were investigated and the deserving written about. The truce with W.C. Tuttle was broken, patched up and broken again. The readers and learners read and learned. Anand and Vidiadhar continued not to speak, and this silence between the cousins was beginning to be known at the college, which Vidiadhar had also managed to enter, though at a suitably low form. Govind beat Chinta, wore his threepiece suits and drove his taxi. The widows stopped taking sewing lessons at the Royal Victoria Institute, gave up the clothesmaking scheme and all other schemes.*
>
> (V.S. Naipaul: A House for Mr Biswas. Harmondsworth: Penguin, 1969, p. 495.)

Sometimes poets or other literary writers (or linguists) might deliberately construct a 'cohesion-free' text to topicalise cohesion rules by flouting them. It is fairly easy, however, to show that cohesion is not sufficient to create a coherent text. Any of the devices mentioned could be misused, creating the appearance of coherence by the use of cohesion devices, in particular lexical cohesion, shown in bold face below, and temporal connectors, shown underlined:

> *Morgen mittag, ¾ 12 Uhr, sind es 200 Jahre, dass der fromme Schweppermann von der Neuhauser Straße zusammen mit seinem Freund **Columbus** den Malzkaffee **entdeckte**. Lange vorher schon, als **König** Herodes in einer Wirtschaft dem **Grafen Zeppelin** zeigte, wie **man ein Ei auf die Spitze stellt**, kam der **Stein** ins Rollen, den der Riese **Goliath** dem **David** an den Kopf warf. Einige Wochen später sah sich **König** Barbarossa genötigt, …*
>
> (Karl Valentin)

This is presumably why DE BEAUGRANDE / DRESSLER (1981) introduced the distinction between **coherence** and **cohesion** (*Kohärenz / Kohäsion*) into the debate. In their approach, and in most of the mainstream literature on textlinguistics, coherence is mainly understood as topical (or thematic) coherence (→ 6.1.3), i.e. a text may be supposed to be coherent when it can be said to have a certain **topic** or complex of topics that are somehow derived from each other in the text, relying on the semantic and encyclopaedic knowledge of the reader. But what exactly coherence then is in contrast to cohesion, has remained somewhat mysterious since then (→ 6.1.4 for an alternative suggestion).

6.1.3 Thematic progression

In the early seventies, DANEŠ (1970) had shown that texts could be analysed by discovering certain patterns of **topic development** in them. To explain this, the notion of **topic,** or **theme** (*Thema*), is crucial. The topic or theme can be informally defined as that part of the sentence that denotes what the sentence is 'about'. And what is said about the topic is the **comment**. The analogous complementary notion for theme is **rheme** (*Rhema*) (→ Box 39).

Box 39: Theme vs. rheme / topic vs. comment

The notions of **theme** (*Thema*) and **rheme** (*Rhema*) have long been being discussed in the European tradition of linguistics, primarily in the **Prague School** (*Prager Schule*), under the name of **functional sentence perspective** (*Funktionale Satzperspektive*) (MATHESIUS 1975); or by FIRBAS (1992), under the name of **communicative dynamism**. Another prominent theoretician of theme / rheme distinctions is HALLIDAY (1985; HALLIDAY / MATTHIESSEN 2004). Theme and rheme are used and relevant both in syntactic description and in text analysis, and not to be confused with the theme as case role (→ 1.2.2.6, and below). The theme is often said to be what the sentence 'is about'; the rheme, then, would be what is said about that theme.

There are analogous notions of **topic** and **comment** (HOCKETT 1958, p. 191-208) in the American tradition.

The relevance and validity of syntactic analyses in terms of 'theme / rheme' or 'topic / comment' is rather controversial and is not followed up any further in this textbook. The notion of 'theme' is, however, highly relevant in text analysis. That's why it is explained here.

All these approaches, very similar to each other, are often said to make a distinction similar to the **figure / ground** (→ 1.2.3.2) alignment, but this is not really the case.

• The figure / ground distinction is concerned with cognitive conceptualisations of scenes, mainly through the distribution of syntactic roles and the choice of predicates with suitable argument frames.

• The theme / rheme distinction is signalled in English through constituent order (theme tends to come before rheme) and intonation (rheme tends to receive main sentence stress) (→ 2.3.4.2). Furthermore, theme / rheme is dependent on the discourse context and can be said to be concerned with what is communicated, i.a., with what is given and what is new in a sentence.

☞ The latter aspect of the theme / rheme distinction is often called **information structure** (*Informationsstruktur*).

Many syntactic descriptions from different approaches, however, use the term **topicalisation** (*Topikalisierung*) to describe a constituent order in which an unusual element is fronted, usually accompanied by unusual intonation as well (*Linguistics I detest; Gefragt hat ihn keiner*). We say that "*Linguistics*" and "*Gefragt*" are topicalised in the above examples.

✐ Note that the term *theme* is used in a completely different sense in generative approaches to syntax (→ 1.2.2.6). In this sense, the term *theme* is widely used, even among non-generative linguists. The two notions are easily confused due to the homonymy, but they actually seldom overlap:

A theme in the generative framework is a case role that typically surfaces as the object of a clause, although there are a few verbs, such as verbs of movement and position (*stand, be in, roll*), which take themes as their subject.

> The theme in the Euroean tradition, as we said above, is very likely to surface as the <u>subject</u> in an English clause. Since DANEŠ himself uses the term *theme* in the sense of 'topic', we are adopting it here in explaining his approach. The term *theme* is also used in this sense in the British tradition of functional syntax (by HALLIDAY, e.g.). Otherwise, to avoid confusion, we prefer the term *topic*, which is the usual term in the American tradition.

Depending on whether the topic remains constant, is split up, or changes from one sentence to the next – the new topic usually being derived in this case from what was said about the old one in the previous sentence – one can distinguish several patterns of **thematic progression,** among others:

- Constant theme:

  > **Phoebe** *walked over to the mantelpiece,* **her** *face abnormally white against the vivid red hair.* **She** *was a tall woman* **who** *was rarely seen out of checked shirts and old Levis.* (Minette Walters, *The Ice House*, p. 10)

  "Phoebe" is the theme of both sentences in the above example. It is also the subordinate theme in the relative clause within the second sentence. This is signalled linguistically by word order in English: In both sentences, the reference to Phoebe comes first: her name *"Phoebe"* in the first sentence, the pronoun *"she"* in the second. So does, of course, the relative pronoun *who.* (this is why relative clauses are a major device to subordinate a constant theme.)

- Linear progression:

  > *Her gardener, a man of massive proportions, was pounding across the grass,* **naked to the waist***, his huge belly lapping at his trousers like some monstrous tidal wave.* **The semi-nudity** *was surprising enough, for Fred held strong views about his position at Streech Grange.*
  > (Minette Walters, *The Ice House*, p. 2)

In this example, the theme of the first sentence is the gardener. Part of what is said about him in this sentence (*"naked to the waist"*) is then taken up as the theme of the following sentence (*"The semi-nudity"*). The text thus progresses smoothly from one theme to the next.

- Split theme:

  > **Silverborne Police Station** *…, baked in the sun amid its more traditional neighbours.* **Inside***, the air-conditioning had broken down again and as the hours passed and the atmosphere overheated so did* **the policemen***.* **They** *grew sticky and squabbled amongst themselves like young children.* **Those who could***, got out;* **those who couldn't***, jealously guarded their electric fans and prayed for a quick end to their shift.*
  > (Minette Walters, The Ice House, p. 9)

The above text fragment gives us an example of each of the three types of thematic progression mentioned:

- The first sentence introduces "*Silverborne Police Station*" as the first theme. This is taken up again by "*inside*" (viz., 'inside Silverborne Police Station') in the second (constant theme according to DANEŠ).
- The second sentence also introduces "*the policemen*" who are taken up by "*they*" in the following sentence as the new topic: linear progression according to DANEŠ: The theme has shifted from the police station to the policemen in it.
- The policemen, theme of the third sentence, remain topical in the fourth, but they are split up in two groups: "*those who could*" and "*those who couldn't*" (split theme according to DANEŠ).

It could be argued in the light of DANEŠ's approach that cohesion for the most part is only a reflection of the text's having a **topic** (or **theme**): If the text has a topic, this topic and related things have to be mentioned again and again. Shifts from one subtopic to another have to be brought about smoothly, so that the text in many cases looks like a tightly woven network of anaphoras, substitutions, and also lexical cohesion phenomena, since what is relatable as subtopics of a single topic is very likely to be semantically related in the linguistic system as well.

To illustrate this, let us return to one of the above examples, repeated here for convenience:

A *season* of growth

Flowers in the spring, *swaying in the wind; from a distance, a wash of red; up close, stains of blue, flashes of yellow and purple and white; hundreds of species, millions of plants: nature's* **commonplace** *diversity. So* **commonplace**, *indeed, that it is matched many billions of times within* **your body**. **Each cell** *of the immune system has such a meadow on its surface: millions of proteins of hundreds of types.* (Economist, 24.2.1995)

The first sentence introduces a theme "*flowers in the spring*" which is in part derived from the title word "*season*". "*Commonplace*", the theme of the next sentence, is derived from the last words of the previous sentence by lexical repetition. And "*each cell*", the theme of the third sentence is in a part – whole relation to the last word of the previous sentence ("*body*").

Thus the thematic progression in this passage is well supported by cohesion devices; seen the other way round, the cohesion devices in this passage mainly have the function of pushing thematic progression forward.

6.1.4   Coherence relations

Other linguists (GRIMES 1975, B.F. MEYER 1975, P.G. MEYER 1975, GRAUSTEIN / THIELE 1978 and a few others) argued very early in the development of textlinguistics that cohesion devices were secondary to coherence. They tried to show that there is more to text coherence than either cohesion or topic continuity.

The basic idea shared by all of them was that texts are held together not by the visible (or audible) cohesion devices, but by certain relations between clauses and/or sentences, which may sometimes be overtly expressed, and supported by cohesion phenomena, sometimes left more or less unexpressed. Texts could thus be analysed completely in terms of such relations, obtaining between all the consecutive clauses, sentences, or larger chunks of text.

> Such intratextual, interclausal relations were later called "rhetorical relations" (MANN / THOMPSON 1986) or **coherence relations** (HOBBS 1983). We shall adopt the latter term here.

We may distinguish at least five conceptual domains from which coherence relations may come. They can be seen as types of reasons why speakers or writers have added this particular sentence.

- **Topic**: The types of thematic progression discovered by DANEŠ (→ 6.1.3) may be seen as one basic type of coherence relations which serve to develop a topic, derive new ones, split the topic up, etc.

- **Clarification**: Sometimes, however, mere topic development is superseded by strategies of clarification, such as

  - **Explication**:

    There is, e.g., the question of increasing physical mobility. People move about, from the country to the towns.

    In the above example, the second sentence explicates the abstract term "*physical mobility*" that occurs in the first.

  - **Contrast** (*Antithese, Kontrastierung*):

    *A **herd of animals** is led by the strongest and fittest. In **human society** a different process has been at work for some time.*

In this example, the second sentence establishes a contrast to the first, which is supported by the lexical cohesion relation of antonymy between "*herd of animals*" and "*human society*". Contrasting is a fairly common strategy of clarification.

> Note again that this is a special sense of the term *contrast*, related to the one used to describe antonymy (→ 4.2.2.4), but not really related to the sense described in → Box 23.

- **Time**: Temporal relations between sentences or clauses are quite common and necessary in narrations, and are not always signalled explicitly.

  *He sat back on his heels for a moment, puffing on his pipe, **then** resumed his search, poking his stick at intervals into the nettles at the base of the icehouse roof but finding no other obvious points of weakness. He returned to the door and a closer examination of the brambles.*
  (Minette Walters, The Ice House, p. 23)

In the above example, we find two temporal relations, one within the first sentence, signalled by "*then*", one between the first and the second sentence, and not signalled at all.

- **Causality**: Coherence relations derived from causal relations abound in all kinds of text. They are always superimposed on a temporal relation because a causal relation presupposes a temporal relation of some kind. But a causal relation is regularly more informative than a temporal one. Like temporal relations, causal relations may, but need not, be signalled explicitly by conjunctions. In narrative discourse, causality is often left unexpressed:

  The ground itself told him little. The summer had been an exceptional one and the last four weeks of almost perpetual sunshine had baked it hard.
  (Minette Walters, The Ice House, p. 22)

There is obviously an implicated causal connection between the two sentences in this example: It may be said that the second sentence states the cause due to which the first sentence was true. In technical discourse, we are more likely to find explicitly stated causality:

  *The word 'guilty' is almost inappropriate for the accusatorial system **since** so little time is spent in looking into degrees and nature of guilt.*
  *Stress, violence and crime **come about as a result** of the way in which these various mechanisms interact.*

- A fifth kind of coherence relations that are different from, and supersede, all the others arises from **argumentation**, or reasoning.

> Note that the meaning of the term *argumentation* has absolutely nothing to do with the use of the term *argument* in valency theory (→ 1.2.1.1) and predicate logic (→ 4.4.5.1).

Often another sentence or clause is added because the writer or speaker wants to strengthen or qualify the argument in some way.

  *Penal methods by themselves will not put an end to crime. **Even** at their **fiercest**, as in nineteenth-century England, when **220** offences, **many of them minor larcenies**, were punishable by **death**, they did not succeed.*

The second sentence in the above example is meant as a support for the argument put forward in the first. This support is further strengthened by the *when*-clause which mentions a particularly striking example (marked by "*even*"). The argumentative strength of this example is further enhanced by the parenthesis "*many of them minor larcenies*": The more in number ("*220*"), and the less important ("*minor*") the larcenies and the more severe the punishment ("*death*"), the stronger the whole argument. It can thus be said that the *when*-clause in the above example is much more than a mere temporal clause: It is clearly there to strengthen the argument, not only to establish a temporal relation to another clause.

6.2   The analysis of conversation

Conversation and other kinds of verbal face-to-face communication have been an increasingly popular object of research over the last few decades. Textlinguistics had never really come to grips with interactional discourse, so new approaches had to be found (see SCHIFFRIN 1994 for an overview). An important distinction is that between

- **formal** and
- **informal** speech situations (*formelle / informelle Sprechsituationen*).

In a conversation taking place in the family or among friends, or even in casual talk among strangers in a disco or on a train, nothing is pre-arranged as a rule. The topic of the conversation is often coincidental, often not even agreed upon fully by the participants. Other situations determine much more strongly the structure and topics of conversational interactions taking place within them. (We will take up this distinction in section → 6.3.1). Just imagine

- a discussion in a talk show,
- a scientific conference,
- counselling encounters such as doctor – patient or social worker – client,
- therapeutic discourse (as in psychoanalysis),
- legal court proceedings,
- religious services etc.

It is obvious that they all differ considerably along the following parameters:

- **Turn-taking**: The decision whose 'turn' it is at a certain point in a conversation is not regulated at all in informal situations, but often clearly assigned to specific persons (chairpersons, judges, priests) in the most formal situations, where it is also subjected to strict rules.
- **Adjacency pairs** are pairs of speech acts that typically follow each other in conversations, such as question – answer, request – response, apology – acceptance, etc. They are a major structuring principle in interactional discourse, and are usually as important as coherence relations are in written texts. Adjacency pairs can also be embedded within each other:

Customer:	*Do you have Marlboros?*
Shop assistant:	*Hard or soft?*
Customer:	*Soft please.*
Shop assistant:	*Okay.*

  (LEVINSON 1983, 361)

In this mini-dialogue, the customer's first question is not answered before the fourth line; between first and fourth line, we find what is called an **insertion sequence** that consists of another question – answer pair and has the function of clarifying the customer's wish.

- **Openings** and **closings** of conversations (*Gesprächseröffnungen, Gesprächs-beendigungen*) are also interesting points for investigation. In the more formal situations, the person who assigns turns is usually also in charge of opening and closing the proceedings. This is sometimes done in a formal declaration (→ 5.1):

  The meeting is now open.
  The meeting is closed.

In more formal situations, other, more delicate, ways have to be found to open or close a conversation in order to avoid rudeness.

- **Thematic progression** is usually much more chaotic in informal conversations than in written discourse or formal situations, where only one or a small number of participants determine the topics that can be dealt with:

  This is beside the point.
  We now come to the next point of our agenda.

In informal situations it may be hard work to introduce a new topic and to maintain it, and this hard work has become the subject of intensive study.

6.3   Discourse in the technical age

6.3.1   The oral – written dichotomy

Textlinguistics and conversation analysis represent two very different kinds of approaches to connected discourse. Although they could in principle both be applied to all kinds of discourse, they may be said to be orientated towards two radically different prototypes of text:

- **Textlinguistics** looks to planned, edited discourse, primarily found in the written, or to be more precise, in the printed medium (→ Box 40), in other words, in written texts.
- **Conversation analysis** preferably studies informal, interactive oral discourse.

The dichotomy between these two types of discourse has been the subject of intensive discussion in linguistics over the last three decades. It had been noticed that they do not primarily differ in the **modality** (communication mode, *Modalität*) in which they are found (viz., written or oral), but rather in other linguistic features.

> ● Note that this use of the term *modality* has nothing to do with modality as a category in the verbal syntagm (→ 1.1.3.4.6).

Box 40: Modality, medium, channel

There is a plethora of terms in linguistics and communication and media studies for this and related kinds of category, but their scope is not always entirely clear. The term *communication mode* is occasionally used for 'modality' and should perhaps be preferred. But it is not entrenched enough for use in a textbook. Some theorists seem to equate the concept of modality with 'medium', but this is contradicted by others (SCHNEIDER 2006).

The concepts are closely associated with that of **channel** (*Kanal*). A channel is (a part of) a physical or technical connection transporting certain physical aspects of a signal between sender and receiver of a message. In oral face-to-face communication, e.g., the channels are usually the air carrying the sound waves and the visual and possibly other (tactile, olfactory, etc.) contacts between the interlocutors. A given channel allows only certain kinds of modalities while excluding others. A purely visual channel, e.g., allows written language, facial expression and gestures, including sign language (→ www.narr-studienbue cher.de on psycholinguistics), but no oral communication. A purely acoustic channel, such as used on the telephone, does not permit gestures or facial expression to be transmitted.

A given complex configuration of channels may be called a **medium** (such as the printed medium, television as a medium, the internet etc). In this sense, *medium* is a true singular form of *media*, and we use term in this sense.

In this textbook, however, we primarily have occasion to use the term *medium* in a sense that is also very common in the literature (as there seems to be no alternative): for characterising a certain language or language variety in a specific 'mediating' function. In this sense it is typically used in situations in which a specific communication problem has to solved by using a specific language variety. We then speak of "English as a medium of instruction" or "Pidgin as an oral medium". From now on we are not going to warn you about the different senses of *medium* at each point as the term is always accompanied by a clarifying modifier.

Pragmatically speaking, the **context of situation** (→ 5.5, Fig. 88) of the discourse types is radically different.

In the printed medium, there is no immediate speech situation in which writer and reader could interact:

> "The writer is a lonely figure cut off from the stimulus and corrective of listeners. He must be a predictor of reactions and act on his predictions. He writes with one hand tied behind his back being robbed of gesture. He is robbed too of his tone of voice and the aid of clues the environment provides. He is condemned to monologue; there is no one to help out, to fill the silences, put words in his mouth or make encouraging noises." (ROSEN 1971, 142)

In face-to-face interaction, speaker and hearer are in visual and auditory contact, share a common frame of reference in terms of 'here' and 'now', and identify each other individually, that is, they may call themselves 'I' or 'me' and address each other as 'you'. They must react to each other's contributions 'in real time', that is, immediately, spontaneously, and without delay. In consequence, the vocabulary and grammar of prototypical written and oral discourses differ considerably (OCHS 1979; CHAFE 1985; TANNEN 1982; BIBER 1986):

- **Informal, unplanned spoken discourse** is, i.a., characterised by simpler morphosyntactic structures such as
    - avoidance of relative and complex adverbial clauses,
    - use of syntactic parallelism: *He knows English, he knows French, he knows Spanish, he knows German...* (cf. below),
    - requests for back-channel responses (*isn't it?, don't you think?* etc.),
    - smaller vocabulary,
    - more general word meanings (*thing, place, make, give, take, cool,* etc.),
    - more informal words,
    - place and time adverbs (*here, there, now, then,* etc.)
    - preference for deictic (→ 6.3.1) pronouns (*this, that, here, now*),
    - use of 1st and 2nd person pronouns,
    - high incidence of the pronoun *it,*
    - emphatic particles (*really, just*),
    - concreteness via giving specific details,
    - direct quotations,
    - questions,
    - emphasis on actions and agents rather than states and objects,
    - reports of speaker's thoughts.
- In contrast, **planned written discourse** is characterised by complex morphosyntactic structures such as
    - relative clauses
    - use of the passive
    - 'cleft' constructions:

        It was on the conscience of the German Protestants that the Nazi crimes weighed most heavily.

    - avoidance of redundant parallelism:

        He knows English, French, Spanish, and German (cf. above).

    - nominalisations:

        They carried out a visual inspection.

        rather than

        They inspected it.
        They took a look at it.

    - participles (→ 1.1.3.4.7)
    - attributive adjectives (→ 1.2.2.4)
    - series of phrases, in particular prepositional phrases:

        the conquest of England in 1066 by the Normans

- – embedded clauses
- – preference for articles rather than pronouns (*the, a*)
- – a larger, more precise and more formal vocabulary (see previous set of examples)

> 📖 Find samples of planned and unplanned discourse and analyse them according to the above criteria.

On the other hand, it has long been noticed that the two types of discourse as thus characterised are idealisations. A whole range of other discourse types or speech situations exist in between, which, interestingly, often have to do with modern communication technology as it has been developing over the last century. On the basis of certain pragmatic features, a scale of typical communication situations can be set up (see tables on next pages).

- • First, there are the **channel** (*Kanal*) (→ Box 40) parameters, that is, the question of how the connection between speaker and hearer or writer and reader is physically brought about and what **modality** of communication is technically possible between them: oral or written, auditory or visual or tactile, or others?
- • Second, there are the **deixis** parameters. *I*, *you*, *here* and *there* and many other words are called **deictic expressions** (*deiktische Ausdrücke*) because their reference is dependent on who is speaking where and when. Thus, the question arises what elements of a situation are jointly accessible to speaker / writer and hearer / reader and can be referred to by deictic expressions. Is it possible to say 'I' and 'you'? Is there a common 'here' and 'now'?

On the basis of these two different kinds of parameters, the following speech situations and text types can be characterised as crucially different in terms of the oral-literate continuum. The table on the next page (Fig. 89) analyses a few typical speech situations and text types.

Each speech event or text type in the top rows of the table is described in terms of the set of parameters in the left column. Although binary decisions seem to be involved in setting up the table, in many cases the pluses and minuses just denote a more-or-less rather than a yes-or-no. The features are set up so that '+' invariably means more closeness and accessibility between speaker / writer and hearer / reader, whereas '–' means more distance and less accessibility. The use of '+/–' is meant to point to divergences within the text type or it denotes the presence of a feature that is highly debatable. Obviously, there are more pluses on the left of the table and more minuses on the right.

> 📖 Try to analyse some more recently developed types of communication, such as e-mail, text messaging, internet chat, hypertext in terms of Fig. 89!

Fig. 89: Situation elements, speech events and text types

	face-to-face talk	telephone calls	private letters	lectures	television news	radio news	newspaper report	academic book
channel parameters								
concomitant actions	+	–	–	+	+/–	–	–	–
co-present objects	+	–	–	+	+	–	–	–
gestures	+	–	–	+	+	–	–	–
facial expression	+	–	–	+	+	–	–	–
intonation	+	+	–	+	+	+	–	–
back channel	+	+	–/+	+/–	–	–	+/– (letters to the editor)	– (except in reviews)
deixis								
I-you	+	+	+	+	–	–	–	+/–
temporal ('now')	+	+	–	+	+	+	–/+ ('today')	–
spatial ('here')	+	–	–	+	–	+/–*	+/–*	–

* + in local media, - in (inter)national media

The scale evident in Fig. 89 above has also largely been confirmed by BIBER's computer-assisted study (1986; 1988) of certain objective linguistic characteristics that had been mentioned in the literature as typical of written or oral discourse (see the lists above). On the basis of the different relative frequencies found for these features, so-called factor scores (a value on a predefined numerical scale) were computed for different situations and text types along different dimensions. On one of these dimensions (named 'interactive vs. edited'), he came up with very much the same scale of communication situations or text types, apart from minor deviations (see Fig. 90).

Fig. 90 BIBER's factor one: interactive vs. edited
(adapted from: BIBER 1986, 398)

Factor score	Text type
320	Telephone and face-to face conversation
260	Interviews
200	Spontaneous speeches
180	Planned speeches
150	Professional letters
130	Broadcasts
100	Romantic fiction
90	General fiction
50	
40	Belles-lettres, Editorial letters, Hobbies, Popular lore
30	Official documents, Academic prose
20	Press reports
0	

6.3.2 Media discourse

Nowadays, most people in industrial societies are exposed to media language (mostly from television) for more hours a day than they are engaged in live conversation with people in their immediate surroundings. ILLICH (1983) argues that just as home-made food is gradually fading out, being replaced by industrial products, home-made speech is also receding, leading to a decline in the use of dialects and local languages, and perhaps eventually to their extinction (→ 7.2.1) (see also LIPPI-GREEN 1997, 133-151). On the other hand, CHAMBERS (2005) has tried to show that media discourse does not influence people's speech behaviour, but vice versa (cf. WOLFRAM / SCHILLING-ESTES 1998, 113-123).

Apart from these sociolinguistic controversies, the study of the language of the media is rewarding in its own right. Communication situations created in the media can be very complex and defy all traditional classification:

⚓ Just imagine a television talk show, with an audience in the studio, and the possibility of phoning in. The participants on the panel are speaking to each other in a pretended face-to-face interaction, where in many cases, or to a great extent, contributions and exchanges have been planned and rehearsed beforehand. In any case, the participants are not only speaking to each other, but also, more or less, to the audience both in the studio and outside. The interaction itself, even if nothing has been rehearsed, is not completely spontaneous either, but regulated by the talk-master, who assigns turns, suggests topics for discussion, and cuts off discussants who are about to become a nuisance or otherwise do not fit into the scheme for the programme. The audience in the studio joins in by applauding, laughing, booing, heckling, and other typical forms of audience participation, but not even this may be completely spontaneous. Often, the audience is prompted to applaud. Sometimes, individual members of the audience may be drawn in, by being interviewed briefly, etc. Finally, the audience outside may be given the opportunity of feedback by phoning in. The whole event, although entirely oral, is an inextricable mixture of planned and spontaneous, formalised and informal, one-way and two-way communication.

In this way, all the pragmatic and textlinguistic approaches and methods mentioned in the last two chapters may be applied to media discourse; in addition to this, other aspects of media discourse are relevant: e.g. the context in which media discourse is produced, who is responsible for the utterances, who is actually the 'speaker' or 'author', what other factors influence the production of the text etc. In the same way, the audience and their behaviour can be studied. It is also obvious that media discourse is more than just a verbal text broadcast through a specific medium (→ Box 40): Other components, such as pictures, gestures, actions, and many other things, are an essential part of it.

Media discourse cannot be analysed by linguistic methods alone, but has to be studied in a joint effort of several disciplines (→ 10.2.6.3.2 for literature).

7   Sociolinguistics

7.0   The realm of sociolinguistics

Sociolinguistics (*Soziolinguistik*) is commonly used as a cover term for the discipline that is concerned with the relationships between language and society. This branch of linguistics aims at investigating linguistic diversity or language behaviour induced by social factors. Languages are thus not seen as self-sufficient entities. Rather, linguistic output in its variation and functions is seen as being deeply rooted both in a culture and in the interaction of its members. Being an interface between linguistics and other social sciences, sociolinguistic study draws on additional findings from such fields as sociology, anthropology, ethnology, or history. It has gained considerably in importance over the past few decades.

Some researchers have established a narrow distinction between sociolinguistics and the **sociology of language** (*Sprachsoziologie*). Prototypically, the sociology of language is concerned with language use and its influence on social organisation (e.g. FISHMAN 1968, 1972), whereas sociolinguistics focuses – conversely – on the influence of society on linguistic structure (e.g. LABOV 1966, 1972). Both approaches roughly correspond to the following model:

Fig. 91: Approaches to language and society

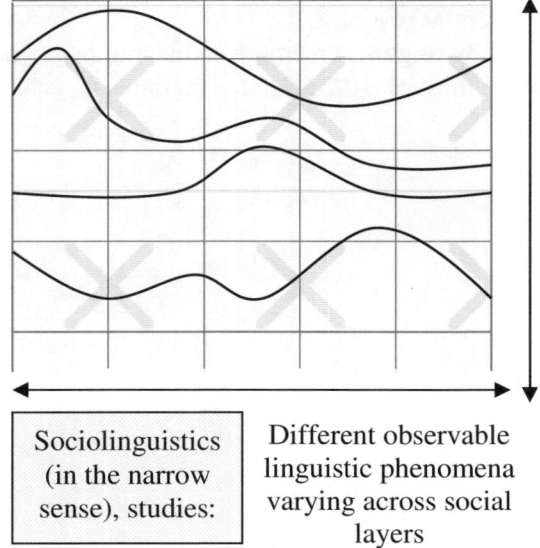

Sociology of language,
studies:

Social layering (stratification)
or different social groups
characterized (i.a.) by
linguistic differences

Sociolinguistics
(in the narrow
sense), studies:

Different observable
linguistic phenomena
varying across social
layers

In fact, there is of course considerable overlap between both fields which often differ in emphasis only. The methods employed can range from the purely empirical to the purely theoretical. The graphs in Fig. 91 indicate the intertwinement of the approaches, i.e. specifically, the possible observability of individual linguistic phenomena in different social stratifications.

The subsequent sections do not attempt to give a comprehensive overview of all varieties of English. Its focus is rather on theoretical concepts and method. We will take up topics relating to socially (or: societally) conditioned influences on the system of language and its variation.

7.1   Dialect, sociolect, and the standard

7.1.1   Dialect vs. language vs. accent

Language and *dialect* are the best-known folk terms for socially defined language varieties. *Dialect* and *accent* are often used interchangeably, inappropriately fuzzily, and – in terms of linguistics – misleadingly. Customary statements such as "Dialects are not real languages" or "His language is accent-free" tend to miss the point linguists usually make. Correspondingly, at least eyebrows should be raised by every individual interested in language when hearing such statements. In linguistics, thus, more precise definitions of the terms are needed in order to establish a purposeful working terminology. We will see that explicitness is indeed necessary to account for the subtle differences in this respect.

First of all, the distinction between **language** (*Sprache*) and **dialect** (*Dialekt*) is more than the mere distinction between a certain prestigious '**high**' **variety** (*hochsprachliche Varietät*) and a certain non-prestigious '**low**' **variety** (*nicht-hochsprachliche Varietät*).

We could start on by assuming that languages such as English or German are subdivided into several dialects which are

- spoken in different regions and which
- differ from each other more or less as regards pronunciation, vocabulary and grammar.
- The different dialects would, for all the differences between them, remain **mutually intelligible** .
- They are all genetically (→ 3.2.1.0) closely related to each other.

But how come we nevertheless consider Mandarin and Cantonese as dialects of Chinese even though they are, when spoken, mutually unintelligible? How come Czech and Slovak are labelled different languages, though their lexical and grammatical differences are marginal?

The assumption of a hierarchical structure of language and dialect is not without problems. From a purely linguistic point of view, there is no difference between a language and a dialect – both have a set of words (i.e. the lexicon) and grammatical rules at their disposal which have to be applied by the members of a

speech community (*Sprachgemeinschaft*) (➔ 1.1.1.2, ☞ box) in order to speak the respective language (or dialect) 'correctly'. It is thus important to note that all language varieties, what ever they are called, are subject to socially controlled norms. even though they are not written down anywhere. Many sociolinguists, to avoid the evaluative implications inherent in the language – dialect dichotomy, insist that the 'high' variety of a language is just another dialect among many. This would be a 'broad' notion of dialect, and any variety of a language could be called a dialect.

There is, on the other hand, a need in sociolinguistic studies to distinguish between 'high' and 'low' varieties.

In this context, 'language' is not a linguistic, but rather a political label, used to establish socio-cultural difference. Thus, according to this definition, e.g. Czech and Slovak are different languages with different written norms, nowadays relating to different nations – whereas Mandarin and Cantonese are regional varieties both spoken within the territory of China that share a written norm. After the end of the Yugoslavian federation, the so-called Serbo-Croatian language (*Serbokroatisch*) that we had been told was the common language of most states of Yugoslavia (it was, incidentally, written in two different alphabets), practically ceased to exist. We are now witnessing hectic **language planning** (➔ 7.2.3) attempts at establishing separate Croatian, Serbian and even Bosnian languages.

We can record that, as the Yiddish linguist Max WEINREICH (1945) once put it, in the original Yiddish in a latinised transcription: "A shprakh iz a dialect mit an armey un flot", usually quoted as

A language is a dialect with an army and a navy.
(http://www.bisso.com/ujg_archives/pix/armyNavyFull.jpg).

By the way, WEINREICH was only quoting an anonymous discussion participant in one of his lectures. This aphorism, for all its sarcasm, should be taken seriously. A dialect that has acquired a political status and an institutional backing of some kind is infinitely more likely to be called a language than, say, a powerless rural variety.

Mutual intelligibility (*gegenseitige Verständlichkeit*) of varieties is thus not the crucial factor that distinguishes one language from another, but rather the speakers' attitude to them.

A narrow definition of 'dialect', fulfilling the need for a term covering 'low' varieties of a language, would be as follows: A dialect is a language variety that is

- regionally restricted,
- used in limited domains of life (It may only be used in the family or in in-group situations, but not in formal situations or on 'official' occasions, e.g.) and is
- usually part of a geographical **dialect continuum** (*Dialektkontinuum*).

Such a continuum can, say, still be observed from Newcastle to Dover, or even from Bordeaux to Sicily, or on the western fringe of the German-speaking area, in the area around Aachen, extending across four different countries and three language borders (guess which!). This means that dialects have no sharp and fixed boundaries; linguistic differences tend to be small in the immediate vicinity and add up gradually to mutual unintelligibility the more geographically distant two dialects are from each other. They may even transcend national borders. Due to this dialect continuum, the exact number of dialects (e.g. of English) is hard to tell. We can only witness the existence of certain linguistic features in dialect A, whereas these are realised in a (slightly) different way in the neighbouring dialect B and so on.

Classical **dialectology** (*Dialektologie*) is especially concerned with such geographically determined language variation in a continuum. E.g., dialect atlases show the distribution of linguistic features such as lexical elements with the help of **isoglosses** (*Isoglossen*), i.e. abstract lines on a map that mark the 'boundaries' of the regionally distinctive use of these features. We have to keep in mind, however, that these isoglosses are only abstract and unstable approximations of constantly changing linguistic realities. Let us have a look at some examples from the lexicon and the grammar of English dialects (TRUDGILL [2]1999, 92, 103ff.):

Fig. 92: Lexical differences between English dialects

Belfast:	*gutties*	
Bristol:	*daps*	
Liverpool:	*gollies*	'trainers' or 'gymshoes'
London:	*plimsolls*	
Newcastle:	*sandshoes*	

Fig. 93: Grammatical differences between English dialects

Devon:	*There idden many can sheary now.*
	'There aren't many who can shear now.'
Merseyside:	*How are youse?*
	'How are you [plural]?'
Staffordshire:	*Cost lend us a quid? – No, I conna.*
	'Can you lend me a pound?' – 'No, I can't.'

Any language with a substantial number of speakers will develop dialectal variety. A reason for this is that spoken language changes differently in different areas (e.g. within England). Thus, as dialects mostly are purely oral media without codified standardisation (→ 7.1.3), dialects are not uniform. Some may be more conservative than others, and some may even be mutually unintelligible although they 'belong to the same language'.

> 📖 Do you happen to know dialects of German which you don't understand? Describe where they are spoken and what makes them unintelligible to you!

A further option enabling us to differentiate between 'language' and 'dialect' has been offered by the conception of *Ausbau* and *Abstand* (KLOSS 1967). The term ***Ausbausprache*** has been used to characterise a language that has evolved from a dialect by the expansion of its functional domains. This elaboration depends in most cases on institutional **language planning** (→ 7.2.3) efforts and is reinforced by socio-psychological factors. Standardisation and the choice of an orthography are two of the most important aspects in the creation of an *Ausbausprache*. Such *Ausbau* often, but not necessarily, creates linguistic autonomy. This autonomy is achieved, i.e. created and negotiated by institutions and the speech community respectively during the phase of functional expansion.

⚐ *Lëtzebuergesch* (**Luxemb(o)urgish**, *Luxemburgisch*), a language spoken by the native population of the Grand Duchy of Luxembourg, is an interesting example of an *Ausbausprache*. *Lëtzebuergesch* (in its self-designation) was traditionally regarded as a dialect of German, namely as a variety of Moselle Franconian (*Moselfränkisch*). By systematically expanding the domains in which it could be used, mostly at the cost of (Standard) German, speakers have tried to convert their dialect into a language. These efforts have met with some surprising, though not overall, success. Lëtzebuergesch can now be spoken in Parliament and in schools, is used in church, in advertisements, on road signs (along with French), in primary education, and in several other domains, in addition to all private occasions. In many of these domains, it has, however, to compete not only with Standard German, but also with French. From a sociolinguistic point of view, it is no longer appropriate to call Lëtzebuergesch a dialect of German. It has become a language which supports and expresses the Luxembourgers' national identity (HOFFMANN 1981). It has been said that the Luxembourgish language was 'born' during World War II under German occupation, when the Nazis tried to claim Luxembourgish as a German dialect. In a census conducted in 1941 by them, in which they had hoped the Luxembourgers would identify themselves as speakers of German, it emerged (in a pretest) that an overwhelming majority of the population – more than 95% – would reject the alternatives given (French or German) and give "Luxembourgish" as their mother tongue. The census was quickly stopped when this became apparent (NEWTON 1996).

The term *Abstandssprache*, on the other hand, denotes a language that is defined on the grounds of the autonomy given in its linguistic structure alone, although by sociolinguistic criteria alone, it would be regarded as a 'mere dialect' (e.g. Basque or Breton in France, Sorbian in Germany). These language forms do not have a 'high' variety around them that would be genetically related (→ 3.2.1.0), hence we call them languages to avoid discriminating against them. *Abstandssprachen* are usually an indication of very old indigenous minorities. Thus, linguistic distance or mutual intelligibility can be factors to check the discreteness of such languages.

The notion of *Abstandssprache* shows that the above-mentioned criterion of a written norm should not be applied too dogmatically. There are many languages in the world that do not have a written norm, that are actually never written (e.g. several indigenous African languages). We can call them languages nevertheless, because they are sufficiently different from other 'high' varieties in use in the area in question (e.g. English), and are also different enough (show enough *Abstand*) from neighbouring 'low' varieties (e.g. other indigenous languages). From

the notion and reality of *Ausbausprache* we can learn that the primary requirement for the distinctness of languages is the speakers' awareness of their social
distinctness. As the examples of Czech and Slovak, Croatian and Serbian, Luxembourgish and German prove, linguistic autonomy can be rather a social than a
solely linguistic category.

As mentioned above, all dialects have systematic grammars (even if they have
never been investigated by linguists) and lexical inventories that can differ considerably and unpredictably.

The importance of linguistic awareness concerning linguistic differences may
also gain importance for dialects. We may know from our own experience that a
speaker who makes use of a dialect, especially outside its original area, may do
so – consciously or not – in order to express his or her personal, local identity.
Moreover, this speaker may want to show via the usage of a dialect that he or she
is a member of a distinct, prestigious in-group whereas speakers of other regional
speech communities are not. Imagine a Scotsman who maintains his Glaswegian
dialect when visiting London – this speaker makes a clear statement with respect
to the identity of the persons involved in a conversation with him, and also runs
the risk of not being understood at all.

Outside its original geographical or social domain, but also within, a dialect
speaker is always at risk of not being (entirely) understood. Today, the total
amount of dialect variation tends to diminish in modern societies in favour of a
supra-regional levelling and focussing (WOLFRAM / SCHILLING-ESTES 1998,
117, also see → Fig. 94 below) of the differences.

It is expedient for the description of many contemporary sociolinguistic situations to distinguish between **traditional** and **modern** dialects (TRUDGILL 2002).
Traditional dialects are what most people think of when they hear the word *dialect*. Fig. 94 lists some characteristic differences in an admittedly idealised way.

Fig. 94: Traditional vs. modern dialects

Traditional dialects	Modern dialects
are typically spoken in remote rural areas.	are typically spoken in urban areas.
are fairly stable, i.e. show little varia-tion when studied on a local level.	show a considerable amount of varia-tion, even on an individual level and in small communities.
used to form a geographical dialect continuum as described above.	form a network of geographically sep-arated, but sprawling urban focuses influencing the surrounding dialects, but also each other.
are used in limited (and diminishing) domains of life.	are used in more and more domains of life.
differ considerably from the standard language in both pronunciation, lexi-con and grammar.	do not differ drastically from the stan-dard, are often mutually intelligible over great distances.

Ever since the industrial revolution and increasing mobility swept away traditional dialects in many urbanising areas of Europe, leaving spots of uncharted territory in the old dialect continuum, new regionally defined dialects have begun to emerge which at first were completely overlooked by classical dialectologists. With increasing urbanisation and globalisation, this development has recently gathered momentum.

WOLFRAM / SCHILLING-ESTES (1998, 113f.), referring to the USA, mention four factors influencing present-day dialect development which, *mutatis mutandis*, also apply to Europe:

(1) changing relations among cultural contact groups,
(2) new patterns of migration …,
(3) the redefinition of cultural centers, and
(4) improved means of transportation and improved access to formerly remote areas.

Consequently, traditional dialects, even if mastered passively, are losing speakers, and the remaining speakers are losing domains in which to use the dialect. It can hardly be practised and is not taught to the next generation. Thereby, especially among the younger generation, a traditional dialect does not belong to the individual's linguistic repertoire any more. Additionally, mass media such as nationwide TV programmes and newspapers may contribute to the decrease of dialect variation in general.

Let us consider our above-mentioned Scotsman again. If he lives and works in London for several years, it will be hard for him to keep up his dialect. His linguistic behaviour is, though unwillingly, becoming less isolated as it gradually adapts to that of the speech community he is surrounded by. As regards the preservation of local identities via dialects the levelling of which is observable today, the overall picture turns out to be twofold. On the one hand, the language situations in which dialects are still used can lead to most successful witty conversations – on the other hand, the use of dialect can lead to a stereotyping on behalf of the speakers. In the latter case, the stigmatisation of some regional differences in language behaviour may result in a low standing of speakers of these dialects, whereas others are held in higher esteem by outsiders.

The most prominent feature that indicates the origin of a speaker, however, is neither the grammar nor specific elements of the lexicon (e.g. *Brötchen*, *Rundstück*, *Schrippe*, *Semmel*, etc. which denote a bread roll in distinct regions of Germany). Rather, it is the **accent** (*Akzent*) of a speaker that most strikingly reveals his or her linguistic background, as it were.

Thus, accents distinguish varieties on a purely phonological basis, e.g. we could imagine speakers of so-called standard British English with a Yorkshire or a Berlin accent, or speakers of *Kölsch* with a Turkish accent. Since all speakers pronounce, all speakers have an accent – some are just more regionally coloured than others.

☞ *Accent* refers to differences in pronunciation only, whereas *dialect* refers to a combination of lexical, grammatical, and phonological (i.e. accent) differences.

📖 Think about your personal inclination (or bias) towards German dialects or accents of a, say, Rhenish, Bavarian, or Saxonian type, and their speakers respectively. Make notes about the dialects, regional varieties or accents you know best and try to pinpoint linguistically what is different about them. Which of their linguistic characteristics do you feel to be stigmatised? Do you yourself speak a dialect? Where do you dare to speak it? Do other members of your family speak a dialect? How does their speech differ from yours?

Received Pronunciation (**RP**) (→ 2.1.1.1) can be considered as a prestigious, regionless accent – though it originally was characteristic of the speech of a distinctive area of England. The RP accent is commonly also called 'BBC English' or 'the Queen's English' – although it is taught in schools throughout England, it remains a prestigious marker of the upper class and is used by not considerably more than 5% of the English population nowadays. In the United States of America, the most common range of accents is called **General American**, which is a more 'democratic' accent, as it were, as it is spoken by larger parts of the population in large parts of the country. Our phonetic descriptions in section → 2.1.1 were based on RP and General American.

The more characteristics of an 'English English' accent deviate from RP, the 'broader' the accent appears. Let us have a look at some examples:

⚱ **Cockney** is the traditional urban dialect of London, and many Londoners speak English with a Cockney accent, even if they don't speak the dialect (TRUDGILL [2]1999). The most striking phonological features of Cockney are

- the lowering of the diphthong [eɪ] to [æɪ] or [aɪ] (which in fact is only one in a series of vowel and diphthong shifts affecting RP /iː/, /eɪ/, /aɪ/ and /ɔɪ/). Note the famous hospital joke:

    [ˈjʊəˈɡəʊɪŋˈhəʊmtəˈdaɪ].

- the replacement of postvocalic [t] by [ʔ] (glottal stop):

    He got a lot of water bottles.
    [ɪɡɒʔəlɒʔəwɔːʔəbɒʔɒz]
    (For more examples, → 2.1.1.2)

- and the notorious [h]-dropping, such as in

    heavy-handed [eviændɪd]

But Cockney as a dialect is also lexically remarkable for its extensive use of metaphors (→ Box 34; 4.1.2.2; 4.3.2) to find unusual designations for everyday things. The so-called Cockney rhyming slang is notorious. This makes deep Cockney practically incomprehensible to outsiders, almost turning it into a secret language. Lack of space prevents us from going into more detail here.

A further development in the London area, which has the potential of developing into a modern dialect, has recently become known as **Estuary English** (ALTENDORF 1999; 2003). It is more prestigious than Cockney and is spoken by increasing numbers of people who, given their education and income, would have used Received Pronunciation until a few decades ago. This shows that also prestige standards are liable to shift – in fact, there is a tendency in the British Isles nowadays in favour of several regional varieties, thus diminishing the importance of RP in, e.g., formal communicative situations.

The vast majority, however, speak with an accent that resembles some mainstream varieties, either standard or non-standard. To show the range of variation, here are some instances of regional pronunciation variety in England (TRUDGILL [2]1999, 68):

Fig. 95: Pronunciation differences between English dialects

'Very few cars made it up the long hill.'

Northeast
(e.g. Newcastle):   /veri: fjuː kaːz meːd ɪt ʊp ðə lɒŋ hɪl/
Northwest Midlands
(e.g. Birmingham):   /verɪ fjuː kaːz meɪd ɪt ʊp ðə lɒŋg ɪl/
Central Southwest
(e.g. Salisbury):   /veri: fjuː kaːrz meɪd ɪt ʌp ðə lɒŋ ɪʊl/

Regional variation is usually much smaller between American accents.

7.1.2   Sociolect

A variety that is defined on purely social grounds is called a **sociolect** (*Soziolekt*). Besides his or her possibly regional speech character, every speaker is member of one, most probably several social groups. Depending on the speech situation, i.e. the immediate social setting the conversation takes place in, we speak differently to different people. Once again, our choice of a linguistic variety proves to be audience-sensitive.

This means that we adapt e.g. to the formality or the emotionality of a situation and are able to switch 'styles' as we see fit, given that we are used to the respective situations (which are culturally dependent) and thus know about the suitability and unsuitability of a certain style. In other words, we usually talk differently with some friends in a pub compared to more formal situations such as, say, an oral exam or a reception where the Queen is present (not that the latter is likely to be a frequent occurrence).

Formal situations seem to increase the awareness of our own linguistic behaviour. In such situations, it is highly probable that we (more or less consciously) move our speech output closer to a prestigious model such as RP.

In sum, every social domain has its own social variety; these varieties can, of course, overlap. Examples of such domains are family, work, hobby, church, news broadcasts, to name but a few. In this context, the range of linguistic features employed by speakers in particular social domains is called **register**.

Sociolects can function as in-group varieties, i.e. as elements of social differentiation. Individuals who belong (or want to belong) to a certain group e.g. as a gang member, a player in a soccer team, a soldier, a musician, a preacher, a doctor, a scientist, etc. employ special, technical terminology which usually only the members of the group concerned understand ad hoc. The use of a sociolect establishes bonds within a peer group on the one hand, whereas on the other hand it excludes others who are not, as it were, let into the secrets of the variety. Thus, sociolectal variation is a reflection as well as a constitutive factor of the organisation of our everyday life and society as a whole.

We all perform certain roles. In doing so, sociolects are used to express identity and solidarity. E.g., the deliberately informal speech (or **slang**) of some youths shows their self-positioning via deliberate choice of language variety: outside the so-called mainstream and usual prestige standards, but inside a self-defined in-group with its own prestige norms.

♦ *Slang* is a term that is often mixed up with *dialect* or even *accent*. It is neither of the two. It may be called a kind of sociolect. It is a deliberately informal, rapidly changing variety of speech typically used by smaller groups within society, typically young or of low social status. Deviations from the standard and, of course, the rapid changes mentioned are mostly found on the lexical level, which makes slang rather opaque to outsiders. This is precisely what is intended. The notion of '**covert prestige**' becomes very relevant here. It is a matter of prestige in slang-using groups, of course, to always know the latest lexical innovations.

☞ The term *covert prestige* is used in sociolinguistics to refer to the prestige of a non-standard variety of a socially underprivileged group. It may not be 'covert' at all given the appropriate situation. In a village pub or a sports association, it may be socially quite unacceptable to speak a 'prestigious' standard variety. Just try speaking with an RP accent in a Catholic pub in Belfast! (Of course, your accent must be convincing enough for this sociolinguistic experiment to succeed...)

In total, sociolectal choice can serve as a powerful instrument to connect and to demarcate. Another example is the use of RP as a social accent by some speakers during a conversation in order to establish (perhaps fictitious and artificial) class divisions. People who see themselves as belonging to the upper class and those who may be upwardly mobile or socially insecure and thus want to 'upgrade' their status may act this way to (re)position themselves in the social hierarchy.

The occasional wrong use or over-use of forms considered desirable can be a consequence of this. Such **hypercorrection** (*Hyperkorrektur*), i.e. the misapplication of lexical and grammatical models, shows e.g. in words such as

platypi,
stati

(instead of *platypuses, statuses*) or in the following example, which for the sake of clarification is somewhat exaggerated:

Whom knows that the romance between you and I will become more serious soonly?

'Who knows that the romance between you and me will become more serious soon?'

A renowned study (LABOV 1966) that is often seen as a benchmark by sociolinguists was carried out in New York City and focused on a possible social stratification of post-vocalic /r/ (as in e.g. *car, floor*, etc.). LABOV found that the use of this variable correlated significantly with the social level of the interlocutor. Thus, at several locations in New York City, the realisation of the variant [r] when following a vowel (e.g. [kɑːr], [flɔːr]) is used as a prestige feature. Thereby, it was shown that variation in speech can indeed evidence social status (or status ambitions).

In this context, a **variable** denotes a specific linguistic feature that may have **variants** likely to be of social significance.

☞ The term *variable* is applied in a different sense in formal semantics (→ 4.4.5). The term *variant* as an adjective is also used in linguistic typology (→ 1.4) to characterise languages of a specific type.

In LABOV's study, post-vocalic /r/ represents such a variable, having the possible variants [r] or zero. The realisation of a such a linguistic variable by a variant is dependent on other parameters, e.g. gender, age, and occupation of the individual informants as well as the interview setting.

Interestingly enough, 'posh' Englishmen and -women do not pronounce post-vocalic /r/. With them, the prestige norm is currently the converse: Those who pronounce it dissociate themselves overtly, i.e. audibly, from any upper-class group membership.

Other interesting variables in this respect are the so-called 'h-dropping' in word-initial position or the realisation of [ɪŋ] as [ɪn] word-finally. Thus, if a speaker uses for example [aʊs] (*house*) or [dʒʌmpɪn] (*jumping*) although knowing the upper-class alternative, he or she makes a clear-cut social statement. However, speakers are not consistent in the usage of such variables. This may serve as a confirmation from sociolinguistics that grammars are in fact **probabilistic** (→ 1.2.3.1). Historical linguists might speak of **free variation** (→ Box 33). In contemporary empirical research we can know better. What we can do as observers is detect certain individual percentages, i.e. tendencies, in certain communicative contexts. Accordingly, we might draw conclusions in terms of the social placement of the speaker on the basis of his or her individual linguistic output.

Additionally, factors such as education, religion, and ethnicity are of relevance with respect to sociolects. As gender, age, occupation, etc., these factors (or better: their dynamic combinations) define our social standing and thus shape our linguistic behaviour to a considerable degree. In this context, the term **ethnolect** (*Ethnolekt*) is used especially to classify those varieties which serve as a distinct marker of ethnic identity and tradition, e.g. the speech of Afro-Caribbean emigrants living in London.

Another well-known and, meanwhile, well-studied ethno- or sociolect of English is **Black English** (also known as **African American Vernacular English** (AAVE); on the term *vernacular*, see → 7.1.3, ☞ box). It is spoken by many, though not all, African Americans of different social class, as well as by some members of other ethnicities in the United States (this is why it may no longer be an ethnolect). Many non-linguists believe that the 'street slang' based on Black English that has been cultivated by, e.g. hiphop culture is all there is to Black English, but the variety is also used in everyday dinner table conversations, literary works, and even, occasionally, in linguistic publications. Black English shares many typical phonological and grammatical features of non-standard (in particular Southern) American English, but also has a few unique traits. Speakers of Black English are often 'credited' with "double negation" (→ 3.2.3.2, ☙ box), but this feature is shared by many non-standard 'white' varieties as well. For many African Americans, their non-standard speech is an important part of their ethnic identity, although others have a very negative image of their own speech. Black English has been the subject of heated, ideologically mined debates not only in American education policy, but also in sociolinguistics. (An excellent overview of all these questions is provided by MUFWENE et al. 1998.)

☞ The term **Black English** may seem somewhat politically incorrect to some. We stick to this more 'traditional' term here more or less for reasons of sloth and in an admittedly stubborn resistance to the ever-turning wheel of euphemism and pejoration (→3.2.4; 3.2.5.4) which cannot be stopped unless at one point the pejoration mechanism is stopped. Constantly seeking politically more correct terms only speeds up pejoration. We think that the term *black* is still sufficiently neutral to make further exercises in PC superfluous. We hardly dare mention that LABOV's first publications in the late 1960s used the term *Negro English*.

7.1.3   The standard

It is a common folk belief that so-called language standards existed before dialects developed that deviated from them. These original standards thus are, in this view, still today best suited to convey the 'original' or 'pure' meaning of 'correct' words. This belief is, as we can already infer from the preceding subchapters, mistaken. This popular conception notwithstanding, we need a better working definition.

A common denominator most linguists can agree on is that a **standard** (*Standardsprache*) is a codified variety that serves the complex communicative needs of a major speech community (→ 1.1.1.2, ☞ box). We may take this as a basis for further elucidation.

A standard is, for the most part, an overtly prestigious and officially sanctioned variety that has acquired formal functions, e.g. it is used in education, literature, etc. Originally based on a dialect, it becomes detached from its local roots during a process of standardisation. Finally, given that the speech community widely 'accepts' the standard and attributes high status to it, it may, with time, become a target norm throughout. The promotion of standardised English in Britain was influenced by several historical factors. In this respect, especially the triumphant progress of the printing press and the institution of grammar schools had considerable effects. The choice of a standard-to-be, however, is often decided by historical accident. In Britain, e.g., the choice fell on a variety that was spoken in and around the then economic, political, and intellectual centres, namely London, Oxford, and Cambridge. This variety still has a considerable number of native speakersthough it is spoken with different regional accents and stylistic variation.

The standardisation of an institutionalised, prescriptive linguistic norm is especially connected to writing. It is thereby predominantly a matter of vocabulary and grammar which become codified, i.e. in this context systematically arranged in authoritative dictionaries and grammar books with the help of a fixed orthography. The collective acceptance of this system is a social process. A new standard must prove useful and must meet the functional requirements – or it will barely manage to survive outside elitist circles. It is a typical feature of present-day English that it has developed a twofold standard which serves as a model for English speech communities worldwide.

- On the one hand, British Standard English or **British English** (**BrE**) is the standard European, African and South Asian countries mostly follow.

- American Standard English or **American English** (**AmE**), on the other hand, is the norm for many countries in the Americas plus the Philippines (cf. Fig. 96). Thus, due to the imbalanced historical development of the United Kingdom and the United States, some differences show today also as regards the codification of rules for linguistic standardisation:

Fig. 96: Grammatical differences between American and British English

AmE	BrE
I would like for you to do this.	*I would like you to do this.*
It has gotten cold in here.	*It has got cold in here.*
Her car is different than mine.	*Her car is different from mine.*

Besides, there exist different degrees of 'standardness' according to the formality of an utterance or a text. In the following instance, we could even find some more stages:

Fig. 97: Different degrees of formality

more formal

He has not seen those elephants.
He hasn't seen those elephants.
'e ain't seen them elephants.

less formal

The least formal variety above is generally regarded as 'sub-standard'. From the point of view of linguistics, a standard is neither more correct nor more grammatical than other, non-standard varieties (such as most dialects and sociolects), even though some purists may dissent from this view. Standards are a matter of power and convention; their availability throughout whole **language communities** is reinforced by their accessibility and prestige.

☞ We use the term *language community* to refer to the totality of speech communities, and, possibly, isolated individuals, that have access to and competence in a certain 'language' in the sense of section → 7.1.1 and use it at least occasionally. Thus, an ex-German emigrant Jew in Israel might still be part of the German language community without being part of any German-speaking speech community. On the other hand, speakers of German emigrant dialects such as Pennsylvania Dutch are members of a kind of 'German' speech community without being part of the German language community.

From earliest childhood, or at the latest from the time we start to become literate, we usually are confronted with a form of standard – be it at school, in our favourite book, in a news broadcast on TV, in a tabloid, etc. Standard has been and still is prestigious and a marker of success and thus often serves as a linguistic model for developments in non-standard varieties, too. This continuous tendency, however, does not and will not affect the integrity of dialectal and sociolectal variation as such.

☞ The term **vernacular** (*Umgangssprache*, *Vernakularsprache*) is occasionally used to denote a widespread colloquial sub-standard variety, including both regional and social varieties. Thus, negative connotations of the notions 'sub-standard' and 'non-standard' might be avoided. In historical linguistics, it also describes, in contrast to the only 'standard' language at that time, Latin, the emerging early popular languages such as Old French, Old English, and Old High German.

7.2   Languages in contact

7.2.1   Minority vs. majority

A **majority language** (*Mehrheitssprache*) is a language of any kind that is spoken by the majority of a country's population. Consequently, a **minority language** (*Minderheitssprache*) denotes a language which is spoken by a community outnumbered by at least one other.

As a consequence of increasing globalisation and large-scale global mobility, many societies throughout the world are now multilingual. This means in our context that minority languages (such as Spanish or native American languages in the USA) exist side by side with majority languages. Majority languages (e.g. Spanish in Spain, English in the USA) usually have the benefit of a higher standing in terms of functional status and prestige.

Often, minority languages are thus marginalised languages. In being marginalised and even occasionally isolated and stigmatised (e.g. in the educational sector), they can become endangered and, in the long term, extinct. In the event of whole language communities (→ 7.1.3, ☞ box) being 'absorbed' by larger ones, we are witness to a general tendency: On a global scale, the total amount of language diversity is diminishing. Several sociolinguists draw a pessimistic picture in this respect. They forecast that by the end of our century, more than 50% of the present language diversity will be lost. We can conjecture that English will most probably not be an endangered language in the near future. Quite the reverse: In the British Isles, e.g., Celtic (minority) languages have for a long time led a shadowy existence in view of the English language spoken by those in power. Whereas e.g. Cornish died out in the 19th century, measures have been taken against a vanishing of Welsh (→ 7.2.3). Such efforts show that the discussion of majority and minority languages highly depends on the viewpoint – the majority language of large parts of a nation may be a minority language on a regional level (e.g. English in some parts of Wales) or in another nation (e.g. German in Belgium).

The division into majority and minority languages raises ethical questions relating to equality, discrimination, and language rights. One could mention the example of British Sign Language (→ www.narr-studienbuecher.de on psycholinguistics) as a particular minority language of the deaf community in the United Kingdom, showing us the underlying problematic nature quite plainly. The terms 'majority' and 'minority' themselves show how languages are, often due to political and economic reasons, classified in hierarchical terms which, by analogy, give way to a misconception of an 'order' of language communities (→ 7.1.3, ☞ box) within a country. Minority languages such as Basque or the (surviving) Native American languages are languages of identification and prestige for many who currently speak them. Future generations, depending on individual attitude, might favour the majority language instead. E.g., the son of a Chinese immigrant in the USA who is eager to find a well-paid job might rather opt for English to realise his aims than stick to his linguistic heritage at any cost.

An ecological metaphor is used by some linguists to clarify such dynamic 'natural' processes of positioning, spreading, dominating, shifting, endangering, defending, assimilating, (re)vitalising, etc. of languages and of language communities (→ 7.1.3, ☞ box). In this view, every language 'lives' within a **linguistic ecology** (*Sprachökologie*) and is influenced by their immediate linguistic environment (FILL 1993). Just as there are bigger and smaller plants, just as there are creatures that devour others, just as there are biological niches in which specialised animals can survive, just as there are human beings who decrease the overall number of species and those who try to prevent some from extinction, languages are subject to comparable, interacting evolutionary processes. The sociolinguist MÜHLHÄUSLER once said that English is the "weed" among the languages (personal communication).

7.2.2   Bi- and multilingualism

As we grow up, we gain skills in our first language, including some of its sociolinguistic variation. At the same time, we learn about the organisation of our social surroundings and the conventions of mutual co-operation (e.g. language behaviour). The way we communicate is thus on the one hand part of our individual social history, and on the other hand part of our cultural heritage. To sum up, as we acquire language(s), we acquire culture(s). While growing up, children can be exposed to more than one language. E.g., a child of an English mother and an Italian father will learn both languages more or less simultaneously, depending on the respective input. Soon, this bilingual child will learn to separate both languages and to differentiate between English and Italian varieties. The proficiency in both languages is not necessarily equal (or balanced), however.

This leads us to a somewhat broader definition of bilingualism: **Bilingualism** (*Bilingualismus*) refers to at least some proficiency in two languages, either simultaneously learnt or via formal education. Consequently, there are several degrees of individual bilingualism, from rudimentary and imbalanced proficiency to (near-)mastery of the languages involved. Bilingualism thus covers a whole spectrum of understanding / speaking and reading / writing skills in two different languages.

E.g., the ability to understand a written text in language A or B may be very different from producing a text in these languages. (By the way, how's your spoken Latin?) Analogously, **multilingualism** (*Multilingualismus*, *Mehrsprachigkeit*) usually refers to more than two languages.

In a conversation, bilinguals / multilinguals, especially those being fluent in the languages involved, choose more or less automatically between the languages according to their interlocutors, the functional domain, or personal experience and preference. In this event, it may happen that languages (or varieties of these) are blended within an utterance, either unwillingly or as a stylistic device. This blending or switching of linguistic codes, termed **code-switching**, is a reflection of the languages in contact within the speaker him- or herself. Such interferences are possible on all levels, i.e. they can comprise elements of all sizes from all parts of the lexicon-grammar continuum: words, phrases, constructions, whole sentences etc. Let us consider some examples:

(1) *Kwani ni ngumu sana ku-**train** wengine?*
    'Why is it difficult to train others?'
    (Swahili / English; MYERS-SCOTTON 1993)

(2) *Dann hab' ich meinen **Trip** ge**cancel**t.*
    'Then, I cancelled my trip.'
    (German / English)

(3) *You are working here, **o**?*
    'You are working here, aren't you?'
    (English / Tok Pisin)

(4) *Ngodei xixi dou **keep in contact**.*
    'We always keep in contact.'
    (Cantonese Chinese / English; LI WEI 1998)

Example (1) shows a sentence-internal insertion of the English lexical element *train*. In such instances, however, it is hard to tell whether code-switching applies or rather the borrowing (→ 3.2.5.1) of a single lexeme from another language.

Likewise, the 'Dinglish' (a popular term for a blend of *deutsch* and *English*) expressions in (2) do not allow an unambiguous interpretation as regards code-switching. The German syntax and morphology suggests borrowing, though.

Example (3) shows an instance of tag-switching. This special kind of code-switching refers to the attachment of a tag in another language to a sentence, either at the beginning or at the end. In (3), a Tok Pisin question tag is added to an English sentence for emphatic reasons.

Example (4) is a more complex code-switch, as it affects whole sentence constituents. We could imagine instances in which the code-switching complexity even increases, e.g. when several code-switches occur within a single sentence or when, additionally, different accents are involved.

A code-switch, however, is not a variable (→ 7.1.2) in the strict sense. Non-fluent speakers may compensate for proficiency gaps by inserting elements (e.g. words, expressions, idioms, etc.) from another language which simply springs to mind. Even so, code-switching is not primarily a question of fluency or non-fluency. Rather, when talking with monolinguals (if there are such) or other bilinguals / multilinguals, code-switching can be a part of communicative strategy, *n'est-ce pas*? Used deliberately, it effectively contributes to our social self-positioning via language (GUMPERZ 1982).

Bilingualism or multilingualism – be it acquired in childhood or as an adult – is a reflection of the fact that modern societies are becoming more and more multicultural. Multiculturalism is (and will remain) by no means a transient phenomenon, but rather a vital characteristic of the communities we are members of. Multilingual communities, thus, are becoming the norm rather than exceptions. Further, the more our life is taking place in the 'global village', the more the dynamic relationship between languages, i.e. speech communities (→ 1.1.1.2, ☞ box) and cultures, becomes apparent. Metropolises around the world, or Europe in particular, are multilingual playgrounds par excellence where purely monolingual speakers become rare. On a global scale, most speech communities are (at least) bilingual of some sort, thus reflecting the heterogeneity of its members. E.g., Welsh or Hopi speakers usually have proficiency in another language (i.e. the majority language English) nowadays, enabling them to partake in cross-social discourse.

With respect to bilingualism, the terms *bilingualism* and *diglossia* are occasionally confused. In contrast to bilingualism, however, **diglossia** (*Diglossie*) usually refers to two co-occurring, alternative varieties of one and the same language which are used in non-overlapping domains and serve distinct purposes throughout the language community (→ 7.1.3, ☞ box).

The classical example of diglossia used to be the coexistence of Katharevousa and Dhimotiki as varieties of **Greek** (which could also be called different standards). Whereas the former used to be used in religious services, newspapers, official announcements, non-fictional literature etc. and thus constituted rather a formal style, the latter was used in colloquial, informal situations, but also in fictional literature. These 'high' and 'low' varieties and their respective occurrence in certain domains have been subject to intense debate in Greece for many decades. During the last three decades, however, changes have been initiated so that the 'pure' (this, incidentally is the meaning of *Katharevousa*) high variety is more or less only used in church, and a typical sociolinguistic continuum of socially, functionally and situationally determined variation with variables and variants (→ 7.1.2) has been developing.

Another example would be High German, which is used as a formal, mainly written standard in parts of **Switzerland**, whereas the Swiss German dialect (*Schwyzerdütsch*) is used as a non-formal standard at the same time, only in different domains.

The term **diglossia** is sometimes also used to include situations of linguistic division of labour in which different languages are involved (FISHMAN 1967). In this case, diglossia siomply comes to mean 'societal bilingualism'. FISHMAN distinguished different combinations of bilingualism and diglossia in this sense. The following examples may serve to illustrate this:

- diglossia without bilingualism: classical Arabic and colloquial Arabic in Egypt;
- bilingualism without diglossia: (almost) German and English in Germany;
- diglossia and bilingualism: Luxembourgish (actually: trilingualism);
- neither diglossia nor bilingualism: well-known examples difficult to fnd nowadays.

7.2.3   Language policy

In the past decades, especially in the event of the independence of many nations formerly under colonial rule, language policy has become a sociolinguistic issue of increasing importance. In such newly forming nations, many problems have to be tackled. Some of these problems are related to the definition and the realisation of political and social goals. In this respect, linguistic issues are an important factor of possible planning activities.

Language policy (*Sprachpolitik*) refers to the deliberate interference in the 'natural' development (and thus change) of a language or a language variety. Usually, such steps are taken under the aegis of official politics and/or independent language institutions (e.g. special academic circles or Churches). Policies with respect to language are by no means restricted to newly founded nations. Many speech and language communities (→ 7.1.3, ☞ box) nowadays havelinguistic 'guardian angels' of some kind.

⌘ An example from Europe is the German-speaking community in Belgium (not more than approximately 70,000 inhabitants of a rural area on the eastern fringe of the country), which profits from the laboriously negotiated and delicate Belgian language policy (and, let's face it, from the vicinity of the vast German language community in Germany) and has its own Prime Minister and government in Eupen, its capital.

Especially multilingual communities have to face intrinsic obstacles. E.g., which language is (or which languages are) to be used in formal education? What is the role played by minority languages? How much prescriptivism is beneficial, how much is advisable at all? Do political and economic interests possibly conflict with already established prestige patterns or the public attitude to the use of the respective language(s) in general? To what extent do the aims of linguists and politicians irreconcilably clash? These and other difficulties arise when planning language (and thus: language behaviour). Therefore, we can often be witness to a compromise as a result which is intended to suit a majority, not to mention the intellectual elite.

Language policy, especially in terms of language standardisation (→ 7.1.3), involves matters of language codification. Such **language planning** (*Sprachplanung* or **corpus planning** (*Korpusplanung*), as it is called, includes the setting-up of uniform rules for orthography, vocabulary, and grammar, as well as necessary structural modifications of these.

As for orthography: On a global scale, the Roman alphabet definitely is on the advance and has been adopted by many language communities without a written tradition (e.g. in large parts of Africa or in the South Pacific) or with a different written tradition (e.g. Arabic letters in pre-Atatürk Turkey). Nevertheless, 'our' Roman alphabet is just one option of many. Instead, a planning committee might opt for a slightly (or even entirely) different writing system in order to create an individual system with which the language community, itself individual, can identify without having to 'import' a system which has long been established elsewhere. In such cases, however, the writing system is more complicated for outsiders to learn and may be a handicap for the participation in supra-national networks.

As for grammar, a probable consequence of standardisation efforts is the publication of grammar books, using a uniform orthography as mentioned above. In the event of selecting and fixing grammatical rules, the grammar of a pre-existing, prestigious variety is one of the possible sources.

In the same way, dictionaries are compiled which more or less determine the lexical inventory of so-called standard (and thus also of non-standard) language. These have to be revised occasionally in order to keep up e.g. with the ongoing meaning change of existing words or the coining of words and new borrowings (→ 3.2.5.1) respectively.

An example in this respect are the purist tendencies of some authorities in France to 'cleanse' the French language of foreign, mostly English loanwords such as *hamburger* or *week-end* and to replace them by more 'genuine' expressions or neologisms. Such politically motivated, conservative prescriptivism, however, neglects the nature of language (and language behaviour): It changes according to the attitudes prevalent among the language community (→ 7.1.3, ☞ box). If the community does not accept language prescriptivism or understand its underlying logic, all efforts become pointless.

In Germany, recent spelling reforms have caused a stir and, what is more, a lot of insecurity. There, it will take time until the new set of rules is – more or less firmly – established (cf. → 2.5.1).

In addition to corpus planning, **status planning** (*Statusplanung*) refers to an expansion of the functional range of a language (→ 7.1.1, *Ausbausprache*). The use of a language in the educational and religious sectors or the deliberate maintenance of multilingualism e.g. via the regional or national promotion of the prestige of a minority language are instances of status planning.

A crucial question involved in every language policy is the question of cost, however. Corpus and status planning are expensive as regards e.g. the institutional infrastructure or the provision of (up-to-date) school books, for example. We could imagine a situation in which the financial situation of a multilingual nation prevents a policy that is considered adequate, say, to promote literacy in several languages spoken within the community. In such a situation, there is the imminent danger of discrimination against whole language communities or even of a total absence of a uniform language policy with official backing.

With respect to discrimination, the efforts to standardise Basque represent a counter-example: Modern Unified Basque, itself a minority language in France and Spain, having acquired autonomy status, is an amalgamation of the four main dialects (MESTHRIE et al. 2003). Ethnic awareness of minorities is opposed to a 'one nation, one language' policy.

In multilingual states such as Belgium, Canada, India, or Switzerland, a language policy or even **language planning** (*Sprachplanung*), as a part of socio-economic planning activity in general, even seems unavoidable in order to guarantee nationwide communication. However, we have to keep in mind that corpus and status decisions are artificial interventions in language development.

When talking about language policy, we must be aware that there are no generally applicable theories or guidelines. As a reflection of different prerequisites and foci, every policy has to be discussed individually. Nowadays, planning is done even across national borders, e.g. the agreement on internationally used scientific or economic terminologies. Another instance is the choice of languages in multinational organisations such as the European Union or the United Nations. Whereas currently twenty-three languages – think of the motive behind the diversity, but also of the running costs – are officially spoken in the European Parliament, the UN recognises six official languages: English, French, Spanish, Russian, Chinese, and Arabic.

7.3   English as a world language

It is controversial where precisely English ranks in the top five of languages in the world, as far as the sheer number of native speakers is concerned. There are statistics claiming that English is only outshone by Mandarin Chinese in these terms. Nowadays, more than 400 million (with an upward tendency) speak English as their first language. What is more important, English has for a number of decades been the world's most widely used language. It is a means of communication that is able to instantly connect native speakers who are geographically dispersed over a vast area, from New York to Sydney and from the Channel Islands to Hawaii. Even more importantly, large numbers of non-native speakers use it or need a knowledge of it.

This situation has given occasion to the rise of a new field of linguistic study, namely English as a **world language** (*Weltsprache*).

At this point, it should be emphasised that the reasons for the global dominance of English are neither God-given nor associated with any intrinsic qualities of the language itself nor connected with the popular preconception that English is 'somewhat easier to learn' than other languages. In fact, English is in many respects a fairly difficult language to learn (SMITH 2005). Rather, the spread of English is chiefly linked to historical accident. Mainly as a consequence of the era of colonialism and settlement (primarily under the umbrella of the former

British Empire, and its successor the Commonwealth) and the political power associated with that, the English language took hold in many corners of the world, far from the original 'habitat' of the English speech community (→ 1.1.1.2, ☞ box). Today, the omnipresent cultural influence of the USA (combined with their political power) is one of the main factors responsible for the present ongoing rise of English.

For the above-mentioned historical reasons, English is today the **native** or **first language** (*Muttersprache*, *Erstsprache*) of the majority of the population in numerous countries, e.g. in the United States of America, the United Kingdom, Ireland, Canada, Australia, and New Zealand. In some of the countries listed, English has acquired the status of a **national language** (*Staatssprache*), including various implications for language policy and prestige. The two major national varieties British English and American English (→ 7.1.3) are exercising a great influence on the establishment of further individual nationwide standards. We can thus identify a model of the spread of English:

Fig. 98: The spread of English (adapted from KACHRU 1988)

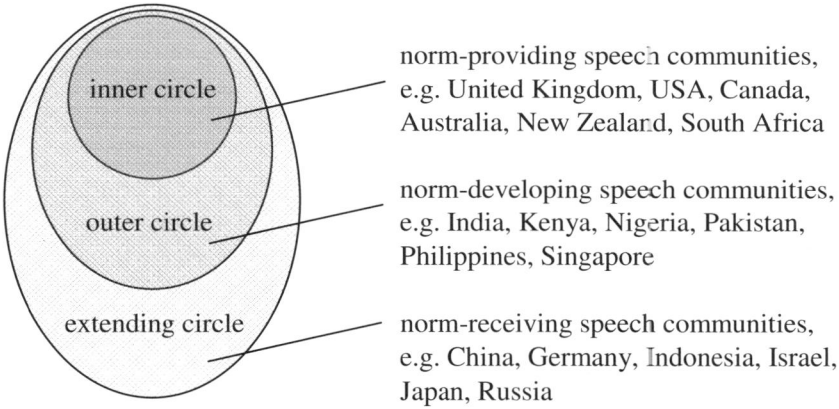

norm-providing speech communities, e.g. United Kingdom, USA, Canada, Australia, New Zealand, South Africa

norm-developing speech communities, e.g. India, Kenya, Nigeria, Pakistan, Philippines, Singapore

norm-receiving speech communities, e.g. China, Germany, Indonesia, Israel, Japan, Russia

In many former British colonies, English is used as an **official** (*Amtssprache*) or **second language** (*Zweitsprache*) (or has acquired a special status of a different kind, e.g. as a medium of higher education) in over 80 of the world's territories, among them South Africa with a sizeable population of native speakers, India and Nigeria. It is remarkable that like them, quite a number of states on declaring their independence from British hegemony decided to keep English, the language originally imposed by the Empire, as a lingua franca.

The term **lingua franca** (*Verkehrssprache*) denotes any language, variety or code that is used as a convenient means of communication throughout a geographical area or in a certain domain. E.g., where there is no common linguistic ground as in the multinational state of India with its many indigenous languages, English is being retained as a quasi-neutral auxiliary language, i.e. as a lingua franca which, in this case, does not give preference to a special speech community over another within India itself.

This does not mean that every citizen in such nation states (e.g. India) actually is, or can be expected to be, fluent in English. There, however, English often becomes a functional medium in such important (prestigious) areas as the law, the press, education, etc. A large proportion of the literature published in such countries is in English, thus constituting a huge world readership and possible international recognition for any author who chooses to write in this language.

Thus, individual '**Englishes**', i.e. regionally restricted varieties such as Canadian English (*Kanadisches Englisch*), Australian English, Papua New Guinean English or South African English have emerged, each including various subvarieties. These deviate from the BrE / AmE standard and sub-standard norms in various characteristics, each to a different extent (→ 10.2.7.3 for literature).
Examples:

- spoken Australian English

  This is the mate that's book on Uluru I borrowed. He's very good mate.
  'This is the friend whose book on Ayers Rock I borrowed. He's a very good friend.'

- spoken Indian English

  He has bought one book and masala yesterday. What he is wishing to do only?
  'He bought a book and spices yesterday. What is he (possibly) intending to do?'

Now they want the same speech in English? But I just delivered it in English!

However, pronunciation and prosody remain the most striking features which render these new Englishes distinctive. The cartoon highlights the possible lack of intelligibility of some varieties (MEHROTRA 1998).

Faced with such a variety of Englishes, first and foremost in spoken language, it is im-mensely helpful to have a linking element, i.e. a guarantee of stability, constancy and continuity of the written form which all users can un-derstand regardless of their own local variety. Thus, this is a powerful argument against a spelling reform of English – notwithstanding the fact that the spelling system is potentially deceptive, especially for non-native speakers.

As hinted at above, there are also several other countries where English has no official status, but where there are nevertheless substantial numbers of speakers who learn English as a second (or third, etc.) language. Bhutan, Brunei, South Korea, and also Germany are examples of such countries. **English as a foreign language (EFL)** (*Englisch als Fremdsprache*) is thus a medium likely to be chosen for communication across frontiers or with people who are not the speaker's compatriots.

Furthermore, apart from the territorial spread, English is also prevalent and thus becomes institutionalised within certain domains of social intercourse. E.g., in a voluntary measure reflecting the everyday realities of a multilingual state in the centre of Europe, the Swiss national railway company has recently introduced English as the official language of their staff and network. The use of English in trilingual Belgium can also be observed to be gradually expanding. Thus, Belgacom (a Belgian telephone company) has given English names to its departments, to avoid having to find names in the three languages with official status (Dutch, French, German) for all of them.

The spheres of activity in which English is the established medium (or: the lingua franca) internationally are both of central importance and on the increase, e.g.: aviation; shipping; tourism; finance and business; fashion; pop music and youth (sub)culture; scholarship, science and technology – in particular, computer and information technology, latterly even more widespread due to the internet. In these domains, English is and will for the time being remain the common ground, i.e. the language most likely to enable ad hoc communication.

English has even displaced French as the language of international diplomacy and negotiation. One does not have to be an uncritical advocate of the French language and French language policy to regard such a development as a mixed blessing. Critical witnesses of this development, the advantages of which seem apparent, might see it as a process of (albeit often self-imposed) linguistic imperialism.

No language is, or ever has been, studied and learnt on a larger scale throughout the world than English. Based on a rough yet recent optimistic estimate, the total number of speakers with at least some competence of English now exceeds two thousand million (CRYSTAL 2008). Taking into account that even in China and Russia there are now vast nationwide English-learning programmes (which pay tribute to the global importance of the language), one can imagine that there will be a constant, considerable andinevitable increase in the number of speakers in the years to come.

The map on the following page gives an overview of those countries and regions in which English enjoys a particular status of the types outlined above. Additionally, the historical norm development is visualised with the help of branches.

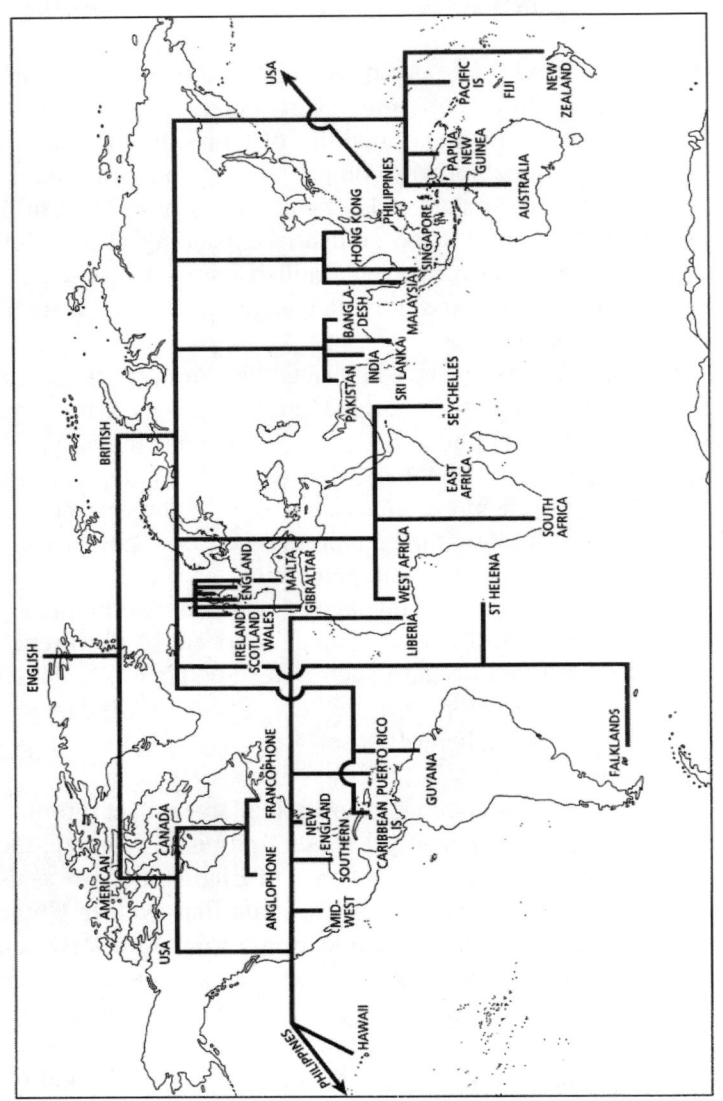

Fig. 99: English as a world language (MCARTHUR 1998, 96)

7.4 Pidgins and creoles

Pidgins and creoles as worldwide phenomena of contact languages have had a considerable influence on linguistic discourse in recent years. Though researchers have discussed such languages since the end of the 19th century, a strong bias against their being 'real' languages persisted for a long time.

Nowadays, in the postcolonial era, about 200 languages classified either as pidgin or creole exist. Their significance to linguists lies primarily in their lexical and grammatical features, which are remarkably similar all over the world, and in their fascinating genesis. For their speakers, they are simply indispensible as lingua francas and, in the case of creoles, as a possible focus of ethnic identity. (→ 10.2.7.4 for literature).

7.4.1 Pidgins

A **pidgin** (*Pidginsprache*) is usually defined as a contact language that comes into existence due to the need for communication between members of mutually unintelligible speech communities (→ 1.1.1.2, ☞ box), i.e. of groups that do not share a common language basis. Pidgins are phenomena the origin of which is prototypically connected to historical contexts of social (or political) hierarchy. Thus, the colonial movement (including the trade of slaves or goods, plantation economy, missionary work, etc.) led by several European states, among them Portugal, Spain, France, the Netherlands, Germany, and – last but not least – the British Empire, was of crucial importance in 'giving birth' to pidgin languages. Accordingly, the core regions of intensive intercultural contact between the colonizers and colonized were located especially in the Caribbean and the South Pacific. Even today, we can witness a multitude of (former) pidgin languages in these regions.

Let us construct a simplified historical scenario: In the 18th century, a British ship arrived at the West African coast. Making use of superior weaponry, its crew carried out the order to ship native Africans to a British colony in the Caribbean. Once arrived there, the Africans, which stemmed from different tribes and thus had different first languages, were forced by the colonizers to work as slaves on plantations far from their homes and original speech communities. In such a plantation setting, there existed an immediate need to communicate. On the one hand, the (in our case) British supervisors had to talk, e.g. to give orders, to the workforce of mixed linguistic descent – conversely, they wanted to understand the slaves' feedback. On the other hand, the workforce had to find a common means for communication among themselves. In such a context, in which the whites were reluctant to learn African languages (which were considered inferior) and the native Africans did not have enough access to English to use it among themselves, a new language could come into existence ad hoc.

In general, this new language consists of a mixture of a language which is typically European, the so-called **superstrate** (*Superstrat*), and of at least two other, typically non-European native tongues (the **substrate** (*Substrat*) languages). The new instrument for communication is mostly short-lived and often does not 'survive' an initial **jargon** stage. Such jargons are, in the context of contact languages, unsystematic linguistic experiments characterised by many one- or two-word phrases and heavily relying on gestures and facial expressions to be understood. (You may imagine yourself having to inquire about the route in, say, a Mongolian village.) Afterwards, however, lexicon and grammar can stabilize and become rule-based due to linguistic negotiation within the new contact community – a pidgin has emerged. In a pidgin, and this is a remarkable characteristic of virtually all pidgins throughout the world, the language mixture is of the following particular kind: The superstrate language, e.g. English, contributes the larger part of the lexicon, whereas the larger part of a pidgin's grammar stems from its substrates, e.g. two distinct African languages. A pidgin functions independently of its language parents, as it were. It is a fully-fledged, autonomous language. Pidgins are, however, purely oral media which are at first hardly spoken outside the context of their origin, i.e. the prototypical plantation setting.

The lexical inventory of pidgins does not significantly exceed 1000-2000 entries. In addition to this fairly small amount, even more lexemes than in Present-Day English have only few syllables (mostly one to three), which means that the range of possible phoneme combinations (which is already diminished by a smaller number of phonemes and stricter phonotactic constraints) to form words from is further limited. How can one make oneself understood with such a small vocabulary? The speakers of pidgins, 'language creators' par excellence, soon develop auxiliary devices. Among these, **circumlocution** (*Periphrase*), i.e. periphrasing with the help of the small lexical stock proves to be a useful tool. An example from the pidgin stage of Tok Pisin (from English *talk* and *pidgin*), which has been spoken in Papua New Guinea, is as follows:

Fig. 100:   An example from Tok Pisin

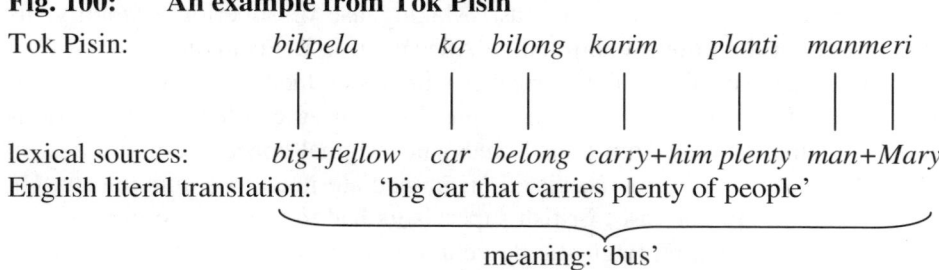

Tok Pisin: *bikpela   ka bilong karim   planti   manmeri*

lexical sources: *big+fellow   car belong carry+him plenty   man+Mary*
English literal translation: 'big car that carries plenty of people'

meaning: 'bus'

Like the lexicon, the grammar of pidgins is kept simplified and transparent. For the most part, neither subordinated phrases nor a passive voice nor allomorphy exist. The syntax, even in questions, is fixed: subject first, verb second, (optional) object third. By this means, the doer of an action can be easily recognized. Additionally, a slow speech tempo promotes the speakers' mutual understanding.

7.4.2   Creoles

A **creole** (*Kreolsprache*) is prototypically defined as a pidgin that has become a first language. The transition from a pidgin as outlined above to a creole is not a matter of course – rather, it only occurs if the language maintains and even spreads its communicative functions. Then, not only adults speak it (e.g. as a possible lingua franca in a particular colonial contact situation), but also children. Thus, the speech community of the former 'linguistic compromise' pidgin can grow considerably.

Let us continue our scenario: On the Caribbean plantation, the workforce (of distinct African descent) lived together for a long time. The consequences of this were, among other things, intermarriages and children. Often, these children were raised using the only language both parents were competent speakers of – namely, pidgin. Thus, the children became the first generation of creole speakers. Alongside that, the language came to be used in all domains of the speakers' everyday life and was not restricted to certain functions any more (e.g. as a language of work in a colonial setting). In our case, the creole even obtained prestige – the speakers liked to speak it without any feeling of inferiority. Thus, the language was further stabilized and also spread beyond the borders of the plantation. It even survived the colonial era and is now, while constantly changing as all other 'natural' languages do, spoken throughout the whole Caribbean island.

Of course, every creole has an individual history. Today, we can encounter creoles in the Caribbean (e.g. *Jamaican Creole*), on the Cape Verde Islands (*Cape Verdian Creole*), on the Ivory Coast (*Krio*), or in East Africa (*Shaba Swahili*), e.g. In general, creoles have a higher degree of complexity concerning lexicon and grammar. This has to do with the above-mentioned expansion of communicative functions. Furthermore, a creole may not remain an exclusively oral medium. Given an orthographic system, literacy and the felt need of members of the speech community, it can be used to create literature – from handbooks to novels, from school books to poetry.

As regards the lexicon: The (former) pidgin vocabulary is semantically expanded, new borrowings (→ 3.2.5.1) come into the language, and word-formation patterns continue to be creatively used. For example, the pidgin Tok Pisin circumlocution *bikpela ka bilong karim planti manmeri* (English *bus*; → 7.4.1) is substituted in creole Tok Pisin by *bus* (from English *bus*). On the one hand, the seemingly unwieldy clusters become replaced; on the other hand, the number of lexemes increases with effects on transparency and learning of the language.

Creole grammar is a little 'trickier' than pidgin grammar. Now, there are for example subordinate clauses and affixation as well as grammaticalised particles to express tense, mode, and aspect. Let us consider a straightforward example from the creole of Hawai'i (mostly called *Hawaiian Pidgin*, though in fact a creole):

Fig. 101: An example from Hawaiian Pidgin

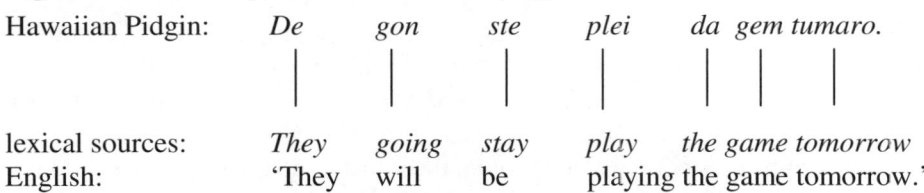

Hawaiian Pidgin:	*De*	*gon*	*ste*	*plei*	*da gem tumaro.*
lexical sources:	*They*	*going*	*stay*	*play*	*the game tomorrow*
English:	'They	will	be	playing the game tomorrow.'

Additionally, a higher speech tempo and an individual prosody often make a creole extremely difficult, if not impossible to understand for outsiders – even if you are a native speaker of English and the superstrate language of the creole is English as well.

Pidgins and creoles certainly appear to be 'unusual' languages at first sight. The most striking difference from so-called traditional languages such as English, French, German, etc. is the social context of their genesis and their rapid development (within decades).

However, they prove to be functional (as a lingua franca), they are rule-governed, they can develop linguistic variety and continua (e.g. dialects and sociolects; → 7.1), and they can die, just like the above-mentioned 'traditional' languages that are conventionally modelled into family trees as genetically related father or sister tongues (→ 3.2.1.0). Thus, pidgins and creoles are natural and effective means of communication which arise due to the sheer need to interlocute among members of a particular group.

Many unsatisfying theories have been brought forward to explain the high degree of similarity of pidgins and creoles worldwide. The universality theory is one of them; its representatives state that the similarities are due to an innate core grammar which is common to all human beings. Yet, many questions are still unanswered in this respect. However, this theory does ring a bell – it is no accident that Chomsky's conception of language competence (→ Box 4) comes to mind. In any case, pidgins and creoles provide valuable insights into how languages change (even within one or two generations) and might even help to elucidate the mystery of language origin in general.

The whole field of **creolistics** (*Kreolistik*) – which includes research on pidgins and jargons – is highly interdisciplinary by nature. Many disciplines of the social sciences contribute to a fuller understanding of underlying phenomena of these languages. For linguists with a focus on the English language, particularly those pidgins and creoles that bear witness to an English (pre-eminently lexical) heritage are of special interest.

7.5   Language and gender

Since the mid-1970s, and especially in the last few years, the differences between men and women in their language use have been identified as a topic of special interest. This particular field of study dealing with the linguistic behaviour in inter-sex (e.g. of man – woman) and intra-sex (e.g. of man – man or woman – woman) interaction and its explanations respectively is commonly labelled **language and gender** (*Sprache und Geschlecht*).

In this field of linguistic study, gender is seen as the key parameter of the choice and the performance of language. The reasons for this are rooted in the evident biological gender dichotomy of mankind. A question that springs from this is: How far is this biological distinction of sexes salient to our identity and, consequently, influential in discourse as an important means of social interaction? Moreover, several linguists who deal with language and gender state that gender is rather a socially constructed category than a mere binary opposition of the sexes. Thus, gender refers to learnt continua of societal order that our linguistic performance is a mirror of.

From this perspective, gender is represented differently in different societies. The following example of speakers of Karajá will clarify this (TALBOT 1998): Karajá is spoken by a small indigenous language community (➔ 7.1.3, ☞ box) in Brazil. In this language, the sex of the speaker is marked phonologically, i.e. every lexeme exists in a male as well as in a female form. Men use the male forms, women use the female forms, exclusively. Thus, both sexes overtly express their role within the community by choosing the appropriate word forms. It soon becomes clear that such rigid marking of identity which is realized (and even further entrenched) via language behaviour only functions in language communities in which male and female social roles are highly fixed and kept separate. In Karajá, the gender differences become strongly emphasized; other more industrialised societies, however, tend to have developed gender roles which are structured more flexibly. This means that the gender roles of, say, speakers of Japanese or English are less clearly defined nowadays – relating to the fact that many domains of modern social life formerly attributed either to a 'male' or 'female' sphere have merged, i.e. differences are increasingly levelling out. Accordingly, the English language does not show sex-exclusive realizations of the extreme Karajá type. Rather, the lack of clear-cut gender boundaries in society is, as it were, counterbalanced by sex-preferential patterns of language, i.e. forms of linguistic expression that are preferred by either men or women, depending whom they are talking to.

These sex-preferential patterns, some of which will be exemplified below, help us speakers to 'construct' ourselves as men or women within our social networks. Language is thus one of the battlegrounds of the struggle of the sexes within society. In this regard, every language, and thereby its speech community (➔ 1.1.1.2, ☞ box) reveals individual, culture-specific strategies.

Gender-differentiated language use occurs on many levels. E.g., women are occasionally said to use a more affective, though more cooperative, interpersonal style in conversation than men; on the other hand, the strategy of men's speech is, according to their different socialisation, reported to be more competitive and information-focused. Language use is, however, not uniform. From women's talk to women, for example, we cannot deduce generalisations of the sort that there is always a certain, inferable strategy of language use. Early research in the field adopted a stratificationist view (i.e. the informants were grouped according to their membership of a social class – be it upper class, working class, or in-between) to prove the hypothesis that women, especially women in paid employment, tend to use more prestigious or acrolectal ($\rightarrow$ 7.6) forms of language than men. Some of these sex-preferential patterns turned out to be phonological in nature.

E.g., word-final -ng as in *living*, *walking*, etc. is realised (within a certain local setting) more consistently as the prestigious, standard-like [ŋ] by women, whereas men are more likely to use the local variant [n] – regardless of their social class ($\rightarrow$ 7.1.2).

Thus, such variants contribute to the enforcement of gender identity (TRUDGILL 1972, MILROY 1992). Nonetheless, such quantitative findings based on class stratification leave many questions open. Do women really seem – albeit subconsciously and often contrary to their self-evaluation – to be more status-conscious than men and thereby have a stronger desire for overt prestige in their language? If they do, is it due to a feeling of less social security in a world still dominated by men? Do men really use non-standard forms, which may obtain a certain covert prestige ($\rightarrow$ 7.1.2, ☞ box) among them more frequently? If they do, is it because they are judged more by their deeds than by their appearance, including their use of language?

In recent years, female linguists in particular have criticised such subliminal misogynist attitudes which reflect, in their view, the gender stereotypes and cli-chés prevalent in many societies as a whole. As representatives of **feminist linguistics** (*feministische Linguistik*), they address questions dealing with special problems of **linguistic sexism** (*Sprachsexismus*). Among them, the analyses of systematic features which are a reflection of sexist social conditions (i.e. here: social conditions discriminating against women) are especially interesting from a sociolinguistic viewpoint in a narrower sense.

In the case of sexism in language, the following phenomena are usually identified:
– Many languages have grammatical structures and rules which mirror an un-disputedly dominating position of men in (earlier) societies. Parallel to this an-drocentric order, the grammars of those languages attribute a privileged role to the grammatical gender 'masculine'. For the most part, more morphological distinctions are made with the masculine, and when talking about men *and* women, it is considered sufficient to use the masculine form (cf. the French personal pronouns: When talking of several individuals and there is only one male person

among them, the appropriate personal pronoun is the 3rd person plural masculine form is *ils*, not its feminine counterpart *elles*).

– The prototypical meaning of many actually 'neutral' words is male. Thus, due to cultural conditioning, with words such as *neighbour*, *guest*, *leader*, etc. many first of all think of a man – unless the context unambiguously suggests a different interpretation. Likewise, many visualise a male person as a norm in their mind when speaking or hearing of a *surgeon*, a *poet* or a *chimney sweeper*, though of course a woman could be meant in all these cases. This phenomenon is frequent especially with respect to (still) existing stereotypical images of a profession – or do you think of a male person with words such as *nurse* or *secretary* in the first place?

Though such linguistic structures are ceasing to be taken as much for granted as they formerly used to be, changing them is no easy task. They are, as outlined above, in part firmly established in our language as well as in our consciousness, which itself is shaped by our socio-cultural environment.

However, especially in the USA, a lot of new gender-neutral terms have been coined to replace the old, purely male-connoted ones. Such new terms could be subsumed under the heading of 'political correctness' – though PC, as it is occasionally abbreviated, has obtained slightly negative overtones.

🖐 Let us have a look at some examples:
- The cultural convention of distinguishing marital statuses is traditionally reflected in the English language via the honorific titles *Mr*, *Mrs*, and *Miss* (e.g. in a letter). *Mr* is used invariably for men, be they bachelors or married, whereas *Mrs* and *Miss* – though containing additional disambiguating information as regards semantics – overtly denote the 'availability status' of the woman under concern (cf. *Fr.* and *Frl.* in German). This linguistic feature has been identified as promoting an asymmetrical treatment of the sexes. Subsequently, a new option, namely *Ms* (/mɪz, məz/), was created. Like *Mr*, *Ms* does not indicate a distinct marital status, but serves as a more neutral form of address, as it were.
- To avoid sexual bias, the use of *they* as a gender-neutral, 3rd person pronoun is making its way more and more in some varieties of English, especially British English. Occasionally, it even replaces the singular neuter *it* and thus avoids inferiority connotations. Nowadays, adding to the horror of male chauvinist purists, the following sentences are accepted as grammatically (and politically) correct by the majority of English native speakers:

A person came into the room, didn't they?
Does your child need help with their English?
A doctor should talk with their patients.

Especially in formal texts we can find instances like the following:

A dentist is obliged to inform his or her patients about the details of an operation.

In this example, instead of a generic usage of the pronoun *he* in order to refer to the dentist, an additional feminine pronoun 'completes' the reference by including women overtly. Thus, a one-sided interpretation is avoided.

> ○ With German grammar, however, solutions of the above-mentioned kind
>
> > *Does your child need help with their English?*
>
> would not be possible. German has not only obligatory number and gender agreement, but also disturbing homonymies between 3rd person singular feminine, 3rd person plural, and 2nd person polite address. Thus, only the second of the following instances is grammatical; a gender-neutral expression as in English is neither existent nor necessary here:
>
> > **Braucht Ihr Kind Hilfe mit ihrem Englisch?*
> > *Braucht Ihr Kind Hilfe mit seinem Englisch?*
>
> There still exists considerable insecurity and disagreement among speakers of German as to whether expressions such as '*die Bewerberinnen und Bewerber*' or alternative awkward creations such as '*die BewerberInnen*' are a suitable or actually an inappropriate way to avoid sexist language.

Also in English, the intention to use language in a non-offensive way (or, conversely, in a way denigrating males) has led to some peripheral and occasionally peculiar word creations, e.g. *womankind* ('*mankind*') or *herstory* ('*history*'). The PC debate, however prescriptive the attitude of its representatives, has resulted in an increasing awareness of language with regard to gender. At the same time, a good deal of linguistic inventiveness ensued from it. Some creations and their use have become widely common – among them gender-neutral terms such as *chairperson* instead of *chairman*, or *parenting* instead of *mothering*. A further practice which can be found e.g. in advertisements nowadays is the use of the 2nd person instead of the 3rd person pronoun:

> *You should be dynamic, committed and inventive. You will be a graduate with a minimum of eight years' commercial experience...; you will assume senior level responsibility....*

However, the lack of alternatives in many cases shows that a lot of creativity will still be needed. The pressure of such creative need even seems to be increasing. Some journalists, for example, work with style guides in order not to use discriminating vocabulary; moreover, feminist dictionaries have been published in which proposals for the avoidance of stereotypes are collected (KRAMARAE / TREICHLER 1985).

To sum up: The biological gender dichotomy between men and women (including children) results in zeitgeisty cultural constraints which themselves are in a reciprocal relationship with language use. Gender is 'performed' with the help of language; learnt stereotypes still have a certain normative force in this respect. However, with increasing awareness that traditional masculine hegemony is under threat, traditional role models are changing accordingly. 'Male' and 'female' are thus not seen as monolithic, diametrically opposed entities, but as fluid elements of a continuum. Gender-specific strategies along this continuum include lexical and grammatical domains as well as communicative functions of language.

Further detailed issues of interest in the field of language and gender, which also reach into other related fields of linguistics, should perhaps be mentioned for the sake of more completeness. They are, among others:

- the division of conversational 'labour' (e.g. speech proportions) among men / women and possible miscommunication,
- compliments and politeness in general as elements of the conversation strategy of women (vs. men),
- the different strategies of storytelling used by men and women,
- the use of greater intonational dynamism by women (in comparison with men),
- the representation of masculinity / femininity in the media,
- different patterns of language use with respect to boys and girls,
- the dissimilar language processing of men and women in the brain.

7.6   On variation and conditioning factors of its use

All language is social. This sounds like a trivial statement as the main function of language is meaningful communication, which itself is a means of social intercourse. The social rootedness of language effects its variation, which has been the main theme of this chapter on sociolinguistics. Several varieties, i.e. identifiable particular kinds of language, have been particularised. Sociolinguistic research in general is an account of the networks, situations, and conditions in which these varieties are used or come into contact or conflict with each other, and the influence of official language regulations on the use of the varieties.

What is more, in describing language behaviour with respect to the use of varieties, the notions of attitude, awareness, identity, and – expressly – prestige have been a leitmotif of this chapter. In other words, the guiding question of all sociolinguistic research has been:

Who speaks what language (or variety) to whom in what situation about what topic?

What many language situations have in common is that some sort of 'high' language variety is distinguished from some sort of 'low' variety. Occasionally, the terms 'acrolect' and 'basilect' are used correspondingly:

- An **acrolect** (*Akrolekt*) usually denotes a prestigious standard, thus 'high' variety, whereas a
- **basilect** (*Basilekt*) represents the opposite end of the dialect continuum, thus a 'low' variety whose characteristics are most remote from the standard.

- In this respect, **mesolects** (*Mesolekte*) are all intermediate varieties, as it were, that exist between these extremes.

Such a hierarchy of standard and sub-standard is an artificial one, however, and does not imply the 'correctness' of a certain language use – rather, it hints at the organisation of the speech community (→ 1.1.1.2, ☞ box) and the social forces that govern it. Every speech community has a plethora of varieties, which are systematically interwoven, at its disposal. Each variety, inclusive of code-switching, is meaningful in itself as it carries, beside the meaning of the words, social information on the speaker, conveyed consciously or subconsciously when communicating.

The individual awareness and classification of a variety is, however, at times defective. E.g., people may not be using the standard even if they think they do, but rather a **vernacular** (→ 7.1.3).

In sum, there is thus an interplay (or better: interdependence) between social structure and the structuring of linguistic variation within a community. The dynamism of communication itself can function to negotiate, establish, and maintain relationships within and between constantly changing societies (or, broadly speaking, cultures).

As speakers (or writers) use linguistic variation as a social tool, it can be instrumentalised by prescriptivist institutions, e.g. in the choice of a certain variety as a carrier of nationalism in postcolonial countries. Planning the prestige of a variety or language is an intricate matter and subject to continuous debate – in this respect, linguists are often in conflict with politicians' interests. Whereas one group might favour the revitalisation of an almost extinct minority language (cf. Irish Gaelic), others might assess such efforts as uneconomical and 'retro'.

There are many factors that determine the use of a certain variety (or language). Several of them, though by no means all, are listed in Fig. 102.

Fig. 102: Prominent conditioning factors of language use

Individual factors	Group-inherent factors	Institutional factors
• age • gender • education • objectives • lifestyle • employment • home / mobility • attitude to group membership	• group / class membership and solidarity • frequency of contact • standard of living	• labour market and infrastructure • educational sector • politics and economics in general • degree of isolation of society • religion • lobbies • media • codification
P R E S T I G E		

A variety (or language) is realised according to individual, group-immanent, and institutional factors which are interwoven. In this regard, the factor of prestige – positive or negative – is singled out due to its being an omnipresent principle that governs our linguistic behaviour. For example, the use of a vernacular can have (covert) prestige among a certain in-group – it is a matter of perspective whether [bʌtə], [bʌdə], [bʌʔə], [bʌɾɾ] or [bʊtə] are prestigious realisations of the word *butter*.

➤ Last but not least, speaking of the conditioning factors of language use, we may consider a sidenote with respect to the history of English.

One of the many examples that feature a socially motivated language change with lasting effects up to the here and now is the remarkable disappearance of the overt distinction of 2nd person personal pronouns. In standard English (e.g. BrE), we can witness today that utterances like *You are wonderful* are potentially ambiguous – only the context makes clear whether *you* refers to one person or several. Additionally, matters of formality and social hierarchy (cf. German *du* vs. *Sie*) are not marked therein. This was not always so.

In the first place, the distinction between *thou* and *ye* (including objective and non-nominative forms; → 3.2.2.3) was one of number only. Then, however, in the Middle English period, *thou* began to be used as the prototypical form for addressing in informal or contemptuous contexts and, particularly, a person who is inferior on the social ladder. Consequently, *ye* was reserved to deferentially address superiors (and equals). Hence, by using and thus choosing a single pronoun, the social hierarchy of the interlocutors, and their power divide respectively, was mirrored or set via language. In fact, the usage of pronouns acquired an extra, namely a social dimension which had to be observed if, e.g., a speaker did not want to be recognised as a disrespectful, clumsy fellow.

This development notwithstanding, it came to pass that the 2nd person singular form *thou* gradually fell out of written use during the Early Modern English period, thus reflecting a preceding change in spoken language in the 15th century. The object form *you* took its place and became regular and multifunctional as it is today. However, the former usage was preserved in a niche of conservative and highly formal contexts, thus contributing to a style that was soon (and is now) felt as solemn, but archaic; cf. this extract from the Gospel of Matthew:

*My God, my God, why hast **thou** forsaken me?* (KJV [1611] 1997)

This Bible verse must grab our attention. It shows that addressing God as *thou* is not inept or heretical – rather, confusingly, it reflects the original singular – plural or later non-deferential – deferential distinction (*thou* vs. *ye*). Ironically, the once non-deferential *thou* now seems to be reserved for addressing God.

The reasons for the above-mentioned changes, i.e. the rise and fall of a marker of distinction, are not entirely resolved. Yet, according to a strong hypothesis, it was the social factor that had the lion's share in it. A thorough transformation, including urbanisation and a breaking-up of rigid traditional hierarchies, shook the post-Middle Age societal organisation of the British. As power relationships revolved, a widening middle class chose to simplify pronominal complexity and thus to avoid (linguistic and social) insecurity and confusion by having a quasi-neutral, single solidarity marker (i.e. *you*). Interestingly, the distinction survivede.g. in some northern English dialects.

In view of European languages, English is today quite alone in not overtly distinguishing all singular and plural pronoun forms. In fact, however, we should not bemoan the loss of a once developed linguistic marking that contributed to communicative (or, to be specific, pragmatic) precision. Instead, we may gain the insight that the inclusion of a diachronic sociolinguistic perspective can, beyond doubt, add to a fuller understanding of the mechanisms of the perpetual changes in language.

8 Epilogue: Specific characteristics of human languages vs. animal communication

At the end of this introduction, we want to raise one more very important, partly controversial and fascinating question of language theory, an anthropological question which touches upon our self-image as human beings and our place in nature: How can we distinguish human language from other systems of animal communication? This question has become known as the problem of **species-specificity** (to use a trendy German expression, the question of the *'Alleinstellungsmerkmal'*) of human language.

It has already been mentioned that most human beings (except for the deaf community) use a sound-signalling system for communication. As for animal communication systems, the use of sounds is by no means the sole strategy. There are a number of species that do not produce sounds to communicate with one another. Some crabs, e.g., wave their claws in order to convey messages and honey bees perform a complicated sequence of movements that we usually refer to as a 'dance'. The use of sounds, however, is more widespread and is employed by a variety of different animal species, e.g. birds, grasshoppers, dolphins, cows, and monkeys.

Indeed, sound signals have considerable advantages which were definitely instrumental in developing human language into the kind of semiotic system that it is now and certainly has been for quite a few millennia:
- They can be used in the dark,
- they leave the body free for other activities and
- they allow messages to be sent over some distance.

The American linguist Charles HOCKETT provided a useful list of some features characteristic of human language which are not shared by other animals. We shall deal with the most important of these in the following sections (cf. LYONS 1992, PINKER 1995)

8.1 Arbitrariness

When we examine animal communication systems, we find that usually, there is a recognisable link between the signal and the message the animal wants to convey, e.g. whenever a cat tries to frighten off an opponent, it is likely to arch its back and thus appear both larger and ready to pounce. Thus, most signs used in the animal kingdom are **iconic** (→ Box 26) or **indexical** (→ Box 27) or both at the same time.

When we consider human language, we learn that, in the great majority of cases, there is no intrinsic link between the signal and the message we wish to convey. E.g., there is absolutely no logical or causal connection between a tree in the real world and the word *tree* we use to refer to it. We say the symbols (i.e. lexical morphemes consisting of phonemes in spoken language and of letters in written language) that are used are **arbitrary** (→ Box 19).

△ One of the few exceptions to this principle are, to a certain degree, instances of **onomatopoeia** such as the words *bang*, *quack-quack* or *splash* (→ Box 19). But as already remarked above, even in these cases we always find a certain degree of arbitrariness as onomatopoeic words are always language-specific, consisting of phonemes of a specific language, and may sound quite different in different languages (or are German roosters any different from English ones because they crow, according to German linguistic lore, *kikeriki*, whereas in English, they go *cock-a-doodle-doo*?).

There are no clear examples of indexical signs in human language, except perhaps in certain features of **intonation** (→ 2.3.4.1); these very features, however, tend to be regarded as non-linguistic for this very reason.

Nevertheless, the principle of arbitrariness has recently been challenged by certain linguists who believe in the pervasiveness of **iconicity** (→ Box 26) in language in general (see, for example, RAFFAELE 1995, FISCHER / NÄNNY 2001). To avoid misunderstandings here, it should first of all be repeated that the principle of arbitrariness is only valid for simple linguistic signs consisting of only one morpheme, but not for complex signs, which are of course motivated by their component morphemes, and certainly not for complex constructions, which may be iconic to a certain degree. But as the phenomena of grammaticalisation (→ 3.2.3) and lexicalisation (→ 3.2.5.3) show, original motivation may easily turn into arbitrariness in a diachronic process. It is quite possible that originally all morphemes were motivated in some way or other, but eventually the principle of arbitrariness asserted itself as a universal tendency, assigning marginal status to iconic signs in language.

8.2   Duality / double articulation

Any animal that uses vocal signals has a restricted stock of basic sounds, depending on the species it belongs to. Most animals can make use of each basic sound only in isolation, i.e. the number of messages an animal can convey is restricted to the given number of respective basic sounds. Again, human language works differently. Each language, as we have seen in section → 2.2.3, has a stock of discrete, i.e. segmentable and substitutable **phonemes**. Usually, each phoneme is meaningless in isolation and has to be combined with other phonemes if we want to make a meaningful utterance. E.g., /d/, /ɒ/, and /g/, if taken separately, have no meaning whatsoever. We can, however, combine them in various ways to make them meaningful, as in *dog* and *god*.

This organisation of human language into two layers – a layer of sound units that can combine into a second layer of larger units – is called **duality** or **double**

articulation *(doppelte Gliederung)*. Compared to animal communication systems, the double articulation of our human sign systems enables us to formulate a far greater number of messages and thus is considerably more complex and flexible.

8.3 Displacement

The vast majority of animals can only communicate about things in their immediate surroundings, e.g. a marmot only utters a danger cry when danger is actually present ($\rightarrow$ 8.1). Thus, their 'performance' is triggered by an immediate stimulus; the 'communicative' response resulting from the stimulus is automatic, unsuppressable. By contrast, human beings can communicate about things that are remote in time and place as well, and they can choose when and where to communicate their message (if at all). This phenomenon has been termed **displacement** *(zeitliche und räumliche Situationsunabhängigkeit)*.

$\triangle$ It only exceptionally occurs in the animal world, e.g. in the communication of honey bees: If a worker bee has found a new source of nectar, it or she returns to the hive and performs a specific dance, informing the other bees of the exact location of the nectar which may be hundreds of yards away. This commonly called 'bee language', however, is very restricted in other respects ($\rightarrow$ 8.4). I.a., it is unsuppressable behaviour. This also means that bees cannot lie; it need hardly be mentioned that human beings can. The ability to deliberately use a sign system for lying has been implicitly suggested as the origin of language by KELLER (1990, 33ff.); but that does not mean that deception does not occur in the animal kingdom. It remains, however, an open question how 'deliberate' animals can be.

8.4 Creativity / productivity and recursiveness

Most animals are rather limited in their ability to communicate – they just have a restricted number of messages at their disposal which they can send or receive. Even honey bees are restricted in this respect: They can only communicate about restricted topics such as nectar and they cannot even communicate about that if the nectar is in the wrong place. In one experiment, nectar was located <u>above</u> the beehive, and the bees were not able to communicate this fact because their language lacks a sign for 'above' (VON FRISCH 1993). And certainly bees cannot communicate about yesterday's nectar or maliciously lead their hive-mates astray by deliberately performing misleading dances.

Human beings, on the other hand, can communicate about anything they can conceive of in past, present, and future, be it true or false, be it in nearby and remote, and real and imagined places. What is more, they can produce new utter-

with, we should ask ourselves whether the results might not be simply over-interpreted.

Critics say the apes did not really learn any true American Sign Language. A deaf scientist, a native signer of American Sign Language who belonged to the Washoe team, later reported:

> Every time the chimp made a sign, we were supposed to write it down in the log. [...] They were always complaining because my log didn't show enough signs. All the hearing people turned in logs with long lists of signs. They always saw more signs than I did. [...] I watched really carefully. The chimp's hands were moving constantly. Maybe I missed something, but I don't think so. I just wasn't seeing any signs. (PINKER 1995, 337f.).

In fact, the chimps were relying heavily on the gestures in their natural repertoire. What is most important to show their behaviour does not compare to human language behaviour: They did not stick to any grammar rules and it never became ultimately certain that they really followed a syntax, let alone recursive rules ($\rightarrow$ 8.4). What is more, the average length of the chimps' sentences remained constant, even after several years of intensive training. By contrast, the average length of a child's sentences would have greatly increased in such a long time.

Washoe and the other chimps seldom signed spontaneously, they did not take turns in conversation and they rarely made 'statements' that 'commented' on some action or event. Virtually all their communicative signs directed at people were demands, for something they wanted, usually food or tickling. Their signing behaviour in other situations seems to suggest that they had not really grasped the function of the signs they had learned. This would be a stage human children leave behind them as soon as they start using language. In sum, it is highly probable that the individual chimp's environmental conditions strongly influence the degree to which it can be motivated to learn an artificial communication system (MARQUARDT 1984, 69). Child language acquisition is considerably more robust in this respect.

Today, ambitious claims about chimpanzee language are a thing of the past. PINKER (1995, 342) arrives at the following sobering conclusion:

> The chimpanzees' resistance is no shame on them; a human would surely do no better if trained to hoot and shriek like a chimp, a symmetrical project that makes about as much scientific sense.

We shall have to accept the fact that language, with its characteristics described above, is unique to human beings. The members of the human species are, as it were, left alone with their language. Thus, the evolutionary gap between our closest genetic relatives, the chimpanzees, and ourselves, although surprisingly small in terms of genes, is immense in terms of the complexity, richness, capacity, and flexibility of the communication systems concerned.

9 Exercises

This part contains exercises relating to the individual chapters or subchapters. The exercises are partly meant for self-study, but also for discussion in class. The former kind simply gives the student an opportunity to test the knowledge and skills acquired in working with this book. The latter are also meant as a challenge to those students who wish to go beyond the topics covered in this introduction. They encourage students to find creative solutions to new problems. These exercises are marked with a § sign. Not all of them can be solved with this introduction serving as cook-book.

9.1 Exercises relating to chapter 1

9.1.1 Grammar in general

1. Briefly explain the most important differences between morphology and syntax in your own words.
2. What criteria can be used to distinguish word classes in English?
3. What part is played by the category of gender in modern English?
4. Which grammatical categories are marked by which grammatical morphemes (auxiliaries, suffixes, etc.) in the following verbal syntagms?
   4.1 He might have been going to be working.
   4.2 The building had been being built for ages.
5. Name the word classes (noun, verb, adjective, etc.) to which the words in the following sentences belong.
   5.1 She must return to her casting appointment fast.
   5.2 The ghastly quarrel between us subsided in the excitement of moving.
   5.3 This book covers American history from the Declaration of Independence to World War I.
   5.4 These book covers are very dirty.

9.1.2 Syntax

1. Find phrase structure rules or draw tree diagrams for the following English sentences. Also describe the sentences in terms of constructions using formulae such as in 1.2.3.2.
   1.1 The Prime Minister of Zimbabwe reassured prospective investors in his country yesterday.
   1.2 She leant her head tiredly against the back of her chair.
   1.3 The girl with the basket only sold a single violet during the day.
   1.4 A horrifying pirate ship suddenly appeared on the horizon.

2. Explain the syntactic ambiguity of the following sentences with the help of tree diagrams or construction formulae:

   2.1 He greeted the girl with flowers.
   2.2 The police stopped drinking after twelve .
   2.3 John was reading a book on Times Square.
   2.4 They arrived at a decision on the boat.
   § *2.5 Visiting relatives can be a bloody nuisance.*

3. Explain briefly the different approaches to describing sentence structure in Generative Grammar and Construction Grammar.

4. What is it that distinguishes a grammatical subject in English? And in German?

5. In what way does Generative Grammar explain the fact that in every language there are in principle infinitely many different sentence structures, although there are only a limited number of different syntactic categories?

6. Try to provide syntactic descriptions for the following English (or pseudo-English) sentences. Give reasons why in some of the sentences it is difficult or impossible to do this. What are the differences between these sentences?

   6.1 She must return to her office immediately.
   6.2 The nasty quarrel between us subsided in the excitement of moving.
   6.3 'Twas brillig, and the slithy toves did gyre and gimble in the wabe.
   § *6.4 Me an' me Mom long time no talk.*
   § *6.5 The book has Martha quite enthusiastic.*
   § *6.6 Girl the boy garden in the kissed.*

7. Describe the construction which the following sentences have in common.

   7.1 They were picking their way through the jungle.
   7.2 She elbowed her way through the crowded bus.
   7.3 He bullied his way to the top.

9.1.3 Morphology

1. Segment the following English words into morphemes. State the kind of morphemes you find in your analysis (e.g. prefix, suffix) and their function (e.g. derivation, inflection), and explain your segmentation. When in doubt, use a good dictionary!

1.1	*compositionality*	1.7	*workaholic*
1.2	*derivationalist*	1.8	*misrepresentation*
1.3	*kindergarten welt-anschauung*	1.9	*unhelpfulness*
1.4	*§necrophiliac*	1.10	*disarmament*
1.5	*disproportionately*	1.11	*§misconception*
1.6	*§biodegradable*	1.12	*arachnophobia*

2. Try to list all the allomorphs of the <u>German</u> plural morpheme.

3. Try to list all the inflectional morphemes of English with their allomorphs.

4. Classify the following morphemes according to the diagram in Fig. 22 at the end of section 1.3.7. Discuss and argue for your decisions!

4.1 -s in *she get-s*
4.2 -ist in *dramatist*
4.3 vis- in *visual, vision*
4.4 declar- in *declaration*

§ *4.5 re-* in *rediscover*
4.6 -groom in *bridegroom*
4.7 eco- in *ecology*
4.8 -gate in *Clintongate*

5. What kinds of morphological procedures are applied to form the following English word forms (inflection, derivation, compounding, etc.)? What else can you say about this particular form?

(Example of a good answer: "The form *brought* is formed by a kind of morphological process which is inflectional. It may be a past tense or a past participle of *bring*. It uses a rare stem alternation plus an irregular allomorph of the inflectional suffix. This form is hence very irregular. It was irregular in Old English already: It was a 'weak' verb with a rare stem alternation. A comparable form is *thought*.")

5.1 oxen
5.2 formulae
5.3 radar
5.4 been

5.5 advisable
5.6 fridge
5.7 poltergeists
5.8 length

9.2   Exercises relating to chapter 2

1. Explain briefly and in your own words the difference between phonetics and phonology.

2. Find minimal pairs for the following phonemic contrasts of English:

2.1 /b/ – /p/	2.3 /f/ – /v/
2.2 /θ/ – /s/	2.4 /n/ – /ŋ/

3. What are the distinctive articulatory features which distinguish the following contrasting phonemes:

3.1 /p/ – /t/	3.3 /t/ – /s/
3.2 /l/ – /n/	3.4 /ð/ – /θ/

4. Describe the following sounds by way of articulatory features:

4.1 [g]	4.3 [n]
4.2 [z]	4.4 [p]

5. Are the following sound pairs allophones of one phoneme or different phonemes? Give reasons for your decisions.

5.1 [ç] (as in German *ich*) – [x] (as in German *ach*) in Standard German

5.2 [l] (as in *lip*) – [ɫ] (as in *pill*) in British English

5.3 [v] – [w] in English

6. Each of the following groups of sounds contains one element which doesn't really fit in. Which is it, and why? (Several solutions may be possible.)

6.1 [m n ŋ g]	6.3 [ɪ w ʊ e]
6.2 [d t g n]	6.4 [ɑ ɒ ɔ ɪ]

7. Name two different functions of intonation in English.

8. Name a function which pitch level has in some languages, but not in English.

9. State the rule for the distribution of allomorphs of the suffix -s (3rd person singular) in the following word forms. Base your analysis on the pronunciation and not on the spelling. (To achieve this, transcribe the words in a broad transcription before starting the analysis.)

   wants, sees, wishes, grins, buzzes, loves, scrambles, laughs, omits, adds, clips, kisses, budges, sobs, goes

10. State the rule for the distribution of allomorphs of the prefix in- (negation) in the following words. Base your analysis on the pronunciation and not on the spelling. (Look up the pronunciation in a dictionary if you're not sure!) To prevent interference from the spelling, it is advisable to produce a phonetic transcription of the words before starting.

    impossible, illegal, irregular, incongruent, infinite, indivisible, insipid

§11. Comment on the spelling-to-sound relationship in two European languages you are familiar with. Which spelling system reflects more precisely the phoneme system of the respective languages? Are there any other criteria for the evaluation of a spelling system? What might be the reasons for inconsistencies in the spelling – pronunciation relationship in the languages in question?

§12. Discuss the complementary distribution of [ŋ] and [h] in English. Should this lead to an analysis where the two sounds are allophones of one phoneme?

13. Provide a phonemic analysis of your own variety of German: State all the phonemes with their allophones, give examples and find minimal pairs where possible.

14. Describe a typical German learner's variety of English. State all the neutralisations and other adaptations that take place.

9.3 Exercises relating to chapter 3

§1. Describe an ongoing sound change which you have observed in your native language or in present-day English (not a historical sound change!).

2. Name a number of words which have existed in German or English for only a few years.

3. Name a number of words which are about to disappear from present-day German or English.

4. Name a number of words which have recently percolated from one linguistic domain of German or English (e.g. academic language, technical language, sports language, media language, politicians' language, underworld jargon, young people's language, slang) into another (e.g. general language use, or another of the above-mentioned domains).

§5. Describe an ongoing meaning change that you have observed in your native language or in present-day English. Is it a case of lexicalisation? What mechanisms are involved?

§6. Describe a case of ongoing grammaticalisation in a language you are familiar with.

7. Is language change an improvement from a diachronic point of view? Substantiate your arguments with the help of examples.

8. In how far is language change characterised by the loss of formerly functional features? If it is, can it be equated with language decay in general or are there counter-movements?

9.4   Exercises relating to chapter 4

1. Analyse the meaning differences within the following lexical fields using semantic features. Use a major monolingual dictionary (Longman, Collins, Webster) if you're not sure about a meaning. Draw up a matrix like the one in Fig. 76 in section 4.2.3

   1.1 filly, foal, gelding, horse, mare, stallion, steed
   1.2 armchair, bench, chair, couch, settee, stool
   1.3 brook, lake, ocean, pond, river, sea, stream

2. Check whether in the following pairs of propositions the truth of the second proposition is entailed by the truth of the first one. What makes this difficult in some cases?

	Does A	entail B?
2.1.	FIDO FOULED UP ALL MY TU-LIPS.	FIDO FOULED UP ALL MY FLOWERS
2.2	MARY SAW A BIG MOUSE.	MARY SAW A BIG ANIMAL.
§2.3	JOHN LIKES FLOWERS	JOHN LIKES TULIPS
2.4	JOHN SAW A MAN	JOHN SAW A PERSON

3. Decide whether the following words are homonymous or polysemous. Give reasons for your decision. In the cases of polysemy, decide whether the meanings/senses are related by metaphor or by metonymy.

   3.1 bark (of a tree – of a dog)
   3.2 steer (... a car – young bull)
   3.3 fork (for eating – in a road)
   3.4 school ('The whole school went on an outing today' – 'the linguistic school of Noam Chomsky')

4. Write a short essay on one of the following topics:

§ 4.1 Arbitrariness and motivation in the vocabulary

4.2 The problem of vagueness and fuzziness in semantics

§ 4.3 Criteria for judging the quality of dictionaries

4.4 Differences between feature semantics and cognitive semantics

5. Which of the following statements are typical of a prototype approach to semantic categorisation rather than of a componential approach?

5.1 The category that a word may refer to is defined by one set of distinctive features which exhaustively describes the meaning of that word.

5.2 The category that a word may refer to is defined by a network of family resemblances among things that belong to the category.

5.3 Category membership can be a matter of degree, i.e. there are often members in a semantic category that are 'better examples' than others.

5.4 All members in a semantic category have at least one property in common.

5.5 In semantic analysis, metaphorical and metonymic uses of a word must be strictly kept apart from its literal uses.

6. Try to devise image schemata for the following prepositions, along the lines of Fig. 78:

in, under, on, above, over, along

7. Try to think about contexts in which the following, logically deficient sentences make sense. Also indicate the kind of deficiency (contradiction, tautology, anomaly, etc.):

7.1 John is neither here nor there.
7.2 My husband is married to his job.
7.3 Boys will be boys.
7.4 A rose is a rose.
7.5 Bachelors are unmarried men.
7.6 Cary Grant was a male bride.
7.7 My computer is neurotic.

9.5 Exercises relating to chapter 5

1. Name the illocutionary act that is typically performed by uttering the following sentences in the situation indicated in brackets. Do you find that such an analysis is really satisfactory in all cases?

1.1 I will! (marriage vows)
1.2 Have you heard the latest? (informal gossip)
1.3 I can give you a lift downtown. (towards the end of a party)
1.4 I'm so glad you passed the exam. (university campus)

2. Check whether in the following pairs of sentences the first one presupposes the second proposition.

	Does A	presuppose B?
2.1	*The man I met yesterday was bald.*	I MET A MAN YESTERDAY.
2.2	*Noam knows that the moon is not made of green cheese.*	THE MOON IS MADE OF GREEN CHEESE.
2.3	*Jane wants to marry a millionaire.*	JANE'S FIANCÉ OR BOY-FRIEND IS A MILLIONAIRE.
2.4	*Mr Parker believes the earth is flat.*	THE EARTH IS FLAT.

3. Try to think of at least three situations in which each of the following sentences could be uttered, with a different illocutionary function respectively, and describe these situations and functions.

   3.1 I'll come back tomorrow.
   3.2 Do you know who's coming to the meeting?
   3.3 The exhibition is now open.

§4. In what way are the following answers, even if true, misleading or evasive? Which conversational maxims are being violated or observed? What conclusions can one justifiably draw? Which heuristics according to LEVINSON (2000) may the hearer apply?

   4.1 Mother: *Have you done your homework and cleaned your shoes?*
   Child: *I've done my homework.*
   4.2 Customer in the stationery shop: *Where can I find pencils?*
   Shop assistant (who has had a row with his boss and does not feel like bending down): *You can get pencils at Woolworth's round the corner.*
   4.3 Wife: *Did you buy salt?*
   Husband: *I tried to.*
   4.4 Boss: *How's the new colleague making out?*
   Head of Department: *He's always punctual and has neat handwriting.*
   4.5 Host: *We could go to that new steakhouse round the corner tonight.*
   Guest: *I'm a vegetarian.*

§5. Analyse the cartoon at the end of section 5.5 in terms of a theory of background.

9.6 Exercises relating to chapter 6

1. In the following text identify and describe where you can find anaphoric expressions, lexical cohesion, or other linking devices. Why is the text peculiar in spite of the occurrence of these expressions?

It was a dark and stormy night. The ship was ploughing the sea at top speed. Ship *It made Jane seasick. Suddenly, a pirate ship appeared on the horizon. The* Jane *girl screamed. Meanwhile, on a farm in Kansas, a small boy was growing up. At that very moment, a young intern at City Hospital was making an important discovery. Could it be that the boy from Kansas was the half-brother of the girl who had been abducted by the pirates?* Jane

§2. Try to identify coherence relations in the following text fragment and describe them in terms of section 6.1.4

People usually think of 'stress' as something the world inflicts on them. Worry and hassle are blamed for all kinds of ailments, from asthma to headaches, from high blood pressure to stomach ulcers. And we often blame other people for making us feel bad: When we call someone a 'pain in the neck', we are describing the physical and psychological effect they have on us.

But although it is tempting to regard stress as some nasty germ attacking us from outside, the truth is that we are largely responsible for what stress does to our bodies. Once we make ourselves aware of how our bodies respond to worry, fear, anger and fatigue (all of which are forms of stress), we can start learning to relax.

§3. In what ways does hypertext differ from ordinary text? Are or were there conventional texts that share or foreshadow certain features of hypertext?

4. Analyse the following short conversations. Identify and describe adjacency pairs. Does the passage contain a typical conversation opening or closing? §What is remarkable about this?

4.1 (At a party. Beth and Fred are the hosts:)
A: *(a) Hello, I'm Sally Jones.*
B: *(b) Hi, I'm John, John Smith.*
A: *(c) I'm Beth's sister.*
B: *(d) Oh, I work with Fred.*

4.2 (Neighbours visiting each other; hosts are Henry and Zelda)
Henry: *(a) Y'want a piece of candy.*
Irene: *(b) No.*
Zelda: *(c)* ^{Z}*She's on a diet.*
(^{Z} = Simultaneous utterances)

4.3 (Library information desk)

L = librarian

P = patron

L: *(a) May I help you?*

P: *(b) Yes. Can you tell me where I might find a numismatic catalog and if it can be taken from the library for a couple of days?*

L: *(c) Is numismatics coins?*

P: *(d) Yeah.*

L: *(e) Yes there- we do have some circulating books.*
    (f) It would be on the second floor
    (g) and the call number for the coin books is 737.

conv. closing

5. Analyse the situation elements of the following communicative situations / text types in terms of Fig. 89 in section 6.3.1:

5.1 Fax

5.2 E-mail

5.3 Television talk show

5.4 Messaging by mobile phone

9.7   Exercises relating to chapter 7

§1. Many people nowadays are exposed to media discourse more than they are to live real-time conversation. Discuss the sociolinguistic implications of this development, drawing from your own experience, and state your opinion.

§2. Describe the language situation of a place or region you are familiar with. Which languages / language varieties / dialects are used? To what extent are they mutually intelligible? Do the speakers know several dialects of one language or different languages? Is there a functional differentiation of different languages or language varieties?

3. Specify two to four linguistic minorities in Europe and characterise briefly their situation: In what region of which state does each minority live? Which language / dialect do the speakers use? What is the lingua franca? Is the language / dialect accepted as such by the state? Are there any language-related conflicts around this minority?

4. Enumerate some factors that influence a speaker's choice of a specific linguistic variety in a specific situation (e.g., regional dialect, nationwide colloquial speech, slang, standard, foreign language). Give an example.

5. Mention of some linguistic facts or examples of speech behaviour by which the oppression of women in language and communication is manifested. What suggestions have been made or could be made in order to change this situation? Are there any differences between different countries or different languages in this respect?

9.8   Exercises relating to chapter 8

1. Explain the most important differences between some animal 'language' of your choice and human language. Touch on aspects like discreteness, arbitrariness, and double articulation.
2. What do you think of the arguments adduced for or against the thesis that chimpanzees can learn human language?

10 Bibliographical section

In the first part of this section (10.1), we point out a few useful websites for linguists.

In part 10.2., we give you a number of recommendations concerning important linguistic literature, starting with basic reference works, introductions and the like (10.2.0), and then listing useful literature about the major subfields of linguistics, basically in the order in which they are dealt with in this book. In the case of textbooks, where up-to-dateness is most important, we have generally listed the latest edition that we could trace, ignoring later unrevised reprints. In the case of classics, we have tried to identify the first edition, occasionally quoting later editions where this seemed appropriate to us. In compiling this list, we have given special emphasis to those areas that, for lack of space, could not be covered adequately in this book. The list is not meant as a reading list to be ticked off one title after another, but as a resource for you to select literature from to browse through when you want to go more deeply into a certain topic area. What you will actually read in the end, will depend very much on availability of the literature, as well as on your own preferences.

In the third part (10.3), you find a list of all the literature mentioned in the book, in alphabetical order of the citation forms. In this part we usually quote the edition used by the authors in working for this book.

10.1   Some useful links for linguists

10.1.1 General sources

Linguist List site: http://www.linguistlist.org/
SIL Links: http://www.sil.org/linguistics/topical.html
Yahoo: linguistics and human languages:
http://dir.yahoo.com/Social_Science/linguistics_and_human_languages/
Linguistics Links on the Web: http://www.essex.ac.uk/linguistics/clmt/other_sites/

10.1.2 Grammar

Construction Grammar: http://www.constructiongrammar.org/
Berkeley Construction Grammar: http://www.icsi.berkeley.edu/~kay/bcg/ConGram.html
Lexical Functional Grammar (The Essex Web Site):
http://www.essex.ac.uk/linguistics/LFG/
Lexical Functional Grammar (The Stanford Web Site): http://www-lfg.stanford.edu/lfg/
Systemic-Functional Linguistics: http://www.wagsoft.com/Systemics/
Word Grammar: http://www.phon.ucl.ac.uk/home/dick/wg.htm

10.1.3 Phonetics and phonology

The International Phonetic Association (IPA): http://www2.arts.gla.ac.uk/IPA/ipa.html

10.1.4 Lexicology and semantics

FrameNet: http://www.icsi.berkeley.edu/~framenet/
WordNet: a lexical database for the English Language (Princeton University): http://wordnet.princeton.edu/
Semanticsarchive.net: http://semanticsarchive.net/

10.1.5 Sociolinguistics

William Labov: http://www.ling.upenn.edu/~wlabov/home.html
Sociolinguistics by Cindy Pattee, University of Oregon: http://logos.uoregon.edu/explore/socioling/

10.1.6 Psycholinguistics

The MRC Psycholinguistic Database: http://www.psych.rl.ac.uk/

10.1.7 Corpus linguistics

Bookmarks for Corpus Linguistics (David Lee): http://devoted.to/corpora/
British National Corpus: http://www.natcorp.ox.ac.uk/
Corpus Linguistics by Tony McEnery and Andrew Wilson: http://bowland-files.lancs.ac.uk/monkey/ihe/linguistics/contents.htm
Linguistic Data Consortium: http://www.ldc.upenn.edu/
University Centre for Computer Corpus Research on Language (Lancaster University): http://www.comp.lancs.ac.uk/computing/research/ucrel/
W3C Corpus Linguistics (The University of Essex): http://www.essex.ac.uk/linguistics/clmt/w3c/corpus_ling/content/introduction.html

10.2　Important basic literature

10.2.0 General literature

10.2.0.1 Bibliographies

Bibliographie Linguistischer Literatur = Bibliography of Linguistic Literature 1-. (Annual publication / on-line version: BLLDB). Frankfurt a.M.: Klostermann.
Kranz, Dieter. 1994. *Arbeitsmittel der Anglistik: ein Studienbuch*. (Grundlagen der Anglistik und Amerikanistik. 18). Berlin: Erich Schmidt.

10.2.0.2 General readers

Bolton, Whitney French; Crystal, David. 1987. *The English language*. (The new history of literature. 10). New York: Bedrick.

Newmeyer, Frederick J. (ed.) 1988. *Linguistics: the Cambridge survey*. 1-4. Cambridge: Cambridge Univ. Pr.

Tonkin, Humphrey; Reagan, Timothy (eds.) 2003. *Language in the twenty-first century: selected papers of the millennial conferences of the Center for Research and Documentation on World Language Problems, held at the University of Hartford and Yale University*. Amsterdam: Benjamins.

10.2.0.3 Reference works

Aarts, Bas; McMahon, April (eds.) 2006. *The handbook of English linguistics*. Oxford: Blackwell.

Ahrens, Rüdiger; Bald, Wolf-Dietrich; Hüllen, Werner (eds.) 1995. *Handbuch Englisch als Fremdsprache (HEF)*. Berlin: Erich Schmidt.

Aitchison, Jean. 2003. *A glossary of language and mind*. Edinburgh: Edinburg Univ. Pr.

Aronoff, Mark; Rees-Miller, Janie (eds.) 2001. *The handbook of linguistics*. Oxford: Blackwell.

Bright, William E. (ed.) 1992. *International encyclopedia of linguistics. 1-4*. New York: Oxford Univ. Pr.

Bussmann, Hadumod. ²1990. *Lexikon der Sprachwissenschaft*. Stuttgart: Kröner.

Bussmann, Hadumod. 1996. *Routledge dictionary of language and linguistics*. London: Routledge.

Campbell, George L. 1995. *Concise compendium of the world's languages*. London: Routledge.

Cobley, Paul (ed.) 2001. The Routledge companion to semiotics and linguistics. London: Routledge.

Collinge, Neville Edgar. 1990. *An encyclopaedia of language*. London: Routledge.

Comrie, Bernard (ed.). 1987. *The world's major languages*. London: Routledge

Crystal, David. 1992. An encyclopedic dictionary of language and languages. Oxford: Blackwell.

Crystal, David. ⁴1997. *A dictionary of linguistics and phonetics*. (Language library). Oxford: Blackwell.

Crystal, David. ²2003. *The Cambridge encyclopedia of the English language*. Cambridge: CUP.

Ellis, Nick C. 2008. *Handbook of cognitive linguistics and second language acquisition*. London: Routledge.

Finch, Geoffrey. 2000. *Linguistic terms and concepts*. Houndmills: Macmillan.

Gramley, Stephan; Pätzold, Kurt-Michael. ²2004. *A survey of Modern English*. London: Routledge.

Herbst, Thomas; Stoll, Rita; Westermayr, Rudolf. 1991. *Terminologie der Sprachbeschreibung: ein Lernwörterbuch für das Anglistikstudium*. Ismaning: Hueber.

Kürschner, Wilfried. 1989. *Grammatisches Kompendium: systematisches Verzeichnis grammatischer Grundbegriffe*. (UTB. 1526). Tübingen: Francke.

Malmkjær, Kirsten (ed.) ²2002. *The linguistics encyclopedia*. London: Routledge.

McArthur, Tom (ed.) 1992. *The Oxford Companion to the English language*. Oxford: Oxford Univ. Pr.

Peters, Pam. 2004. *The Cambridge guide to English usage*. Cambridge: Cambridge Univ. Pr.

Richards, Jack; Platt, John; Weber, Heidi. 1985. *Longman dictionary of applied linguistics*. Harlow, Essex: Longman.

Ruhlen, Merritt. 1991. *A guide to the world's languages: with a postscript on recent developments*. London: Arnold.

Trask, R.L. 1997. *A student's dictionary of language and linguistics*. London: Arnold.

Trask, R.L. 1998. *Key concepts in language and linguistics*. Amsterdam: Erasmus.

Trask, R.L. [2]1999. *Language: the basics*. London: Routledge.

Werlich, Egon. [8]1978. *Wörterbuch der Textinterpretation*. Dortmund: Lensing.

10.2.0.4 Basic theoretical literature / Classics of linguistics

Bühler, Karl. 1982 [[1]1934]. *Sprachtheorie: die Darstellungsfunktion der Sprache*. (UTB. 1159). Stuttgart: G. Fischer.

Chomsky, Noam. [10]1972 [[1]1957]. *Syntactic structures*. (Janua linguarum: series minor. 4). The Hague: Mouton.

Gabelentz, Georg von der. 1999 [[1]1891]. *Die Sprachwissenschaft: ihre Aufgaben, Methoden und bisherigen Ergebnisse*. (UTB. 2036). Tübingen: Francke.

Halliday, M.A.K. 2002. *On grammar*. (Collected Works. 1) / Webster, J. J. (ed.) London: Continuum.

Halliday, Michael. 2003. *On language and linguistics*. (Collected Works. 3) / Webster, J. J. (ed.) London: Continuum.

Hjelmslev, Louis. 1968. *Die Sprache: eine Einführung*. (Original title: *Sproget: en introduction*. [1963]). Darmstadt: Wiss. Buchges.

Hjelmslev, Louis. 1970. *Language: an introduction*. (Original title: *Sproget: en introduction*. [1963]). Madison: Univ. of Wisconsin Pr.

Humboldt, Wilhelm von. 1963 [[1]1825-1836]. *Werke 3*. Berlin: Rütter & Loering.

Humboldt, Wilhelm von. 1994 [[1]1825-1836]. *Über die Sprache*. / Trabant, Jürgen (ed.) (UTB. 1783). Tübingen: Francke

Jackendoff, Ray. 2007. *Language, consciousness, culture: essays on mental structure*. Cambridge, Mass: MIT Press.

Morris, Charles. 1946. *Signs, language and behavior*. New York: Braziller.

Peirce, Charles Sanders. 1998 [[1]1931-1958]. *Collected papers*. Cambridge, MA: Harvard Univ. Pr.

Saussure, Ferdinand de. 1916. *Cours de linguistique générale*. Lausanne: Payot.

Saussure, Ferdinand de. 1964. *Course in general linguistics*. London: Owen.

Saussure, Ferdinand de. 1967. *Grundfragen der allgemeinen Sprachwissenschaft*. Berlin: Mouton de Gruyter

Whorf, Benjamin Lee. 1956. *Language, thought and reality*: selected writings of Benjamin Lee Whorf. / Carroll, John B. (ed.) New York: Wiley

10.2.0.5 General introductions

Aitchison, Jean. [4]1995. *Linguistics: an introduction*. London: Hodder & Stoughton.

Akmajian, Adrian; Demers, Richard Arthur; Harnish, Robert M. [4]1995. *Linguistics: an introduction to language and communication*. Cambridge, Mass.: MIT Pr.

Blake, Barry J. 2008. *All about language: a guide*. Oxford: Oxford Univ. Pr..

Brinton, Laurel J. 2000. *The structure of Modern English: a linguistic introduction*. Amsterdam: Benjamins.

336

Burton, S.H. [2]1992. *Mastering English language*. Houndmills: Palgrave Macmillan.

Crystal, David. 1988. *The English language*. London: Penguin.

Ellis, Donald G. [2]1999. *From language to communication*. London: Erlbaum.

Finch, Geoffrey. 2002. *Word of mouth: a new introduction to language and communication*. Houndmills: Palgrave Macmillian.

Finch, Geoffrey. [2]2003. *How to study linguistics*. Houndmills: Macmillan.

Finegan, Edward. [3]1999. *Language: its structure and use*. Orlando: Harcourt Brace College Publishers.

Fromkin, Victoria; Rodman, Robert. [5]1993. *An introduction to language*. Fort Worth: Harcourt Brace College Publ.

Fromkin, Victoria A. 2000. *Linguistics: an introduction to linguistic theory*. Oxford: Blackwell.

Hudson, Grover. 2000. *Essential introductory linguistics*. Oxford: Blackwell.

Kortmann, Bernd. 2005. *English linguistics: essentials*. Berlin: Cornelsen.

Kuiper, Koenraad. [2]2003. *An introduction to English language: words, sounds and sentences*. Houndmills: Palgrave Macmillan.

Mair, Christian. 2008. *English linguistics: an introduction*. Tübingen: Narr.

Matthews, Peter. 2003. *Linguistics: a very short introduction*. Oxford: Oxford Univ. Pr.

Penhallurick, Rob. 2003. *Studying the English language*. Houndmills: Macmillan.

Plag, Ingo; Braun, Maria; Lappe, Sabine; Schramm, Mareile (eds.) 2007. *Introduction to English linguistics*. Berlin: Mouton de Gruyter.

Poole, Stuart C. 1999. *An introduction to linguistics*. Houndmills: Macmillan.

Thompson, Neil. 2003. Communication and language: a handbook of theory and practice. Houndmills: Palgrave Macmillan.

Todd, Loreto. 1989. *An introduction to linguistics*. Harlow: Longman.

Winkler, Elizabeth Grace. 2007. *Understanding language: A basic course in linguistics*. London: Continuum.

Yule, George. [2]1996. *The study of language*. Cambridge: Cambridge Univ. Pr.

10.2.0.6 Schools of linguistics

Chomsky, Noam. 1981. *Lectures on government and binding*. (Studies in Generative Grammar. 9). Dordrecht: Foris Publ.

Chomsky, Noam. 1995. *The minimalist program*. (Current studies in linguistics. 28). Cambridge, MA: MIT Press.

Chomsky, Noam. 2006. *Language and mind*. Cambridge: CUP.

Croft, William; Cruse, Alan D. 2004. *Cognitive linguistics*. Cambridge: Cambridge Univ. Pr.

Fillmore, Charles. 1987. *Fillmore's Case Grammar*. / Dirven, René; Radden, Günter (eds.) (Studies in descriptive linguistics. 16). Heidelberg: Groos.

Givón, Talmy. 1993. *English grammar: a function-based introduction*. 1-2. Amsterdam: Benjamins.

Haegeman, Liliane; Gueron, Jacqueline. 1999. *English grammar: a generative perspective*. (Blackwell textbooks in linguistics. 14). Oxford: Blackwell.

Halliday, Michael Alexander Kirkwood. [2]1994. *Introduction to functional grammar*. London: Arnold.

Harris, Roy. 1998. *Introduction to integrational linguistics.* Oxford: Pergamon / Elsevier.

Langacker, Roland W. 1987. *Foundations of cognitive grammar.* 1. Stanford, CA: Stanford Univ. Pr.

Langacker, Ronald W. 1991. *Foundations of cognitive grammar.* 2. Stanford, CA: Stanford Univ. Pr. üüü

Lee, David. 2001. *Cognitive linguistics: an introduction.* New York: Oxford Univ. Pr.

10.2.0.7 Exercises

Cowan, William; Rakusan, Jaromira. [2]1987. *Source book for linguistics.* (Benjamins paperbacks. 5). Philadelphia: Benjamins.

Demers, Richard A.; Farmer, Ann K. [3]1996. *A linguistics workbook.* Cambridge, MA: MIT Pr.

Parker, Frank. 1990. *Exercises in linguistics.* Boston, MA: College-Hill Pub.

Rutherford, William E. 1997. *A workbook in the structure of English: linguistic principles and language acquisition.* Oxford: Blackwell.

Wardhaugh, Ronald. 1972. *Workbook to accompany 'Introduction to linguistics'.* New York: McGraw-Hill.

10.2.1 Grammar

10.2.1.1 Grammars of Modern English

Biber, Douglas; Johansson, Stig; Leech, Geoffrey; Conrad, Susan; Finegan, Edward. 1999. *Longman grammar of spoken and written English.* Harlow: Longman.

Börjars, Kersti; Burridge, Kate. 2001. *Introducing English grammar.* London: Arnold.

Crystal, David. [5]1991. *Rediscover grammar.* Harlow, Essex: Longman.

Dirven, René (ed.) 1989. *A user's grammar of English: word, sentence, text, interaction.* 1-4. (Duisburger Arbeiten zur Sprach- und Kulturwissenschaft. 4). Frankfurt am Main: Lang.

Huddleston, Rodney; Pullum, Geoffrey K. 2005. *A student's introduction to English grammar.* Cambridge: Cambridge Univ. Pr.

Jespersen, Otto H. 1909-1931. *A modern English grammar: on historical principles.* 1-7 Heidelberg: Winter.

Quirk, Randolph; Greenbaum, Sidney; Leech, Geoffrey; Svartvik, Jan. [12]1994. *A comprehensive grammar of the English language.* London: Longman.

10.2.1.2 Syntax

Aarts, Bas. [3]2008.. *English syntax and argumentation.* Houndmills: Macmillan.

Anderson, John M. 1997. *A notional theory of syntactic categories.* (Cambridge studies in linguistics. 82). Cambridge: Cambridge Univ. Pr.

Baker, Mark C. 2008. *The syntax of agreement and concord.* Cambridge: Cambridge Univ. Pr..

Brown, Keith; Miller, Jim (eds.) 1996. *Concise encyclopedia of syntactic theories.* Oxford: Pergamon.

Burton-Roberts, Noel. [2]1997. *Analysing sentences: an introduction to English syntax.* London; New York: Longman.

Carnie, Andrew. 2007. *Constituent structure.* Oxford: OUP.

Chomsky, Noam. [10]1972 [[1]1957]. *Syntactic structures.* (Janua linguarum: series minor. 4). The Hague: Mouton.

Cowper, Elizabeth A. 1992. *A concise introduction to syntactic theory.* Chicago: Univ. of Chicago Pr.

Croft, William. 2001. Radical construction grammar: syntactic theory in typological perspective. Oxford: Oxford Univ. Pr.

Fillmore, Charles et al. 1988. "Regularity and idiomaticity in grammatical constructions: the case of *let alone.*" *Language* 64, 501-538.

Foley, William A.; Van Valin, Robert D. 1984. *Functional syntax and universal grammar.* (Cambridge studies in linguistics. 38). Cambridge: Cambridge Univ. Pr.

Freidein, Robert. 2007. *Generative grammar: theory and its history.* London: Routledge.

Givón, Talmy. 1984. Syntax: a functional-typological introduction. 1. Amsterdam: Benjamins.

Givón, Talmy. 1990. Syntax: a functional-typological introduction. 2. Amsterdam: Benjamins.

Goldberg, Adele E. 1995. Constructions: a construction grammar approach to argument structure. Chicago: Univ. of Chicago Pr.

Goldberg, Adele E. 2003. "Constructions: a new theoretical approach to language." *Trends in cognitive sciences* 7, 219-224.

Goldberg, Adele E. 2006. *Constructions at work: the nature of generalization in language.* Oxford [u.a.] : Oxford Univ. Press.

Kay, Paul; Fillmore, Charles J. 1999. "Grammatical constructions and linguistic generalizations: the *What's X doing Y?* construction." *Language* 75, 1-33.

Langacker, Ronald. 2008. *Cognitive grammar: an introduction.* Oxford: Oxford Univ. Pr..

McCawley, James D. 1991. *The syntactic phenomena of English.* 1-2. Chicago: Univ. of Chicago Pr.

Östman, Jan-Ola (ed.) 2008. *Construction Grammars: cognitive grounding and theoretical extensions.* Amsterdam: John Benjamins.

Radden, Günter; Dirven, René. 2007. *Cognitive English grammar.* Amsterdam: John Benjamins.

Radford, Andrew. 2004. *English syntax: an introduction.* Cambridge: Cambridge Univ. Pr.

Taylor, John. 2002. *Cognitive grammar.* Oxford: Oxford Univ. Pr.

Van Valin, Robert. 2001. *An introduction to syntax.* Cambridge: Cambridge Univ. Pr.

10.2.1.3 Morphology

10.2.1.3.1 Theory. General

Aronoff, Mark. 1996. *Morphology now.* New York: SUNY Press.

Bauer, Laurie. 1988. *Introducing linguistic morphology.* Edinburgh: Edinburgh Univ. Pr.

Bubenik, Vit. 1999. *An introduction to the study of morphology.* (LINCOM coursebooks in linguistics. 7). München: LINCOM.

Carstairs-McCarthy, Andrew. 2002. An introduction to English morphology: words and their structure. Edinburgh: Edinburgh Univ. Pr.

Friederich, Wolf. 1976. *Englische Morphologie.* (Hueber Hochschulreihe. 39). München: Hueber.

Haspelmath, Martin. 2002. *Understanding morphology.* London: Arnold

Matthews, Peter H. [2]1991. *Morphology.* Cambridge: Cambridge Univ. Pr.

Plank, Frans. 1981. *Morphologische (Ir-)Regularitäten: Aspekte einer Wortstrukturtheorie.* (Studien zur deutschen Grammatik. 13). Tübingen: Narr.

Welte, Werner. [2]1996. *Englische Morphologie und Wortbildung: ein Arbeitsbuch mit umfassender Bibliographie.* (Hamburger englische Linguistik. Praktika. 1). Frankfurt am Main: Lang.

10.2.1.3.2 Word-formation

Bauer, Laurie. 1983. *English word-formation.* (Cambridge textbooks in linguistics). Cambridge: Cambridge Univ. Pr.

Harley, Heidi. 2006. *English words: a linguistic introduction.* Oxford: Blackwell.

Lieber, Rochelle. 1992. Deconstructing morphology: word formation in syntactic theory. Chicago: Univ. of Chicago Pr.

Marchand, Hans. [[1]1960] [2]1969. *The categories and types of present-day English word-formation: a synchronic-diachronic approach.* München: Beck.

Plag, Ingo. 2003. *Word-formation in English.* Cambridge: Cambridge Univ. Pr.

Shopen, Timothy (ed.) 1985. *Language typology and syntactic description.* 3. Cambridge: Cambridge Univ. Pr.

Stekauer, Pavol. 2000. *English word formation: a history of research (1960-1995).* Tübingen: Narr.

10.2.1.4 Typology and universals

Comrie, Bernard. [2]1989. *Language universals and linguistic typology: syntax and morphology.* Oxford: Blackwell.

Croft, William. 1990. *Typology and universals.* Cambridge: Cambridge Univ. Pr.

Foley, William A. 2000. *Anthropological linguistics: an introduction.* (Language in society. 24). Oxford: Blackwell.

Greenberg, Joseph H. 1974. *Language typology: a historical and analytic overview.* (Janua linguarum. Series minor. 184). The Hague: Mouton.

Hawkins, John A. 1986. *A comparative typology of English and German: unifying the contrasts.* London: Croom Helm.

Shopen, Timothy (ed.) 1985. *Language typology and syntactic description.* 1-3. Cambridge: Cambridge Univ. Pr.

10.2.2 Phonetics and phonology. Graphemics

Arnold, Roland; Hansen, Klaus. [8]1992. *Englische Phonetik.* Leipzig: Langenscheidt.

Bolinger, Dwight. 1986. *Intonation and its parts: melody in spoken English.* Stanford: Stanford Univ. Pr.

Carr, Philip. 1999. *English phonetics and phonology: an introduction.* Oxford: Blackwell.

Chomsky, Noam; Halle, Morris. 1991. *The sound pattern of English.* Cambridge, MA: MIT Pr.

340

Clark, John; Yallop, Colin. [2]1995. *An introduction to phonetics and phonology*. (Blackwell textbooks in linguistics. 9). Oxford: Blackwell.

Coulmas, Florian. 1994. *The writing systems of the world*. (Aristotelian society series. 5). Oxford: Blackwell.

de Lacey, Paul. 2007. *The Cambridge handbook of phonology*. Cambridge: Cambridge Univ. Pr..

Dretzke, Burkhard. 1998. *Modern British and American pronunciation: a basic textbook*. (UTB. 2053). Paderborn: Schöningh.

Fudge, Erik. 1984. *English word-stress*. London: Allen & Unwin.

Giegerich, Heinz J. 1992. *English phonology: an introduction*. Cambridge: Cambridge Univ. Pr.

Gimson, Alfred Charles. [5]1994. *An introduction to the pronunciation of English*. London: Arnold.

Gussenhoven, Carlos; Jacobs, Haike. 1998. *Understanding Phonology*. London: Arnold.

Hale, Mark; Reiss, Charles. 2008. *The phonological enterprise*. Oxford: Oxford Univ. Pr..

International Phonetic Association. 1984. *Principles of the International Phonetic Association*. London: IPA.

International Phonetic Association. 1999. *Handbook of the International Phonetic Association: a guide to the use of the international phonetic alphabet*. Cambridge: Cambridge Univ. Pr.

Sampson, Geoffrey. 1985. *Writing systems: a linguistic introduction*. London: Hutchinson.

Scherer, Günther; Wollmann, Alfred. [3]1986. *Englische Phonetik und Phonologie*. (Grundlagen der Anglistik und Amerikanistik. 6). Berlin: Erich Schmidt.

Siegrist, Ottmar K. 2003. *Wörterbuch der englischen Falschaussprachen durch Deutschsprachige*. Heidelberg: Universitätsverl. Winter.

Trubetzkoy, Nikolai S. [3]1971. [[1]1936]. *Grundzüge der Phonologie*. Göttingen: Vandenhoeck & Ruprecht.

Wells, John C. 1990. *Longman pronunciation dictionary*. London: Longman.

10.2.3 The history of English

10.2.3.0 Introductions to historical linguistics

Aitchison, Jean. [2]1994. *Language change: progress or decay?* Cambridge: Cambridge Univ. Pr.

Crowley, Terry. [3]1997. *An introduction to historical linguistics*. Oxford: Oxford Univ. Pr.

Joseph, Brian D; Janda, Richard D. 2003. *The handbook of historical linguistics*. Oxford: Blackwell.

Lass, Roger. 1997. *Historical linguistics and language change*. Cambridge: Cambridge Univ. Pr.

Lehmann, Winfred P. [3]1992. *Historical linguistics: An introduction*. London / New York: Routledge.

Moessner, Lilo. 2003. *Diachronic English linguistics: an introduction*. (Narr Studienbücher). Tübingen: Narr.

Trask, Robert L. 1996. *Historical linguistics*. London: Arnold.

10.2.3.1 History of the English language

10.2.3.1.0 Language histories. Historical grammars. Historical and etymological
    dictionaries

Baugh, Albert C.; Cable, Thomas. [5]2002. *A history of the English language*. London:
Routledge & Kegan Paul.

Berndt, Rolf. 1982. *A history of the English language*. Leipzig. VEB Verlag Enzyklopä-
die

Brinton, Laurel J.; Arnovick, Leslie K. 2006. *The English language: a linguistic history*.
Oxford: OUP.

Fisiak, Jacek. 1993. *An outline history of English*. Poznań: Kantor Wydawniczy Saww.

Freeborn, Dennis. 1992. *From Old English to Standard English*. Basingstoke: Macmillan
Press

Görlach, Manfred. 1997. *The linguistic history of English*. London: Macmillan.

Hock, Hans Henrich. [2]1991. *Principles of historical linguistics*. Berlin: Mouton de
Gruyter.

Hogg, Richard et al. (eds.). 1992-1999. *The Cambridge history of the English language:
Vols. 1-4*. Cambridge: Cambridge Univ. Pr.

Jespersen, Otto. 1976. *Growth and structure of the English language*. Oxford: Blackwell

Jucker, Andreas H. 2000. *History of English and English historical linguistics*. Stuttgart,
etc. Klett.

Knowles, Gerry. 1997. *A cultural history of the English language*. London: Arnold.

Mugglestone, Lynda. 2006. *The Oxford history of English*. Oxford: OUP.

Strang, Barbara M. H. [2]1974. *A history of English*. London: Methuen.

Traugott, Elizabeth Closs. 1972. *A history of English syntax*. New York: Holt, Rinehart
and Winston.

Jespersen, Otto H. 1909-1931. *A modern English grammar: on historical principles*. 1-7
Heidelberg: Winter.

Luick, Karl. 1914-1940. *Historische Grammatik der englischen Sprache*. 2 Bde. Stuttgart: Tauchnitz.

Klein, Ernest. 1971. *A comprehensive etymological dictionary of the English language*.
Amsterdam, etc.: Elsevier.

10.2.3.1.1 Old English

Bosworth, Joseph; Northcote Toller, T. 1898. *An Anglo-Saxon dictionary*. London: Oxford Univ. Pr. Supplement by T. Northcote Toller with revised and enlarged addenda by
Alistair Campbell (Oxford Univ. Pr. 1921).

Hall, John R. Clark; Meritt, Herbert D. 1962. *A concise Anglo-Saxon dictionary*. Cambridge: Cambridge Univ. Pr.

Hogg, Richard M. (ed.). 1992. *The Cambridge history of the English language. 1: The
beginnings to 1066*. Cambridge: Cambridge Univ. Pr.

Campbell, A. 1959. *Old English grammar*. Oxford: Clarendon.

Lass, Roger. 1994. *Old English:. a historical linguistic companion*. Cambridge: Cambridge Univ. Pr.

Smith, Jeremy J. 1999. *Essentials of early English*. London: Routledge.

10.2.3.1.2 Middle English

Kurath, Hans; Kuhn, Sherman M. 1954-. *Middle English dictionary*. Ann Arbor: University of Michigan Press.

Stratmann, Francis Henry. 1891. *A Middle-English dictionary*. Rearranged, revised and enlarged by Henry Bradley. Oxford: Oxford Univ. Pr..

Blake, Norman (Hg.). 1992. *The Cambridge history of the English language. 2: 1066-1476*. Cambridge: Cambridge Univ. Pr.

Fisiak, Jacek. 1968. A *short grammar of Middle English*. London: Oxford Univ. Pr.

Markus, Manfred. 1990. *Mittelenglisches Studienbuch*. Tübingen: Francke.

Moessner, Lilo. 1989. *Early Middle English syntax*. Tübingen: Niemeyer.

Moessner, Lilo; Schaefer, Ursula. ²1987. *Proseminar Mittelenglisch*. Tübingen: Francke.

Mossé, Fernand. 1952. A *handbook of Middle English*. Transl. by James A. Walker. Baltimore: John Hopkins Press.

10.2.3.1.3 Early and Late Modern English

Algeo, John (Hg.). 2001. *The Cambridge history of the English language. 6: English in North America*. Cambridge: Cambridge Univ. Pr..

Barber, Charles. ²1997. *Early Modern English*. Edinburgh: Edinburgh University Press.

Burchfield, Robert. (Hg.). 1994. *The Cambridge history of the English language. 5: English in Britain and overseas: origins and development*. Cambridge: Cambridge Univ. Pr..

Görlach, Manfred. 1991. *Introduction to Early Modern English*. Cambridge: Cambridge Univ. Pr.

Lass, Roger (Hg.). 1999. *The Cambridge history of the English language. 3: 1476-1776*. Cambridge: Cambridge Univ. Pr..

Nevalainen, Terry. 2007. *Introduction to Early Modern English*. Oxford: OUP.

Romaine, Suzanne (Hg.). 1998. *The Cambridge history of the English language. 4: 1776-1997*. Cambridge: Cambridge Univ. Pr..

10.2.3.2 Language change

10.2.3.2.1 General

Heringer, Hans Jürgen. 1985. "Not by nature nor by intention: the normative power of linguistic signs." In: Ballmer, Thomas T. (ed.) 1985. *Linguistic dynamics: discourses, procedures and evolution*. (Research in text theory. 9). Berlin: De Gruyter, 251-275.

Keller, Rudi. 1990.[²1994]. *Sprachwandel: von der unsichtbaren Hand in der Sprache*. (UTB. 1567). Tübingen: Francke

Labov, William. 1994. *Principles of linguistic change. 1*: Internal factors. (Language in society. 20). Oxford: Blackwell.

Labov, William. 2001. *Principles of linguistic change. 2*: Social factors. (Language in society. 29). Oxford: Blackwell.

Labov, William. 2008. *Principles of linguistic change. 3*: Cognitive factors. Oxford: Blackwell.

Roberts, Ian G. 2006. *Diachronic syntax*. Oxford: OUP.

ances and, within certain limits, even new words (→ 1.3.4, 1.3.5) whenever they want to. A conscious use of gestures and facial expressions adds to this.

This is why we say that human language is characterised by **creativity** or productivity (*Kreativität / Produktivität*) (→ Box 15). By following (subconsciously or consciously) acquired grammatical rules, we can utter a sentence or form a word that has never been said before.

Thus, unlike most animals, we are not forced to choose from a limited and restricted repertoire of utterances and we can usefully employ it for any purpose. In this context, it should be mentioned once more that **recursiveness** (*Rekursivität*) is an extremely useful feature of human language.

All we need for recursion is, e.g., the ability to embed a noun phrase within another noun phrase (→ 1.2.2.3) or a clause within a clause (→ 1.2.1.3) repeatedly, as illustrated once again in the following example (PINKER 1995, 368):

He knows that she thinks that he is flirting with Mary.

8.5   Can animals learn human language?

Referring to the anatomical condition of our vocal tract, we can explain why other primates are not able to learn to speak. Nevertheless, several experiments have been made to teach individual chimpanzees special communication systems similar to human language. Chimpanzees were considered to be able to acquire language because neuroanatomists had discovered areas in monkey brains that correspond in location, input-output cabling, and cellular composition to the human language areas. Beginning in the late 1960s, many scientists have been captivated by the prospect of teaching language to animals. Indeed, several famous projects claimed to have succeeded in doing so. This is the reason why a lot of attention was focussed on experiments like those conducted with the chimpanzee Viki, who was given arduous training in speech. She was forced to use her vocal apparatus, which is, in fact, not designed for speech and which she could not voluntarily control. Finally, Viki learned to make three utterances that charitable listeners could identify as *mama, papa* and *cup*. When she got excited, however, she would confuse these words. Strictly speaking, she could only respond to stereotyped formulae such as *Kiss me* and *Bring me the dog*, but was completely at a loss when faced with a new combination such as *Kiss the dog*.

Another ambitious project was conducted with several chimps, among them a female chimpanzee called Washoe, who, after many years of intensive training, was said to have a command of several hundred signs of American Sign Language (→ www.narr-studienbuecher.de on psycholinguistics), and also seemed to have learnt a kind of syntactic system.

If we consider this seemingly astonishing success a little more closely, however, we might become more sceptical with regard to such projects. To begin

10.2.3.2.2 Grammaticalisation

Heine, Bernd; Claudi, Ulrike; Hünnemeyer, Friederike. 1991. *Grammaticalization: a conceptual framework*. Chicago: Chicago Univ. Pr.

Heine, Bernd; Kuteva, Tania. 2007. *Genesis of grammar: a reconstruction*. Oxford: Oxford Univ. Pr..

Hopper, Paul J.; Traugott, Elizabeth Closs. 1993. *Grammaticalization*. (Cambridge textbooks in linguistics). Cambridge: Cambridge Univ. Pr.

Lehmann, Christian. 1995. *Thoughts on grammaticalization*. (Lincom studies in theoretical linguistics. 1). München: Lincom Europa.

Traugott, Elizabeth Closs; Heine, Bernd (eds.) 1991. *Approaches to grammaticalization. 1-2*. (Typological studies in language. 19). Amsterdam: Benjamins.

10.2.4   Lexicology and semantics

10.2.4.0 Dictionaries. Lexicography

Atkins, Sue; Rundell, Michael. 2008. *Oxford Guide to Practical Lexicography*. Oxford: Oxford Univ. Pr..

Collins Cobuild English Dictionary for Advanced Learners. [3]2001. Sinclair, John (ed.) London: Harpercollins.

Longman Language Activator. [2]2002. Harlow: Longman.

Oxford English Dictionary (OED) (on-line version: www.oed.com)

Partridge, Eric. 1978. *A dictionary of clichés*. London: Routledge.

Partridge, Eric. 1991. *Concise dictionary of slang and unconventional English* / Beale, Paul (ed.) London: Routledge.

Partridge, Eric. 1992. *A dictionary of catch phrases: American and British, from the sixteenth century to the present day*. / Beale, Paul (ed.) London: Routledge.

Random House Webster's College Dictionary. Updated annually. New York: Random House Reference

Webster 1986. *Webster's third new international dictionary of the English language* / Babcock, Philip (ed.). Springfield MA: Merriam Webster.

10.2.4.1 Introductions to semantics

Cruse, Alan. 2000. *Meaning in language: an introduction to semantics and pragmatics*. Oxford: Oxford Univ. Pr.

Goddard, Cliff. 1998. *Semantic analysis: a practical introduction*. (Oxford textbooks in linguistics). Oxford: Oxford Univ. Pr.

Hofmann, Thomas R. 1993. *Realms of meaning: an introduction to semantics*. Harlow; Essex: Longman.

Jackson, Howard. 1988. *Words and their meaning*. (Learning about language). London: Longman.

Jeffries, Lesley. 1998. *Meaning in English: an introduction to language study*. Houndmills: Macmillan.

Kreidler, Charles W. 1998. *Introducing English semantics*. London: Routledge.

Lappin, Shalom (ed.) 1997. *The handbook of contemporary semantic theory*. Oxford: Blackwell.

Leech, Geoffrey Neil. [2]1983. *Semantics*. Harmondsworth: Penguin.

Saeed, John I. 1997. *Semantics*. Oxford: Blackwell.

Stechow, Arnim von; Wunderlich, Dieter (eds.) 1991. *Semantik = Semantics: Ein internationales Handbuch der zeitgenössischen Forschung*. (Handbücher zur Sprach- und Kulturwissenschaft. 6). Berlin: De Gruyter.

10.2.4.2 Structural semantics

Lehrer, Adrienne. 1974. *Semantic fields and lexical structure*. Amsterdam: North-Holland.

Lehrer, Adrienne; Kittay, Eva Feder (eds.) 1992. *Frames, fields and contrasts: new essays in semantic and lexical organization*. Hillsdale, NJ: Lawrence Erlbaum.

Leisi, Ernst. [2]1985. [[1]1973]. *Praxis der englischen Semantik*. (Sprachwissenschaftliche Studienbücher: Abt. 1). Heidelberg: Winter.

Lipka, Leonhard. [2]1992. *An outline of English lexicology: lexical structure, word semantics, and word-formation*. (Forschung & Studium Anglistik. 3). Tübingen: Niemeyer.

Lutzeier, Peter Rolf (ed.) 1993. *Studien zur Wortfeldtheorie = Studies in lexical field theory*. (Linguistische Arbeiten. 288). Tübingen: Niemeyer.

Lyons, John. 1977. *Semantics*. 1-2. Cambridge: Cambridge Univ. Pr.

Lyons, John. 1995. *Linguistic semantics: an introduction*. Cambridge: Cambridge Univ. Pr.

10.2.4.3 Cognitive semantics

Fillmore, Charles J. 1975. "An alternative to checklist theories of meaning." *Proceedings of the Annual Meeting of the Berkeley Linguistics Society* 1, 123-131.

Fillmore, Charles J.. 1977. "Scenes-and-frames semantics." In: Zampolli, Antonio (ed.) 1977. *Linguistic structures processing*. (Fundamental studies in computer science. 5). Amsterdam: North-Holland, 55-81.

Fillmore, Charles J. 1982. "Frame semantics." In: Linguistic Society of Korea (ed.) 1982. *Linguistics in the morning calm: selected papers from SICOL-1981*. Seoul: Hanshin, 111-137.

Fillmore, Charles J. 1985. "Frames and the semantics of understanding." *Quaderni di semantica* 6, 222-254.

Fillmore, Charles; Atkins, Beryl. 1992. "Toward a frame-based lexicon: the semantics of RISK and its neighbors." In: Lehrer, A.; Kittay, E. F. (eds.) 1992. *Frames, fields and contrasts: new essays in semantic and lexical organization*. Hillsdale, NJ: Lawrence Erlbaum, 75-102

Gärdenfors, Peter. 1999. "Some tenets of cognitive semantics." In: Allwood, J; Gärdenfors, P. (eds.) 1999. *Cognitive semantics: meaning and cognition*. Amsterdam: Benjamins, 19-37

Johnson, Mark. 1987. *The body in the mind: the bodily basis of meaning, imagination, and reason*. Chicago: Univ. of Chicago Pr.

Lakoff, George. 1987. *Women, fire and dangerous things: what categories reveal about mind*. Chicago: Univ. of Chicago Pr.

Langacker, R. 2002. *Concept, image and symbol: the cognitive basis of grammar*. Berlin / New York: Mouton de Gruyter.

Petruck, M. R. L. 1996. "Frame Semantics". In: Verschueren, J.; Östman, J.-O., Bloom-maert, J.; Bulcaen, C. (eds.) 1996. *Handbook of pragmatics.* Philadelphia: John Benjamins, 1-13.

Schank, Roger C.; Abelson, Roger P. 1977. *Scripts, plans, goals and understanding.* Hillsdale, N.Y.: Lawrence Erlbaum

Schwarz, Monika; Chur, Jeannette. ²1996. *Semantik: ein Arbeitsbuch.* Tübingen: Narr.

10.2.4.4 Formal semantics

Cann, Ronnie. 1993. *Formal semantics: an introduction.* Cambridge: Cambridge Univ. Pr.

10.2.5 Pragmatics

10.2.5.0 Theory / Introductions

Ariel, Mira. 2008. *Pragmatics and grammar.* Cambridge: CUP.

Brown, Penelope; Levinson, Stephen. 1988. *Politeness: some universals of language usage.* (Studies in interactional sociolinguistics. 4). Cambridge: Cambridge Univ. Pr.

Cutting, Joan. ²2008. *Pragmatics and discourse: a resource book for students.* London: Routledge.

Davis, Stephen (ed.) 1991. *Pragmatics: a reader.* New York: Oxford Univ. Pr.

Huang, Yan. 2006. *Pragmatics.* Oxford: OUP.

Horn, Laurence R.; Ward, Gregory (eds.) 2004. *The handbook of pragmatics.* Oxford: Blackwell.

Klein, Wolfgang. 1983. "Vom Glück des Mißverstehens und der Trostlosigkeit der idealen Kommunikationsgemeinschaft." *Zeitschrift für Literaturwissenschaft und Linguistik 50,* 128-140.

Leech, Geoffrey Neil. 1983. *Principles of pragmatics.* (Longman linguistics library. 30). London: Longman.

Levinson, Stephen C. 1983. *Pragmatics.* Cambridge: Cambridge Univ. Pr.

Mey, Jacob L. 1993. *Pragmatics: an introduction.* Oxford: Blackwell.

Östman, Jan-Ola; Verschueren, Jef. 2007. *Handbook of pragmatics: 2007 installment.* Amsterdam: John Benjamins.

Verschueren, Jef. 1999. *Understanding pragmatics.* London: Arnold.

10.2.5.1 Speech act theory

Austin, John Langshaw. 1962. *How to do things with words.* (The William James lectures. 1955). Oxford: Clarendon Pr.

Austin, John Langshaw. 1972. *Theorie der Sprechakte.* (Universal-Bibliothek. 9396-98). Stuttgart: Reclam.

Hindelang, Götz. ²1994. *Einführung in die Sprechakttheorie.* (Germanistische Arbeitshefte. 27). Tübingen: Niemeyer.

Schiffrin, Deborah. 1994. "Speech act theory." In: Schiffrin, Deborah. 1994. *Approaches to discourse.* (Blackwell textbooks in linguistics. 8). Oxford: Blackwell, 49-96.

Searle, John Rogers. 1969. *Speech acts: an essay in the philosophy of language.* Cambridge: Cambridge Univ. Pr.

346

Searle, John Rogers. 1971. "What is a speech act?" In: Rosenburg, Jay F.; Travis, Chares (eds.) 1971. *Readings in the philosophy of language*. Englewood Cliffs: Prentice Hall, 614-628.

Searle, John Rogers. 1975. "A taxonomy of illocutionary acts." In: Gunderson, K. (ed.) 1975. *Language, mind and knowledge*. (Minnesota studies in the philosophy of science. 7). Minneapolis: Univ. of Minnesota Pr., 344-369.

Searle, John Rogers. 1975. "Indirect speech acts." *Syntax and semantics* 3, 59-82.

Searle, John Rogers. 1979. *Expression and meaning: studies in the theory of speech acts*. Cambridge: Cambridge Univ. Pr.

10.2.5.2 Conversational maxims

Grice, Herbert Paul. 1975. "Logic and conversation." In: Cole, P; Morgan, J.L. eds. 1975. *Syntax and semantics* 3. New York: Academic Pr., 41-58.

Levinson, Stephen C. 2000. *Presumptive meanings: the theory of generalized conversational implicatures*. Cambridge, MA: MIT Pr.

Schiffrin, Deborah. 1994. "Pragmatics." In: Schiffrin, Deborah. 1994. *Approaches to discourse*. (Blackwell textbooks in linguistics. 8). Oxford: Blackwell, 190-231.

10.2.5.3 Relevance theory

Blakemore, Diane. 1992. *Understanding utterances: an introduction to pragmatics*. Oxford: Blackwell.

Sperber, Dan; Wilson, Deirdre. [2]1995. ([1]1986). *Relevance: communication and cognition*. Oxford: Blackwell.

10.2.6   Textlinguistics. Conversation analysis. Discourse analysis

10.2.6.1 Textlinguistics

Bhatia, Vijay K; Flowerdew, John; Jones, Rodney H. (eds.) 2008. *Advances in discourse studies*. London: Routledge.

Brown, Gillian; Yule, George. 1983. *Discourse analysis*. Cambridge: Cambridge Univ. Pr.

Chimombo, Moira; Roseberry, Robert L. 1998. *The power of discourse: an introduction to discourse analysis*. London: Erlbaum.

De Beaugrande, Robert Alain. [7]1994. *Introduction to textlinguistics*. London: Longman.

De Beaugrande, Robert; Dressler, Wolfgang Ullrich. 1981. *Einführung in die Textlinguistik*. (Konzepte der Sprach- und Literaturwissenschaft. 28). Tübingen: Niemeyer.

Gee, James Paul. 1999. *An introduction to discourse analysis: theory and method*. London: Routledge.

Harweg, Roland. [2]1979 ([1]1968). *Pronomina und Textkonstitution*. (Poetica Beih. 2). München: Fink.

Heinemann, Wolfgang; Viehweger, Dieter. 1991. *Textlinguistik: eine Einführung*. (Reihe Germanistische Linguistik. 115). Tübingen: Niemeyer.

Hoey, Michael. 2001. *Textual interaction: an introduction to written discourse analysis*. London: Routledge.

Van Dijk, Teun A. 1980. *Textwissenschaft: eine interdisziplinäre Einführung*. (dtv Wissenschaft. 4364). München: dtv

10.2.6.2 Analysis of conversation:

Blakemore, Diane. 1988. "The organization of discourse". In: Newmeyer, Frederick (ed.) 1988. *Linguistics: the Cambridge Survey*. 4. Cambridge: Cambridge Univ. Pr., 229-250.

Brinker, Klaus et al. (eds.) 2000. *Text- und Gesprächslinguistik: ein internationales Handbuch zeitgenössischer Forschung*. Berlin: Mouton de Gruyter.

Coulmas, Florian ed. 1981. *Conversational routine: explorations in standardized communication situations and prepatterned speech*. (Janua linguarum. Series maior. 96; Rasmus Rask studies in pragmatic linguistics. 2). The Hague: Mouton.

Liddicoat, Anthony J. 2006. *An introduction to conversation analysis*. London: Continuum.

Martin, J.R.; Rose, David. ^{2}2007. *Working with discourse: meaning beyond the clause*. London: Continuum.

Paltridge, Brian. 2006. *Discourse analysis: an introduction*. London: Continuum.

Schiffrin, Deborah. 1994. *Approaches to discourse*. (Blackwell textbooks in linguistics. 8). Oxford: Blackwell.

Stenström, Anna-Brita. 1994. *An introduction to spoken interaction*. (Learning about language). London; New York: Longman.

Van Dijk, Teun A. 1997. *Discourse studies: a multidisciplinary introduction. 1-2*. London: Sage.

Tannen, Deborah. 2007. *Talking voices: repetition, dialogue, and imagery in conversational discourse*. Cambridge: CUP.

Wardhaugh, Ronald. 1985. *How conversation works*. Oxford: Basil Blackwell.

10.2.6.3 Discourse in the technical age

10.2.6.3.1 Orality / literacy

Barton, David. 1996. *Literacy: an introduction to the ecology of written language*. Oxford: Blackwell.

Biber, Douglas. 1988. *Variation across speech and writing*. Cambridge: Cambridge Univ. Pr.

Chafe, Wallace L. 1983. "Integration and involvement in spoken and written language." In: Borbé, Tasso (ed.) 1983. *Semiotics unfolding: 2*. (Approaches to semiotics. 68). Berlin: Mouton, 1095-1102.

Chafe, Wallace L.; Danielewicz, Jane. 1987. "Properties of spoken and written language." In: Horowitz, Rosalind; Samuels, S.J. (eds.) *Comprehending oral and written language*. New York: Academic Pr., 83-113.

Cornbleet, Sandra; Carter, Ronald. 2001. *The language of speech and writing*. London: Routledge.

Downing, Pamela; Lima, Susan D.; Noonan, Michael (eds.) 1992. *The linguistics of literacy*. (Typological studies in language. 21). Amsterdam: Benjamins.

Grabe, William. 1996. "Written language: English." In: Hartmut, Günther; Otto, Ludwig (eds.) 1996. *Schrift und Schriftlichkeit. Writing and its use. Ein interdisziplinäres Handbuch internationaler Forschung. 2*. (Handbücher zur Sprach- und Kommunikationswissenschaft. 10). Berlin: De Gruyter, 1495-1499.

Günther, Hartmut; Ludwig, Otto (eds.) 1994-1996. Schrift und Schriftlichkeit. Writing and its use. Ein interdisziplinäres Handbuch internationaler Forschung. 1-2. (Handbücher zur Sprach- und Kommunikationswissenschaft. 10). Berlin: De Gruyter.

Olson, David R.; Torrance, Nancy; Hildyard, Angela (eds.) 1985. Literacy, language, and learning: the nature and consequences of reading and writing. Cambridge: Cambridge Univ. Pr.

Tannen, Deborah. 1982. "Oral and literate strategies in spoken and written narratives." Language, 581-21.

10.2.6.3.2 Media language

Bell, Allan. 1993. *The language of news media*. (Language in society. 17). Oxford: Blackwell.

Bell, Allan; Garrett, Peter (eds.) 1998. *Approaches to media discourse*. Oxford: Blackwell.

Burton, Graeme. 1990. More than meets the eye: an introduction to media studies. London: Arnold.

Cook, Guy. 1992. *The discourse of advertising*. London: Routledge.

Fowler, Roger. 1991. Language in the news: discourse and ideology in the press. London: Routledge.

Höflich, Joachim R. 1997. "Technisch vermittelten Kommunikation." *Zeitschrift für Semiotik* 19,203-327.

Leitner, Gerhard. 1996. "The sociolinguistics of communication media." In: Coulmas, Florian (ed.) 1996. *The handbook of sociolinguistics*. (Blackwell handbooks in linguistics). Oxford: Blackwell,187-204.

Ludes, Peter. 1998. Einführung in die Medienwissenschaft: Entwicklungen und Theorien. Berlin: Erich Schmidt Verlag.

Nöth, Winfried (ed.) 1997. *Semiotics of the media: state of the art, projects, and perspectives*. (Approaches to semiotics. 127). Berlin: Mouton de Gruyter.

Reah, Danuta. 1998. *The language of newspapers*. London: Routledge.

Thornborrow, Joanna (ed.) 1997. "Broadcast talk." *Text* 17,157-262.

Van Dijk, Teun A. (ed.) 1985. Discourse and communication: new approaches to the analysis of mass media discourse and communication. (Research in text theory. 10). Berlin: De Gruyter.

Van Dijk, Teun A. 1988. News analysis: case studies of international and national news in the press. Hillsdale: Erlbaum.

Watson, James; Hill, Anne. [3]1993. *A dictionary of communication and media studies*. London: Arnold.

White, D. 1988. "Advertising." In: Bullock, Alan; Stallybrass, Oliver (eds.) 1988. *The Fontana dictionary of modern thought*. London: Collins. (s.v.)

10.2.7   Sociolinguistics and dialectology

10.2.7.0   General

Ammon, Ulrich; Dittmar, Norbert (eds.) 1987-1988. *Sociolinguistics = Soziolinguistik: an international handbook of the science of language and society*. 1-2. (Handbücher zur Sprach- und Kommunikationswissenschaft. 3, 1-2). Berlin: De Gruyter.

Cobarrubias, Juan; Fishman, Joshua A (eds.) 1983. *Progress in language planning: international perspectives*. (Contributions to the sociology of language. 31). Berlin: Mouton de Gruyter.

Coupland, Nikolas; Jaworski, Adam (eds.) 1997. *Sociolinguistics: a reader and coursebook.* Basingstoke: Macmillan.

Holmes, Janet. [3]2008 [[1]1992]. *An introduction to sociolinguistics.* Harlow: Pearson Longman.

Hudson, R.A.. 1996. [2]*Sociolinguistics.* (Cambridge textbooks in linguistics). Cambridge: Cambridge Univ. Pr.

Kortmann, Bernd; Schneider, Edgar W. eds. 2008. *Varieties of English.* Volumes 1-4. Berlin: Mouton de Gruyter.

Mesthrie, Rajend et al. 2003. *Introducing sociolinguistics.* Edinburgh: Edinburgh Univ. Pr.

Milroy, Lesley; Gordon, Matthew. 2003. *Sociolinguistics: method and interpretation.* (Language in society. 34). Oxford: Blackwell.

Romaine, Suzanne. [2]2000. Language in society: an introduction to sociolinguistics. Oxford: Oxford Univ. Pr.

Singh, Rajendra. 1996. *Lectures against sociolinguistics.* New York: Lang.

Spolsky, Bernard. [5]2004. *Sociolinguistics.* Oxford: Blackwell.

Trudgill, Peter; Cheshire, Jenny (eds.) 1997. *The sociolinguistics reader. 1: Mutlilingualism and variation.* London: Arnold.

Trudgill, Peter. 1995. *Sociolinguistics: an introduction to language and society.* London: Penguin.

Trudgill, Peter. 2002. *Sociolinguistic variation and change.* Edinburgh: Edinburgh Univ. Pr.

Wardhaugh, Ronald. [4]2003. *An introduction to sociolinguistics.* (Blackwell textbooks in linguistics. 4). Oxford: Blackwell.

10.2.7.1 Dialects, accents and the standard

Altendorf, Ulrike. 2003. *Estuary English: levelling at the interface of RP and South-Eastern British English.* Tübingen: Gunter Narr.

Hughes, Arthur; Trudgill, Peter. [3]1997. *English accents and dialects: an introduction to social and regional varieties of British English in the British Isles.* London: Arnold.

Trudgill, Peter. [2]1999. *The dialects of England.* Oxford: Blackwell.

10.2.7.2 Bilingualism

Fill, Alwin. 1993. *Ökolinguistik: eine Einführung.* Tübingen: Narr.

Haugen, Einar et al. (eds.) 1981. *Minority languages today.* Edinburgh: Edinburgh Univ. Pr.

Hélot, Christine; de Mejia Anne-Marie. 2008. *Forging multilingual spaces: integrated perspectives on majority and minority bilingual education.* Multilingual Matters Ltd.

Romaine, Suzanne. [2]2004. *Bilingualism.* (Language in society. 13). Malden: Blackwell.

10.2.7.3 Varieties around the world

Algeo, John (Hg.). 2001. *The Cambridge history of the English language. 6: English in North America.* Cambridge: Cambridge Univ. Pr..

Blair, David; Collins, Peter (eds.) 2001. *English in Australia.* (Varieties of English around the world: general series. 26). Amsterdam: Benjamins.

Burchfield, Robert. (Hg.). 1994. *The Cambridge history of the English language. 5: English in Britain and overseas: origins and development*. Cambridge: Cambridge Univ. Pr..

Kachru, Yamuna; Smith, Larry. 2008. *Cultures, contexts, and World Englishes*. London: Routledge.

Mair, Christian. 2006. *Twentieth-century English: history, variation and standardization*. Cambridge: CUP.

McArthur, Tom. 2003. *The Oxford guide to world English*. Oxford: Oxford Univ. Pr.

Mehrotra, Raja Ram. 1998. *Indian English: texts and interpretations*. (Varieties of English around the world. 7). Amsterdam: Benjamins.

Mesthrie, Rajend; Bhatt, Rakesh M. 2008. *Word Englishes: the study of new linguistic varieties*. Cambridge: CUP.

Meyerhoff, Miriam. 2006. *Introducing sociolinguistics*. London: Routledge.

Trudgill, P.; Cheshire, J. (eds.) 1998. *The sociolinguistics reader. 1: Multilingualism and variation*. New York: Oxford Univ. Pr.

10.2.7.4 Pidgins and creoles

Arends, J.; Muysken, P.; Smith, N. (eds.) 1995. *Pidgins and Creoles: an introduction*. (Creole language library. 15). Amsterdam: Benjamins.

Bickerton, Derek. 1981. *Roots of language*. Ann Arbor, MI: Karoma.

Clark, Jeniffer. 2008. *The emergence of pidgin and creole languages*. Oxford: OUP.

Mühlhäusler, Peter. [2]1997. *Pidgin and creole linguistics*. London: Univ. of Westminster Pr.

Sebba, Mark. 1997. *Contact languages: Pidgins and Creoles*. Basingstoke: Macmillan.

Spears, Arthur K.; Winford, D (eds.) 1997. *The structure and status of pidgins and creoles* (Creole language library. 19). Amsterdam: Benjamins.

10.2.7.5 Language and gender

Cameron, Deborah. [2]1998. *The feminist critique of language*. London: Routledge.

Cameron, Deborah. 1995. "Rethinking language and gender studies: some issues for the 1990s." In: Mills, Sara ed. 1995. *Language and gender: interdisciplinary perspectives*. Oxford: Blackwell.31-44.

Coates, Jennifer (ed.) 1998. *Language and gender: a reader*. Oxford: Blackwell.

Crawford, Mary. 1995. *Talking difference: on gender and language*. (Gender and psychology series). London: Sage.

Goddard, Angela; Patterson, Lindsey Meân. 2000. *Language and gender*. London: Routledge.

Hellinger, Marlis. 1991. *Kontrastive feministische Linguistik*. Ismaning: Hueber.

Johnson, Sally; Meinhof, Ulrike (eds.) 1997. *Language and masculinity*. Oxford: Blackwell.

Lakoff, Robin. 1975. *Language and woman's place*. New York: Harper & Row.

Mills, Sara. 1998. *Feminist stylistics*. London: Routledge.

Penelope, Julia. 1990. *Speaking freely: unlearning the lies of the fathers' tongues*. New York: Pergamon.

Romaine, Suzanne. 1998. *Communicating gender*. London: Erlbaum.

Smith, Philip Maynard. 1985. *Language, the sexes and society.* (Language in society. 8). Oxford: Basil Blackwell.

Talbot, Mary M. 1998. *Language and gender: an introduction.* Cambridge: Polity Pr.

Tannen, Deborah. 1993. *Gender and conversational interaction.* Oxford: Oxford Univ. Pr.

Tannen, Deborah. 2002. *You just don't understand: women and men in conversation.* London: Virago.

Trudgill, Peter; Cheshire, Jenny (eds.) 1998. *The sociolinguistics reader. 2: Gender and discourse.* New York: Oxford Univ. Pr.

10.2.8 Psycholinguistics. Neurolinguistics. Biolinguistics

(No longer a chapter in this textbook, see www.narr-studienbuecher.de. Below you find some basic literature.)

10.2.8.1 Psycholinguistics

Aitchison, Jean. [4]1998. *The articulate mammal: an introduction to psycholinguistics.* London: Routledge.

Aitchison, Jean. [3]2004. *Words in the mind: an introduction to the mental lexicon.* Malden: Blackwell.

Altmann, Gerry T. M. 1997. *The ascent of Babel: an exploration of language, mind, and understanding.* Oxford: Oxford Univ. Pr.

Butzkamm, Wolfgang; Butzkamm, Jürgen. 2004. *Wie Kinder sprechen lernen: kindliche Entwicklung und die Sprachlichkeit des Menschen.* Tübingen: Francke.

Ellis, Andrew W.; Beattie, Geoffrey. 1986. *The psychology of language and communication.* London: Weidenfeld & Nicholson.

Forrester, Michael A. 1996. *Psychology of language: a critical introduction.* London: Sage.

Garman, Michael. [3]1996. *Psycholinguistics.* Cambridge: Cambridge Univ. Pr.

Harley, Trevor A. [3]1998. *The psychology of language: from data to theory.* Hove: Psychology Pr.

Kess, Joseph F. 1992. *Psycholinguistics: psychology, linguistics and the study of natural language.* Amsterdam: Benjamins.

Jäger, Ludwig et al. 2002. *Fliegende Hände.* Aachen: Desire.

MacWhinney, Brian (ed.) 1999. *The emergence of language.* London: Erlbaum.

McNeill, David. 1987. *Psycholinguistics: a new approach.* New York: Harper & Row.

Radach, Ralph et al. (eds.) 2004. *Eye-movements and information processing during reading.* (European Journal of Cognitive Psychology: Special issue. 16). Hove: Psychology Pr.

Pinker, Steven. 1999. *How the mind works.* New York: W.W. Norton & Company.

Pinker, Steven. 1995. *The language instinct: the new science of language and mind.* London: Penguin.

Smith, Frank. [6]2004. *Understanding reading: a psycholinguistic analysis of reading and learning to read.* London: Lawrence Erlbaum Associates.

Steinberg, Danny D. [4]1996. *An introduction to psycholinguistics.* London: Longman.

Taylor, Insup; Taylor, Martin. 1990. *Psycholinguistics: learning and using language.* Englewood Cliffs: Prentice Hall.

10.2.8.2 Neurolinguistics

Ahlsén, Elisabeth. 2006. *Introduction to neurolinguistics*. Amsterdam: John Benjamins.

Caplan, David. 1998. *Neurolinguistics and linguistic aphasiology: an introduction*. Cambridge: Cambridge Univ. Pr.

Damasio, Hanna B. 1995. *Human brain anatomy in computerized images*. Oxford: Oxford Univ. Pr.

Huber, Walter; Poeck, Klaus; Springer, Luise. 1991. *Sprachstörungen. Ursachen und Behandlung von Sprachstörungen (Aphasien) durch Schädigungen des zentralen Nervensystems*. Stuttgart: TRIAS Thieme Hippokrates Enke.

Lamb, Sydney M. 1999. *Pathways of the brain: the neurocognitive basis of language*. Amsterdam, PA: Benjamins.

Loritz, Donald. 2002. *How the brain evolved language*. Oxford: Oxford Univ. Pr.

Obler, Loraine K.; Gjerlow, Kris. 1999. *Language and the brain*. Cambridge: Cambridge Univ. Pr.

Posner, Michael I.; Raichle, Marcus E. 1997. *Images of mind*. New York: Scientific American Library.

Weiller, C. 2000. "Bildgebende Verfahren – Aktivierungsstudien mit PET und fMRT." In: Strum, W. et al. (eds.) 2000. *Lehrbuch der klinischen Neuropsychologie: Grundlagen Methoden Diagnostik Therapie*. Lisse, NL: Swets & Zeitlinger.204-218.

10.2.8.3 Biolinguistics

Bickerton, Derek. 1991. *Language and species*. Chicago: Univ. of Chicago Pr.

Hurford, James R.; Studdert-Kennedy, Michael; Knight, Chris. 1998. *Approaches to the evolution of language*. Cambridge: Cambridge Univ. Pr.

Jenkins, Lyle. 2000. *Biolinguistics: exploring the biology of language*. Cambridge: Cambridge Univ. Pr.

Jenkins, Lyle. 2004. *Variation and universals in biolinguistics*. Amsterdam: North Holland.

Lenneberg, Eric H. 1967. *Biological foundations of language*. New York: Wiley.

Marquardt, Beate. 1984. *Die Sprache des Menschen und ihre biologischen Voraussetzungen*. (Tübinger Beiträge zur Linguistik. 236). Tübingen: Narr

10.3   Literature mentioned in the text

Aitchison, Jean. [2]1994. *Language change: progress or decay?*. Cambridge: Cambridge Univ. Pr.

Aitchison, Jean. [4]1995. *Linguistics: an introduction*. London: Hodder & Stoughton.

Aitchison, Jean. [4]2002. *The articulate mammal: an introduction to psycholinguistics*. London: Routledge.

Aitchison, Jean. [3]2004. *Words in the mind: an introduction to the mental lexicon*. Malden: Blackwell.

Altmann, Gerry T.M. 1997. *The ascent of Babel: an exploration of language, mind, and understanding*. Oxford: Oxford Univ. Pr.

Anderson, Stephen R. 1992. *A-morphous morphology*. (Cambridge studies in linguistics). Cambridge: Cambridge Univ. Pr.

Arnold, Roland; Hansen, Klaus. [8]1992. *Englische Phonetik*. Leipzig: Langenscheidt.

Barber, Charles. 2005 [[1]1976]. *Early Modern English*. Edinburgh: Edinburgh Univ. Pr.

Baugh, Albert C.; Cable, Thomas. [4]1993 [[1]1935]. *A history of the English language*. Englewood Cliffs: Prentice Hall.

Biber, Douglas. 1986. "Spoken and written textual dimensions in English: resolving the contradictory findings." *Language* 62,384-414.

Biber, Douglas. 1988. *Variation across speech and writing*. Cambridge: Cambridge Univ. Pr.

Biber, Douglas; Johansson, Stig; Leech, Geoffrey; Conrad, Susan; Finegan, Edward. 1999. *Longman grammar of spoken and written English*. Harlow: Longman.

Blass, Regina. 1990. *Relevance relations in discourse: study with special reference to Sissala*. (Cambridge studies in linguistics. 55). Cambridge: Cambridge Univ. Pr.

Brinton, Laurel J.; Arnovick, Leslie K. 2006. *The English language: a linguistic history*. Oxford: Oxford Univ. Pr.

Brown, Penelope; Levinson, Stephen. 1988. *Politeness: some universals of language usage*. (Studies in interactional sociolinguistics. 4). Cambridge: Cambridge Univ. Pr.

Butzkamm, Wolfgang; Butzkamm, Jürgen. [2]2004. *Wie Kinder sprechen lernen: kindliche Entwicklung und die Sprachlichkeit des Menschen*. Tübingen: Francke.

Carroll, Robert et al. (eds.) 1997 [1611]. *The Bible: Authorized King James Version*. Oxford: Oxford Univ. Pr.

Chafe, Wallace L. 1985. "How we know things about language: a plea for catholicism." In: Tannen, Deborah (ed.); Alatis, James E. (ed.). 1985. *Languages and linguistics: the interdependence of theory, data, and application*. (Georgetown University round table on languages and linguistics. 1985). Washington, D.C.: Georgetown Univ. Pr.214-225.

Chambers, Jack K. 2005. "Talk with talk." *Do you speak American?* (http:// www.pbs.org/ speak/ahead/mediapower/media/).

Chomsky, Noam. 1957. *Syntactic structures*. (Janua linguarum: series minor. 4). S'-Gravenhage: Mouton.

Chomsky, Noam. 1965. *Aspects of the theory of syntax*. Cambridge, MA: MIT Pr.

Chomsky, Noam. 1972. *Topics in the theory of generative grammar*. The Hague: Mouton de Gruyter.

Chomsky, Noam. 1981. *Lectures on government and binding*. (Studies in Generative Grammar. 9). Dordrecht: Foris Publ.

Chomsky, Noam. 1995. *The minimalist program*. (Current studies in linguistics. 28). Cambridge, MA: MIT Press.

Chomsky, Noam; Halle, Morris. 1968. *The sound pattern of English*. New York: Harper & Row.

Clark, Herbert H.; Carlson, T.B. 1982. "Speech acts and hearers' beliefs." In: Smith, Nelson Voyne (ed.). 1982. *Mutual knowledge*. Cambridge: Academic Pr.1-36.

Comrie, Bernard. 1981. *Language universals and linguistic typology: syntax and morphology*. Oxford: Blackwell.

Comrie, Bernard. [2]1989. *Language universals and linguistic typology: syntax and morphology*. Oxford: Blackwell.

Comrie, Bernard. 2001. "Different views of language typology". In: Haspelmath, Martin et al. (eds.). 2001. *Language typology and language universals*. Berlin [u. a.]: Walter de Gruyter.

354

Cook, Guy. 1992. *The discourse of advertising*. London: Routledge.

Croft, William. 2001. *Radical construction grammar: syntactic theory in typological perspective*. Oxford: OUP.

Croft, William; Cruse, Alan D. 2004. *Cognitive linguistics*. Cambridge: Cambridge Univ. Pr.

Crystal, David. 2008. "Two thousand million? Updates on the statistics of English." *English Today* 24(1), 3-6.

Dahl, Östen. 1985. *Tense and aspect systems*. Oxford: Blackwell.

Dahl, Östen. 1994. "Perfect." In: Asher, R.E. (ed.). 1994. *The encyclopedia of language and linguistics*. 6. Oxford: Pergamon Pr. 3000-3001.

Daneš, František. 1970. "Zur linguistischen Analyse der Textstruktur." *Folia linguistica* 4, 72-79.

De Beaugrande, Robert; Dressler, Wolfgang Ullrich. 1981. *Einführung in die Textlinguistik*. (Konzepte der Sprach- und Literaturwissenschaft. 28). Tübingen: Niemeyer.

Dirven, René; Pörings, Ralf (eds.). 2002. *Metaphor and metonymy in comparison and contrast*. Berlin: de Gruyter.

Fill, Alwin. 1993. *Ökolinguistik: eine Einführung*. Tübingen: Narr.

Fillmore, Charles J. 1968. "The case for case." In: Bach, Emmon (ed.); Harms, Robert T. (ed.). 1968. *Universals in linguistic theory*. New York: Holt, Rinehart & Winston, 1-88.

Fillmore, Charles; Kay, Paul; O'Conner, Mary Catherine. 1988. "Regularity and idiomaticity in grammatical constructions: the case of *let alone*." *Language* 64, 501-538.

Firbas, Jan. 1992. *Functional sentence perspective in written and spoken communication*. Cambridge: Cambridge Univ. Pr..

Fischer, Olga (ed.); Nänny, Max (ed.). 2001. *The motivated sign: iconicity in language and literature*. 2. Amsterdam: Benjamins.

Fishman, Joshua A. 1967. "Bilingualism with and without diglossia, diglossia with and without bilingualism." *Journal of social issues* 23, 29-38.

Fishman, Joshua A. 1968. *The sociology of language: an interdisciplinary social science approach to language in society*. The Hague: Mouton.

Fishman, Joshua A. 1972. *The sociology of language: an interdisciplinary social science approach to language in society*. Rowley, MA: Newbury House.

Foley, William A.; Van Valin, Robert D. 1984. *Functional syntax and universal grammar*. (Cambridge studies in linguistics. 38). Cambridge: Cambridge Univ. Pr.

Frisch, Karl von. [10]1993. *Aus dem Leben der Bienen*. Berlin: Springer.

Fromkin, Victoria; Rodman, Robert. [5]1993. *An introduction to language*. Fort Worth: Harcourt Brace College Publ.

Fry, Dennis. 1977. *Homo loquens: man as a talking animal*. Cambridge: Cambridge Univ. Press.

Gärdenfors, Peter. 1999. "Some tenets of cognitive semantics." In: Allwood, J. (ed.); Gärdenfors, P. (ed.). 1999. *Cognitive sementics: meaning and cognition*. Amsterdam: Benjamins, 19-37.

Gimson, A.C. [5]1994. *Gimson's pronunciation of English*. London: Arnold.

Givón, Talmy. 1984. *Syntax: a functional-typological introduction*. 1. Amsterdam: Benjamins.

Givón, Talmy. 1990. *Syntax: a functional-typological introduction*. 2. Amsterdam: Benjamins.

Gleason, Jean B. [5]2003. *The development of language*. Boston: Allyn & Bacon.

Goldberg, A.E. 1995. *Constructions: a construction grammar approach to argument structure*. Chicago: Univ. of Chicago Press.

Goldberg, Adele E. 2003. "Constructions: a new theoretical approach to language." *Trends in cognitive sciences* 7, 219-224.

Goldberg, Adele E. 2006. *Constructions at work: the nature of generalization in language*. Oxford [u.a.] : Oxford Univ. Press.

Graustein, Gottfried; Thiele, Wolfgang. 1978. "Beziehungsinhalte als Ausdruck semantischer Kohärenz bei der Analyse englischer Texte." *Linguistische Arbeitsberichte* 19, 27-36.

Grice, Herbert Paul. 1975. "Logic and conversation." *Syntax and semantics* 3, 41-58.

Grimes, Joseph. 1975. *The thread of discourse*. (Janua linguarum. Series minor. 207). The Hague: Mouton.

Gruber, Jeffrey S. 1976. *Lexical structures in syntax and semantics*. (North-Holland linguistic series. 25). Amsterdam : North-Holland.

Gumperz, John J. 1982. *Discourse strategies*. (Studies in interactional sociolinguistics. 1). Cambridge: Cambridge Univ. Pr.

Gussenhoven, Carlos. 2000. "On the origin and development of the Central Franconian tone contrast." In: Lahiri, Aditi (ed.). 2000. *Analogy, levelling, markedness: principles of change in phonology and morphology*. (Trends in linguistics: studies and monographs. 127). Berlin: Mouton, 215-260.

Gussenhoven, Carlos; Jacobs, Haike. 1998. *Understanding Phonology*. London: Arnold.

Haase, Martin. 2001. "Sprachtypologie und Universalienforschung bei Joseph H. Greenberg". In: Haspelmath et al., 280-283.

Haegeman, Liliane. 1991 [2]1994. *Introduction to government and binding theory*. Oxford: Blackwell.

Haegeman, Liliane (ed.). 1997. *Elements of grammar: handbook of generative syntax*. (Kluwer international handbooks for linguistics. 1). Dordrecht: Kluwer.

Haegeman, Liliane; Gueron, Jacqueline. 1999. *English grammar: a generative perspective*. (Blackwell textbooks in linguistics. 14). Oxford: Blackwell.

Halliday, Michael Alexander Kirkwood. 1985. *An introduction to functional grammar*. London: Arnold.

Halliday, Michael Alexander Kirkwood; Hasan, Ruqaiya. 1976. *Cohesion in English*. (English language series. 9). London: Longman.

Halliday, Michael Alexander Kirkwood; Matthiessen, Christian. 2004. *An introduction to functional grammar*. London: Arnold.

Harweg, Roland. 1968. *Pronomina und Textkonstitution*. (Poetica Beih. 2). München: Fink.

Haspelmath, Martin et al. (eds.). 2001. *Language typology and language universals. An international handbook. 1-2*. Berlin / New York: Walter de Gruyter (= Handbücher zur Sprach- und Kommunikationswissenschaft. 20.1-20.2)

Hawkins, John A. 1986. *A comparative typology of English and German: unifying the contrasts*. London: Croom Helm.

Hjelmslev, Louis. 1943. *Omkring sprogteoriens grundlæggelse*. (Festskrift udg. af Københavns Universitet i Anled. of Univ. Aarsfest. 1943). København: Luno.

Hjelmslev, Louis. 1953. *Prolegomena to a theory of language*. (Indiana University publications in anthropology and linguistics. Memoir. 7). Baltimore: Waverly Pr.

Hjelmslev, Louis. [2]1969. *Prolegomena to a theory of language*. Madison: Univ. of Wisconsin Pr.

Hobbs, Jerry R. 1983. "Why is discourse coherent?." In: Neubauer, Fritz (ed.). 1983. *Coherence in natural-language texts*. Hamburg: Buske, 29-70.

Hockett, Charles F. 1958. *A course in modern linguistics*. New York: The Macmillan Company.

Hoffmann, Fernand. 1981. "Triglossia in Luxemburg." In: Haugen, Einar (ed.); et al. 1981. *Minority languages today: a selection from the papers read at the First International Conference on Minority Languages held at ..* Edinburgh: Edinburgh Univ. Pr., 201-207.

Horn, Laurence R. 1984. "Toward a new taxonomy for pragmatic inference: Q-based and R-based implicature." In: Schiffrin, Deborah (ed.) 1984. *Meaning, form, and use in context: linguistic applications*. (Georgetown University round table on languages and linguistics. 1984). Washington: Georgetown Univ. Pr., 11-42.

House, Juliane; Kasper, Gabriele. 1981. "Politeness markers in English and German." In: Coulmas, Florian (ed.). 1981. *Conversational routine: explorations in standardized communication situations and prepatterned speech*. (Janua linguarum. Series maior. 96; Rasmus Rask studies in pragmatic linguistics. 2). The Hague: Mouton, 157-185.

Humboldt, Wilhelm von. 1963. *Werke*. 3. Berlin: Rütter & Loering. [1. Aufl. 1825-1836]

Illich, Ivan. 1983. "Vernacular values and education." In: Bain, Bruce (ed.). 1983. *The sociogenesis of language and human conduct*. New York: Plenum Pr., 461-495.

Itkonen, Esa. 2005. *Analogy as structure and process: approaches in linguistic, cognitive psychology, and philosophy of science*. Amsterdam, etc.: Benjamins (= Human cognitive processing. 14).

Johnson, Mark. 1987. *The body in the mind: the bodily basis of meaning, imagination and reason*. Chicago: Chicago Univ. Pr.

Jucker, Andreas H. 2000. *History of English historical linguistics*. (Uni-Wissen. Anglistik/Amerikanistik). Stuttgart (et al.): Klett.

Kachru, Braj B. 1988. "The sacred cows of English." *English Today* 16(4), 3-8.

Kay, Paul; Fillmore, Charles J. 1999. "Grammatical constructions and linguistic generelizations: the *what's X doing Y?* construction." *Language* 75, 1-33.

Keller, Rudi. 1990. *Sprachwandel: von der unsichtbaren Hand in der Sprache*. (UTB. 1567). Tübingen: Francke.

Kloss, Heinz. 1967. "'Abstand' languages and 'Ausbau' languages." *Anthropological linguistics* 9, 29-41.

Kortmann, Bernd. 1991. "The triad 'tense – aspect – Aktionsart': problems and possible solutions." *Belgian journal of linguistics* 6, 9-30.

Kortmann, Bernd. 1997. *Adverbial subordination: a typology and history of adverbial subordinators based on European languages*. Berlin: Mouton de Gruyter.

Kramarae, Cheris; Treichler, Paula. 1985. *A feminist dictionary*. London: Pandora.

Labov, William. 1966. *The social stratification of English in New York City*. Washington: Center for Applied Linguistics.

Labov, William. 1972. *Sociolinguistic patterns*. Oxford: Blackwell.

Labov, William. 1973. "The boundaries of words and their meanings." In: Bailey, Charles-James N. (ed.); Shuy, Roger W. (ed.). 1973. *New ways of analyzing variation in English*. Washington: Georgetown Univ. Pr., 340-374.

Lakoff, Robin Tolmach. 1973. "The logic of politeness: or minding your p's and q's." *Papers from the Regional Meeting of the Chicago Linguistic Society* 9, 292-305.

Lakoff, George. 1987. *Women, fire, and dangerous things: what categories reveal about the mind*. Chicago: Univ. of Chicago Pr.

Lane, Harlan. 1993. *The wild boy of Aveyron*. London: Allen & Unwin.

Langacker, Roland W. 1987. *Foundations of cognitive grammar*. 1. Stanford: Stanford Univ. Pr.

Langacker, Ronald W. 1988. "An overview of cognitive grammar." In: Rudzka-Ostyn, Brygida (ed.). 1988. *Topics in cognitive linguistics*. (Amsterdam studies in the theory and history of linguistic science. 50). Amsterdam: Benjamins, 3-48.

Langacker, Roland W. 1991. *Foundations of cognitive grammar*. 2. Stanford: Stanford Univ. Pr.

Lee, David. 2001. *Cognitive linguistics: an introduction*. New York: OUP.

Leech, Geoffrey Neil. 1983. *Principles of pragmatics*. (Longman linguistics library. 30). London: Longman.

Levinson, Stephen C. 1983. *Pragmatics*. (Cambridge textbooks in linguistics). Cambridge: Cambridge Univ. Pr.

Levinson, Stephen C. 2000. *Presumptive meanings: the theory of generalized conversational implicature*. Cambridge, MA: MIT Press.

Li Wei. 1998. "Banana split? Variations in language choice and code-switching patterns of two groups of British-born Chinese in Tyneside." In: Jacobson, Rodolfo (ed.). 1998. *Codeswitching worldwide*. (Trends in linguistics: studies and monographs. 106). Berlin: Mouton de Gruyter. 153-176.

Lippi-Green, Rosina. 1997. *English with an accent: language, ideology, and discrimination in the United States*. London: Routledge.

Lux, Friedemann. 1981. *Text, Situation, Textsorte*. (Tübinger Beiträge zur Linguistik. 172). Tübingen: Narr.

Lyons, John. 1977. *Semantics. 1-2*. Cambridge: Cambridge Univ. Pr.

Lyons, John. 1992. *Language and linguistics*. Cambridge: Cambridge Univ. Press. [Repr.]

Malmkjær, Kirsten (ed.) 1995. *The linguistics encyclopedia*. London: Routledge. [Paperback]

Mann, William C.; Thompson, Sandra A. 1986. "Relational propositions in discourse." *Discourse processes* 9, 57-90.

Marchand, Hans. [2]1969 [[1]1960]. *The categories and types of present-day English word-formation: a synchronic-diachronic approach*. München: Beck.

Marquardt, Beate. 1984. *Die Sprache des Menschen und ihre biologischen Voraussetzungen*. (Tübinger Beiträge zur Linguistik. 236). Tübingen: Narr.

Mathesius, Vilém. 1975. *A functional analysis of present-day English*. (Janua linguarum. Series practica 208). The Hague: Mouton.

Mehrotra, Raja Ram. 1998. *Indian English: texts and interpretations*. (Varieties of English around the world. 7). Amsterdam: Benjamins.

Mesthrie, Rajend et al. 2003. *Introducing sociolinguistics*. Edinburgh: Edinburgh Univ. Pr.

Meyer, Bonnie J.F. 1975. *The organization of prose and its effects on memory*. Amsterdam: North-Holland Publ. Co.

Meyer, Paul Georg. 1975. *Satzverknüpfungsrelationen: ein Interpretationsmodell für situationsunabhängige Texte*. (Tübinger Beiträge zur Linguistik. 61). Tübingen: Narr.

358

Milroy, Leslie. 1992. "New perspectives in the analysis of sex differentiation in language." In: Bolton, Kingsley (ed.); Kwok, Helen Lesley (ed.). 1992. *Sociolinguistics today: international perspectives*. London: Routledge, 163-179.

Mitchell, Bruce; Robinson, Fred C. [5]1997 [[1]1964]. *A guide to Old English*. Oxford et al.: Blackwell.

Moessner, Lilo. 2003. *Diachronic English linguistics: an introduction*. (Narr Studienbücher). Tübingen: Narr.

Mooij, J.J.A. 1976. *A study of metaphor*. (North-Holland linguistic series. 27). Amsterdam: North-Holland

Myers-Scotton, Carol. 1993. *Social motivations for codeswitching: evidence from Africa*. Oxford: Clarendon.

Newton, Gerald. 1996. *Luxembourg and Lëtzebuergesch: language and communication at the crossroads of Europe*. Oxford: Clarendon.

Ochs, Elinor. 1979. "Planned and unplanned discourse." *Syntax and semantics* 12, 51-80.

Peirce, Charles Sanders. 1998. *Collected papers*. 2. Cambridge, MA: Harvard Univ. Pr. [Repr. of the 1931-58 edition]

Petruck, M. R. L. 1996. "Frame semantics." In: Verschueren, J. et al. (eds.). 1996. *Handbook of pragmatics*. Philadelphia: Benjamins, 1-13.

Pierrehumbert, Janet; Hirschberg, Julia. 1990. "The meaning of intonational contours in the interpretation of discourse." In: Cohen, Philip R. (ed.); Morgan, Jerry (ed.); Pollack, Martha E. (ed.). 1990. *Intentions in communication*. (Bradford book). Cambridge, MA: MIT Press, 271-311.

Pinker, Steven. 1995. *The language instinct: the new science of language and mind*. London: Penguin.

Plank, Frans. 1981. *Morphologische (Ir-)Regularitäten: Aspekte einer Wortstrukturtheorie*. (Studien zur deutschen Grammatik. 13). Tübingen: Narr.

Quirk, Randolph; Greenbaum, Sidney; Leech, Geoffrey; Svartvik, Jan. 1985. *A comprehensive grammar of the English language*. London: Longman.

Quirk, Randolph; Greenbaum, Sidney; Leech, Geoffrey; Svartvik, Jan. [9]1991. *A comprehensive grammar of the English language*. London: Longman.

Quirk, Randolph; Greenbaum, Sidney; Leech, Geoffrey; Svartvik, Jan. [12]1994. *A comprehensive grammar of the English language*. London: Longman.

Radach, Ralph et al. (ed.). 2004. *Eye-movements and information processing during reading*. (European Journal of Cognitive Psychology: Special issue. 16). Hove: Psychology Pr.

Radford, Andrew. 1981. *Transformational syntax: a student's guide to Chomsky's Extended Standard Theory*. (Cambridge textbooks in linguistics). Cambridge: Cambridge Univ. Pr.

Radford, Andrew. 1988. *Transformational grammar: a first course*. New York: Cambridge Univ. Pr.

Radford, Andrew. 2004. *English syntax: an introduction*. Cambridge: Cambridge Univ. Pr.

Raffaele, Simone (ed.). 1995. *Iconicity in language*. (Current issues in linguistic theory. 110). Amsterdam: Benjamins.

Rohdenburg, Günter. 1990. "Aspekte einer vergleichenden Typologie des Englischen und Deutschen kritische Anmerkungen zu einem Buch von John A. Hawkins." In: Gnutzmann, Claus (ed.). 1990. *Kontrastive Linguistik*. (Forum angewandte Linguistik. 19). Frankfurt a.M.: Lang, 133-152.

Rosen, Harold. 1971. "Towards a language policy across the curriculum." In: Barnes, Douglas; Britton, James (contr.); Rosen, Harold (contr.). 1971. *Language, the learner, and the school*. Harmondsworth: Penguin. [Rev. ed.], 117-159.

Saeed, John I. 1997. *Semantics*. Oxford: Blackwell.

Sauer, Hans. 1992. *Nominalkomposita im Frühmittelenglischen: Mit Ausblicken auf die Geschichte der englischen Nominalkomposition*. (Buchreiher der Anglia, Zeitschrift für englische Philologie. 30). Tübingen: Niemeyer.

Saussure, Ferdinand de. 1965. *Cours de linguistique générale*. Paris: Payot.

Saussure, Ferdinand de. 1966. *Course in general linguistics*. New York: MacGraw-Hill.

Scalise, Sergio. 1988. "Inflection and derivation." *Linguistics* 26, 561-581.

Schank, Roger C.; Abelson, Robert P. 1977. *Scripts, plans, goals and understanding: an inquiry into human knowledge structures*. Hillsdale, NJ: Erlbaum.

Schiffrin, Deborah. 1994. *Approaches to discourse*. (Blackwell textbooks in linguistics. 8). Oxford: Blackwell.

Searle, John Rogers. 1969. *Speech acts: an essay in the philosophy of language*. Cambridge: Cambridge Univ. Pr.

Searle, John Rogers. 1975a. "A taxonomy of illocutionary acts." In: Gunderson, K. (ed.). 1975. *Language, mind and knowledge*. (Minnesota studies in the philosophy of science. 7). Minneapolis: Univ. of Minnesota Pr., 344-369.

Searle, John Rogers. 1975b. "Indirect speech acts." *Syntax and semantics* 3, 59-82.

Searle, John Rogers. 1980. "The background of meaning." In: Searle, John R. (ed.); Kiefer, Ferenc (ed.); Bierwisch, Manfred (ed.). 1980. *Speech act theory and pragmatics*. (Synthese language library. 10). Dordrecht: Reidel, 221-232.

Skousen, Royal; Lonsdale, Deryle; Parkinson, Dilworth B. 2002. *Analogical modeling: an exemplar-based approach to language*. Amsterdam, etc.: Benjamins.

Smith, Frank. [6]2004. *Understanding reading: a psycholinguistic analysis of reading and learning to read*. London: Lawrence Erlbaum Associates.

Smith, Ross. 2005. "Global English: gift or curse?." *English today* 21, 56-62.

Schneider, Jan Georg. 2006. "Gibt es nichtmediale Kommunikation?" In: *Zeitschrift für angewandte Linguistik* 44, 71-90.

Sperber, Dan; Wilson, Deirdre. 1981. "Irony and the use-mention distinction." In: Cole, Peter (ed.). 1981. *Radical pragmatics*. New York: Academic Pr. 295-318.

Sperber, Dan; Wilson, Deirdre. 1986 [[2]1995]. *Relevance: communication and cognition*. Oxford: Blackwell.

Sweetser, Eve. 1990. *From etymology to pragmatics: metaphorical and cultural aspects of semantic structure*. (Cambridge studies in linguistics. 54), Cambridge: Cambridge Univ. Pr.

Talbot, Mary M. 1998. *Language and gender: an introduction*. Cambridge: Polity Pr.

Tannen, Deborah. 1982. "Oral and literate strategies in spoken and written narratives." *Language* 58, 1-21.

Taylor, John. 2002. *Cognitive grammar*. Oxford: Oxford Univ. Pr.

Trask, R.L. 1999. *Key concepts in language and linguistics*. London: Routledge.

Trier, Jost. 1934. "Das sprachliche Feld. Eine Auseinandersetzung." *Neue Jahrbücher für Wissenschaft und Jugendbildung*. 10, 428-449.

Trudgill, Peter. 1972. "Sex, covert prestige and linguistic change in the urban British English of Norwich." *Language and society* 1, 179-195.

Trudgill, Peter. [2]1999. *The dialects of England*. Oxford: Blackwell.

360

Trudgill, Peter. 2002. *Sociolinguistic variation and change*. Edinburgh: Edinburgh Univ. Pr.

Van Dijk, Teun A. 1980. *Textwissenschaft: eine interdisziplinäre Einführung*. (dtv Wissenschaft. 4364). München: Deutscher Taschenbuch Verlag.

Wanner, Dieter. 2006. *The power of analogy: an essay on historical linguistics*. Berlin: Mouton de Gruyter (= Trends in linguistics: studies and monographs. 170).

Weiller, C. 2000. "Bildgebende Verfahren − Aktivierungsstudien mit PET und fMRT." In: Sturm, Walter (ed.); Herrmann, Manfred (ed.); Wallesch C.W. (ed.). 2000. *Lehrbuch der klinischen Neuropsychologie: Grundlagen Methoden Diagnostik Therapie*. Lisse, NL: Swets & Zeitlinger, pp.

Weinreich, Max. 1945. "Der YIVO un di problemen fun undzer tsayt." *YIVO bletter* 25, 3-18

Wells, John C. 1990. *Longman pronunciation dictionary*. London: Longman.

Wierzbicka, Anna. 1988. *The semantics of grammar*. (Studies in language companion series. 18). Amsterdam: Benjamins.

Wierzbicka, Anna. 1992. *Semantics, culture and cognition: universal human concepts in culture-specific configurations*. New York: Oxford Univ. Pr.

Wierzbicka, Anna. 1996. *Semantics: primes and universals*. Oxford: Oxford Univ. Pr.

Wierzbicka, Anna. 1999. *Emotions across languages and cultures: diversity and universals*. Cambridge [u.a.] : Cambridge Univ. Pr. [u.a.]

Wolfram, Walt; Schilling-Estes, Natalie. 1998. *American English*. Malden, MA : Blackwell

Zipf, George Kingsley. 1929. "Relative frequency as a determinant of phonetic change." *Harvard studies in classical philology* 40, 1-95.

Zwicky, Arnold M.; Pullum, Geoffrey K. 1983. "Cliticization vs. inflection: English *n't*." *Language* 59, 502-513.

11 Index

This index contains
- all the relevant terminology that is used in this book.
- Furthermore, this index contains names of linguists (in SMALL CAPITALS) that are well known and discussed at some length, or from whom crucial examples or arguments were taken over.
- And it contains names of languages, dialects and countries that are mentioned. As the whole book is about English linguistics, English, of course, is not listed as a keyword.

AAVE *see* Black English
abbreviation 90
Abkürzung *see* abbreviation
ablaut 23, 33, 79, 90, 172, 173
absolute construction 45
Abstandssprache 284
accent 286
accusative 38
acoustic phonetics 99
acrolect 313
acronym 91
active voice 29
actor 58, 66
adjacency pair 272
adjective 15
adjective declension 22, 180
adjectives (comparison of) *see* comparison of adjectives
adjunct 40, 55, 56, 231
adjunct / complement 40, 55
adverb 17
adverbial 39, 50, 53, 56
adverbial clause 43, 44
affix 76, 94
affricate 114
African American Vernacular English *see* Black English
Afro-Caribbean speech 291
agent 58, 59
agglutinating language 96, 98
agreement 19, 20, 21, 32, 35

AITCHISON 206, 210, 218
Albanian 172
allograph 154
allomorph 77
allophone 121, 138
alphabetic writing 145, 153, 299
alveolar 115
ambiguity 212, 244
ambiguity (syntactic) *see* syntactic ambiguity
AmE *see* American English
amelioration 195
American English 31, 45, 101, 108, 109, 125, 144, 147, 192, 193, 291, 292, 301, 311, 360
American National Corpus 5
American Sign Language 321
amplitude 117
analogical levelling 179
analogy 178
analysability (in language typology) 96
analytic language 96
anaphora 262
ANC *see* America National Corpus
Angles 159
anomalous 241
anteriority 26
anticipatory assimilation 151
antonymy 222
approximant 114, 115, 123
Arabic 46, 79, 127, 217, 298, 299, 300

arbitrariness 63, 317, 318
areal typology 172
argument (in predicate logic) 33, 59, 242
argumentation 271
ARNOLD / HANSEN 145
article 17
articulatory gesture 101
articulatory phonetics 99
aspect 18, 24
aspirated 122, 125
aspiriert see aspirated
assertive 248
assimilation 125, 151
attribute 43, 55
attributive adjective 19, 55, 85
attrition (phonetic) 148
auditory phonetics 99
Ausbausprache 283
Australia 301
Australian English 302
auxiliary (verb) 15, 31, 32, 149
back vowel 102
background 240, 259
Balkan sprachbund 172
basilect 313
Basque 284, 294, 300
Belgium 294, 298, 300, 303
benefactive 58
beneficiary 58
Beowulf 161
Bhutan 303
BIBER 15, 26, 33, 40, 45, 275, 278
Bible translation 162
biconditional 236
bilabial 115
bilingualism 295
Black English 188, 291
BLASS 255
blend 86
BNC *see* British National Corpus
borrowing 198
bound morpheme 75, 94
brace construction 142
BrE *see* British English

Breton 284
Britain *see* United Kingdom
British English 104, 115, 122, 147, 149,
    152, 155, 292, 301, 311
British National Corpus 5
British Sign Language 294
broad transcription 123
broadening (of meaning) *see* semantic
    broadening
Brunei 303
Bulgarian 172
Canada 300, 301
Canadian English 302
Canterbury Tales 162
case 18, 21
case role 57
categorial perception 119
categorisation 226
causality 271
Caxton 162
Celtic languages 159, 160
central vowel 102
centring diphthong 108, 176
CHAFE 275
channel 274, 276, 277
Chaucer 162
Chinese 98, 157, 294, 300
CHOMSKY 2, 6, 45, 55, 59
CHOMSKY / HALLE 134, 139
circumlocution 306
circumstance adverbial 53
clarification 270
CLARK / CARLSON 259
clause 42
clipping 91
clitic 77, 94, 148
close vowel 102
closed class 75, 94
coalescent assimilation 151
coarticulation 125, 151
Cockney 112
coda 136
code-switching 296
cognate language 168

cognate word 168
Cognitive Grammar 61
Cognitive Linguistics 61
cognitive semantics 225
coherence / cohesion 266
coherence relation 270
cohesion 262
cohesion / coherence 266
collocation 212
combining form 77, 87, 94
comment 266, 267
commissive 248
communication mode see modality (of communication) , see modality (of communication)
communicative competence 246
communicative dynamism 267
comparative (form of adjectives) 22
comparative linguistics 94
comparative reconstruction 166, 167
comparison 18
comparison of adjectives 22
competence 9
competence (communicative) see communicative competence
competence / performance 6, 246, 308
complement 40, 55, see also adjunct / complement
complement (QUIRK) see predicative
complement clause 44
complementary distribution 124
complementation see complement clause
complementiser 43
complex sentence 42
componential analysis 224
compositionality 60, 61, 233
compound 84
compound sentence 42
compounding (in Old English) 183
compounding / syntax interface 86
comprehensibility 207
COMRIE 96
conceptualisation 226
conceptualist approach 225

concord see agreement
concordance 5
conjugation 80, 182, 192
conjunction (logic) 234, 235
conjunction (syntax) 35
conjunction (textlinguistics) 265
conjunction (word class) 17, 42, 150
connected speech 148
connective see logical connective
connector 265
connotation 212
consecutio temporum see sequence of tenses
consonant 101, 110
constituency test 48
constituent structure 48
construction 62, 71
Construction Grammar 2, 60, 61
Construction Grammar vs. Generative Grammar 72
content (in cognitive grammar) 62
content (propositional) see propositional content
content plane (in HJELMSLEV) 63, 64, 130, 140, 144, 209, 210, 211
content word 18, 94
context 258
context of situation 259, 274
continuant 114
continuum 62, 71, 72, 75, 101, 116, 140, 276, 282, 313
contradiction 241
contradictory contrast 223
contrast see also antonymy
contrast (contradictory) see contradictory contrast
contrast (in descriptive linguistics) 121, 217
contrast (in text linguistics) 265, 270
contrastive linguistics 5, 94
conventional sign see symbol
conversation (closing of) 273
conversation analysis 261
conversation opening 273
conversational implicature 252

conversational maxim 251
converse 223
conversion 83
Cook 239
cooperativeness 251
cooperativeness principle 256
coordinating conjunction 17
core 11
Cornish 160
corpus linguistics 5
corpus planning 298
covert prestige 289, 310, 315
creativity 55, 320
creole 307
creolistics 308
Croatian 282, 285
Croft 61
Croft / Cruse 65, 66, 71
cuneiform writing 157
Czech 281, 282, 285
Danelaw 161
Daneš 266, 269, 270
dative 38
De Beaugrande / Dressler 266
dead metaphor 229
declaration 248
declension 22, 80, 179, 180
definite article 17
degeneration *see* pejoration
deictic expression 276
deixis 276
Deklination see declension
deletion test 48
demonstrative pronoun 17
denotation 211
dental 115
derivation 80, 81
derivational morpheme 76
derivationalist / lexicalist 74
descriptive grammar 7, 46
descriptive meaning 211
determiner 17, 150
diachronic linguistics 158
diachrony / synchrony 87, 158

dialect 281
dialect (traditional vs. modern) 285
dialect continuum 282
dialectology 283
dictionary 210
differentiation of meaning 220
diglossia 297
digraph 154
diphthong 103, 108
direct object 35, 38
direct passive 69
directional opposition 223
directive 248
discontinuous constituent 142
discourse 3, 9, 61, 261, 273
discourse analysis 261
discreteness 141, 144
disjunction 235
disjunction (logic) 234
displacement 319
distinctiveness 121
donor language 198
do-periphrasis 188
do-periphrasis (in Proto-Germanic) 183
doppelte Gliederung see duality
do-so test 50, 216
double articulation *see* duality
double negation *see* negative concord
dual 19, 181
duality 318
Dutch 26, 146, 157, 303
dysphemism 205
Early Modern English 163, 342
economy principle 207
EFL *see* English as a foreign language
elevation *see* amelioration
elision 148, 177
Elizabethan Age 162
ellipsis 262
embedded clause 42
empiricism 2
encyclopaedic knowledge 227, 266
English (origin of name) 160
English as a foreign language 303

Englishes 302
entailment 221, 237, 240
equivalence 236
equivalence (logic) 234
Eskimo 217
essential condition 249
Estuary English 112
ethnolect 291
etymological doublet 200
etymology 167
EU *see* European Union
euphemism 205
European Union 300
exclusive *or* 235
existential quantifier 243
experiencer 58, 59
explication 270
expression plane (in HJELMSLEV) 62, 63, 64, 130, 140, 144, 153
expressive 248
extension 211
external history 159
eye dialect 192
feature analysis 224
felicity condition 248
feminine 20
feminist linguistics 310
figure / ground 70, 226, 267
FILL 295
FILLMORE 57, 61, 230
final obstruent devoicing 132
finite clause 44
finiteness 32
first language 301
FISHMAN 280, 297
flap 114
for ... to infinitive clauses 45
form (in cognitive linguistics) 64
form (in HJELMSLEV) 62, 209, 211
form / function 64, 131
form / meaning *see* form / function
form / meaning (in cognitive linguistics) 62
form / substance (in HJELMSLEV) 130, 144, 153, 210, 211

formal / informal (speech situations) 272
formal semantics 209, 233
formant 117
formelle / informelle Sprechsituation see formal / informal speech situations
form-meaning pairing 64
fortis 111, 112
frame 230
France 305
Franks Casket 161
free morpheme 75, 94
free variation 186
FREGE's principle *see* compositionality
French 6, 24, 25, 32, 37, 46, 63, 64, 76, 78, 80, 81, 84, 88, 97, 98, 103, 113, 116, 125, 128, 139, 142, 155, 156, 161, 162, 163, 172, 177, 184, 189, 192, 194, 196, 197, 198, 199, 200, 201, 202, 203, 208, 220, 275, 284, 293, 299, 300, 303, 308, 310, 333
French-based loans 201
fricative 114
FRISCH *see* VON FRISCH
Frisians 159
front vowel 102
function word 14, 18, 47, 62, 75, 94, 140, 148, 202
functional approach 59
functional sentence perspective *see* theme / rheme
fundamental frequency 117
fusion *see* synthesis (in language typology)
future 23, 31
fuzziness 62, 77, 194, 228
Gaelic 160
gender 18, 19
General American 103, 287
generate 54
Generative Grammar 2, 54, 72
Generative vs. Construction Grammar 72
genetically related language *see* cognate language, *see* cognate language, *see* cognate language
genitive object 38

German V, IX, 6, 7, 11, 13, 14, 18, 19, 20,
    21, 22, 24, 26, 28, 30, 34, 36, 37, 38, 42,
    46, 59, 63, 64, 76, 77, 78, 79, 80, 81, 82,
    84, 85, 86, 87, 88, 89, 90, 93, 94, 98, 99,
    102, 105, 106, 107, 108, 109, 110, 111,
    112, 113, 114, 119, 127, 128, 129, 132,
    133, 139, 142, 146, 152, 154, 157, 158,
    160, 161, 165, 167, 168, 169, 171, 172,
    173, 176, 177, 179, 180, 181, 183, 187,
    190, 191, 192, 193, 194, 195, 197, 198,
    199, 203, 207, 208, 217, 218, 219, 221,
    235, 242, 251, 275, 281, 282, 283, 284,
    285, 286, 287, 293, 294, 296, 297, 298,
    299, 303, 308, 311, 312, 315, 318, 323,
    324, 325, 326
Germanic 90, 191, 220
Germany 303, 305
gerund 33, 44
GIMSON 116, 149
glide 114, 115, 123
glottal 115
glottal stop 112
goal 58
going to 26
GOLDBERG 61, 66, 67, 69, 71
gradable antonymy 223
grammar 1, 11
grammatical category 18
grammatical gender 20
grammatical morpheme 76, 94
Grammatical morpheme 75
grammaticalisation 31, 143, 148, 177, 178,
    183, 189, 190, 191, 193, 194, 206, 257,
    307, 318, 326
grapheme 154
graphemics 154
Great Britain see United Kingdom
Great Vowel Shift 134, 174
Greek 20, 24, 31, 36, 46, 63, 77, 80, 87, 88,
    89, 90, 94, 97, 98, 135, 139, 155, 163,
    166, 172, 173, 178, 181, 184, 188, 191,
    193, 194, 199, 200, 202, 207, 297
GRICE 251, 253, 255
Grimm's Law 169

ground see figure / ground
GUMPERZ 296
HAEGEMAN / GUÉRON 45, 49, 52, 53, 59
half-close vowel 102
half-open vowel 102
HALLIDAY 59
HALLIDAY / HASAN 262, 263, 264
HARWEG 264
Hastings (Battle of) 161
have a [V]$_N$ construction 68
head 55, 84
height (of vowels) 102
Helsinki Corpus 5
hereby-insertion test 250
heuristics (for implicatures) 253
hierarchy 51
high variety 281
high vowel 102
Hindi 127
historical linguistics 5, 158
HJELMSLEV 62, 130, 131, 140, 144, 209,
    210, 211
HOBBS 270
HOCKETT 317
homography 213
homonymy 213
homophony 213
HOUSE / KASPAR 251
HUMBOLDT 96
Hungarian 157
hybrid formation 81
Hybridbildung see hybrid formation
hypercorrection 289
hypernym 221
hyperonym 221
hyponymy 221
icon 63, 142
iconicity 141, 142, 194, 317, 318
idiom 60
ILLICH 278
illocutionary act 248
illocutionary force 247
illocutionary point 249
illocutionary verb 249

image-schema 226
imperative 31
imperfective 24
impersonal passive 30, 37
implication 234, *see* entailment
implication, material *see* material
    implication
implicature 196, 237, 240
i-mutation *see* umlaut
inclusive *or* 235
indefinite article 17
indeterminacy 228
index 144
indexical 317
India 107, 300, 301, 302
Indian English 302
indicative 31
indirect object 34, 38
indirect speech act 250
Indo-European *see* Proto-Indo-European
inferencing 257
Inferenz see *inferencing*
infinitive 32, 44
inflecting language 96, 98
inflection 80
inflectional form 73
inflectional morpheme 76
information structure 146
informativeness principle 256
initialism 90
inkhorn controversy 202
insertion sequence 272
intelligibility *see* mutual intelligibility
intension 211
interactive oral discourse 273
internal reconstruction 170
International Phonetic Alphabet 99, 139
International Phonetic Association 99
intonation 265, 267, 277, 313, 318
intransitive verb 34
introspective method 10
inversion 35
IPA 99
Ireland 301

Irish 160
isogloss 283
isolating language 96
isomorphism 142
JAKOBSON 120, 218
Japanese 157
jargon (as a pre-pidgin stage) 306
Johnson, Samuel 163
Jutes 159
juxtaposition 84, 88
KELLER 208
kenningar 183
KLOSS 283
knowledge (of grammar) 1, 65
labiodental 115
LABOV 280, 290
LAKOFF / JOHNSON 229
LAKOFF, George 61
LAKOFF, ROBIN 252
LANGACKER 16, 61, 70
language (vs. dialect) 281
language acquisition 86, 321
language and gender 309
language community 293
language planning 164, 282, 284, 298, 300,
    348
language policy 298
language typology 94
language variation 5, 280, 281, 313
language-internal approach 225
language-world approach 225
langue / parole 6, 12, 121, 175, 246
Late Modern English 163
lateral 114
Latin 7, 19, 20, 26, 32, 34, 36, 76, 77, 78,
    80, 81, 84, 87, 88, 89, 90, 94, 98, 135,
    139, 154, 155, 159, 162, 163, 166, 169,
    177, 184, 186, 188, 189, 191, 192, 193,
    197, 198, 199, 200, 201, 202, 203, 207,
    208, 236, 259, 264, 293, 295
lax vowel 102
length (of vowels) 101
lenis 111, 112
let alone construction 68

368

Lëtzebuergesch see Luxembourgish
LEVINSON 253, 272
lexeme 209
lexical cohesion 264
lexical field 217
lexical morpheme 75, 94
Lexical morpheme 75
lexical tone *see* tone language
lexicalisation 82, 92, 224
lexicalist / derivationalist *see* derivationalist
  / lexicalist
lexically conditioned 78
lexicography 5, 210
lexicology 210
lexicon 210
lexicon-syntax continuum *see* syntax-
  lexicon continuum
Limburgs 146
lingua franca 301
linguistic creativity 55
linguistic ecology 295
linguistic relativity theory *see* SAPIR-
  WHORF hypothesis
linguistic sexism 310
linguistic universal 95
liquid 114, 116
litotes 188
loan 198
loans from Old Norse 181
local adverb 17
location 58
logical connective 234
logical form 234
logical operator 234
logography 157
long vowel 101, 104, 106
loudness 117
Low German 160, 169
low variety 281
low vowel 102
lower articulator 115
LUX 259
Luxembourg 284
Luxembourgish 29, 284, 285, 298

LYONS 63, 141, 217, 317
majority language 294
MANN / THOMPSON 270
manner (maxims of) 251, 252
manner adverb 17
manner adverbial 53
manner of articulation 110, 113
marked 28, 232
markedness 28
MARQUARDT 321
masculine 20
material implication 236
meaning 209, 210
meaning (as a criterion for word classes) 16
meaning (in cognitive linguistics) 62, 64,
  72, 131, 225
meaning (of a sentence) *see* sentence
  meaning
meaning (of an utterance) *see* utterance
  meaning
meaning (of intonation) 144
meaning relation 220
medium 274
meinen see speaker's meaning
mental lexicon 210
mentalism 2
mention / use 4
mesolect 314
metalanguage 3, 4
metaphor 196, 197, 215, 227, 228
metonymy 196, 215, 227
mid vowel 102
Middle English 161, 342
MILROY 310
minimal pair 127
minority language 294
modal verb 31, 194
modality (of communication) 273, 276
modality (verbal category) 18, 30, 31
modifier 55, 84
monophthongisation 109
mood 18, 30, 193
morpheme 74
morpheme-by-morpheme translation 97

morphological change 178
morphological process 79
morphological rule 74
morphological structure 73, 74
morphologically conditioned 77
morphology 11, 73
morphophonology 133
morphosyntactic word 12
Moselle Franconian 146, 284
motivated 63
movement 47
MÜHLHÄUSLER 295
multilingualism 295
multiple negation *see* negative concord
mutual intelligibility 281
narrow transcription 122, 123
narrowing (of meaning) *see* semantic
    narrowing
nasal 114, 116
nasal vowel 103
national language 301
Native American languages 294
native language 301
natural gender 19
necessary condition 236
negation (multiple) *see* negative concord
negative concord 19, 187, 188
neoclassical compound 77, 87
neologism 203, 299
Netherlands 305
neuter 20
neutralisation 132, 136, 175
New Zealand 301
Nigeria 301
nominative 36
nonce-formation 204
non-finite clause 44
norm 9
Norman Conquest 161
Norman French 161
noun 15
noun attribute 44
noun complement 44
noun declension *see* declension

noun phrase 52
NP *see* noun phrase
nucleus *see* peak
number 18, 28
object 34, 39, 40, 50, 52, 56
object clause 44
object complement *see* object predicative
object language 4
object predicative 39, 69
obligatorification 190
obligatory adverbial 39
obligatory constituent 39
observer's paradox 4
obsolescence 205
obstruent 116
OCHS 275
OED see Oxford English Dictionary
official language 301
Old English 19, 21, 22, 28, 31, 36, 38, 51,
    80, 81, 84, 93, 113, 128, 155, 159, 160,
    161, 166, 168, 169, 170, 171, 172, 173,
    174, 176, 178, 179, 180, 181, 182, 183,
    184, 185, 189, 190, 194, 195, 199, 200,
    201, 257, 293, 324, 341
Old Norse 161
Old Saxon 160
onomatopoeia 142, 318
onset 136
opacity (of vocabulary) 199
open class 75, 94
open vowel 102
operator *see* logical operator
opposition 121, *see* contrast (in descriptive
    linguistics)
optional adverbial 39
optional constituent 39
oral discourse 273
oral vowel 103
orientation 26
orthography *see* spelling
Ottoman empire 172
outer history *see* external history
Oxford English Dictionary 164
palatal 115

palatal vowel see front vowel

Papua New Guinea 302

paradigmatic / syntagmatic 175

paradigmatic relation 212

parameter of variation (across languages)
    95

paraphrase 238

parole 6, 12

part of speech 15

partial assimilation 151

participle 44

particle 17

passive construction 69

passive voice 29

past tense 23

patient 58

peak 136

pedagogical grammar 7

PEIRCE 63

pejoration 195

Pennsylvania Dutch 293

perfect 24, 25, 26

perfective 24

performance see competence / performance

performative utterance 249

performative verb 249

periphery 11

periphrasis 189

person 18, 28

personal pronoun 17

Philippines 292

phoneme 120, 318

phoneme loss 176

phoneme merger 175

phoneme split 170

phonemic spelling 155

phonemic transcription 123

phonemics see phonology

phonetic attrition 177, 178, 190

phonetic transcription 99, 122

phonetics 99

phonological transcription 122

phonological word 12

phonologically conditioned 78

phonology 99, 120

phonotactics 135, 136, 151, 306

Phonotaktik see phonotactics

phrase structure 54

pictogram 157

pidgin 305

PIERREHUMBERT / HIRSCHBERG 144

PINKER 317, 320, 321

pitch 117, 140

place adverbial 53

place of articulation 110, 115

plosive 113

plural 18

point of reference 26

polarity 223

politeness 250, 252

polysemy 213

Portugal 305

possessive determiner 17

posteriority 26

pragmatic competence see communicative
    competence

pragmatics 245

pragmatics / semantics see semantics /
    pragmatics

Prague School 120, 218, 267

predicate (in predicate logic) 33, 242

predicate (in traditional syntax) 37, 51, 52

predicate logic 242

predicative 38, 39, 40

predicative adjective 19

prefix 76, 82, 94, 184

preposition 16, 150

prepositional passive 69

prescriptive grammar 7, 46

present tense 23

Present-Day English 164

presupposition 238, 259

presupposition trigger 239

preterite see past tense

primary / secondary stress 138

printed medium 273

printing press 162

probabilistic 61, 187, 290

productivity 91, 320

progressive (historical development) 190

progressive aspect 24

progressive assimilation 151

pronominalisation 262

pronoun 17, 150

pronoun system (development) 180

pronunciation rules 157

proposition 236

propositional content 236, 247

propositional logic 236

prosody 135

Proto-Indo-European 166, 170, 208

prototype 228

pseudo-loan 203

psycholinguistics 119, 210

pull chain 174

punctuation 145

push chain 174

quality (maxims of) 251, 252

quantifier 243

quantity (maxims of) 251, 252

quasi-suffix 86, 94

question test 36, 38, 39, 42, 48

QUIRK 15, 25, 33, 37, 38, 40, 45, 67

Radical Construction Grammar 61

reanalysis 190

Received pronunciation 176

Received Pronunciation 103, 287

recipient passive 30

reconstruction (comparative) see
    comparative reconstruction

recursiveness 55, 320

reduplication 89

reference 210, 225

reference potential 211

Reformation 162

register 289

regressive assimilation 151

relation (maxim of) 251, 252

relative clause 43, 45

relative pronoun 43

relevance (maxim of) see relation (maxim
    of)

Relevance (principle of) 255

Renaissance 162

resultative construction 69

retroflex 107

Rheinische Akzentuierung 146

rheme 266, *see* theme / rheme

Rhenish dialects 24, 146, 171

rhotic dialect 109

rhyme 136

rhythm 139

Ripuarian 146

Roman alphabet 153, 299

Romance languages 22, 98

root 76

Roumanian 172

rounded vowel 102

RP *see* Received Pronunciation

Runic script 155, 161

Russian 20, 24, 98, 124, 127, 157, 203, 300

Ruthwell Cross 161

S *see* sentence

SAEED 234, 237, 243

SAPIR-WHORF hypothesis 219

Satzklammer see brace construction

SAUSSURE 6, 63, 121, 158, 216, 246

Saxons 159

schematic construction 65

SCHIFFRIN 272

Schwyzerdütsch see Swiss German

scope 8, 244

SEARLE 247, 248, 249, 250, 259

second language 301

secondary stress *see* primary / secondary
    stress

secretion 87

segment 101

segmental phonology 120

selectional restriction 241

semantic bleaching 190

semantic broadening 195

semantic feature 224

semantic field 212

semantic field theory 217, 220, 232

semantic narrowing 195

semantics 209

semantics / pragmatics 246

semiotics 63

semi-vowel *see* glide

sense 211, 217

sense relation 220

sentence 42, 52

sentence meaning 233, 245

sentence semantics 209

sentence stress *see* intonation

sequence of tenses 264

Serbian 172, 282, 285

Serbo-Croatian 282

sexism *see* linguistic sexism

Shakespeare 163

short vowel 101, 103, 105

sibilant 115

sign language 294, 320, 321

simple aspect 24

simplicity principle 256

sincerity condition 249

singular 18

slang 289

Slavonic languages 36

Slovak 281, 282, 285

so do test 50

sociolect 288

sociolinguistics 280

sociology of language 280

sonorant 116

sonority hierarchy 116

Sorbian 284

source 58

South Africa 11, 301

South Korea 303

Spain 305

Spanish 294, 300

Spätneuenglisch see Late Modern English

speaker's meaning 245, 247, 252, 258

species-specificity 317

spectrograph 117

speech act 247

speech community 3, 282

speech-act verb 249

spelling 11, 84, 99, 106, 107, 126, 133, 135, 136, 154, 155, 157, 213, 284, 292, 298, 299, 302, 307

spelling pronunciation 177

spelling reform 157

SPERBER / WILSON 4, 255

sprachbund 172

Sprachtabu see taboo

spread vowel 102

standard 292

standardisation 163

status planning 299

stem 76

stigmatisation 207

stop *see* plosive

stress 79, 85, 106, 132, 135, 138, 174, 177, 198

strong form 148

strong verbs 173

structuralist semantics 225, 230

subject 34, 35, 50, 51, 52

subject clause 43, 44

subject complement *see* subject predicative

subject predicative 38, 69

subjunctive 31, 193

subordinated clause 42

subordinating conjunction 17, 43

substance *see* form / substance (in HJELMSLEV)

substantive construction 65

substitution (text grammar) 263

substitution test 49

substrate 306

sufficient condition 236

suffix 76, 94, 184

superlative 22

superstrate 306

suppletion 133

suprasegmental phonology 120, 135

Swahili 98

Swedish 146

Swiss German 297

Switzerland 297, 300

syllable 136

syllabography 157

symbol (in SAUSSURE's sense) 63

synchronic linguistics IX, 13, 87, 133, 158, 216

synchrony / diachrony *see* diachrony / synchrony

syncretism 182

synonymy 220

syntactic ambiguity 47, 86

syntactic function 35

syntagmatic relation 212

syntax 11, 45

syntax (iconicity in) 142

syntax-lexicon continuum 71, 72

synthesis (in language typology) 96

synthetic language 96, 97

system of language 6

taboo 205

TANNEN 275

tautology 241

TAYLOR 225

telegraphic style 36, 37

temporal adverb 17

tense 18, 23

tense vowel 102

text 261

text analysis 261

text coherence 261

text comprehension 261

text constitution 261

text production 261

text reception 261

textlinguistics 261

textual context 258

thematic progression 268, 273

thematic roles 57

theme (in discourse) 266, 269

theme (thematic role) 58

theme / rheme 267

time 23

time (in discourse) 270

time adverbial 53

tone language 146

topic 266, 269, 270

topic / comment 267

topic development 266

topicalisation 267

total assimilation 151

trajector / landmark 226

transformation 47

Transformational Grammar 47

transitive verb 34

tree diagram 51

TRIER 217

trill 114

TRUBECKOJ, N.S. *see* TRUBETZKOY, N.S.

TRUBETZKOY 120

TRUDGILL 283, 288, 310

truth condition 233, 245

truth table 235

truth value 233

truth-conditional semantics 225

Tudor Vowel Shift *see* Great Vowel Shift

Turkish 97, 98, 157, 172, 286, 299

turn-taking 272

UK *see* United Kingdom

umlaut 78, 171, 180

Umlaut 133

UN *see* United Nations

undergoer 66

unique morpheme 92, 94

United Kingdom 294, 301

United Nations 300

United States of America 301, *see also* American English

universal *see* linguistic universal

universal quantifier 243

unmarked 28

unreleased plosive 126

unrounded vowel 102

upper articulator 115

USA 294, 295, 301

usage-based approach 187

usage-based model 61

use / mention 4

use of language 6

utterance meaning 245, 247

uvular 115

vagueness 216
valency 34
VAN DIJK 261
variable (in formal logic) 243
variable (in sociolinguistics) 290, 297
variance (in morphology) 96, 98
variant (in sociolinguistics) 290, 297
variant (of linguistic unit) *see* Allo...
variation *see* language variation
variation (across languages) 95
velar 115
velar vowel see back vowel
verb 15, 50
verb phrase 51
verbal context 258
verbal syntagm 27
verbal syntagm (historical development)
   185
vernacular 64, 155, 291, 293, 314
Vietnamese 98
V$_{intr}$ away construction 68
vocabulary 210
vocal folds 110
vocal tract 100
voice 18, 29
voiced 110, 112
voiceless 110, 112
VON FRISCH 319
vowel 101
vowel alternation 78
vowel chart 104

vowel diagram 104
vowel gradation *see* ablaut
vowel height 102
vowel length 101
vowel weakening 177
Wales 294
weak form 77, 94, 148
weak verbs 174
Webster, Noah 163
Welsh 160, 218
WIERZBICKA 59
word 12
word class 15
word formation (historical development)
   76, 81, 184
word order (historical development) 185
word semantics 209
word stress *see* stress
world language 300
writing (alphabetic) see alphabetic
written grammar 6
written language 7, 153, 273, 292
Wycliffe 162
Yiddish 26
Yugoslavia 282
zero allomorph 79
zero morpheme 79
Zipf' s Law 208
Zipf's Law 91, 256
Zulu 11
ZWICKY / PULLUM 192

Thomas Herbst /
Susen Schüller

Introduction to Syntactic Analysis

A Valency Approach

narr studienbücher
2008, XII, 212 Seiten,
€[D] 19,90/Sfr 35,90
ISBN 978-3-8233-6390-3

This book provides an introduction to the analysis of sentences for students of English. It outlines principles of syntactic analysis and develops the categories used for a framework in which the concept of valency plays a major role.

The basic categories of syntactic description are elucidated in great detail: word classes, phrases, clauses. One major chapter deals with the notion of valency and how it can be implemented in a description of the English language.

The main purpose of this book is to describe a framework which will enable students to scrutinise English sentences.

The final chapter provides a practically oriented outline of how the categories identified in the preceding parts of the book can be adopted in an analysis of English sentences. The method outlined consists of eight clearly defined steps and is demonstrated in detail in the analysis of a number of authentic English sentences.

Narr Francke Attempto Verlag GmbH + Co. KG
Postfach 2560 · D-72015 Tübingen · Fax (07071) 9797-11
Internet: www.narr.de · E-Mail: info@narr.de

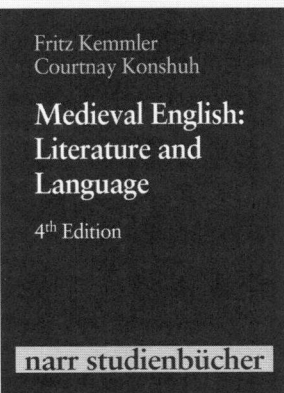

Fritz Kemmler / Courtnay Konshuh

Medieval English: Literature and Language

An Introduction

narr studienbücher
4., überarb. und erweiterte Auflage 2008,
X, 394 Seiten, zahlreiche Abb.,
€[D] 24,90/SFr 44,00
ISBN 978-3-8233-6430-6

This new and innovative approach to English Medieval Studies takes what is often judged as two separate fields, Old and Middle English, and unites them under their linguistic and literary continuities. Through this comprehensive approach, the reader will become familiar not only with the stages and the changes the language has undergone from the Anglo-Saxon invasions up to the late Middle Ages, but also how modern English evolved out of this.

An introductory grammar shows the continuous development of Old English to Middle and Early Modern English, with examples taken from a selection of carefully annotated texts. From historiography to works of religious instruction, battle poetry to love lyric, these show the progressive developments both in the English language and medieval English culture.

This collection will introduce beginning students to the diverse and fascinating world of Medieval English, enabling them to read and translate most texts, and also to have an understanding of Medieval life.

Narr Francke Attempto Verlag GmbH + Co. KG
Postfach 25 60 · D-72015 Tübingen · Fax (0 7071) 97 97-11
Internet: www.narr.de · E-Mail: info@narr.de

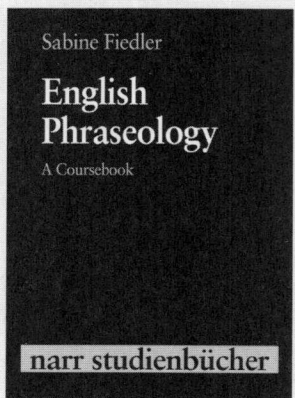

Sabine Fiedler

English Phraseology

A Coursebook

narr studienbücher
2007, 198 Seiten,
€[D] 19,90/Sfr 33,80
ISBN 978-3-8233-6338-5

This book introduces students of English to one of the most fascinating and at the same time most difficult parts of language: Phraseology. Commonly known as phrases and idioms, phraseological units are fascinating because of their colourful authenticity and the insight they provide into a language community's culture and history. Due to their frequently unpredictable meanings and their connotations these units are problematic, especially for foreign learners. The book was conceived for university classes as a coursebook with exercises, but it can also be used for self-study. It familiarizes readers with the key concepts in phraseology research and examines the behaviour and functions of phraseological units in discourse. With more than 200 examples drawn from a wide variety of written and spoken sources (including, above all, literary texts, newspapers, advertisements, comics, and films), the book illustrates the significant role that phraseology plays in the English language.

Narr Francke Attempto Verlag GmbH + Co. KG
Postfach 2560 · D-72015 Tübingen · Fax (07071) 9797-11
Internet: www.narr.de · E-Mail: info@narr.de

Michael Meyer

English and American Literatures

UTB basics
3., überarb. und erw. Auflage 2008
VIII, 241 Seiten, zahlreiche Abb.,
€[D] 14,90/Sfr 27,90
ISBN 978-3-8252-2526-1

English and American Literatures bietet kompaktes Basiswissen über:

- die Analyse lyrischer, narrativer und dramatischer Texte
- literaturwissenschaftliche Methoden und Theorien
- die Vorbereitung auf Referate, Hausarbeiten und Prüfungen

Der Band ist in englischer Sprache verfasst und auf die Gegebenheiten an Universitäten im deutschsprachigen Raum zugeschnitten. Er ist sowohl als Grundlage für Einführungskurse in die englische und amerikanische Literaturwissenschaft als auch zum Selbststudium geeignet.

»Das Buch ist uneingeschränkt empfehlenswert.«
Der fremdsprachliche Unterricht Englisch

Narr Francke Attempto Verlag GmbH + Co. KG
Postfach 25 60 · D-72015 Tübingen · Fax (0 7071) 97 97-11
Internet: www.francke.de · E-Mail: info@francke.de

Siepmann / Gallagher /
Hannay / Mackenzie

Writing in English:
A Guide for
Advanced Learners

UTB M
2008, X, 460 Seiten,
€[D] 22,90/SFr 41,00
ISBN 978-3-8252-3124-8

Endlich ein Schreiblehrbuch, das gezielt auf die sprachlichen
Probleme und Fehler fortgeschrittener deutschsprachiger Schrei-
ber des Englischen eingeht! Die Autoren arbeiten »typisch deutsche« Schwierigkeiten systematisch auf und bieten konkrete
sprachliche Hilfen für die Gestaltung wissenschaftlicher Texte
wie Hausarbeiten und Essays an. Die modulare Gliederung des
Buches ermöglicht den Nutzern, ihren persönlichen Kompe-
tenzen entsprechend individuelle Lernwege zu gehen.

Narr Francke Attempto Verlag GmbH + Co. KG
Postfach 25 60 · D-72015 Tübingen · Fax (0 7071) 97 97-11
Internet: www.francke.de · E-Mail: info@francke.de